T0230137

Lecture Notes in Computer Science

Lecture Notes in Computer Science

Edited by G. Goos and J. Hartmanis

499

Dimitris Christodoulakis (Ed.)

Ada: The Choice for '92

Ada-Europe International Conference
Athens, Greece, May 13–17, 1991
Proceedings

Springer-Verlag

Berlin Heidelberg New York London Paris
Tokyo Hong Kong Barcelona Budapest

Editorial Board

D. Barstow W. Brauer P. Brinch Hansen D. Gries D. Luckham
C. Moler A. Pnueli G. Seegmüller J. Stoer N. Wirth

Volume Editor

Dimitris Christodoulakis
University of Patras, Computer Engineering Department and
Computer Technology Institute, 26500 Patras, Greece

CR Subject Classification (1991): D.1.2−5, D.2, D.3

ISBN 3-540-54092-X Springer-Verlag Berlin Heidelberg New York
ISBN 0-387-54092-X Springer-Verlag New York Berlin Heidelberg

This work is subject to copyright. All rights are reserved, whether the whole or part of the material
is concerned, specifically the rights of translation, reprinting, re-use of illustrations, recitation,
broadcasting, reproduction on microfilms or in other ways, and storage in data banks. Duplication
of this publication or parts thereof is only permitted under the provisions of the German Copyright
Law of September 9, 1965, in its current version, and a copyright fee must always be paid.
Violations fall under the prosecution act of the German Copyright Law.

© Springer-Verlag Berlin Heidelberg 1991
Printed in Germany

Printing and binding: Druckhaus Beltz, Hemsbach/Bergstr.
2145/3140-543210 − Printed on acid-free paper

Preface

The annual Ada-Europe Conference goes from strength to strength. It is the most important event in Europe for the promotion and development of the Ada programming language and of Ada-based software engineering methodology. The 1991 conference has repercussions beyond the confines of Europe. This year it takes place in the epochal shadow of the impending and historic event which is probably the most momentous in the whole of Europe's long history - the creation of the 1992 Single Market.

A total of 25 papers were selected from over 60 extended abstracts received in response to the call of papers. Each paper was separately refereed by 3 individuals and was read by the members of the programme committee. The committee then met in Athens and carefully considered each paper before coming to a consensus on the 25 papers selected for presentation at the conference. Technical excellence and originality were the principal selection criteria, but readability and relevance to the conference theme were also taken into account.

I thank and commend all authors who submitted extended abstracts, whether accepted or not. For their thoroughness and dedication in reviewing the submitted abstracts I would like to thank the conference chairman Apostolos Coucouvinos and the members of the Programme Committee: Angel Alvarez (Spain), Toomas Kaer (Sweden), Jan van Katwijk (Netherlands), Barry Lynch (Ireland) and Sotiris Samaras (Greece).
I gratefully acknowledge the referees who assisted the programme committee: J. Kok, J. Bamberger, J.G.P. Barnes, J. Bundgaard, G. Green, M. Nagl, I.C. Pyle, I.C. Wand, P. Wehrum, G. Winterstein, R. De Benito, D. Craeynest, A. Burns, H.-J. Kugler, I. Richmond, J. A. de la Puente, K. De Vriendt, G. Glynn, J.-P. Rosen, G. Mendal, K. Gilroy, M. Gerhardt, E. Colbert, J. Squire, R. Bowerman, C. Hayden, B. Stowe, C. Roby, D. Dikel, D. Ahern, M. Kamrad and C. Brandon.

A special mention must go to the local organization of the conference and exhibition by Ada-Greece. Without the help of Mary Zarri of INTRASOFT S.A. and Brian Welsh of Zita Tourist Club none of this would have been possible. My thanks also to Alison Wearing, the treasurer of Ada-Europe for her help in arranging the publication of these proceedings.

Finally, I sincerely thank INTRASOFT S.A. for organizing accommodation for the meeting and for the support that considerably helped the task of the programme committee.

Patras   Dimitris Christodoulakis
March 1991   Programme Committee Chairman

Contents

Part I: Language Issues

Modelling the Temporal Summation of Neural Membranes using the Ada Language

MICHAEL C. CURTIS
ICL SECURE SYSTEMS, WOKINGHAM RG11 5TT, UK

VICTORIA J.D. SIVESS
THE UNIVERSITY OF SOUTHAMPTON SO9 5NH, UK

Abstract

This paper describes a program to model the construction and operation of a neural network and the process of temporal summation across the neural membrane, using the tasking facilities of the Ada language. The program is controlled by an agenda. The system has been written without compromising the safe features provided by the language.

1 INTRODUCTION

In another paper (Sivess 1989) we showed that the Ada language has features which make it suitable for the implementation of neural networks. This is an area in which it is important to develop reliable tools, as much of the work is experimental, and so Ada is good from a software engineering point of view. If we consider a neuron as a component, with various parameters such as threshold value, then this may be programmed naturally using the generic and tasking features of the language.

We decided to investigate further whether Ada can be used for more general Artificial Intelligence applications. This is important because more critical applications are now expected to incorporate A.I. techniques. For instance, (R. McCabe & Shields 1989) describes an adaptive diagnostic system for electronic equipment in the American navy. As an application domain, we took a piece of related work, the temporal summation on a neural membrane. We had previously implemented this in Scheme, a dialect of Lisp, using closures to implement a message passing style and driving the system with an agenda mechanism, as in (Abelson & Sussman 1985). These are powerful mechanisms, and one approach to incorporating such features into an Ada program is to interface to a language such as Lisp or Prolog (Fornarino & Neveu 1989). We aimed in this piece of work to see if we could write a fully-fledged agenda-driven system using Ada alone.

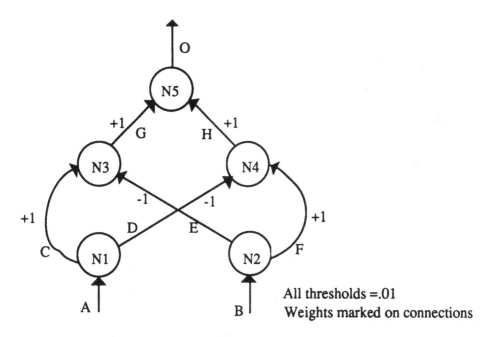

Figure 1: The XOR Network

2 ARTIFICIAL NEURAL NETWORKS

Traditionally, Artificial Intelligence has seen Man as a "processor of symbols" (Newell & Simon 1972). A different view is to regard intelligence as a property emerging from neural behaviour in the brain. This is a systems point of view (Checkland 1985) in which it is meaningless to ascribe the property of intelligence to an individual neuron but it makes sense to describe the whole system or network as intelligent. In artificial neural networks, the neurons are typically simplified and idealised in order to abstract away from the behavioural complexities at the molecular level. They are connected in a structured, usually hierarchical fashion. Each connection has a weighting attached to it. Each neuron sends a value to its output connections if the weighted sum of values on its input connections exceeds a threshold. Learning takes place by adjusting the values of the weights on the connections. Figure 1 shows an example of a small network set up to mimic the behaviour of the boolean *xor* function. So, for instance, when the neurons on what is known as the input layer are both set to 1, the output neuron will return a value of zero, and so on. Note that this example cannot be done without a hidden layer. In learning mode, the input layer is set and the output compared with the target output. Where there is a discrepancy, small adjustments are made to the weights until the input pattern produces the correct output. In the case of a network with hidden layers, these corrections to the weight values must be propagated back through the network using a technique known as backpropagation (Rumelhart & McClelland 1986). Backpropagation represented a breakthrough in learning algo-

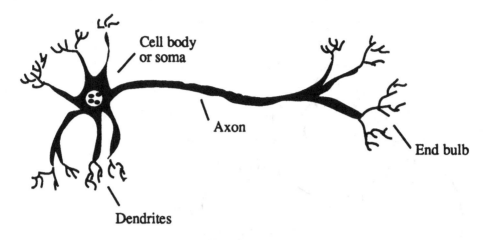

Figure 2: Biological Neuron

rithms for artificial neural networks. Unfortunately, there is no plausible biological explanantion for the process of backpropagation. At the other end of the spectrum, neurophysiologists have worked for a long time trying to develop realistic models of the brain (Carpenter 1990), often using complex systems of differential equations. Some artificial intelligence workers and cognitive scientists have tried to develop more plausible models, on the premise that the stripped down model may lose some computational power.

3 BIOLOGICAL NEURAL NETWORKS

Humans have about 10^{10} nerve cells or neurons, and each has in the order of 10^4 connections. There are many different kinds of neuron but most is known about motor neurons. Figure 2 shows a schematic diagram. Attached to the cell body are many filaments called *dendrites* through which impulses are passed to the cell from other neurons. Some of these impulses are excitatory and some are inhibitory. The inside of the cell body has a negative charge in comparison with the outside of the cell. This is maintained by means of a sodium pump which constantly pumps positive sodium ions out of the cell. On reaching the *cell membrane*, excitatory signals tend to depolarise the membrane while inhibitory ones hyperpolarise it. At the membrane, a process of *neuronal integration* of the incoming corrents takes place, and if the cell membrane becomes sufficiently depolarised, above a certain threshold, sodium floods into the cell body and an impulse or spike is sent out of the neuron down a larger filament known as the *axon*. The cell then returns to its resting potential. The branched end of the axon forms contact with the dendrites or cell bodies of other neurons. At the point of contact is a *synapse* where the electrical impulse causes a chemical transmitter to be released across a gap known as the *synaptic cleft*. The synapse becomes "strengthened" with use and the current is more likely to cross it, and it is in this way that learning takes place at the neuronal level. It is this that is modelled by the changes in weight in an artificial network.

Both the cell body and the synapses require a short period to settle down after being activated and any impulses arriving within this *refractory period* will be ignored.

3.1 Temporal Summation

Neurons exhibit what is known as *temporal summation*. The potential produced by a current from a synapse falls off slowly, and so it is possible to sum the effects of repeated stimulation of a single or different ending. Each neuron has a *time constant* associated with it which determines the capacitative properties of the cell membrane. The program seeks to model this temporal aspect.

4 PROGRAM DESIGN

The program has to provide three main functions:

- The network must first be linked, using parameters such as synaptic strength and the different constants.

- The signal values must be set on the input lines.

- The signals must be propagated through the network.

The top level can be expressed in pseudocode:

```
procedure A_NETWORK is
begin
 create connections;
 create neurons;
 connect neurons together;
 set time to zero;
 set input signals;
 propagate signals through network;
end A_NETWORK;
```

4.1 Data Objects

Five types of data object can immediately be recognised:

- The time

- Signals

- Connections

- Neurons

- The agenda

A *signal* is modelled using a pair (Signal-value, Time). The time is updated, as the signal passes through the network, by various constants such as the time taken to travel along a particular connection and the firing time for a neuron. As a signal passes along a connection, it crosses the synaptic gap and is affected by the synaptic strength. The synapse has a period when it must recover and so if a signal arrives within this time it cannot cross the synapse. The signal arrives at the membrane of the post-synaptic neuron and the process of integration takes place. This involves the neuron summing all signals on the in-coming connections that have arrived within a certain time period.

A *neuron* object has three main operations:

1. designate an input connection

2. designate an output connection

3. indicate that all connections have been made to and from this particular neuron

The object stores lists of all input and all output connections. Each neuron also keeps a local copy of a process that carries out the integration process. When the connections have been completed, the neuron can pass to this process the lists of in and out connections. It then passes a copy of this whole process to each incoming connection which can set the integration process going if ever its signal value changes.

If a neuron fires as the result of this integration process, an operation is placed on the agenda to set all the neuron's outgoing signals. It is this agenda, ordered in terms of time slots, that controls the whole process of propagation of the signals.

A *connection* object then has four operations:

1. have its synaptic strength or weight set

2. accept the integration process from a neuron

3. have its signal value changed

4. return the current value of its signal

The *agenda* is basically a list of actions to be carried out in order, according to some criterion. For instance, in Lenat's AM program, (Lenat 1978), actions are carried out in order of "interestingness" as specified by various heuristics. In this program, actions are ordered according to time. The agenda is accessed using two operations: one of these puts an action onto the agenda, which is kept ordered in terms of time-slot; the other operation propagates all the actions through the network.

5 THE ADA PROGRAM
5.1 Signals
The objects that we are dealing with in this program are active. They represent independent processes that communicate with each other by passing signals and references to other processes. The Ada task and the rendezvous are appropriate for modelling this sort of behaviour. The use of access types to reference tasks enables information on processes to be communicated without making detailed information unnecessarily visible.
A signal is modelled by a record containing two fields, thus:

```
type SIGNAL_TYPE is
record
   VALUE : VALUE_TYPE;
   TIME : TIME_TYPE;
end record;
```

where VALUE_TYPE is a floating point type. TIME_TYPE is a fixed point type.

Signals are set in the connections which modifies the VALUE field according to the weight of the connection. When a neuron gets the signal from an input connection it will set the signals on its output connections to one or zero depending on whether or not it has fired. The TIME field of output signal will be the TIME value of the input connection with a delay added for the passage through the connection and a further delay added for the passage through the neuron.

5.2 Time
The brain has no equivalent of a real-time clock, each neuron is independent of all others with no form of synchronisation. It would not even be reasonable to suppose that each neuron has its own clock, its behaviour is a non-deterministic sequence of chemical reactions. It is convenient to model this by operations taking a certain amount of time to complete and by assuming that actions may take place if other actions occur together, or within a short time interval. The correspondence between

the sequence imposed by the chemistry and our external concept of time is quite vague and it could be affected by many factors such as disease, age or tiredness. There has therefore been no attempt to relate the operation of the network to any clock.

5.3 The Agenda

The agenda is the main controlling mechanism for the whole program. Once the input signals have been set, it is by means of the agenda that these are propagated throughout the network. The agenda consists of a list of (time, action) pairs ordered on the time field. Each action is a piece of code that has to be carried out on a particular set of data; in this case to set a signal on a list of output connections. The agenda should not however know any of the details of the action to be performed, and in particular the specific variables and their values should not be visible. In a language such as Lisp it is possible to pass to the agenda a closure. That is a process with all its run-time bindings including the values of its local variables. This could not, of course, be programmed directly in Ada because of the strong typing and the rules of scope and visibility. The Ada solution is however quite neat and safer than the Lisp alternative.

The problem was to place on the agenda an action to take place at a certain time. The action is going to operate on variables particular to the problem domain, whose values will of course be changing during program execution. The outgoing connections which will be set by the action are local to each particular neuron. If the action is local to the neuron and refers to a list of connections within its scope then it cannot be specified within the agenda package. If the actions and connections must be passed as parameters to the action then they must be visible within the package specification of the agenda.

The solution makes use of the generic features of Ada and the fact that it is possible to have an access type referencing a task. AGENDA is a general purpose, reusable, generic package with specification:

```
generic
    type ITEM_TYPE is limited private;
    type TIME_TYPE is delta <>;
    with procedure ASSIGN(FROM : in ITEM_TYPE;
            TO : in out ITEM_TYPE);
    with procedure PERFORM_ACTION(ITEM : in out ITEM_TYPE);
package AGENDA is
    procedure SET_ACTION(AFTER : in TIME_TYPE;
        ACTION : in ITEM_TYPE);

    procedure PROPAGATE;
```

function FINISHED **return** BOOLEAN;

end AGENDA;

The ASSIGN procedure is necessary to allow the limited private type ITEM_
TYPE to be placed onto a list.

In this case the actual parameter corresponding to the formal ITEM_TYPE is
defined within the body of the NEURAL_NET package thus:


```
type ENVIRONMENT_TYPE is
record
   OUT_CONNECTIONS : CONNECTION_LIST_ACCESS_TYPE;
   SIGNAL : SIGNAL_TYPE;
end record;
type ENVIRONMENT_ACCESS_TYPE is access ENVIRONMENT_TYPE;
task type AGENDA_TASK_TYPE is
   entry PERFORM_ACTION(ENVIRONMENT : in out
            ENVIRONMENT_ACCESS_TYPE);
end AGENDA_TASK_TYPE;

type AGENDA_ACCESS_TYPE is access AGENDA_TASK_TYPE;
type AGENDA_ITEM_TYPE is
record
   ENVIRONMENT : ENVIRONMENT_ACCESS_TYPE;
   ACTION : AGENDA_ACCESS_TYPE;
end record;
```


CONNECTION_LIST_ACCESS_TYPE is an access type to the LIST_TYPE in
the instantiation of the LISTS package for a list of connections.
In other words we are passing an entire environment to the agenda, rather than just
a procedure or task. The actual parameter for the formal PERFORM_ACTION is
then simply defined thus:


```
procedure PERFORM_AGENDA_TASK(
            ITEM : in out AGENDA_ITEM_TYPE) is
begin
```

```
ITEM.ACTION.PERFORM_ACTION(
        ENVIRONMENT => ITEM.ENVIRONMENT);
end PERFORM_AGENDA_TASK;
```

which passes the environment for a particular agenda item to its task and causes it to run.

These tasks of AGENDA_TASK_TYPE are placed onto the agenda by a neuron action task along with its environment. At the appropriate point on the agenda this task will be called on to perform its action, which will be to set the signal part of its environment on each of its list of output connections.

The agenda is dynamic, each task that is run from the agenda may add further items onto the agenda.

5.4 Neurons

The neuron objects are modelled by a pair of tasks:

NEURON_TASK_TYPE, the purpose of these tasks is to hold information on the structure of the network. The neuron has no knowledge of the overall structure but it must contain information on its immediate environment, that is its input and output connections. During the stage when the network is being created it will be passed information on each connection and it then builds up two lists, one for input connections and one for output connections. When the network is complete then it must set up an action, that is a separate task that carries out the process of summing the input signals and checking whether the sum exceeds the threshold value. The value of the threshold is passed to the neuron when it is created. It creates the action task and passes to it the threshold value and the two lists of input and output connections. This action must be performed whenever a signal appears on any of its input connections therefore a reference to this task is passed to each of the input connections.

The specification is:

```
task type NEURON_TASK_TYPE is
    entry SET_THRESHOLD(THRESHOLD : in VALUE_TYPE);
    entry CONNECT_IN(CONNECTION : in CONNECTION_TYPE);
    entry CONNECT_OUT(CONNECTION : in CONNECTION_TYPE);
    entry END_CONNECTIONS;
end NEURON_TASK_TYPE;
```

NEURON_ACTION_TASK_TYPE, these tasks carry out the summation of input signals to determine whether or not the neuron fires. They must accept the threshold value and a list of input connections and a list of output connections then, for each of the input connections it will accept a call to perform its action. The value of the output signal is determined (either zero or one) and the time of the signal modified by a constant amount to represent the delay for a neuron to fire and a delay that is passed to it by the connection, which represents the time for the signal to pass through it, this amount will vary between connections to model the fact that connections can be of very different lengths. The output signal is propagated by placing a new item on the agenda. This agenda item consists of two parts: an environment, which is the output signal and the list of output connections, and a reference to an agenda task whose purpose is to set the signals on those connections.

```
task type NEURON_ACTION_TASK_TYPE is
    pragma PRIORITY(SYSTEM.PRIORITY'LAST);
    entry SET_THRESHOLD(THRESHOLD : in VALUE_TYPE);
    entry SET_IN_CONNECTIONS(TO : in
            CONNECTION_LIST_ACCESS_TYPE);
    entry SET_OUT_CONNECTIONS(TO : in
            CONNECTION_LIST_ACCESS_TYPE);
    entry PERFORM_ACTION(USING_DELAY : in TIME_TYPE);
end NEURON_ACTION_TASK_TYPE;
```

5.5 Connections

Connections are modelled by tasks of CONNECTION_TASK_TYPE, there are three types of connection: INPUT, OUTPUT and HIDDEN. This models the situation where a neuron may obtain its signal directly from some other organ, directly affect a muscle or other organ, or simply form part of the chain that transmits a signal from the input to the output. In fact in this system the action is only different for an OUTPUT connection since the setting of an input signal is the same whether the signal comes from another neuron or an external source. During the construction of the network each connection must be set up with various parameters. These are:

1. The starting WEIGHT, the weight of a connection is used to model the synaptic strength that is the ease with which a signal can pass across the synaptic gap between the axon of one neuron and the dendrites of the next. The value of the signal is multiplied by the weight as it passes through the connection.

2. The WEIGHT_INCREMENT, this is used to model the process of learning. Each time a signal passes through the connection the weight is increased by adding the product of this increment and the absolute value of the signal.

3. The NATURE, one of INPUT, OUTPUT or HIDDEN.

4. The CONNECTION_DELAY, which is added to the signal time as it passes through the connection.

Unless a connection has nature OUTPUT it is passed a reference to a NEURON_ACTION_TASK at the end of the construction phase. A signal can be set on a connection either externally in the case of an INPUT connection or from an agenda task. The value of this signal is modified by the WEIGHT. When a signal is set then the action task is called to sum the signals on all its inputs. This action will obtain the modified signal from the connection.
The connection tasks have specification:

```
task type CONNECTION_TASK_TYPE is
    entry SET_WEIGHT(TO : in WEIGHT_TYPE);
    entry SET_WEIGHT_INCREMENT(TO : in WEIGHT_TYPE);
    entry SET_NATURE(TO : in CONNECTION_NATURE_TYPE);
    entry SET_DELAY(TO : in TIME_TYPE);
    entry SET_SIGNAL(SIGNAL : in SIGNAL_TYPE);
    entry GET_SIGNAL(SIGNAL : out SIGNAL_TYPE);
    entry SET_ACTION(TO_TASK : in
            NEURON_ACTION_ACCESS_TYPE);
end CONNECTION_TASK_TYPE;
```

where NEURON_ACTION_ACCESS_TYPE is an access type to NEURON_ACTION_TASK_TYPE.

5.6 Rendezvous

Since there are a number of tasks that are not only calling each other but in particular placing items on the agenda it is important that certain operations be carried through to completion before others can occur. It must not be possible, for example, for the agenda to complete while a task that is about to place a new agenda item is suspended. For this reason virtually all processing within tasks is performed within the bodies of accept statements. The only exception to this is in the case of the NEURON_ACTION_TASKs which has the entry PERFORM_ACTION called from one of its input connections. It must then call the entry GET_SIGNAL for each of its input connections, including the one from which it has been called. This would cause a deadlock if this were to be done from within the accept body. In order to ensure that the subsequent placing of an item on the agenda occurs as soon as possible these tasks are run at a higher priority than all the others.

5.7 Lists

A number of lists are built and maintained during the construction and propagation of a network, Some lists being accessed by a number of different tasks. A reusable list component was used with the following specification.

```
generic
   type ELEMENT_TYPE is limited private;
   with function ">"(LEFT, RIGHT : in ELEMENT_TYPE)
           return BOOLEAN is <>;
   with procedure ASSIGN(FROM : in ELEMENT_TYPE;
           TO : in out ELEMENT_TYPE);
   package LISTS is
   type LIST_TYPE is limited private;
   procedure INITIALISE(LIST : in out LIST_TYPE);

   procedure INSERT(LIST : in out LIST_TYPE;
           ITEM : in ELEMENT_TYPE);

   procedure START(LIST : in out LIST_TYPE;
           ITEM : in out ELEMENT_TYPE);

   procedure NEXT(LIST : in out LIST_TYPE;
           ITEM : in out ELEMENT_TYPE);

   function END_OF_LIST(LIST : in LIST_TYPE) return BOOLEAN;

   function SIZE_OF_LIST(LIST : in LIST_TYPE) return NATURAL;

   LIST_ERROR : exception;
private
   type NODE_TYPE;
   type NODE_ACCESS_TYPE is access NODE_TYPE;
   type LIST_TYPE is
   record
      SIZE : NATURAL := 0;
      HEAD : NODE_ACCESS_TYPE;
      CURRENT : NODE_ACCESS_TYPE;
   end record;
end LISTS;
```

Three separate instantiations were used, one to provide the agenda, and the others to provide lists of connections and signals in the various tasks. In order to allow access to these lists from a number of separate tasks the package was implemented using a task as a LIST_MANAGER, each instantiation therefore ran as a separate task.

5.8 The Package NEURAL_NET

The following is the final specification for package NEURAL_NET and contains the only objects that are visible to a user. Note that package AGENDA is not visible to the user.

```
package NEURAL_NET is
    MAXIMUM_TIME : constant := 10.0;
    type CONNECTION_TYPE is limited private;
    type NEURON_TYPE is limited private;
    type REAL_TYPE is digits 6;
    subtype VALUE_TYPE is REAL_TYPE;
    subtype WEIGHT_TYPE is REAL_TYPE;
    type TIME_TYPE is delta 0.01 range 0.0..MAXIMUM_TIME;
    type CONNECTION_DIRECTION_TYPE is
            (INWARDS, OUTWARDS);
    type CONNECTION_NATURE_TYPE is
            (INPUT, OUTPUT, HIDDEN);
    procedure CONSTRUCT(
            CONNECTION : in out CONNECTION_TYPE;
            WEIGHT : in WEIGHT_TYPE;
            WEIGHT_INCREMENT : in WEIGHT_TYPE;
            NATURE : in CONNECTION_NATURE_TYPE;
            CONNECTION_DELAY : in TIME_TYPE);

    procedure CONSTRUCT(
            NEURON : in out NEURON_TYPE;
            THRESHOLD : in VALUE_TYPE);

    procedure CONNECT(
            NEURON : in out NEURON_TYPE;
            CONNECTION : in out CONNECTION_TYPE;
            DIRECTION : in CONNECTION_DIRECTION_TYPE);

    procedure FINISH_CONNECTING(
            NEURON : in out NEURON_TYPE);
```

```
procedure SET_INPUT_SIGNAL(
        CONNECTION : in out CONNECTION_TYPE;
        VALUE : in VALUE_TYPE;
        TIME : in TIME_TYPE);

procedure GET_OUTPUT_SIGNAL(
        CONNECTION : in out CONNECTION_TYPE;
        VALUE : out VALUE_TYPE;
        TIME : out TIME_TYPE);

procedure PROPAGATE;

private
  type NEURON_TASK_TYPE;
  type NEURON_TYPE is access NEURON_TASK_TYPE;
  type CONNECTION_TASK_TYPE;
  type CONNECTION_TYPE is access CONNECTION_TASK_TYPE;
end NEURAL_NET;
```

5.9 The XOR Example
The following program implements the XOR network shown in figure 1.

```
with TEXT_IO, NEURAL_NET;

procedure XOR_NET is

  package VALUE_IO is new TEXT_IO.FLOAT_IO(
        NUM => NEURAL_NET.VALUE_TYPE);
  package TIME_IO is new TEXT_IO.FIXED_IO(
        NUM => NEURAL_NET.TIME_TYPE);
  A, B, C, D, E, F, G, H, O : NEURAL_NET.CONNECTION_TYPE;
  N1, N2, N3, N4, N5 : NEURAL_NET.NEURON_TYPE;
  VALUE : NEURAL_NET.VALUE_TYPE;
  TIME : NEURAL_NET.TIME_TYPE;

begin
  NEURAL_NET.CONSTRUCT(CONNECTION => A, WEIGHT => 1.0,
        WEIGHT_INCREMENT => 0.001, NATURE => NEURAL_NET.
        INPUT, CONNECTION_DELAY => 0.1);
  NEURAL_NET.CONSTRUCT(CONNECTION => B, WEIGHT => 1.0,
```

```
        WEIGHT_INCREMENT => 0.001, NATURE => NEURAL_NET.
        INPUT, CONNECTION_DELAY => 0.1);
NEURAL_NET.CONSTRUCT(CONNECTION => C, WEIGHT => 1.0,
        WEIGHT_INCREMENT => 0.001, NATURE => NEURAL_NET.
        HIDDEN, CONNECTION_DELAY => 0.1);
NEURAL_NET.CONSTRUCT(CONNECTION => D, WEIGHT => -1.0,
        WEIGHT_INCREMENT => 0.001, NATURE => NEURAL_NET.
        HIDDEN, CONNECTION_DELAY => 0.1);
NEURAL_NET.CONSTRUCT(CONNECTION => E, WEIGHT => -1.0,
        WEIGHT_INCREMENT => 0.001, NATURE => NEURAL_NET.
        HIDDEN, CONNECTION_DELAY => 0.1);
NEURAL_NET.CONSTRUCT(CONNECTION => F, WEIGHT => 1.0,
        WEIGHT_INCREMENT => 0.001, NATURE => NEURAL_NET.
        HIDDEN, CONNECTION_DELAY => 0.1);
NEURAL_NET.CONSTRUCT(CONNECTION => G, WEIGHT => 1.0,
        WEIGHT_INCREMENT => 0.001, NATURE => NEURAL_NET.
        HIDDEN, CONNECTION_DELAY => 0.1);
NEURAL_NET.CONSTRUCT(CONNECTION => H, WEIGHT => 1.0,
        WEIGHT_INCREMENT => 0.001, NATURE => NEURAL_NET.
        HIDDEN, CONNECTION_DELAY => 0.1);
NEURAL_NET.CONSTRUCT(CONNECTION => O, WEIGHT => 1.0,
        WEIGHT_INCREMENT => 0.001, NATURE => NEURAL_NET.
        OUTPUT, CONNECTION_DELAY => 0.1);
NEURAL_NET.CONSTRUCT(NEURON => N1,
        THRESHOLD => 0.1);
NEURAL_NET.CONSTRUCT(NEURON => N2,
        THRESHOLD => 0.1);
NEURAL_NET.CONSTRUCT(NEURON => N3,
        THRESHOLD => 0.1);
NEURAL_NET.CONSTRUCT(NEURON => N4,
        THRESHOLD => 0.1);
NEURAL_NET.CONSTRUCT(NEURON => N5,
        THRESHOLD => 0.1);
NEURAL_NET.CONNECT(NEURON => N1, CONNECTION => A,
        DIRECTION => NEURAL_NET.INWARDS);
NEURAL_NET.CONNECT(NEURON => N2, CONNECTION => B,
        DIRECTION => NEURAL_NET.INWARDS);
NEURAL_NET.CONNECT(NEURON => N1, CONNECTION => C,
        DIRECTION => NEURAL_NET.OUTWARDS);
NEURAL_NET.CONNECT(NEURON => N1, CONNECTION => D,
        DIRECTION => NEURAL_NET.OUTWARDS);
NEURAL_NET.CONNECT(NEURON => N2, CONNECTION => E,
```

```
          DIRECTION => NEURAL_NET.OUTWARDS);
  NEURAL_NET.CONNECT(NEURON => N2, CONNECTION => F,
          DIRECTION => NEURAL_NET.OUTWARDS);
  NEURAL_NET.CONNECT(NEURON => N3, CONNECTION => C,
          DIRECTION => NEURAL_NET.INWARDS);
  NEURAL_NET.CONNECT(NEURON => N3, CONNECTION => E,
          DIRECTION => NEURAL_NET.INWARDS);
  NEURAL_NET.CONNECT(NEURON => N4, CONNECTION => D,
          DIRECTION => NEURAL_NET.INWARDS);
  NEURAL_NET.CONNECT(NEURON => N4, CONNECTION => F,
          DIRECTION => NEURAL_NET.INWARDS);
  NEURAL_NET.CONNECT(NEURON => N3, CONNECTION => G,
          DIRECTION => NEURAL_NET.OUTWARDS);
  NEURAL_NET.CONNECT(NEURON => N4, CONNECTION => H,
          DIRECTION => NEURAL_NET.OUTWARDS);
  NEURAL_NET.CONNECT(NEURON => N5, CONNECTION => G,
          DIRECTION => NEURAL_NET.INWARDS);
  NEURAL_NET.CONNECT(NEURON => N5, CONNECTION => H,
          DIRECTION => NEURAL_NET.INWARDS);
  NEURAL_NET.CONNECT(NEURON => N5, CONNECTION => O,
          DIRECTION => NEURAL_NET.OUTWARDS);
  NEURAL_NET.FINISH_CONNECTING(NEURON => N1);
  NEURAL_NET.FINISH_CONNECTING(NEURON => N2);
  NEURAL_NET.FINISH_CONNECTING(NEURON => N3);
  NEURAL_NET.FINISH_CONNECTING(NEURON => N4);
  NEURAL_NET.FINISH_CONNECTING(NEURON => N5);
  NEURAL_NET.SET_INPUT_SIGNAL(CONNECTION => A,
          VALUE => 1.0, TIME => 0.01);
  NEURAL_NET.SET_INPUT_SIGNAL(CONNECTION => B,
          VALUE => 1.0, TIME => 0.02);
  NEURAL_NET.PROPAGATE;
  NEURAL_NET.GET_OUTPUT_SIGNAL(CONNECTION => O,
          VALUE => VALUE, TIME => TIME);
  TEXT_IO.PUT("output_value is:");
  VALUE_IO.PUT(VALUE);
  TEXT_IO.PUT(" output time is:");
  TIME_IO.PUT(TIME);
  TEXT_IO.NEW_LINE;
end XOR_NET;
```

5.10 Ada Style

The original intention had been to produce a syntax that reflected the object-oriented, message-passing style in which the system has been written. So that for example instead of the statement:

```
NEURAL_NET.CONNECT(NEURON => N1, CONNECTION => A,
        DIRECTION => NEURAL_NET.INWARDS);
```

we could have the statement:

```
N1.CONNECT(TO_CONNECTION => A,
        DIRECTION => NEURAL_NET.INWARDS);
```

which more accurately reflects the actuality of what is happening, namely that a message is being passed to neuron N1 instructing it to connect itself with connection A. This syntax is possible in Ada but in order to achieve it it would be necessary to place the specification of at least the task type NEURON in the specification of NEURAL_NET. The placing of the specification of a task in a package specification is not desirable in most circumstances and in this case it would preclude us from alternative implementations. The only other possible way of achieving the same effect would be to implement each neuron as a generic package containing CONSTRUCT and CONNECT procedures, this does not seem to be a particular good way of implementing this system.

6 CONCLUSIONS

This work has clearly shown that it is possible to program a fully fledged agenda driven system in Ada. The resulting system is robust and reasonably efficient for the small networks that have so far been used. The advantages of Ada over the more usual languages such as Lisp and Prolog for this type of work are clear. The strong typing made it more difficult to make the usual sort of mistake and the scope and visibility rules meant that we had to be very sure about where objects were declared and how the necessary information could be made available to the parts of the program that needed it. The features of Ada allow an Artificial Intelligence style of programming that is more secure and reliable than the more traditional AI languages.

The program does require a system that allows a large number of tasks. The XOR example uses over 30 tasks and while it runs efficiently on the systems that we have used, the construction of large networks may present a number of difficulties. Of course such systems are best run on machines with large numbers of parallel processors and an Ada compiler that can distribute tasks. In order to increase the practicality of the system we are looking at other units of distribution, currently the only real alternative is to use Ada programs, possibly each with a few tasks, and then use Operating System facilities for distribution and inter-process communication. We are hoping that increased help for distribution will be one of the main priorities for Ada 9X. The other language feature which could make this style of programming much easier would be the ability to treat subprograms as objects and pass them as parameters, again we hope that Ada 9X will give priority to this feature.

References

ABELSON, HAROLD & GERALD JAY SUSSMAN 1985. *Structure and Interpretation of Computer Programs*. The MIT Press.

CARPENTER, R.H.S. 1990. *Neurophysiology*. Edward Arnold, 2nd. edition.

CHECKLAND, PETER 1985. *Systems Thinking, Systems Practice*. John Wiley and Sons.

FORNARINO, C. & B. NEVEU 1989. "Ada and Le_Lisp: a marriage of convenience for A.I.", *in* Diaz-Herrera, J. & Zytgow, J. M., (eds.), *Proceedings of AIDA-89. Fifth Annual Conference on Artificial Intelligence and Ada*. George Mason University.

LENAT, DOUGLAS B. 1978. "The Ubiquity of Discovery", *Artificial Intelligence*, 9: 257–285.

NEWELL, A. & H. SIMON 1972. *Human Problem Solving*. Prentice-Hall.

R. MCCABE, C. HEARTWELL, A. MAGLIERO & T. SHIELDS 1989. "The Adaptive Diagnostic System", *in* Diaz-Herrera, J. & Zytgow, J. M., (eds.), *Proceedings of AIDA-89. Fifth Annual Conference on Artificial Intelligence and Ada*. George Mason University.

RUMELHART & MCCLELLAND, (eds.) 1986. *Parallel Distributed Processing*. MIT Press.

SIVESS, VICTORIA J.D. 1989. "The Design and Implementation of a Neural Network Toolkit Using Ada", *in* Diaz-Herrera, J. & Zytgow, J. M., (eds.), *Proceedings of AIDA-89. Fifth Annual Conference on Artificial Intelligence and Ada*. George Mason University.

THE USE OF ADA IN REACTIVE SYSTEMS:
A 3-DIMENSIONAL MODEL

T. ELRAD[1], V. WINANS

Illinois Institute of Technology
Department of Computer Science
Chicago, IL   60616   USA
EMAIL: CSELRAD@HARPO.IIT.EDU

1 INTRODUCTION

Reactive real time systems present a challenge to designers and programmers because of the dual need for efficient and well-maintained system operations and also the need to provide a system responsive to external and internal events. Reactive systems are systems which respond to external events in order to maintain a particular interaction with their environment [P]. The new generation of military avionics and ground control systems are typically reactive systems. These systems are quite different from transformational systems which are systems whose sole purpose is to accept inputs, transform these inputs in some manner, then produce outputs. Real-time systems might be transformational or reactive systems. For example, systems which must compute a specific function with hard deadlines are real time transformational systems. Systems which have aperiodic, periodic, and sporadic external events are considered to be real-time reactive systems.

An event-driven design is often used in the initial specification and design stages; in particular, the use of statecharts [H1] and similar state-based visual methods have proven to be quite useful in developing these types of systems. One of the design principles of Statemate [H1] and Machine Charts [B2] is that the design and specification of such a system is a tri-modal blend of the functional, the behavioral, and the structural aspects of the final system. The functional aspect of the system details the actions carried out by the system. The behavior of the system describes the dynamic control of these actions: the sequence of events necessary to trigger/terminate these actions, the timing constraints, and the required concurrency. The structural view of the system represents its physical requirements of both the hardware and the software.

---

[1] This work supported in part by a grant from the U.S. Army CECOM Army Research Office, and Battelle under Scientific Services Program #1800.

2 THE MAGIC CUBE

2.1 Traversing the Magic Cube

These three modes which serve as a framework for developing reactive systems can be represented 3-dimensionally by a magic cube, which is an extension of the magic square concept [H1]. The three axis of the cube correspond to the structural, functional, and behavioral aspects of the reactive system. New promising approaches to reactive system development provide a means for capturing all three modes using design/specification languages such as Statemate [H2]. From now on this will be referred to as the specification language. Traversing the magic cube is application specific. Ideally, system development progresses in small increments from one corner of the cube to the farthest corner along a diagonal (Fig. 1). The small increments are accomplished by elucidating the design and specification of the system along each of the three axis simultaneously. This balanced development, with each of the three modes reflecting the needs of the other two, results in the diagonal traversal of the magic cube.

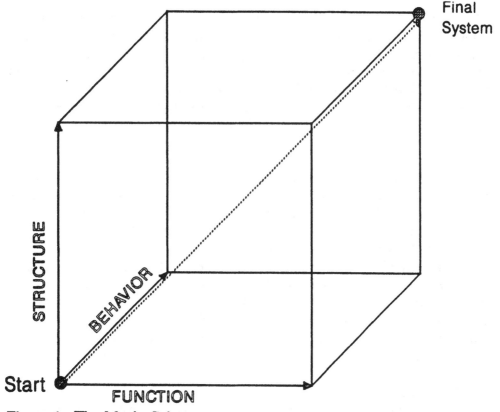

Figure 1. The Magic Cube

2.2 Reactive System Development

This magic cube framework provides a general orientation for the development of reactive systems. Developmental tool packages exist that can assist in converting the design and specification of a reactive system into code. However, the conversion into code points out an additional concern in developing large reactive systems: the suitability of the chosen high-level language for implementing the reactive system.

Specifically, the expressive power and the limited capacity of the language used for implementing the design can result in a reactive system that does not accurately translate the design and specification. The resulting system may suffer from any one or a combination of the following: 1) the structure of the software does not accurately reflect the structure of the specification, 2) the behavior of the system cannot be adequately controlled, especially in real-time situations, 3) the limited capacity of the language results in awkward functionality. The sum of the compromises made between the language used and specification results in an inaccurate but operable reactive system.

The assurance that the implementation language can fully and accurately implement the specification [L] relieves the burden of trial-and-error exhaustive testing of the final system and the subsequent costly adjustments that must be made to the completed system. Rather, utilization of tool packages allow the testing to be performed in the specification phase of the project. Making the necessary changes earlier in the project development conserves time, money, and can ultimately result in a particularly robust reactive system.

2.3 Specification to Implementation

One may argue that the system design and specification should be independent of the intended language for purposes of 1) reusability, 2) portability, and 3) the aesthetics of a design that truly reflect the desired product without unnecessary a priori constraints. Incorporating a language preference, albeit implicit, into the development of the system may appear to increase the degree of complexity in these formative stages. Carefully coordinating the development of the project along three axis simultaneously is challenging in itself; including an intuitive knowledge of a language's expressive power skews the development process more towards the intangible since the language dependence of the design and specification is not explicit.

2.4 Interface

The term "interface" is used to avoid the interpretation that the implementation language should dictate the specification, more that the language should have enough expressive power and flexibility that the design team can have the confidence in the ability of the language to fully translate the specification into code. The application of an intuitive knowledge of the implementation language's particular strengths and weaknesses during the design phase can prevent a later series of compromises at the interface between the implementation language and the specification language.

3 THE 3-D BUILDING BLOCKS LANGUAGE INTERFACE VS. THREE 1-D LINEAR MODULES LANGUAGE INTERFACE.

3.1 Models Definitions

This implementation language-specification language interface can be approached in two ways: 1) three one-dimensional linear modules, or 2) three-dimensional building blocks. A pictorial representation of these two interfaces is shown in Fig. 2.

1-D Model A three 1-D linear modules language is a language in which modules are of three types: structural modules, functional modules, or behavioral modules. Each module encapsulates exactly one of the three modes and hence it is linear in nature. With a three 1-D linear module interface it is not possible to encapsulate structure, function and behavior into a syntactically recognizable software component.

One example of a three 1-D module language interface is the Reactive Systems Model (RSM) [G]. Another examples is when a "time-slice/round-robin" approach to scheduling is used.

3-D Model A 3-D building block language interface is a language which enables a large reactive system to be decomposed into smaller components. Each of the components is itself a piece of the reactive system; it contains all three of the modes and hence is considered a 3-D module. A basic 3-D module has a structural element, a functional element, and a behavioral element. The exact coincidence of the modules with the design and specification signifies that the implementation language can fully and accurately translate the specification of the reactive system. A mismatch of the modules with the specification indicates that some of the aforementioned problems exist in the interface.

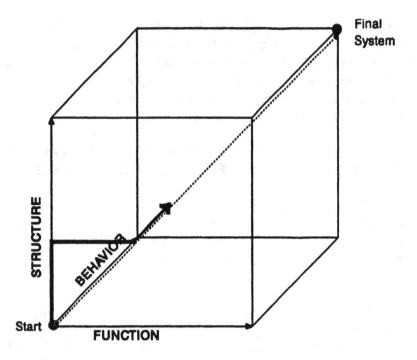

Figure 2a. The Three 1-D Linear Modules

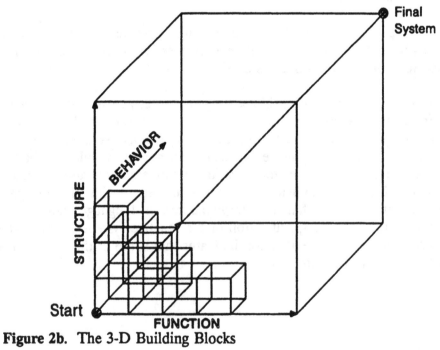

Figure 2b. The 3-D Building Blocks

Another design concern in reactive systems is the flexibility to interleave various system software components laterally and hierarchically [B1]. The 3-D cubes offer the capability of arranging the software components to accommodate numerous software architectures.

3.2 Cohesiveness and Coupling Issues

The ability to traverse the magic cube using the 3-D cubic modules indicates that the chosen implementation language can provide the ultimate balance of structure, function, and behavior. The 1-D modules are likewise stacked together to create the final 3-D cube. The stacking of these 1-D modules results in a superficially equivalent reactive system to the 3-D cubes however, the implementation language of the reactive systems differ greatly.

Intramodular Cohesion Intramodular cohesion is defined as the relationship that exists between the functional, behavioral, and structural aspects within the module. The 3-D cubes, by nature, have strong intramodule cohesion since each of the blocks encapsulates all three aspects of the specification. The 1-D modules exhibit a weak intramodule cohesion due to the domination of one particular aspect or in extreme cases, the actual absence of the other two modes.

Intermodular Coupling Similarly, intermodular coupling defines the implementation language's ability to connect the cubes or modules. The 3-D cubic modules provide weak intermodule coupling and inversely, the 1-D modules exhibit tight intermodule coupling. Languages could be classified according to which of the two interfaces they provide.

4 ADA: A 3-DIMENSIONAL INTERFACE MODEL

4.1 Encapsulation of the Three dimensions

Ada belongs to the 3-D class of languages which encapsulates a balance of progress in these syntactically recognizable units as shown in Figure 3.

Ada's expressive power for reactive real-time systems is evaluated. Using the magic cube and its modular interface model offers several advantages: 1) During the specification for reactive real-time systems to be implemented in Ada, Ada's expressive power/lack of expressive power may be taken into consideration to minimize potential conflicts. 2) Matching Ada against an ideal model of 3-D building blocks of language design will direct us towards possible ways to extend Ada to a powerful language consistent with its own design choice as a 3-D language. 3) The 3-D interface model can be applied to the concept of mega-programming creating a direction for future software developments.

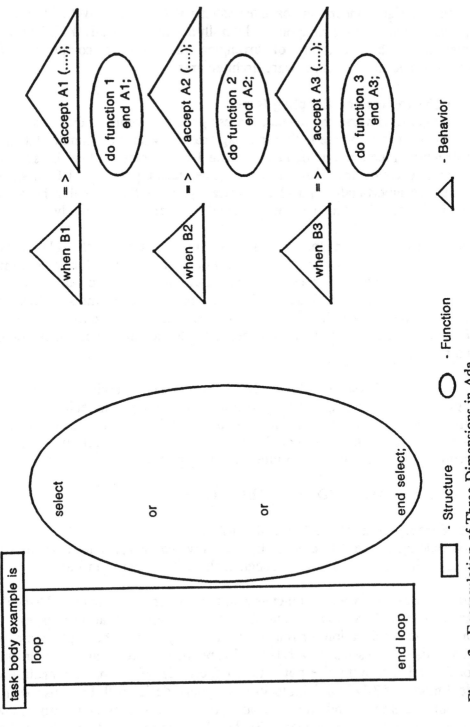

Figure 3. Encapsulation of Three Dimensions in Ada

The Ada tasking model reflects the 3-D cubic building blocks. The Ada task is the natural block which can be manipulated in the three different ways: structurally, functionally, and behaviorally. The structure of the system can be naturally mirrored in the tasks. The tasks can represent the physical character of the system, on a superficial level. They can likewise be communicationally linked together by the rendezvous in virtually any pattern to implement the specified underlying structure of a system. The select statement can be thought of as an expressive unit within the external task, providing another hierarchical inner layer of structure. It is this internal, expressive layer that can be parameterized and molded to system specification. The functionality of the system is carried out through the body of the **accept** statement, or the body of the task. The behavioral dimension is controlled by the guards.

4.2 Mega-programming

Mega-programming can be describe as "component-based software engineering and life cycle management"[2]. Building independently strong cohesive modules equipped with external handles is consistent with this concept of mega-programming. External handles are syntactically recognizable entities that can be dynamically modified from outside the module. These handles are templates to instantiate specific structure, function, and behavior. A 3-D building block is a natural component for software engineering management. A critical issue is the degree to which a 3-D block is manageable and integratable. A rigid, inflexible block would not support mega-programming. A manageable block is a block which can be parameterized along all three axis. External handles should be provided for managing the structure, the functional and the behavior. Integrating the block for multiple uses, either in the same system or for later re-use [R], is facilitated by these external handles. Ada supports life cycle management of function and structure. There is no equivalent support for managing behavior. This is reflected in the number of requirements for the Ada 9X to support user-defined and flexible scheduling capabilities. The focus of this paper is the behavioral dimension of the 3-D cubic interface and its impact on the directions Ada may take in supporting the Ada 9X efforts.

5 THE BEHAVIORAL EXPRESSIVE POWER IN ADA

The behavioral dimension can be thought of as the necessary controls for the functional dimension. The ability of a language to control behavior is a large

---

[2] Barry Boehm, Director of the Information Systems Technology Office, Keynote Address at DARPA, Software Engineering Instutute, *Bridge*, December 1990

part of its expressive power; in a reactive event-driven system, this entails responding to external events which may be widely dispersed in time and physical space. One can term behavior as the execution of the correct response to these external events. A correct response may have time constraints where a deadline must be met, synchronization constraints where a response(s) must be performed on specific cue, and scheduling constraints where a well-ordered response(s) must occur.

5.1 Intermodular Behavior Control

The time and scheduling constraints are directed by the task scheduler which is separated from the 3-D cubic interfaces. The task scheduler provides some of the intermodular behavioral and structural control for the language. As explained earlier, Ada has an inherent capability to control the three dimensions internally in the language itself. The task scheduler can be thought of as the default exterior controls: the basic static controls of an Ada program without specific application or programmer influences. The task scheduler can be thought of as providing the basic intermodular behavioral and structural coupling needed in the 3-D interface model.

5.2 Intramodular Behavior Control

The Comprehensive Race controls [E2] introduce a basis for behavior controls in Ada within the context of the 3-D cubic interface. The behavioral interface must provide the tools to construct a well-controlled environment. This environment provides the backdrop for orchestrating the functions of the specification language.

6 THE COMPREHENSIVE SCHEDULING CONTROLS

The set of all possible scheduling controls used by a language is termed the Comprehensive Scheduling Controls. Figure 4 illustrates the Comprehensive Scheduling Controls hierarchy. The Comprehensive Scheduling Controls are split into two classes: Availability Controls and Race Controls.

6.1 Availability Controls

Availability controls are those controls which enable or disable a nondeterministic choice within the selective wait construct. In a reactive system, the event-driven specification defines the allowable state transitions from the current state; guaranteeing that the reactive system will be restricted to these allowable transitions is an important ability for a language. Availability controls also provide the flexibility to control these alternatives dynamically, which allows the language to accommodate the constantly changing system state.

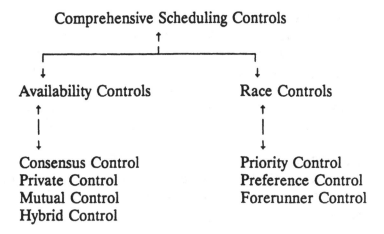

Figure 4. Scheduling Controls Classification

The availability of any of the alternatives for selection is derived from certain constraints applied to each alternative, such as Boolean expressions, communication readiness or any combination of such constraints. Those alternatives in which all the constraints are satisfied are said to be open and available for selection, otherwise the alternatives are said to be closed and unavailable for selection.

In examining the use of availability controls for reactive systems, it is conceivable that these expressions could be utilized to reflect the system's state, enabling a syntactic recognition of the current state of the reactive system. Since the primary functions of the interface modules is to provide a natural transition from specification language into the implementation language, providing these state-oriented syntactic constructs for behavior control is essential. This is not to say that availability controls should be state-oriented; merely that since Ada is to be used for large complex reactive systems, thinking in terms of event-driven designs should lead to variations of some basic behavior controls. Ada offers a "blank slate" for nondeterministic behavior; one of the challenges is to discover ways the language can naturally mimic the event-driven designs of reactive systems with availability controls.

The responsiveness of the system depends on 1) recognition of the triggering event(s), 2) communicating the occurrence of this event to the proper module, and 3) the accurate responses (both function and timeliness) of the module. The separation of concerns [F1] also includes the separation of functional concerns. In the case of reactive systems, the recognition of events is a functional part of the system, as are the operations of the system. Separating these two functions into different modules allows the operational functions to progress smoothly without the need to poll for event occurrences and the need to activate other functional modules. The separation of the event recognition, however, heightens the need for a strong communication-to-function response. In Ada, the communication is performed with a rendezvous, and the accepted entry call determines the proper functional response to the communication. The addition of behavior control can channel responses to strengthen dynamically-specified communication response.

These Availability Controls are classified as Consensus Control, Private Control, Mutual Control and Hybrid Control to reflect the different constraints that may be applied to an alternative to control behavior and are defined below.

Consensus Control. Consensus Control represents the capacity to enable/disable a nondeterministic choice based on pending communication requests originating outside of the local environment of the task. The concensus control would particularly enable a specific channeling of a communication to a response.

Private Control. Private control represents the capacity to enable/disable a nondeterministic choice based on a Boolean expression determined by the local state of the task. This particular control can aid in verifying that local conditions exist for a specific state transition to occur. State transitions may be conditional, and the behavior must be sensitive to these fluctuating conditions. This control can be utilized to reflect the local conditions that must be met for a state transition to occur (ie, a response to be performed). More details can be found in [C].

6.2 Race Controls

During the execution of a concurrent program, tasks are racing to be scheduled when a resource becomes free at the program level, open alternatives are racing to be selected when an alternative construct is executed at the task level or entry calls are racing to be accepted to initiate an intertask communication at the entry level. A event must be selected from the available events. Race controls are those controls which resolve a race for either task scheduling, alternative selection or intertask communication. In describing the difference between availability controls and race controls, it is helpful to note that availability controls determine what could be done whereas race controls determine how to resolve possible conflicts among available choices.

An important aspect of race controls is that they may be used to prioritize the choices for selection. The necessity for deterministic race controls is crucial within real-time and reactive systems as both rely heavily on the enforcement of specific behavior patterns. To reflect the race at each level, race controls are classified as Priority Control, Preference Control and Forerunner Control. The classification of race controls by levels (program, task, and entry) gives a framework for understanding the dynamics of any tasking model used in a language such as Ada, Concurrent C, CSP, or Occam. Many of the problems and deficiencies that occur in the tasking model can be directly explained through the function of an individual race control or through the interaction between the various race controls. This classification scheme allows us to focus on each control as a separate entity with properties that effect the entire system in which it exists. The different types of individual race control are defined as follows:

Priority Control. The control over the program level scheduling of tasks.

Preference Control. The control over the task level scheduling of alternatives within the nondeterministic construct.

Forerunner Control. The control over the entry level scheduling of pending entry calls.

6.3 The Current State of Race Controls in Ada [C],[E2]

Priority Control Ada has an explicit static priority control mechanism. Priority is implemented as a **pragma.**

Preference Control Ada has no preference control. An arbitrary selection is made among open alternatives in the **selective wait.**

Forerunner Control Ada has an implcit static forerunner control mechanism. Entry calls are serviced in a strictly FIFO manner.

Ada can be characterized as being weak and seriously lacking in the area of race controls. The concept of priority is not integrated consistently across all controls. The characteristics of race control range from no control to explicit static to implicit static. A lack of integration contributes to inflexibility in the application of race controls. Control is performed by a static centralized scheduler. The result is that real-time control is virtually impossible.

7 BEHAVIOR REQUIREMENTS UNDER ADA 9X

The Ada 9X draft document [A] proposes several changes that would support the 3-dimensional design interface consistent with its original intent [Figure 3].

7.1 Task Scheduling

The Fourth International Workshop on Real-Time Ada Issues [F2] discussed Ada 9X Draft Requirements Document and proposed the following:

> *Ada 9X shall sllow implementations to provide other methods, in addition to Ada 83's static priorities, for scheduling task execution. Use of an alternative scheduling method shall be reflected in the source code. Greater flexibility shall also be allowed in the syntactic placement of scheduling paramters."*

This particular requirement states the need for expressive priority control. The ideal intermodular relationship can be attained by utilizing the capability to control behavior within the module. Priority control provides an intramodular alternative to the existing intermodular task scheduler. This offers the advantages of 1) the behavior control reflecting the dynamic needs of the local environment, 2) allowing programmer behavior control, and 3) incorporating behavior parameters that can be easily modified to reflect various applications for the purposes of portability and resuability.

7.2 Forerunner Control

Queuing Order Requirement Ada 9X Draft Requirements Document [F2] also proposes The following :

> *Ada 9X shall allow implementations to provide other methods, in addition to first-come-first-serve, for ordering tasks queued on an entry. Use of an alternative queuing method shall be reflected in the program source code.*

Incorporating forerunner control into the Ada 9X language would provide more depth and flexibility to the existing behvavior control. The present queuing order is FIFO and provides a basic service for all incoming entry calls. Offering the programmer the capability to choose a different order for accepting entry calls enables a powerful expressive tool which would enhance both scheduling and synchronization. An intramodular behavior control is the essence of this requirement.

Dynamic Forerunner Control Adding a priority queue is insufficient to fully provide the necessary external handles for mega-programming. There is also a need for a dynamic forerunner control.

7.3 Flexible Select Algorithm
The third requirement [F2] that directly pertains to race controls is the following:

> *Ada 9X shall provide other methods, in addition to "arbitrary", for choosing open alternatives in a select statement. Use of an alternative method shall be reflected in the program source code.*

This provision applies to the preference control. Since there is a lack of preference control in the current version of Ada, this control would strengthen the intramodular cohesiveness of the language. The advantages would be similar to those mentioned earlier for priority control. The particular added advantage for an event-driven reactive system is with preference control. In specifications of reactive systems where state transitions are evoked from a set of states and under specified conditions, the preference control offers a means of dynamically reflecting current states and conditions and the subsequent possible "open" alternatives. The preference control construct offers an obvious means of directly translating the specification language into Ada code, providing an integral part of the 3-D interface.

Dynamic Preference Control Again, a dynamic preference control will assure that the external handles necessary for mega-programming are available.

7.4 Matching Ada to the 3-D Model
The implementation of the above requirements would expand the expressive power in Ada to match the 3-D language interface. Developing the behavioral controls in the language increases the complexity of an already complex language, but one of the current software concerns is the ability to construct large, complex reactive systems. Attempting to meet this need by providing powerful and complex high-level languages is only plausible. If the implementation of a reactive system is to accurately translate a large and complex specification, then it follows that the implementing language must somehow accommodate this complexity. Maximizing the intramodular cohesiveness increases the complexity, yet it provides such a wealth of power that in the long run, a more natural transition between the specification can be accomplished, therby reducing the complexity of the specification language and implementation language interface. Simplifying this interface allows the automatic translation of the specification language into code. Maximizing the intramodular cohesiveness will effectively minimize the basic intermodular coupling Ada currently provides, but this again reflects the need in reactive systems. Reactive systems needs coherent units of operation which can be

loosely or tightly bound together; providing the necessary intramodular cohesiveness offers a vast amount of flexibility in the inter and intra modular interactions.

8 CONCLUSION

Reactive systems present a challenge to designers and programmers. A key issue for understanding their complexity is the strong requirements on all three axis; structure, function, and behavior. Moreover, all three are tightly bound in their intra-structure. Recent developments in specification/design tools for such systems encompass all three aspects and enable verification of the design [H2]. An implementation language with an adequate interface is crucial to keep the system under development sound. Ada has made a major step by first, incorporating behavior into the language rather than omitting it from the language(which would require the use of external tools in order to cast behavior at a later stage). Ada has made a second major step by choosing the 3-D building blocks interface. This enables the decomposition of the system under development into mini 3-D blocks and hence maximizing intramodular cohesiveness within a block and minimizing intermodular coupling among the cubes. A 3-D block is a natural component for software engineering and life cycle management and as such it supports the mega-programming style.

Ada 9X has the opportunity to complete the intramodule behavior control capability. This implies flexible scheduling parameters, flexible select algorithm through a dynamic preference control and flexible queuing ordering through forerunner control; these are a few of the possibilities among other aspects that were not covered here. Furnishing modifiable external handles to manage and integrate a block behavior from outside will provide an excellent opportunity for the mega-programming style.

Acknowledgements: We would like to thank R. E. Winans for assistance with the graphics.

REFERENCES

[A]   ADA 9X Project Report, Draft, ADA 9X Requirements Document, August, 1990

[B1]   J. V. Berk, A.H. Muntz, and P.R. Stevens, " Software Architectural Concepts for Avionics", Proceedings of IEEE National Aerospace and Electronics Conference, May 1989

[B2]   Raymond J. Buhr. Practical Visual Techniques in System Design, Draft Copy, (Prentice-Hall, 1990)

[C]   CECOM, Center for Software Engineering Advanced Software Technology, " Final Report - Comprehensive Race Controls: A Versatile Scheduling Mechanism for Real-Time Applications", CIN: C08 092KU 0001 00, February, 1990,

[E1]   T. Elrad. ADA Real-Time Issues Workshop, Devon, United Kingdom, 1987

[E2]   T. Elrad. "Comprehensive Race Controls: A Versatile Scheduling Mechanism for Real-Time Applications". Proceedings of the ADA Europe Conference, ADA The Design Choice, Ed. Angel Alvarez, Cambridge University Press, June 1989

[F1]   Stuart R. Faulk and David L. Parnas. "On Synchronization in Hard-Real-Time Systems." Communications of the ACM, Vol. 31, No. 3, March 1988

[F2]   The Fourth International Workshop on Real-Time Ada Issues, Pitlochry, Scotland, July 1990

[G]   Vered Gafni. "A Tasking Model for Reactive Systems". IEEE Proceedings Real Time Systems Symposium, 1989

[H1]   D. Harel and A. Pneuli. "On the Devlopment of Reactive Systems". NATO ASI Series, Vol. F13, "Logics and Models of Concurrent Systems", Ed. K. R. Apt (Springer Verlag, Berlin, 1985, pp. 477-498

[H2]   D. Harel et al. "STATEMATE: A Working Environment for the Development of Complex Reactive Systems". Transactions on Software Engineering, Vol. 16, No. 4, April 1990, pp. 403-414

[P]   A. Pneuli. "Applications of Temporal Logic to the Specification and Verification of Reactive Systems: A Survey of Current Trends" in Current Trends in Concurrency (de Bakker et al., eds), Lecture Notes in Computer Science, Vol. 224 (Springer-Verlag, Berlin, 1986, pp. 510-584)

[L]   R. W. Lichota and A.H. Muntz. "Specification Methods and
        Mapping Techniques for Transitioning from Requirements to
        Implementation", Proceedings of the 3rd Workshop on Large
        Grain Parallelism, Pittsburgh, PA, USA, Oct. 1989

[R]   Paul J. Rohde and Capt Larry Jamerson. "Integration of
        Multisensor Fusion and Sensor Management", Northrop
        Corporation Aircraft Division, Hawthorne, CA, USA and Air
        Force Wright Research & Development Center, Wright
        Patterson AFB, Ohio, USA

Ada 9X Real-Time Scheduling Alternatives

Fred A. Maymir-Ducharme

Grumman Data Systems
Woodbury, NY (USA)
fredmd@ajpo.sei.cmu.edu

ABSTRACT
The need to control Ada scheduling at the language level is one of the most popular requests for Ada 9X, as evidenced by the large number of related Revision Requests. Currently, the only alternatives available for Ada 83 require re-writing the executive, which requires modifying the operating system and/or runtime environment. This paper examines the requirements for controlling the scheduling of Ada ready queues, entry queues and select alternatives at the language level. These requirements are reviewed and the solutions currently being considered by various Ada 9X Project teams are presented and analyzed.

These requirements are based on participation at various Special Interest Group on Ada (SIGAda) and Ada RunTime Environment Working Group (ARTEWG) meetings reviewing Ada 9X Revision Requests, Revision Issues and Requirements. The proposed solutions and many of the discussion issues are reported from the 4th International Workshop on Real-Time Ada Issues, which was held in Pitlochry, Scotland, July 21 -25, 1990 and submitted to the Ada 9X Requirements Team, the Mapping Team, and the Designated Reviewers.

1 INTRODUCTION

Scheduling is one of the major set of requirements that must be addressed by Ada 9X. This is evident by the numerous Revision Requests (RRs) submitted [Ada 9X Project, "Revision Request Report," 1990] to the Ada 9X Project Office and the related Revision Issues (RIs) documented [Ada 9X Project, "Revision Issues," 1990]. The following RRs directly address these issues and are addressed by Revision Issues RI-7005 and RI-7007:

RR0013 DYNAMIC PRIORITIES FOR TASKS

RR0015 USE OF TASK PRIORITIES IN ACCEPT AND SELECT STATEMENTS
RR0016 ALTERNATE ADA TASK SCHEDULING
RR0020 MODIFICATION OF TASK PRIORITIES DURING EXECUTION
RR0021 TASK SCHEDULING
RR0037 CONTROL OF CLOCK SPEED AND TASK DISPATCH RATE
RR0072 TASK PRIORITIES (ADA-UK/012)
RR0075 PRIORITY ENTRY QUEUING
RR0076 PRIORITY SELECT
RR0116 ALLOW MODIFIABLE PRIORITIES FOR TASKS
RR0121 INCONSISTENCY IN ADA SEMANTICS OF RACE CONTROLS
RR0124 REVOKE AI-00594/02
RR0125 INTRODUCE INHERITANCE INTO ADA
RR0170 SCHEDULING ALGORITHMS
RR0192 ALLOW DYNAMIC PRIORITIES FOR TASKS
RR0193 CONSISTENT SEMANTICS FOR TASK PRIORITIES
RR0337 DYNAMIC PRIORITIES
RR0347 IMPROVED SUPPORT OF PRIORITY LEVELS
RR0379 SCHEDULING ALGORITHMS
RR0415 TASK PRIORITIES, PROCESSING OF ENTRY CALLS
RR0525 ADA SHOULD SUPPORT INHERITANCE AND POLYMORPHISM
RR0654 DYNAMIC PRIORITIES
RR0656 TIMED EXCEPTIONS
RR0657 PRIORITY IN ENTRY QUEUES
RR0737 ALLOW PREFERENCE CONTROL FOR ENTRIES IN A SELECT STATEMENT
RR0750 SUPPORT FOR INHERITANCE AND POLYMORPHISM

The Ada 9X addresses these issues in two separate requirements [SEI 1990]. These requirements were the first discussed at the workshop and were categorized as "Essential" (Level 1) - necessary in Ada 9X in order to fulfill the requirements of the real-time community.

Requirement 1 - Flexible Scheduling -   Ada 9X shall allow implementations to provide other methods, in addition to Ada 83's static priorities, for scheduling task execution. Use of an alternative scheduling method shall be reflected in the source code. Greater flexibility shall also be allowed in the syntactic placement of scheduling parameters.

Requirement 2 - Flexible Entry Queue Ordering - Ada 9X shall allow implementations to provide other methods, in addition to first-come-first-serve, for ordering tasks queued on an entry. Use of an alternative queuing method shall be reflected in the program source code.

It was agreed at the workshop that flexible scheduling and entry queue ordering were not sufficient requirements to meet the scheduling needs of Ada 9X. The need to control the ordering of the choice of open alternatives in a select statement is evident in several RRs. The dynamic priorities, scheduling mechanisms and priority inheritance proposals discussed herein are recommended by the workshop for Ada 9X to address these issues.

2 DYNAMIC PRIORITIES
The need exists to dynamically change the relative order of execution of tasks for scheduling and mode changes purposes. The most accepted mechanism proposed to address this issue in Ada 9X is dynamic priorities.

2.1 Dynamic Priorities Proposal
The initial dynamic priorities implementation proposed at the workshop was defined as follows:

- Priorities range: -5 .. 5. Range of 11, using 4 bits.
- Default Priorities: The main and library units will default to "O" and all others will default to the priority of the activator.
- A new statement is proposed for setting priorities dynamically. The syntax options are described below:

    set_priority_statement   :==   Set_Priority(task_name   =>
    integer_expression) {,task_name => integer_expression});

    or

    set_priority_statement   :==   Set_Priority((task_name,
    integer_expression) {,(task_name, integer_expression)});

- A new attribute is proposed for reading a task's priority dynamically. The syntax is as follows:

    P'PRIORITY

    where P is the task name, the attribute returns the priority of task P. The scope is defined the same as the task scoping rules in the

Ada LRM [ANSI/MIL-STD-1815A, 1983]. The exception "TASKING_ERROR" will be raised if P has terminated.

In addition to these definitions, the proposal adds that "aborted," "completed," and "unactivated" tasks be valid tasks to assign priorities and read their priorities dynamically. It should be noted that this implementation does not depend on the support of "task_id's," as does the CIFO [ARTEWG 1987] entry on dynamic priorities. The issue of "immediacy" of the updating of priorities is left to be implementation dependent; the intent is to make the new assignment of priorities effective immediately, before the next scheduling event.

2.2 Dynamic Priorities Issues

A discussion on the related issues and concerns ensued shortly after the dynamic priorities proposal above was presented. The issues, concerns and recommendations discussed are listed below:

- It's accepted that the range of priorities needs to be standardized; this will help make Ada software more portable. The priority range defined (-5..+5) was challenged. First of all, 4 bits allow a range of 16, whereas the range defined only allows a range of 11. The initial intent was to save some higher and lower priorities for system specific software.

- A study on the effect of priority ranges on rate monotonic scheduling was cited. The study concludes that with a range of 256 priorities there is no negative effect on rate monotonic; 128 priorities only have a 2% degradation effect, whereas 64 priorities can degrade the rate monotonic scheduling up to 8% and a reduction to 32 priorities can cause a degradation between 8% and 10%; a range of only 16 priorities had a much more severe degradation effect between 50% and 60%. The conclusion derived was that Ada 9X must support a range of 32 priorities.

- The issue on the need to define maximum and minimum priority ranges was brought up. After minimal discussion, it was agreed to define the minimum range of priorities to be 32, and allow the maximum range to be implementation dependent.

- The immediacy of setting priorities is a critical issue. The setting of priorities is defined to have immediate effect, but it cannot be guaranteed that it has taken effect by the time of return from the set_priority_statement. This issue must also be reviewed with respect to feature interactions with priority inheritance.

- The setting of priorities brings up another feature interactions issue - that is the (temporal) difference between the "personal" priority initially set by the system and modified by the set_priority_statement, and the "system" priority that can be changed back and forth by the system for priority inheritance features. The setting of priorities should only apply to the "personal" priority. The "personal" priority was sometimes referred to as "basic" priority; whereas the "system" priority was sometimes referred to as "inherited" priority. The differences (including scoping rules) between these two priorities need to be clearly defined and delineated. The scope for changing priorities should be limited appropriately.

- The default priority scheme was reviewed. The setting of default priorities only applies to the "basic/personal" priority. Some concerns were expressed over giving library units a default priority of "O." It was generally accepted that the main program defaults to "O" and that the priority of a parent task is passed as default to its children. The issues of whether or not mode changes affect default priorities and special cases where when leaving accept code and launching into application code one may not want to retain priorities were brought up and deferred until the discussion on inheritance.

- The question arose regarding whether or not priorities can be assigned to objects or types (e.g., task types.) These issues require additional investigation and should be addressed by the requirements team.

- Inconsistencies within the underlying runtime data structures were discussed. Changes must be sufficiently atomic to ensure consistency in overlapping strings of operations.

- Multiprocessing and the support of dynamic priorities also requires additional investigation. Temporary inconsistencies within multiprocessors is a possible problem that should be reviewed, as well as the overhead associated with having to support dynamic priorities on multiprocessors.

- The suggestion that a "get_priority_statement" be added, instead of the P'PRIORITY attribute function, in order to be more consistent needs to be reviewed. Another consistency issue raised was over the fact that initiating priorities is proposed using pragmas, setting priorities is proposed using a new statement, and getting priorities is proposed using a new attribute.

- The group discussed the feasibility of setting and getting priorities of "aborted, completed or unactivated" tasks. It was agreed that this proposal was consistent with the language treatment of the abort feature.

3 PRIORITY SCHEDULING AND INHERITANCE

The need exists to allow programmers the ability to explicitly control the Ada scheduling mechanisms for the "ready queues," the "entry queues," and the "select statements" in order to avoid service degradation, ensure adequate response time and meet real-time deadline schedules. Another reason cited for the need to control the Ada scheduling involves consistency - users often require deterministic scheduling behavior. Several Ada 9X Revision Request support the need for these features within the Ada language for scheduling and mode change purposes.

The other issue addressed by this section is that of avoiding priority inversion. This proposal describes the general inheritance rules and suggests adding the option to extend these rules to support transitive inheritance. (These features are all defined below).

The initial scheduling features and priority inheritance [Sha *et al.* 1987] rules proposed at the workshop were defined as described below. The proposal differentiates between three levels of implementations: Each subsequent level includes the previous level.

Scheduling mechanisms are defined in Section 3.1 for the following:

- Ready Queues (dispatch scheduler)
- Entry Queues (rendezvous scheduler)
- Select Statement (nondeterministic select scheduler)

Three levels of priority management are proposed; these are described in section 3.2:

- Dynamic Priorities
- "Basic" Inheritance Rules
- Transitive Inheritance Rules

3.1 Scheduling Features Proposed

The first set of scheduling features (level 1) are for ready queues. These features all assume that dynamic priorities are supported and that every task is assigned a priority. The selection of tasks waiting in the ready queues will be done on the basis of priority, instead of the current First In First Out (FIFO) selection basis. In the case where there are more than one task in the ready queue with the same highest priority value, one of the following scheduling paradigms may be used:

- FIFO (Of the tasks with the highest priority, dispatch the one that

was queued first.)
- Round Robin (Use the classical Round Robin scheduling theory.)
- Unspecified (This option may be left to the compiler vendor as an implementation dependent feature.)

The second set of scheduling features are for entry queues. These features assume that all entry queues will select the caller in the entry queue for the rendezvous on the basis of priority. In the case where there are more than one calling tasks with the highest priority, one of the following criteria may be used for the selection between tasks of the highest priority:

- FIFO (Of the tasks with the highest priority, dispatch the one that was queued first.)
- User Defined (The user may select a caller based on the values passed in the call parameters (e.g., Mutual Control [Elrad and Maymir-Ducharme 1988] such as the "suchthat" construct in Concurrent C) or based on some attributes associated with the task (e.g., new values added to the Task Control Block (TCB) such as deadline time or time CPU time used, etc. Similar to the "by" construct in Concurrent C.).
- Unspecified (This option may be left to the compiler vendor as an implementation dependent feature).

The third set of scheduling features controls the selection mechanism of the select statement. The following options are defined:

1. Priority Select - Select the open alternative with the highest priority caller queued. In the case where there are more than one calling tasks with the highest priority queued, one of the following criteria may be used for selection [Maymir-Ducharme and Kamrad 1990]:

   - FIFO (Of the tasks with the highest priority, dispatch the one that was queued first.)
   - User Defined (The user may select a caller based on the values passed in the call parameters or based on some attributes associated with the task (as described above.)
   - Unspecified (This option may be left to the compiler vendor as an implementation dependent feature.)

2. Language Defined Static Order - The calls within the select statement will be considered for selection statically by either of the two following paradigms:

- Select the first open alternative in the order the alternatives are defined within the select statement. This is similar to the "priority_select statement" proposed in Ada Letters [Burns 1987].
- Define a relational order for the selection of alternatives. This may be implemented using labels associated with each alternative and expressions defining which the relational importance of each label. (e.g., LABEL_1 is associated with alternative_1, LABEL_2 is associated with alternative_2, and LABEL_3 is associated with alternative_3. If we define LABEL_3 > LABEL_2 > LABEL_1, then alternative_3 will be selected before alternative_2, which will be selected before alternative_1 - given their guards are open.) This is similar to the CELL language [Silberschatz 1984] nondeterministic construct.

3. User-Specified Dynamic Order - The open alternatives within the select statement will be selected on the basis of dynamic user-specified expressions. These expressions may use the values included in the entry's "IN parameters" (such as the "such_that" construct in Concurrent C) or may define dynamic preferences, which define which alternatives should be considered before the others based on dynamic expressions or values. This is similar to the "preference control construct" [Elrad and Maymir-Ducharme 1986] or the "Pragma PREFERENCE_SELECT" [Maymir-Ducharme and Kamrad 1990].

4. FIFO - The calls within the select statement may be accepted in the order they were made, assuming their guards are open. This can be implemented using a single queue per select statement; the caller with an open guard is selected.

5. Round Robin - Similar to Round Robin queuing, the first alternative is selected (if the guard is open) the first time through the select statement. The second alterative would be given first consideration the second time through the select statement, and so on.

The proposal includes the assumption that the scheduling algorithms implemented be consistent through all of the program. That is, if priority queuing is implemented, then all of the ready queues and all of the entry queues are priority queues, and if a new select statement is implemented, then all of the select statements have the same semantics. This homogeneity is intended to simplify compiler implementations and not add too much additional complexity to the language.

3.2 Inheritance Features Proposed

The non-transitive (Basic) Priority Inheritance is the second level of implementation proposed. The basic premise is to allow a serving task with a low priority to inherit the higher priority of the calling task; thereby allowing the higher priority task to continue, instead of preventing progress due to the serving tasks lower priority. The proposal uses the "waiting rendezvous" scenario to illustrate the semantics of priority inheritance. The server's priority is upgraded dynamically to that of the caller's priority if it is lower to begin with. In the case where a task with higher priority is delayed due to lower prioritized dependent tasks, then each dependent task (with a lower priority) inherits the priority of this task, allowing it to proceed accordingly. The priorities inherited in both cases described above are dynamically changed back to their original value after they complete the rendezvous or dependent actions with the higher priority task. In the case where the priorities are dynamically changed using level 1 features, the tasks will be re-prioritized accordingly to ensure priority inheritance.

The Transitive Priority Inheritance feature is the third level of implementation defined by the proposal. Level 3 includes the implementation of dynamic priorities (level 1) and priority inheritance (level 2.) This feature extends priority inheritance to be transitive; for example: if A inherits a priority from B, and B inherits a priority from C, then A inherits a priority from C. The semantics discussed specified that every task directly or indirectly blocking a high priority task will inherit the priority of the blocked task until the task completes its blocked actions. Priorities will be dynamically updated during runtime at implementation dependent intervals.

3.3 Priority Scheduling and Inheritance Issues

A discussion on the related issues and concerns ensued shortly after the priority scheduling and inheritance proposal above was presented. The issues, concerns and recommendations discussed are listed below:

- Some concern was expressed over the number of options defined for the scheduling of queues and select alternatives. The author responded that the intent of the proposal was to list the various scheduling alternatives proposed and requested for Ada 9X, and then make them coherent. In addition, the question as to the completeness of the list of options was also brought up.
- Discussions over the frequency at which priorities must be updated in order to support priority inheritance. The proposal specifies that priorities change accordingly, if not immediately, then by each context switch. The need to allow some flexibility in this timing constraint in order to accommodate varying hardware and compiler

dependencies was acknowledged.

- The issue of the effect of time outs on inheritance was brought up for future consideration and investigation. Blocking anomalies must also be investigated. The interactions between dynamic priorities and FIFO require additional analysis.
- Some concerns over the perceived loss of FIFO scheduling was brought forward. It was concluded that FIFO should remain as the default, as specified for Ada83.

The group agreed that one of the basic requirements that must be met is the ability to prevent priority inversion, as specified by JIAWG. Transitive priority inheritance will guarantee the prevention of priority inversion. The priority ceiling protocol [Goodenough and Sha 1988] should also be addressed by this proposal at a later time.

The final discussion was on the addition of another scheduling alternative to allow vendors to define their own implementation dependent scheduling. This "blank check explicit option" (chef's choice) alternative allows for future requirements to be met legally by Ada9X and may also act as a competitive incentive for the development of faster and more efficient schedulers.

4.0 SUMMARY AND CONCLUSION

Although several scheduling options were cited for meeting these requirements, such as allowing an occam-style priority select, preference control, or allowing access to parameters in the guards of a select, the workshop felt that it was crucial that any solution consistently be enforced across the dispatching of ready tasks, entry queue ordering and the select algorithm. This could be achieved either by specifying a scheduling algorithm to be used throughout the program, or by allowing programmer control over all queuing activities carried out by the runtime support system.

Being that these scheduling requirements are some of the major requests for revisions to Ada, as well as their interactions and interface with other language features, it is imperative that they be reviewed and scrutinized by as much of the Ada community as possible. Careful consideration needs to be given to the subject of whether these features belong in the Ada language, as opposed to being included in secondary standards or "Ada 9X annexes."

REFERENCES

Ada 9X Project Office, "Ada 9X Project Revision Request Report," Office of the Under Secretary of Defense for Acquisition, Washington, D.C., January 1990.

Ada 9X Project Office, "Ada 9X Revision Issues, Release 2," Office of the Under Secretary of Defense for Acquisition, Washington, D.C., May 1990.

Ada Runtime Environment Working Group. December 1987. A Catalog of Interface Features and Options for the Ada Runtime Environment. Association
for Computing Machinery.

ANSI/MIL-STD-1815A-1983. Reference Manual for the Ada Programming Language, American National Standards Institute, Inc., 1983.

Burns, A. January, February 1987. Using Large Families for Handling Priority Requests, *Ada LETTERS Vol. VII, No. 1*, vii.1-97 - vii.1-104.

Elrad, T. and Maymir-Ducharme, F. 1986. "Distributed Language Design: Constructs for Controlling Preferences," *Proceedings of the 1986 International Conference on Parallel Processing* in St. Charles, Illinois, August 19-22, 1986, pp. 176-183.

Elrad, T. and Maymir-Ducharme, F. "Race Control for the Validation and Verification of Ada Multitasking Programs," *Proceedings of the Sixth Annual National Conference on Ada Technology*, March 14 - 17, 1988.

Goodenough, J. and Sha, L. Fall 1988. The Priority Ceiling Protocol: A Method for Minimizing the Blocking of High Priority Ada Tasks. *Proceedings of the Second International Workshop on Real-Time Ada Issues*. Ada Letters, Vol. VIII, No. 7.

Maymir-Ducharme, F. Fall 1990. Dynamic Priorities, Scheduling Mechanisms and Priority Inheritance Issues. *A Special Edition from SIGAda, The ACM Special Interest Group on Ada, Volume X, Number 9, Fourth International Workshop on Real-Time Ada Issues*, Pitlochry, Scotland.

Maymir-Ducharme, F. and Kamrad, M. June 1990. "Multitasking, Scheduling Approaches for Ada," *Proceedings of the Seventh Washington Ada Symposium*.

Sha, L., Rajkumar, R., and Lehoczky, J.P., "Priority Inheritance Protocols, An Approach to Real-Time Synchronization," technical report CMU-CS-87-181, Carnegie Mellon University, November 1987.

Silberschatz, A. March 1984. Cell: A Distributed Computing Modularization Concept, *IEEE Transactions on Software Engineering, Vol. SE-10*, No. 2, pp. 178 - 185

Software Engineering Institute, "Ada 9X Requirements - DRAFT, Version 2.0," Carnegie Mellon University, July 1990.

Part II: Metrics

Information Engineering for Systems in Ada

A New Metric for Complexity

STEFAN BJÖRNSON

TeleSoft, Sweden

1. ABSTRACT

This paper describes a method for information engineering of Ada systems. It uses the "Principle of Locality" as a metric for structuring. The focus is on the information processed by the system. Information elements are related to Ada packages and procedures in an "Information Processing Matrix" (IP-matrix). A method for establishing the IP-matrix is described. Algorithms for transforming the IP-matrix to optimum diagonal form are also given. A metric for locality of information processing - called *Dispersion Index* - is defined.

The "IP-method" which is proposed in this paper is shown to give an overview over the system with respect to where and how information is processed. It also . highlights structuring properties of the system with respect to how close around its level of abstraction the information in the system is processed. If the recommendations which this method presents are observed, it will be easier to manage implementation and maintenance of the system, since it will be simpler to control side-effects. The dispersion index presents a one-dimensional metric of the quality of system structuring in this aspect.

The concept of mapping information against processing in a tabular form has been presented before and is applied by some Information Engineering (IE) CASE products on the market. Application of IE methods to technical systems is however not commonly done. The definition of a "Dispersion Index" is specific to this paper. The method can be used for the early stages of design as well as for evaluating existing systems. It may be automated to parse and generate reports on existing software.

2. STRUCTURING ADA SYSTEMS

Ada systems are often structured along functional entities. The task the system is intended to perform is divided into subtasks and these are then mapped onto the

Ada objects of packages, tasks and subprograms. Possibly also *subsystems*[1] may be used to structure a large system.

This kind of definition assumes that the design team undertakes a mental leap from the original formulation of the problem to a fully structured system. In actual project work there is a number of non-formalized and undocumented steps in between problem formulation and definition of a system structure.

When focusing on functions, there is a risk that coherence of data in the system will be overseen. If the system is designed such that a certain data element is processed all over, the system will be hard to develop and maintain due to interdependence between development teams and potential side-effects of maintenance actions.

The method which is proposed in this paper focuses on the information flow through the system rather than functional objects of the system. The hypothesis is that Ada objects of subsystems, packages, tasks and subprograms may be related to information elements represented as abstract types and actual variables. The structuring is accomplished by classifying the information according to *level of abstraction* and then making a best fit between the Ada objects and the level of abstraction of the information processed by each object. This analysis will then serve as a guide-line for structuring the system such that the dispersion of information through the system is kept low.

3. THE PRINCIPLE OF LOCALITY

In any system it is beneficial to keep the processing of code and information tight. If a certain information element has a long lifetime within the system, it may call for activation of the same piece of code at a great number of steps in the processing. This will lead to side-effects, if any part of the system is modified. It will also reduce efficiency in processing, since that piece of code has to stay in active memory for a longer time than otherwise might be necessary.

If a certain process has to access a great number of information elements, corresponding adverse effects will arise - these elements have to be kept active and memory management will be less efficient. It is also contrary to good modularization practices to have a process span over a large number of information elements.

This leads to the well-known *principle of locality*, which stipulates that any data in the system should be fully processed within a local context.

The method which is proposed here supports the principle of locality and provides a metric for how well the system conforms to that principle.

---

[1]A *subsystem* is a collection of packages which present a limited scope of their joint specifications to the outer world. It may be thought of as a kind of *superpackage* and defined transitively.

4. LEVEL OF ABSTRACTION

A common method for structuring systems based on a data flow model is to identify the *point of highest abstraction* and make the related process the root of the structure tree.

4.1. Interpretation of "Level of Abstraction"

A user of a computer system will normally regard all other information than input and output as "abstract". The normal train of processing will receive input and transform it to output through a number of computational steps. By this the information will consume more and more computational "energy" (= number of CPU cycles) and generally become more aggregated until it is resolved to output.

In complex systems there is a set of algorithms which constitute the core of the model which the system represents. The information processed by these algorithms will represent the highest level of abstraction. The final transformations to produce output will usually not consume much computing energy. The entire set of operations may be illustrated by an "S-curve", which is familiar from other areas where work is accumulated (eg project team work):

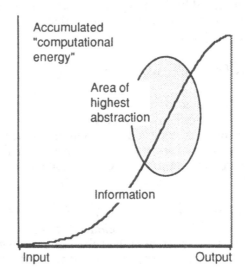

Figure 1 Conceptual illustration of "Level of Abstraction". As CPU cycles are put into aggregating and transforming the information, it becomes more "abstract". The level of abstraction then trails off towards output.

This description is based on the assumption that there is a natural flow of information from input to output. This flow need not be coherent in time, as would be the case for a data registration system. The operation of the system may also be phased such that there are distinct interfaces of output and input between phases. Some of the information in the system can also be characterized as auxiliary, eg control parameters for the system itself, and is not directly transformed to output.

The considerations described here will assist in defining a level of abstraction, but for an actual system there is likely to be a certain degree of ambiguity as to what is most "abstract" relative to input and output.

4.2. A typical model

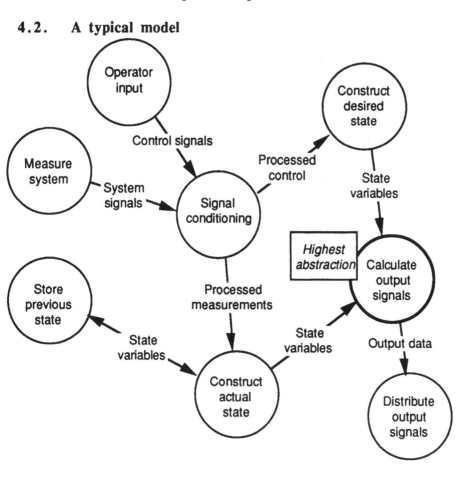

Figure 2. A typical model for a control system which takes input from an operator and from transducers. The task of this system is to adjust the state of the controlled object to a desired state given by the operator.

Here the calculation of the output signals will contain the core of the system model, eg dynamic difference equations, to determine what output to produce in order to make system state match the desired state. This entity will therefore be identified as the point of highest abstraction and is suitable as a root of the system structure tree. An example of such a structure tree is given below.

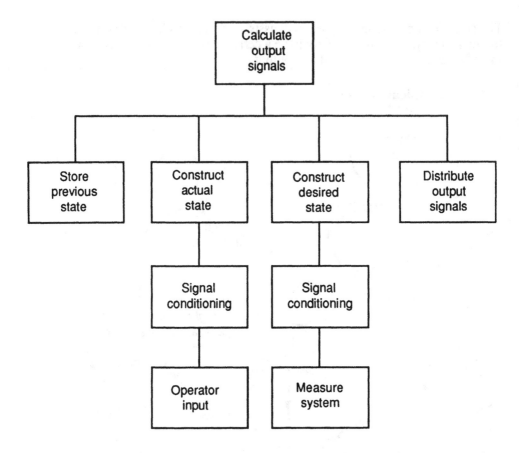

Figure 3. Structure tree for typical control system. The flow of information will be up from the input modules, through the central algorithm of calculation and then to distribution of output.

5. INFORMATION PROCESSING

The processes of the system interact in different ways with the information. In the context of this paper a distinction is made between *creating, updating* and *reading* the information. These different types of interactions represent different degrees of binding between the information and related processes.

The closest binding for a certain information element is to the process which *creates* it. In this context "create" is to be perceived as the act of the *agent process* which infuses the information element into the system, eg a signal-receiving Ada task or a package which contains the information element among the **out** parameters of its interface subprograms. In most cases a system is designed such that only one process creates each element of information. It may however be the case, eg in telecommunication systems or alarm systems, that a certain type of information is created by several different processes.

The next level of connection is presented by the act of *updating*, ie reading and then modifying, a certain information element. Updating will generally be implemented as **in out** parameters of interface subprograms. It can also be related to modification of global variables or globally accessible data base entities.

The least intrusive form of interaction between a process and information in the system is *reading*. That will generally be implemented as **in** parameters of interface subroutines or read access to global variables or data base entities.

For the continuation of this paper these different classes of interaction will be used to give different weights to the relationships between information elements and processes

6. METRIC OF INFORMATION DISPERSION

A specific metric would be desirable in order to evaluate how much spread out the processing of the information elements is relative to their inherent level of abstraction. This metric would provide a way of determining system structuring quality with respect to the principle of locality, structured design and ease of maintenance. It is also natural that such structuring will have a bearing on operation of the system in its practical use.

6.1. The IP-matrix
The relationship between the information and the processing in the system can be shown in an "Information Processing Matrix" (IP-matrix). This matrix maps information elements to processes and shows where the information is created, updated and read, respectively. In the method described here, this matrix is transformed and evaluated to determine how well the system is structured with respect to locality of processing and confinement of information to its relevant level of abstraction.

The IP-matrix will offer an overview over the system. This facilitates analysis of *where-used* such that potential side-effects from modifications can be analysed.

6.2. Establishing the IP-matrix
For a given system, the IP-matrix is created by identifying the main information elements and processes. For an Ada system the main information elements will normally be the variables and parameters which are defined in library units. The processes for an Ada system would similarly consist of Ada compilation units, regarded as a kind of objects. Breaking this down further would include subprograms an tasks in the analysis.

6.3. Creating Columns
The IP-matrix is established by identifying the main information elements of the system. These elements are then sorted according to the accumulated "computational energy" they represent, cf section 4.1. Corresponding columns in the matrix are created to contain the information elements in this order. The elements representing the highest level of abstraction will occur in the middle columns, maybe offset a little towards the right .

6.4. Creating Rows

The rows of the IP-matrix are created by identifying the processes of the system. For Ada systems they are represented by packages, tasks and subprograms down to a granularity level corresponding to the level of detail applied in the information analysis. They need not at this stage to be in any specific order, since the subsequent transformation of the matrix will create an order according to the best fit to level of abstraction.

6.5. The Elements

In order to characterize the interaction between the information and the processes, as described above, the following classification system is used:

Interaction	Classification
Process creates the information for the system	3
Process updates the information in the system	2
Process reads the information from the system	1

Figure 4. Classification of types of interaction between information and processes.

6.6. Example of an IP-matrix

This means that the IP-matrix can take on a form as in the following example:

Process	Information			
	I1	I2	I3	I4
P1	3	3		
P2	1	2	3	
P3		1	1	3

Figure 5. Illustration of IP-matrix for a very small and simple system.

Here I1 and I2 are created to the system by P1. They may for instance be read off a signal input channel and stored in memory. I1 is then read by P2, processed together with I2, which is read and modified by P2, resulting in the output of I3. Finally I2 and I3 are read by P3 and result in I4, which can be perceived as the end product of the system in this simple example.

7. TRANSFORMING THE IP MATRIX

In order to evaluate the current structuring of a system under study, the IP-matrix is transformed to optimum diagonal form.

7.1. Purpose of Transformation

The purpose of this diagonalization is to get a view of the mapping between information elements and processes, considering level of abstraction and degree of interaction. The transformation does not affect the structuring of the system itself. It only highlights its structuring properties.

7.2. Algorithm for Transformation

Diagonalization is achieved by calculating the "centre of gravity" for each row (=process) and then sort the rows in ascending order of centre of gravity. This will give a best fit of order of processing related to level of abstraction, considering the different "weights" of the elements with respect to their interaction with each process.

Centre of gravity:

$$Cg_{i=row} = \frac{\sum\limits_{i=col} j * w_{ij}}{\sum\limits_{j=col} w_{ij}} \tag{1}$$

where w_{ij} represents the "weight" classification for element ij of row=i and column=j.

8. CALCULATING THE DISPERSION INDEX

A metric for the quality of the system design with respect to locality can be expressed by a quantitative measure, here called *dispersion index*. This index accounts for the overall processing of information relative to its corresponding level of abstraction. There will be a penalty on row distance from the diagonal of the IP-matrix as well as on "weight" of the off-diagonal interaction.

8.1. Formula for Dispersion Index

The dispersion index is defined as follows:

$$DI = \sum\limits_{i=col} \sum\limits_{j=row} w_{ij} * (j - d_i)^2 \tag{2}$$

Where w_{ij} is the classification (1, 2 or 3) of each element and d_i is the vertical coordinate of the diagonal through column i. Since the IP matrix is not assumed to have an equal number of rows and columns, d_i cannot be assumed to be an integer.

8.2. Interpretation of Formula

The dispersion index can be given a somewhat generalized physical interpretation as the "moment of inertia" of the IP-matrix around its diagonal. It is also a correlation index for the best fit between information and processes with respect to level of abstraction.

9. RELATION TO OTHER MEASURES OF COMPLEXITY

Some more qualitative measures of inter-modular complexity is described in [MMCL88]. Martin and McClure point out that increased modularity will lead to more complex interfaces between modules.

Conte, Dunsmore and Shen [CDS86] have provided an overview over a number of other metrics of complexity, such as token count, live variable counts and cyclomatic complexity. These metrics are generally more detailed than the one presented here and they also focus on the processing *within* a module rather than information engineering aspects on the entire system.

9.1. COCOMO
This empirical model, introduced by Barry Boehm [BOE81], uses *delivered source lines* as a basis for estimating complexity. Complexity is expressed as time required to develop a deliverable system. The basic COCOMO formula is:

$$Complexity = Constant * kLOC^n \qquad (3)$$

Where "complexity" is expressed as manmonths. The "constant" is normally set to have 0.3 kLOC (thousand lines of code) per manmonth and the exponent n is of the order of 1.03. The count of lines includes only the active code, ie comments, headers and such are excluded. For a more advanced analysis, this formula is refined with various correction factors based on the type of system under development and perceived competence of the developing team.

The COCOMO method of estimation is based on empirical data from a significant number of actual projects. Its main usage is to estimate cost and time for development and maintenance of a system. It does not give specific guidance for system design to *reduce* complexity in this sense.

9.2. Live Variable Count
This is a per-module estimate of complexity. The method [CDS86] accounts for "the burden on the programmers mind", ie how many different variables he must be aware of at each point in the program. There are several ways of defining live variables, but the most suitable seems to be to count a variable as *live* from its first reference to its last. The complexity measure related to live variable count is obtained by adding up the number of live variables for each line in the module. A related measure is obtained by dividing this sum by the number of lines of code in the module.

This method can be used as a guide for programming style, keeping complexity down by reducing number of live variables at each point in the module. It would then also promote the principle of locality.

9.3. Token Count
A method suggested by Halstead in his family of software metrics [HAL77] is to count the number of operators and operands or *tokens* in the program. This method

is somewhat ambiguous as to the definition of a "token". There may also be a discussion about whether to use only *unique* tokens or *total references* to tokens. The method will in any case be an indication of the conceptual burden on a programmers mind.

9.4. Cyclomatic Count

McCabe [MCCA76] has proposed a logic structure metric based on the number of decisions in the program. It is referenced to as *cyclomatic count number (v(G))*. This relates to the number of "linearly independent" paths through the program. Analysis of a flowgraph[2] shows that the cyclomatic number can be expressed as:

$$v(G) = \text{(number of edges)} - \text{(number of nodes)} + 2 \qquad (4)$$

This metric of complexity is based on flow of control rather than data flow. It may be used to guide design, creating modules with a low number of independent paths. It is however likely that this will lead to a more complex inter-module pattern, since the number of necessary paths tends to be inherent in the application problem, cf [MMCL88].

10. ITERATIVE DESIGN WITH THE IP MATRIX

The IP-matrix can be used in early stages of design as well as for evaluating existing code. In preliminary design it may be desirable to operate with generalized entities of information and lump processing into larger entities, such as Ada subsystems. It will then be possible to break out different regions of the resulting IP-matrix and define them in greater detail with further subsystems, packages and subprograms. During this process it may become obvious that the definition of information and processing does not hold for the requirement of locality and thus encourage adjustments in early stages of design.

After the IP-matrix has been defined, it will serve as an overview of the system, showing how processes interact and highlight natural boundaries of responsibility for development, operation and maintenance.

10.1. Defining Subsystems

Clustering of elements in the IP-matrix may show that it is advantageous to break the system down into subsystems. This will create a more structured modularity and reduce potential interdependence between parts of the system. The figure below shows how this would work for a fictive example:

---

[2]An *edge* in a flowgraph is a line connecting blocks of code that indicates flow of control. A *node* in a flowgraph is a block of code.

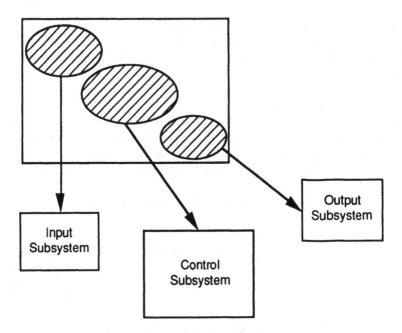

Figure 6. Disjunct regions of a typical IP-matrix may be used to define subsystems.

This is a bottom-up method which helps structure a large number of information elements and processes into more manageable units, based on level of abstraction.

11. EVALUATING AN EXISTING DESIGN

It is also possible to parse existing software to create the IP-matrix based on entities related to Ada syntax, such as types, variables, packages and subprograms, as well as other grouping which may be defined. A typical case will be to relate data flow to flow of control in order to get a more detailed picture than the one given by the context rules of Ada.

11.1. Restructuring to Reduce Dispersion
After establishing and transforming the IP-matrix to diagonal form it may become obvious that the system is not well structured with respect to dispersion of information across levels of abstraction. This may encourage reiteration of the design structuring to reduce the dispersion index. The IP-matrix will show which elements are out of place.

11.2. CASE Tool for the IP Method
A CASE tool for Ada may be envisioned to automate IP-analysis of existing systems. Such a tool would parse the code and create the IP-matrix based on Ada entities. The columns would be set up containing the variables and parameters declared in library units. The rows would be made up by the corresponding library units. The elements would be filled by 1, 2 or 3 for parameters of type **in, in out** and **out** respectively. Certain Ada constructs, such as use of pointers, may lead to de-

pendencies which are hard to analyse semantically. It is therefore likely that a tool of this kind would best be run interactively in a dialogue with the user.

The context rules of Ada will account for *maximum* dependencies. For a practical system there may not be actual dependencies corresponding to these rules. A data flow analyser would give a more exact picture. For the purpose of the IP-method it may however be justified to account for all *potential* dependencies, using Ada visibility rules as a fallback.

After parsing the source and creating an IP-matrix, such a tool would perform the transformation and calculate the dispersion index. As a final step the elements which contribute most to the dispersion index might be highlighted.

12. AN APPLICATION EXAMPLE

This example is taken from "Software Components with Ada" [BOOCH87]. It describes a cruise control system for an automobile. I want to use it here as an illustration, since it is comprehensive and relatively well known.

12.1. General Comment on Examples
Using practical examples in a presentation like this involves a dilemma. On one hand the example should not be so simple that it seems trivial. On the other hand it must not be so complicated that it is hard to explain and understand.

While the cruise control system is not trivial, it is still comprehensible. This system is however not big enough to really demonstrate the usefulness of the IP-method. The purpose of presenting it here is merely to illustrate application of this method to a practical system.

12.2. The Cruise Control System

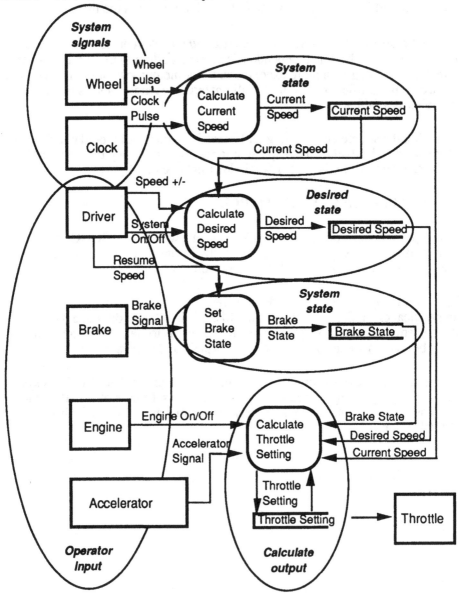

Figure 7. Block diagram for Cruise Control System which will be used here to illustrate application of the IP-method to a less-than-trivial system which is relatively well known as a case study [BOOCH87]

The following input signals are accounted for, and they are here ordered according to perceived level of abstraction and flow from input to output:

I1	System on/off
I2	Increase/decrease speed
I3	Resume speed
I4	Engine on/off
I5	Brake signal
I6	Accelerator signal
I7	Pulses from wheel
I8	Clock pulse

Figure 8. Input signals to Cruise Control System.

and there is one output signal:

I20	Throttle setting

Figure 9. Output signal from Cruise Control System.

Intermediary information:

I10	Current speed
I11	Brake state
I12	Desired speed

Figure 10. Intermediary information (=highest level of abstraction).

Processes:

P1	Calculate current speed
P2	Calculate desired speed
P3	Set brake state
P4	Calculate throttle setting

Figure 11. Processes of Cruise Control System.

12.3. IP-matrix for Cruise Control
The IP-matrix will assume the following form:

Process	Information											
	I1	I2	I3	I4	I5	I6	I7	I8	I10	I11	I12	I20
P1							3	3	3			
P2	3	3							1		3	
P3			3		3					3		
P4				3		3			1	1	1	3

Figure 12. "Raw" form of IP-matrix for Cruise Control System.

The Dispersion Index of this matrix is **81**. A transformation to optimum diagonal form gives the following matrix:

Process	Information											
	I 1	I 2	I 3	I 4	I 5	I 6	I 7	I 8	I 10	I 11	I 12	I 20
P2	3	3							1		3	
P3			3		3					3		
P1							3	3	3			
P4				3		3			1	1	1	3

Figure 13. Transformed IP-matrix for Cruise Control System.

As can be seen, the processes have been classified differently with respect to "Level of Abstraction". The Dispersion Index is now **58.**

12.4. Conclusions from Example
It can also be seen that I10, I11 and I12 are not well handled by P2 and P3. It might be considered to restructure the design to process these information elements closer around their level of abstraction. For this limited example such redesign is however hardly justified.

References:

[CDS86]   Conte, Dunsmore, Shen *Software Engineering Metrics and Models*", Menlo Park, CA: Benjamin/Cummings 1986

[MMCL88]   Martin, McClure *Structured Techniques: The Basis for CASE*, Englewood Cliffs, NJ: Prentice-Hall, 1988.

[BOOCH87] Booch G. *Software Components with Ada*, Menlo Park, CA: Benjamin/Cummings 1987.

[BOE81]   Boehm, B. W. *Software Engineering Economics*, Englewood Cliffs, NJ: Prentice-Hall, 1981.

[HAL77]   Halstead, M. H. *Elements of Software Science*, New York: Elsevier North-Holland, 1977.

[MCCA76]   McCabe, T. J. A Complexity Measure. *IEEE Transactions on Software Engineering* SE-2. 4 (December 1976): 308-220.

AFADA, A Measurement Tool for Ada

C. T. TSALIDIS, A. E. HATZIMANIKATIS

Computer Engineering Department, University of Patras

and

Computer Technology Institute Patras,

Greece

1 INTRODUCTION

ADA is a big and complex language that includes several major sets of features having no analogue in other languages — in particular, tasks and concurrent execution, real-time control of tasks, exception handling and abstract data types. ADA is indented to support the construction of large programs by teams of programmers. Rather than being constructed as a single main program and a hierarchy of subprograms as in Pascal and most other languages, an ADA program is ordinarily designed as a collection of larger "software components" called *packages*.

Ada [9, 6] and its supporting environment protocols were originally designed for mission-critical computer systems. Even if Ada was designed to accommodate the criteria of *reliability* and *maintainability*, the need for a more formalistic and algorithmic method to assure and elucidate the quality of Ada programs is more imperative.

Software quality assurance is one of the most important concerns in software engineering. Numerous software quality studies have been performed over the past few years and a new, quantitative approach to software management and software engineering has emerged. This approach includes the use of models and metrics based on experience, to qualify software products. Lord Kelvin said that if you cannot measure something, then you do not understand it. This is certainly true in software development; thus, various models and metrics have been developed, tested, refined, and established as aids. Models and metrics are tools for the good manager and engineer and can not replace them. This is especially true, because these methods are new and not yet well-established. Some models and metrics have been proposed but not fully tested. Others have been tested only in the environments in which they were developed. However, many are being used and tested in environments other than that of the developer.

ATHENA is a Software Measurement Environment which has been developed with the following objectives:

1. To make the process of applying current software metrics more economical, by reducing the amount of manual inspection and data collection.

2. To be language independent. Different environments can be created for different languages. This makes **ATHENA** a full customizable tool.

3. To be metrics independent. New metrics can be added to the basic kernel set of metrics.

4. To provide graphical representation of collected data and results of metrics.

5. To provide a database of metric information for future research, refinement and validation of metrics.

In this paper we present how we have used the **ATHENA** Software Measurement Environment to construct a metrics processor for ADA, called AFADA. In Section 1 we describe briefly the **ATHENA** architecture. In Section 2 we analyze the four metrics that we have chosen for AFADA, and we describe the way they were implemented using **ATHENA** .

2 ATHENA ARCHITECTURE

It is clear that models and metrics must be established through testing and experimentation. Before using a metric, the manager or engineer should have sufficient knowledge about how much to trust the results of the metric. The purpose of **ATHENA** is to provide an environment for creation, application and testing of current and future software metrics. Special emphasis is given to make **ATHENA** independent of any particular programming or design language, and thus to be able to apply it on documents written in different languages. Various program characteristics can be measured using **ATHENA** , such as: Control & Data Flow, Data Structures, Modularity, Volume, Readability, etc. These characteristics can be measured by more than one metrics, since we accept that there are no perfect metrics and their validity and reliability is very difficult to be estimated.

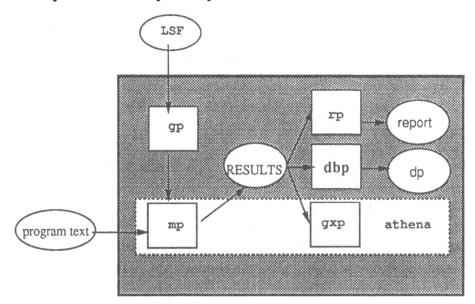

Figure 1: Architecture of **ATHENA**

As shown in Figure 1, where the overall architecture of **ATHENA** is depicted, **ATHENA** consists of:

- a grammar processor (gp)

- a metrics processor (mp)

- a graphics processor (gxp)

- a report processor (rp), and

- a database processor (dbp)

The grammar processor gp is the component that processes the Language Specification File (LSF), to produce the metrics processor mp. The LSF consists of the specification of the language (syntactic) and the description of the measured quantities (semantic). It also defines structures (called *graphs*) that are needed for the measurement of quantities. The metrics processor mp is the component that processes program texts corresponding to the language specification (LSF) and produces the results of the data collected and measured, and optionally pretty prints program texts. The graphics processor (gxp), based on X Windows, processes the results and presents them graphically in various ways. The report processor (rp) processes the result and produces a report. The database processor (dbp) is concerned with the permanent storage and retrieval of results.

2.1 Description of the LSF
ATHENA uses compiler-compiler techniques to construct the metrics processor. Similarly to a compiler, the analysis of the program texts is done in four phases: the Lexical Phase, the Syntax Phase, the Semantic Phase and the Storage Phase (that corresponds to code generator). The first three phases are used not only to analyze the source program, but also to collect data, construct temporal structures and finally compute the quantities that the metrics need. The fourth phase is used to manipulate these quantities by evaluating metrics and finally storing the results for later use.

In each one of the first three phases different kinds of quantities can be measured. The kind of these quantitities has a strong relationship with the phase in which measured. For example, the quantities measured in the Lexical phase have a strong relationship with the lexical analysis of the program. In this phase we can measure quantities such as *number of lines* or *number of characters in identifiers* etc. In the Syntax phase quantities that are related to the syntax analysis of the program are measured. Such quantities can be *number of procedure calls, number of if-then-else statements* etc. Semantic analysis of a program usually uses dynamic structures as control graphs, data flow graphs, etc. There are various metrics, such as Hall & Preiser's and Tsai's, that use these structures to extract quantities and evaluate their metrics. The metrics processor during the Syntax Phase constructs all these structures (graphs) and the Semantic Phase uses these graphs to extract the required information. To help the user define the quantities and structures (needed for the evaluation of metrics) we use the concepts of *Class* and *Graph*.

Classes
The definition of classes has the format

```
%<ClassKind> '[' <ClassName> ']'
                element {element}
            '[' actions ']'
```

The <ClassKind> denotes the kind of the class, i.e. in which phase it is applied and what kind of element it can measure. The <ClassName> is the name of the class. The elements of a class can be quoted characters, terminals, nonterminals or compound objects of them. This depends on the kind of the class. For example, in Character Classes we can have as elements only quoted characters. Finally, the actions define what must be done if one element of the class is found in source program text. We have two types of actions. The *function calls* and *the execution strings*. If an action is a function call, then this function is called with each appearance of an element taking as argument a characterization of the element. For example, in character classes the functions called take as arguments the characters found in input. The execution strings are strings that include C code that we want to be executed for each element found.

There are four kinds of classes: Character Classes, Token Classes, Grammar Symbol Classes, and Operator Classes.

As an example of a class kind we will see the Operator Class used to define syntax oriented quantities. With this kind of class we define structures of the language that look like the ordinary operators in functional languages. In order to define elements of this class, called *operators*, we have classified operators in four categories. Each operator can be single, consisting of one token, or compound, consisting of more than one tokens, and simple, having one use, or polymorphic, having more than one uses. Thus, the four categories are:

- Single   Simple
- Single   Polymorphic
- Compound Simple
- Compound Polymorphic

There is a set of classes called *predefined* classes. These classes define quantities that are needed for the basic kernel metrics set that **ATHENA** implements. The user doesn't have to define the kind or the actions for the predefined classes. He must only define the `elements` of these classes. The format of the predefined classes is

```
%<ClassName> element {element}
```

An example of such a predefined class is the `%McCabe` class, which defines the grammar symbols that must be counted to evaluate the McCabe metric for structured (without **goto**) programs.

Graphs

The primary definition mechanism that **ATHENA** offers for the definition of graphs is the *Graph Specification Language* (GSL). The basic data type of GSL is a *directed graph* **G**. A graph G is defined as the quadruple (V, E, I, O), where V is the set of nodes, E is the set of arcs, $E \subseteq V \times V$, I is the subset of V called *input nodes* and O is also a subset of V called *output nodes*. Since graphs, in our case, basically represent flow of information, input nodes indicate *start* nodes, where the flow of information begins and output nodes indicate *end* nodes, where the flow of information concludes. So, graphs can be connected at the input and output nodes. The edges of the graph show how the information is processed and transformed going from one node to another.

GSL has four operators [5, 8] for the manipulation of graphs and an assignment operator. The manipulation operators are

- The *sequence operator*, that connects two graphs, $G = G_1 -> G_2$, so that each output node of graph G_1 is connected to every input node of G_2. The input nodes of G_1 and the output nodes of G_2 become the input and output nodes of the resulting graphs. For example if G_1 is the graph representation of statement s_1 and G_2 is the graph representation of statement s_2, then G is the graph of s_1; s_2.

- The *parallel operator*, unifies two graphs, $G = G_1 || G_2$, so that the input and output nodes of the resulting graph G are the union of input and output nodes of G_1 and G_2. For example $G_1 || G_2$ corresponds to **case 1 :** s_1; **case 2 :** s_2; where G_1 and G_2 correspond to s_1, s_2 respectively.

- The *cycle_to* operator, $G = G_1 => G_2$, connects the input nodes of G_2 with the output nodes of G_1 and the output nodes of G_2 to the input nodes of G_1. The input nodes of the resulting graph G are the input nodes of G_1 and the output nodes of G are the output nodes of G_2. For example $G_1 => G_2$ corresponds to **repeat** *s* **until** *e*;, where G_1 corresponds to the *s* statement and G_2 to *repeat* statement or to expression *e*.

- Finally, the *cycle_from* operator, $G = G_1 <= G_2$ is similar to the cycle_to operator. The only difference is that the output nodes of the resulting graph here are the output nodes of G_1. For example $G_1 <= G_2$ corresponds to **while** *e* **do** *s*;, where G_1 corresponds to the *while* statement or expression *e* and G_2 to *s*.

A detailed description of **ATHENA** architecture, the syntax of the LSF, and examples of its use can be found in [5, 8].

3 METRICS FOR ADA

3.1 The Halstead's family of Software Science Metric

The *size* is the most common characteristic of all programs. It is also a factor that determines the complexity, programming effort and time required, and other critical characteristics of software. The size of the program can be easily measured by the *lines of code* metric that survives to this day. This metric, even if it can be easily implemented, it is not very consistent, since some lines are more difficult to code than others.

Description

In Halstead's Software Science [3], a computer program is considered to be a collection of tokens that can be classified as either *operators* or *operands*. The basic measuring quantities of a program are:

n_1 , number of unique operators

n_2 , number of unique operands

N_1 , total occurrences of operators

N_2 , total occurrences of operands

Generally, any symbol or keyword in a program that specifies an action is considered an operator, while a symbol used to represend data is considered an operand [1]. Most punctuation marks are also considered as operators.

Counting the quantities n_1, n_2, N_1, N_2, in a program we can express the size of the program with the formula:

$$N = N_1 + N_2$$

Software Science defines a number of additional metrics that use the above basic quantities:

- The program's *vocabulary* $n = n_1 + n_2$.

- The program's *volume* $V = N \times \log_2 n$.

- The program's *difficulty* $D = n_1 N_2 / n_2$.

- The program's *effort* $E = V \times D$, etc.

Implementation

The Halsteads metrics belong to the basic kernel of metrics. This means that the user must define only the quantities needed for the metric, not the actions. This is accomplished using the the predefined classes **%Hoperator** and **%Hoperand**. We assume that all the parts of an ADA program (i.e. definition and execution), except of comments, consist of operators and operands.

As already stressed, almost all of the keywords and punctuation symbols are operators. Also, we consider as operators the names of procedures or function when they are called. Compound operators (consisting of more than one token) as (**begin end**), (**case is end case**), etc are considered as single operators. On the other side, almost all of the variables presented in the program are considered as operands. The names of procedures or functions, when they are defined, are also considered as operands. We consider as operands not only user defined variables but also standard constants, user-defined types, literals, reserved words used as variables (**null**, **all**, etc.) and file names. The part of the LSF, that defines the Halstead operands and operators for ADA, is the following:

%Hoperator PRAGMA CONSTANT (TYPE IS) (SUBTYPE IS)
RANGE DIGITS DELTA (ARRAY OF)
(RECORD END RECORD) (CASE IS END CASE)
WHEN AND OR XOR (AND THEN) (OR ELSE) NOT
ABS STARS MOD REM (IF THEN END IF) ELSE ELSIF
(LOOP END LOOP) WHILE RETURN GOTO
FUNCTION EXCEPTION (PACKAGE IS END)

(TASK IS END) (TASK BODY IS BEGIN END) ENTRY
DELAY (SELECT END SELECT) TERMINATE
(PACKAGE IS NEW) ...
%Hoperand IDENTIFIER NULL ALL INTEGER NUMBER ...

3.2 McCabe's Cyclomatic Complexity

The control structure of a program is a representation of the actions
that the program accomplishes according to the different input data.
It has a strong relationship with the complexity of a program, since
programs with a great number of control sattements is much more
difficult to be tested and maintained.

Description

McCabe's metric [4] is an old, well known and accepted metric which
measures the complexity of the control structure of the program. Mc-
Cabe assumes that every program can be represented by a graph, in
which the edges represent different control paths and the nodes represent processing segments. From another point of view, the metric is
based on the number of the branches in the control flow of the program. This number can be easily counted on the control graph of the
program. Branches in the control graph usually correspond to *loop* or
conditional statements. The number of branches is proportional to the
level of the complexity of the program. If we have the control graph of
a program which has n nodes, e edges and consists of p connected components, the cyclomatic complexity of the program is expressed with
the formula

$$u = e - n + 2p \tag{1}$$

The number of components p represents the number of different routines (usually the number of subroutines or procedures) in a program.
This permits us to compute the cyclomatic complexity of an Ada program at module level, i.e. considering each module seperately, or at
routine level, i.e considering each routine seperately. It can be shown
that the cyclomatic complexity for a single routine written using structured programming techniques is a function of the number of predicates
in the module (i.e., simple conditions found in conditional or iteration

statements). The resulting equation is

$$v(G)_m = \pi_m + 1$$

where π_m is the number of simple predicates in the mth module. Using the above equation the cyclomatic number for the entire program is

$$v(G) \sum_{m=1}^{M} v(G)_m$$

Implementation

There are two different methods to compute the McCabe's cyclomatic complexity of a routine. First we assume that each routine of the program is written using structured programming techniques without **gotos**. In this case the cyclomatic complexity can be easily measured by counting the number of predicates in the code. This can be achieved by counting certain tokens that represent conditions in the program flow. Such tokens for ADA are **WHILE, IF, ELSIF, AND, OR, . . .** , and can be defined using the predefined class with name %McCabe.

The second method that we will examine is to construct the control graph of the routine using the GSL. After constructing the graph, we can measure the number of nodes and the number of edges. Then we compute the cyclomatic complexity using Equation 1. Because the McCabe's metric is a predefined metric we didn't need to define the function that processes the control graph. We must only define how the graph is constructed from the grammar rules that represent the syntax of ADA. A small but representative part of how this can be achieved is presented below.

```
%%
. . . . . . . . . . . . . . . . . . . . . . . . .
%NewGraph  MCCABE
. . . . . . . . . . . . . . . . . . . . . . . .
%%
. . . . . . . . . . . . . . . . . . . . . . . .
%%
. . . . . . . . . . . . . . . . . . . . . . . .
```

```
statement_list    :        {MCCABE: $$ <- nil. }
                  |    statement   statement_list
                       {MCCABE: $$ <- $1 -> $2.}
                  ;
statement         :    LABEL simple_statement
              {MCCABE: $$ <- putInputInfo($2,#sSymTab($1)#).}
                  |    simple_statement
              {MCCABE: $$ <- $1.}
                  |    LABEL compound_statement
              {MCCABE: $$ <- putInputInfo($2,#sSymTab($1)#).}
                  |    compound_statement
              {MCCABE: $$ <- $1.}
                  ;
simple_statement :    null_statement
              {MCCABE: $$ <- $1.}
                  |    assignment_statement
              {MCCABE: $$ <- $1.}
                  |    exit_statement
              {MCCABE: $$ <- $1.}
                  |    goto_statement
              {MCCABE: $$ <- $1.}
                  |    delay_statement
              {MCCABE: $$ <- $1.}
                  |    raise_statement
              {MCCABE: $$ <- $1.}
                  |    procedure_call
              {MCCABE: $$ <- $1.}
                  |    return_statement
              {MCCABE: $$ <- $1.}
                  |    entry_call
              {MCCABE: $$ <- $1.}
                  |    abort_statement
              {MCCABE: $$ <- $1.}
                  |    code_statement
              {MCCABE: $$ <- $1.}
                  ;
compound_statement :  if_statement
              {MCCABE: $$ <- $1.}
                  |    loop_statement
              {MCCABE: $$ <- $1.}
                  |    accept_statement
              {MCCABE: $$ <- $1.}
                  |    case_statement
              {MCCABE: $$ <- $1.}
```

```
            |  block_statement
         {MCCABE: $$ <- $1.}
            |  select_statement
         {MCCABE: $$ <- $1.}
            ;
assignment_statement   :   variable_name ASG expression ';'
            {MCCABE: $$ <- newG(":=",_ASG,01).}
            ;
if_statement   :   IF condition THEN statement_list elsifclause
               END IF ';'
            {MCCABE: $$ <- newG("if_then",_IF,OL) ->
                ($4 || $5).}
            ;
elsifclause    :   elsif_list ELSE statement_list
               {MCCABE: $$ <- $1 || $3.}
            |  elsif_list
               {MCCABE: $$ <- $1.}
            ;
elsif_list     :     {MCCABE: $$ <- nil.}
            |  ELSIF  condition THEN statement_list elsif_list
               {MCCABE: $$ <- $4 || $5.}
            ;
loop_statement :   name_iteration LOOP statement_list END LOOP name
               {MCCABE: $$ <- newG("loop",_LOOP,OL) <= $3.}
            ;
. . . . . . . . . . . . . . . . . . . . . . . .
```

3.3 Hall's and Preiser's Combined Network Complexity Measures

Today's large software systems are built by teams of programmers, and the design is based on the principle of modularity. A system is decomposed into modules, that have clear and specified interfaces, and each programmer builds a different part of the system. ADA is one of the modern languages that explicitly support modularity and the specification of clear interfaces between modules, through the feature of *packages*. Under this situation, a main factor in the quality of the system becomes the complexity of the modules' interconnections. A variety of metrics have been proposed for the estimation of this complexity. We have chosen to implement, using **ATHENA** , the *Combined Network Complexity Measures*, proposed by Hall and Preiser [2].

Description

Hall and Preiser do not propose a single metric, but rather a set of measures. First of all, they define a network of modules. This network has as nodes the modules that constitute the system, and as edges the inter–module connections. Each edge from node A to node B, represents, either a call from module A to module B or the return of a result from A to B. This way a directed graph, called *network control graph* is created.

The first metric that is applied on such a network is McCabe's metric. The complexity of the network u, based on the well–known formula for the computation of the cyclomatic number of a program, is

$$u = e - n + 2p$$

where e is the number of edges in the network, n is the number of nodes (modules) and p is the number of connected components.

Then, they propose a generalized measure that incorporates resources that are controlled by modules. The definition for this generalized measure is

$$C = \sum_{i=1}^{n}(e_i + \sum_{j=1}^{k} d_j \times r_p)$$

where, n is the number of single paths in the network, k is the total number of resources to be controlled in the network, $r_{1i}, \cdots, r_{ki}$ represent the resources which must be controlled for a given path p_i, $r_p = 0$ if the resource is not required by the node and $r_p = 1$ if the resource is required, d_j is the complexity for allocation of each resource and e_i is the complexity of program invocation and return along each path p_i.

Finally, they combine these measures with measures on the source code of the modules (McCabe's or Halstead's metrics). The combined measure is defined as

$$C_T = w_1 \times CN + w_2 \sum_{i=1}^{k} C_k$$

where, CN is the network complexity (computed by one of the other methods), $C_1, \cdots, C_k$ are the individual module complexities (computed by Halstead's or McCabe's metrics), k is the number of nodes, and w_1 and w_2 are weighting factors assigned by the user.

All of these measures give a good indication of the complexity of a network of modules. In [2] a detailed description of the measures and their implementation, their use for the derivation of simplified measures for hierarchy and pipeline networks of modules, and also a way that these measures can be used for the control of the complexity of a design, are presented.

For example, suppose we have the following definitions in the ADA source code:

```
package A is ...
with B;
.....
end package;

package B is ...
with C,D;
......
end package;

package C is ...
with E;
.......
end package;

package D is ...
with E;
...
end package;

package E is ...
with A;
....
end package;
```

The corresponding network control graph is presented in Figure 2. The measurement for this graph gives results $u = 3$ and $C(N) = 6$, for the McCabe's and the generalized measures respectively. In order to compute the combined measure, the complexity of the packages in terms of McCabe's or Halstead's metrics are required.

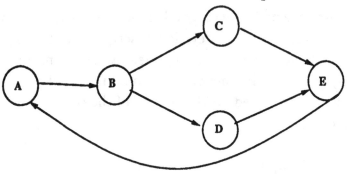

Figure 2: Network control graph

Implementation

The main units of modularity in ADA are packages and tasks, and these can be the nodes of the network control graph. We made a simplified assumption, and accepted that every WITH statement found in a package defines a call to the used package (i.e. an edge of the network).

For the construction of the network we use the Graph Language of the ATHENA environment. A graph is created for every WITH statement, and finally these graphs are merged, so that there is a unique node for every package or task.

The rule of the grammar and the corresponding Graph Language statement used is:

```
%%
. . . . . . . . . . . . . .
%NewGraph HALL
. . . . . . . . . . .
%%
```

```
. . . . . . . . . . . .
unit_name_list : unit_name
                 { HALL : $$ <- $1.}
                 | unit_name ',' unit_name_list
                 { HALL : $$ <- $1 || $2}.
                 ;
with_clause    : WITH unit_name_list ';'
         { HALL : $$ <- newG(#currentUnitName()#,_ID,0L)->$1.}
                 :
. . . . . . . . . . .
```

After the graph is constructed the McCabe's measure on the network is easily computed. For the generalized measure, we make the
assumption that no resources are used by the packages. Finally, the
combined measure can be easily computed, if we have already computed the McCabe's and Halstead's metrics for each package.

3.4 Tsai's Data Structure Complexity Metric

The McCabe's and Halstead's metrics can only be measured during
the late phases of the software life cycle (detailed design and coding).
However, there is a great need for estimation of the software complexity
very early, during the design phase of a project. On the other hand, it is
widely accepted that the complexity of a program is heavily dependent
on the complexity of the data structures of the program. McCabe's
metric computes the complexity of the program based on the control
flow, and pays no attention to the complexity of the data structures.

Tsai et. al. [7] proposed a *Data Structure Complexity Metric*. It
can be computed early in the software life cycle, as data specifications
are usually available very early. The main properties of this metric are
that it conforms to intuition, it measures the structure of data, and not
only their size, it is consistent (if data structure x is a substructure of
data structure y, then $complexity(x) \leq complexity(y)$), it can tolerate
incomplete information, it can be automated and it is insensitive to
the language specific details.

In this section we will give a description of the metric, the algorithm for its calculation and how it can be applied to Ada programs using the Athena Metrics Environment. A detailed description of the metric, and hints for the interpretation of its results can be found in [7].

Description

As we said earlier, the computation of the metric is based on the structure of the data and not on their size. In order to compute the metric, the definitions of the data structures used by the program are needed. From these definitions a directed multigraph is created. The graph has as nodes the data structures themselves, while an edge from node A to node B means that the data structure B is referenced from data structure A (for example, B is a field in record A). Recursive definitions are allowed and some data structures can be atomic and not reference any other structure (predefined types of the language).

The graph is splited into a set of strongly connected components, a self-complexity polynomial is derived for each connected component and, finally, a complexity polynomial is derived for each node (actually, each data structure). The complexity of a data structure is not given by a single number, but rather by a polynomial.

For example, in the following there are the definitions of a set of data structures for ADA:

```
type A is record;
type C is record;
type F is record;
type D is record;
type G is record;
type B is record;
224z
type A_ptr is access A;
type C_ptr is access C;
type F_ptr is access F;
type D_ptr is access D;
type G_ptr is access G;
type B_ptr is access B;
```

```
type E is record            type F is record
    f1 : A_ptr;                 f1 : Integer;
    f2 : Character;             f2 : Character;
    end record;                 end record;

type C is record            type D is record
    f1 : C_ptr;                 f1 : F_ptr;
    f2 : Character;             f2 : G_ptr;
    f3 : C_ptr;                 f3 : D_ptr;
    end record;                 end record;

type G is record            type A is record
    f1 : Integer;               f1 : B_ptr;   f3 : D_ptr;
    f2 : A_ptr;                 f2 : C_ptr;   f4 : C_ptr;
    end record;                 end record;
```

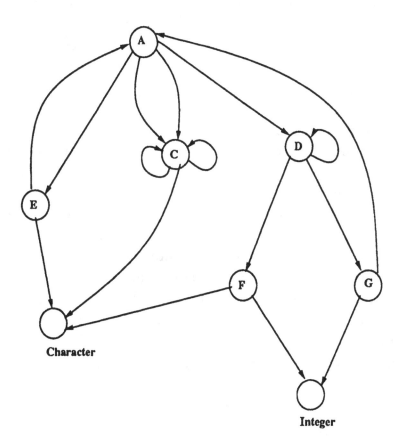

Figure 3: Data structure dependency multigraph

In Figure 3 the directed multigraph describing the dependencies among these data structures is presented.

Applying the Tsai's algorithm on this graph, the following results are derived, as polynomials:

$$
\begin{aligned}
C(Integer) &= 1 \\
C(Character) &= 1 \\
C(C) &= 1 + 3x^2 \\
C(F) &= 3 \\
C(A) &= C(D) = C(E) = C(G) = 7 + 6x^2 + 10x^3
\end{aligned}
$$

The prime index for the complexity of a data structure is the degree of the corresponding polynomial. Simple and atomic data structures (Integer, Character, F) have a zero degree in the corresponding polynomial, while complex data structures (A, D, C, etc.) have degree two or three.

Implementation

The main problem in the automatic computation of Tsai's Data Structure Complexity metric is the creation of the directed multigraph that represents the dependencies between the data structures of a system. We want this graph to be created from the data structure definitions found in the source code. For every type definition found in the source code of a program we create a graph that has as nodes the defined data structure and the data structures used for its definition, and as edges the dependencies between them. This can be easily described in the LSF using the GSL. A small part of the rules of the grammar that are used for the specification of Tsai's metric and the corresponding Graph Language statements are:

```
%%
. . . . . . . . .
%NewGraph TSAI
. . . . . . . . . .
%%
. . . . . . . . . .
```

```
type_declaration   :   TYPE identifier IS type_definition
          { TSAI: $$ <- newG(#sSymTab($2),_ID,OL) -> $3. }
        ;
type_definition    :   enumeration_type
  {TSAI: $$ <- $1. }
  |  real_type
  {TSAI: $$ <- $1. }
  |  record_type
                   {TSAI: $$ <- $1. }
  |  derived_type
                   {TSAI: $$ <- $1. }
  |  integer_type
  {TSAI: $$ <- $1. }
  |  array_type
  {TSAI: $$ <- $1. }
  |  access_type
  {TSAI: $$ <- $1. }
  ;

array_type         :   ARRAY '(' index_type ')' OF component_indication
  { TSAI: $$ <- ($3 || $5). }
  |  ARRAY index_constraint OF component_indication
  { TSAI: $$ <- ($2 || $4). }
  ;
record_type        :   RECORD component_list END RECORD
  { TSAI: $$ <- $2. }
  ;
```

After the graphs are created, one for every type definition, they
are merged, so that all the nodes have a unique name and the edges
from a node represent all the dependencies of the corresponding data
structure. Tsai's algorithm is then applied on this graph. The input
to the Tsai's metric can be only the specifications of the packages or
only the body of a single package.

4 CONCLUSIONS

Based on **ATHENA** , a software measurement environment, a measurement tool for ADA, called AFADA, was constructed. It is our view
that users applying software quality assurance methods should experi-
ment with different metrics and find these that fit best in their develop-

ment environment. They should be provided with tools that make the application of metrics easy and economical. **ATHENA** is a tool that comes to support this approach. AFADA is only an instance of the metrics processors for ADA that can be constructed. Other instances, incorporating different metrics, can be easily created.

References

[1] Conte S.D., Dunsmore H.E., Shen V.Y., *Software Engineering Metrics And Models*, 1986, Benjamin/Cummings Publishing Company, Menlo Park, California.

[2] Hall N. R., Preiser S., "Combined network complexity measures." IBM Journal of Research and Development. 23,1. pp. 15-27, 1984.

[3] Halstead, Maurice H., *Elements of Software Science*. Elsevier, (1977), New York.

[4] Mc Cabe, J. J. "A Complexity Measure", IEEE Transactions on Software Engineering, Vol. SE-2, No 4, (Dec 1976) pp. 308-320.

[5] Esprit project MUSE, "The ATHENA Software Measurement Tool, User's Guide and Reference Manual", April 1990.

[6] Shumate, K. *Understanding ADA With Abstract Types*, John Wiley & Sons, New York, 1989.

[7] Tsai W. T., Lopez M. A., Rodriguez W., Volovik D., "An approach to measuring data structure complexity", IEEE COMPSAC 86, pp. 240-246.

[8] Tsalidis C., Christodoulakis D., "Composing Software Quality Tools with Software Quality Metrics", Second European Conference on Software Quality Assurance, May 30-June 1, 1990, Norway.

[9] Wegner, P. *Programming with Ada: an introduction by measures of graduated examples*. Englewood Cliffs, NJ: Prentice-Hall, 1980.

An Approach To Benchmarking Ada Compilation Systems

Tom Curley

IBM - Federal Sector Division
9201 Corporate Boulevard
Rockville, MD 20850 U.S.A

1.0 ABSTRACT

This paper focuses on the approach used by IBM to benchmark the Ada Compilation Systems being used in the development of the Advanced Automation System (AAS). AAS is a major FAA program that involves a system-wide replacement of the United States air traffic control system. Ada performance risk management, establishment of compilation system performance requirements, and techniques used to monitor and improve compiler performance are discussed.

2.0 INTRODUCTION

In 1981, the Federal Aviation Administration (FAA) devised a comprehensive plan for modernizing and improving air traffic control and airway facilities and services. The largest undertaking in the plan is the Advanced Automation System (AAS). AAS will upgrade the entire air traffic control system to handle traffic loads well into the next century. (In 1988, over 430 million people used air travel in the United States - a figure that is expected to grow at a rate of nearly 5 percent a year and reach over 713 million by the end of the century.) Upgrades include new tower displays and common console equipment (controller workstations) for both enroute and terminal positions, and new software and hardware for tower, terminal, and enroute operations.

One of the major challenges for AAS is the stringent set of requirements. For example, AAS must be available virtually without interruption - no more than two minutes overall system down time per year, and no more than 15 seconds down time per year for the common consoles.

To meet the high availability requirements of AAS, IBM designed a distributed architecture, consisting of IBM System/390 central processors for centralized applications requiring facility-wide data bases, and IBM RISC System/6000 processors for the common consoles. The processors are attached via redundant token rings (referred to as Local Communications Networks (LCN)), backed by an Ethernet[1] network in the event of token ring failure.

The System Level Specification (SLS) for AAS requires a system which maximizes the use of commercial off-the-shelf (COTS) products, including commercial hardware, commercial tools and languages, and commercial operating systems. This is in keeping with the long-range objective of the FAA (and other United States government agencies) to eliminate customized system components, and to develop and use application programs that are reliable and easy to modify and extend.

Before selecting a programming language for AAS, the FAA commissioned an extensive programming language trade study and concluded that Ada would be used for AAS.

---

[1] Ethernet is a registered trademark of the Xerox Corporation

IBM selected the TeleSoft Ada compiler for developing System/370 MVS/XA-targeted software and developed an Ada compiler based on TeleSoft front-end technology for the RISC System/6000-targeted software. (Results presented in this paper pertain to the IBM Ada program offering for IBM System/370 running under the MVS/XA operating system, and the IBM AIX Ada/6000 program product for the RISC System/6000 (RS/6000) running under the IBM AIX Version 3 operating system.)

A program the size of AAS (estimated at 2 million lines of code) requires a powerful development environment. The AAS development environment is a heterogeneous environment consisting of an IBM 3090 central processor, intelligent workstations, and Rational (R1000) development environments networked with a set of IBM communication products. A key component of this environment is the Software Configuration Library Manager (SCLM). SCLM is used for the library management, system build, and integration functions of AAS. The development environment hardware configuration is summarized in Figure 1.

In 1987, during the Design Competition Phase (DCP) of AAS, IBM identified the capacity and maturity of the Ada compilation system as a risk area: specifically, the ability of the compilers, development processors, and target processors to handle the size of AAS software, as well as the compiler's ability to produce code that would meet the real-time performance requirements.

In response to this and other identified risk areas, IBM implemented a risk management program, consisting of (a) identifying risk areas, (b) performing risk analysis, and (c) reporting on risk analysis to internal management and the government. As part of the risk management program, IBM identified factors contributing to risk, and developed strategies to reduce the risk, including contingency plans.

Large scale Ada development can add a unique level of complexity to the problem of risk reduction because of Ada's unique compilation rules, as well as Ada's run time checking and tasking model. Also, the rich expressiveness of the Ada language needs to be well understood when estimating software size, complexity, performance.

To reduce the risks associated with the use of Ada, IBM developed a set of Compiler Performance Measurements (CPMs). CPMs provide a flexible mechanism by which an Ada compilation system can be broken into a set of requirements and progress can be tracked against those requirements. CPMs provide the ability to detect or predict performance bottlenecks that require management attention early in the program. Because realistic estimates of technical risk are attainable only when a system performance requirement or underlying performance parameter has been clearly identified, sound technical risk management depends on the complementary task of defining an accurate and appropriate set of CPMs. For each CPM, key performance parameters were monitored for movement outside the bounds of acceptable performance, thereby indicating risk.

This paper will describe the CPMs used by IBM on AAS to decompose and establish requirements for the Ada Compilation System, as well as the methods used to measure the performance and the efficiency of the code generated by the compilation system.

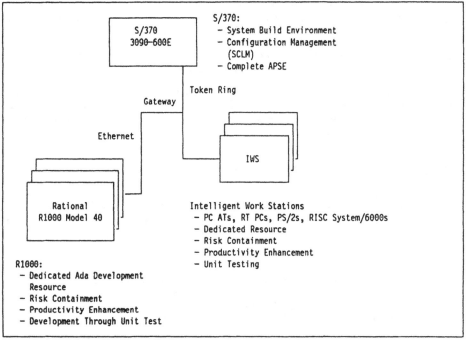

Figure 1. AAS Software Development Environment

3.0 PERFORMANCE CATEGORIES

The first step in analyzing any large problem is decomposing the problem into a set of smaller more manageable tasks. To measure the performance of the Ada compilation system the following categories were defined:

- Development Environment
  - Compilation System Throughput
  - Linker Throughput
  - Disk Storage Utilization
  - Compilation System Capacities
- Target Environment
  - Execution Performance
  - Memory Utilization
  - Run-time System Capacities

A set of Compiler Performance Measurements (CPMs), based on overall system needs, was established for each of these categories. CPMs were defined to ensure that system requirements would be met; they do not necessarily reflect the best results achievable by the compilation system.

Each CPM was defined as either primary or secondary. Primary CPMs were tied to "real" system requirements and had target values associated with them. Secondary CPMs provided a mechanism to explore the
factors which contribute to the associated primary CPM. For example, compilation system throughput is a
Primary CPM measuring lines of code compiled per elapsed minute. Associated Secondary CPMs may be
lines of code compiled per CPU minute, I/O subsystem utilization, compilation system memory usage, and
the effects that various code constructs and coding styles have on throughput rates.

The following sections describe how the CPMs selected for the AAS were established, the factors considered
when defining both Primary and Secondary CPMs, and their role in the decomposition process. Also discussed are the techniques used to measure Ada compilation system performance and monitor progress
against CPMs.

4.0 DEVELOPMENT ENVIRONMENT

When establishing development environment CPMs, IBM's objective was to provide a set of metrics that
could be used to characterize the Ada compilation system from a software development perspective. IBM
considered configuration management, compilation system throughput, operating system linker throughput,
compiler-imposed limitations, and hardware resources.

4.1 AAS Compilation System Throughput CPMs

Many factors must be considered when establishing a requirement for compilation system throughput. Each
compilation system will exhibit different performance characteristics based on the types of applications to be
developed, computer resources (CPU speed, memory, disk resources), the number of developers to be supported, and compiler architecture.

Table 1. Compilation System Throughput CPMs				
	Requirements		Measured Results	
Description	S/370 Host S/370 Target	S/370 Host RS/6000 Target	S/370 Host S/370 Target	S/370 Host RS/6000 Target
Primary CPMs Ada Statements (semi-colons) per elapsed ("wall-clock") minute, while compiling AAS application code under the control of Software Configuration Library Manager (SCLM).				
While generating listings	250	250	272	191
Without generating listings	250	250	355	329
Secondary CPMs				
Ada Statements per CPU minute:				
While generating listings			981	684
Without generating listings			1273	928
Effects of compiler options			Listings	Listings
Disk and I/O Subsystem utilization			Num I/O	Num I/O
Impact of compiler optimization levels			CPU	CPU

4.2 AAS Compilation System Throughput CPMs

The requirements for compilation system throughput were defined by the FAA in the System Level Specification (SLS). IBM felt that it was important to include the configuration management system, SCLM, in the compilation system throughput requirements. SCLM works with the IBM Ada compilers to provide compilation management and configuration control throughout the development and maintenance of AAS. All system components are controlled by SCLM, including Ada design and code, documentation and test cases, as well as other languages such as assembly and C.

The system build component of SCLM provides an easy-to-use interface to compilers and link editors. The build function creates compilation order lists, avoids any unnecessary compiles, and compiles all necessary components. For Ada, SCLM provides special build scopes. SCLM has a "normal" scope that will compile any implicit or explicit 'with' dependencies of the component being built (if the components are out-of-date), and an "extended" scope that compiles entire packages in preparation for binding a main program to produce an object module. The SCLM product checks the last modified date and the last built date to determine if a component has been edited since the last time it was built. If it has not been changed and none of its dependencies have been modified, the component will not be rebuilt. This mechanism ensures that only the minimum recompiles are performed and that the Ada chain reaction of compiles does not occur unnecessarily. A build may also be executed in report mode to ascertain what units are out of date and would need to be recompiled.

Early in AAS development, various benchmarks from the ACM SIGAda Performance Issues Working Group (PIWG), Ada Compiler Evaluation Capability (ACEC) [1] test suites, and IBM-developed benchmarks were used to analyze throughput. As AAS software applications became available, the earlier benchmark suite was replaced with AAS application code.

To measure the compilation system throughput CPM, three AAS application programs were selected. These programs consisted of 4,893, 15,969, and 24,960 semi-colons respectively, totaling 45,822 Ada statements and declarations. IBM did not want to exclude any Ada constructs or impose any restrictions regarding system loading or the generation of compiler reports or optimization levels. The throughput results shown in Table 1, were measured as single jobs executing on an IBM model 3090-600. (The IBM 3090-600, used on AAS, is configured to support 28 batch initiators and 200-300 interactive users, concurrently.)

Early in AAS, software development maximized the use of Ada's separate compilation capabilities, making every subprogram a subunit. The effect was the overuse of subunits, by declaring very small subprograms as subunits. Separate compilation imposes a burden on the compilation system in terms of additional data type and subprogram parameter checking across compilation boundaries. This extra processing is further compounded by subprogram subunits, because they are generally declared in very small physical files.

Analysis performed in April, 1990, revealed that AAS software consisted of 412,292 Ada statements, declared in 4464 compilation units. Seventy-five percent of these compilation units were subprogram subunits that contained less than 100 statements.

The secondary CPM, that monitors I/O subsystem utilization, has been very useful in exploring factors contributing to throughput performance. By monitoring I/O subsystem utilization IBM found that the physical size of the files had a significant impact on throughput performance. The effective throughput rate for files containing greater than 300 Ada statements is anywhere from 4 to 10 times faster than files containing fewer than 50 Ada statements. For example, a file containing 50 statements may require 1 minute to compile, while a file containing 300 statements may only require one minute and ten seconds to compile. Small physical files decrease total throughput because the amount of I/O required for opening, reading, and closing the source files, and the rewriting of the Ada library directory after a successful compilation increases.

Analysis also showed that during compilations the loading, elaborating, initializing, shutting down, and unloading of the compiler was the most time-consuming process. This analysis led to the design of a queuing approach where the compiler would be loaded and initialized once for an entire list of compilation units.

4.3 Linker Throughput CPMs for the AAS Target Linkers

The requirements for linker throughput were defined by the FAA in the System Level Specification. Because AAS uses two different operating systems, MVS/XA for the S/390 and AIX for the RS/6000, requirements were levied against both target linkers. The MVS/XA targeted code uses the S/370 system linker (the S/390 supports program-to-program compatibility with the S/370). For code targeted to the RS/6000, IBM ported the AIX Version 3 linker from AIX to MVS/XA.

Table 2. IBM Linker Throughput CPMs				
	Requirements		Measured Results	
Description	S/370 Host S/370 Target	S/370 Host RS/6000 Target	S/370 Host S/370 Target	S/370 Host RS/6000 Target
Primary CPM				
Object Modules Bound Per Second (Elapsed)	5	5	9	5
Secondary CPMs				
Object Modules bound and linked per CPU second			66	80
Disk Storage and I/O Subsystem Utilization			Num I/O	Num I/O
Operating System Overhead/Configuration			CPU load	CPU load
Elimination of Un-referenced modules and data			Yes	Yes
Object code organization			Yes	Yes
Linker Controls			Yes	Yes
Linker Reports			Yes	Yes

The Bind and Link Process: The primary reason for establishing a requirement for linker throughput was to determine the amount of time required to create an executable module once the compilation process was complete. With traditional languages such as Pascal or C, the compilation process generates blocks of code, which are then collected together by a linker to create an executable module. In Ada, the process of creating an executable module consists of a bind and a pre-link step, followed by an operating system link step. Therefore, the linker throughput CPM was based on the sustainable throughput rate for the bind, pre-link and link steps.

During the bind step, the Ada compiler generates elaboration binding code. Elaboration binding code is a list of calls to the static elaboration CSECTs of every unit that will be linked into the executable module. Static elaboration is the elaboration of a program that occurs prior to entering the main program (primarily the elaboration of package specs and bodies, see Figure 2).

The bind step is followed by a pre-link step. The pre-link is the binding of Ada object modules, and the resolution of references to run-time routines.

The final step in generating an executable module is the operating system link step. The operating link step is done to link in foreign language routines (if pragma interface is used to reference routines written in languages other than Ada), provide support for load-time symbol resolution and relocation, and link operating system support routines required to produce an executable module.

Measuring Linker Performance: Linker throughput was measured in terms of object modules bound per elapsed second. For the purposes of this measurement, an object module was defined as:

1. An independent code or exception section (CSECT or EXINFO) produced from an Ada compilation unit. (CSECTs are pieces of code or data treated as a unit; they are always contiguous.)

2. An independent data section produced from an Ada compilation unit

3. An independent code or exception section linked as a result of calls to Ada run-time software

4. An independent code or exception section resulting from the inclusion of non-Ada code in the program.

To measure linker throughput for the S/370, a report called a link map was used to determine the number of object modules processed by the linker. This report provides a lower bound for the throughput rate, because the bind step on the S/370 compiler eliminates all un-referenced modules. On the RS/6000, a file produced by the Ada binder that contains a list of all referenced object files was used. The object files listed in this file were processed by a tool that provides a list of all of the CSECTs to be processed by the linker.

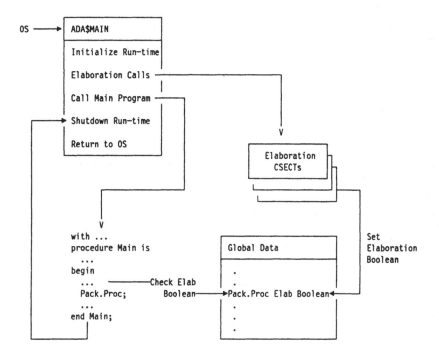

Figure 2. Elaboration Binding

AAS Target Linkers: For code targeted to the S/370, the Ada binder generates a CSECT, called ADA$MAIN. The ADA$MAIN CSECT contains the elaboration binding code of the main program. The bind step for the S/370 Ada compiler will also eliminate all un-referenced modules.

The Ada binder used to bind code targeted to the RS/6000 is structured differently than the S/370 Ada binder. The fundamental difference is that the pre-link step is not done for RS/6000 targeted code. The RS/6000 binder takes the object code created by the Ada compiler and generates a file called (MAIN.o) that specifies the elaboration order of the main program (analogous to ADA$MAIN). The binder also generates a file called (MAIN.bcf) that lists all of the object files that contain CSECTs referenced by the main program. These object files are in extended Common Object File Format (XCOFF). XCOFF is a deriva- tive of the Common Object File Format (COFF), used by most UNIX [2] operating systems, that has been modified to provide support for load-time symbol resolution and relocation **3**. Normally, an XCOFF object file consists of a text (code) CSECT, a data (constant) CSECT, a Blank Static Storage (BSS) CSECT, a Table Of Contents (TOC) CSECT for each address constant, and additional data or BSS CSECTs for each external variable defined, including run-time routines and non-Ada code.

The RS/6000 linker discards all CSECTs that are unused and sorts the remaining CSECTs. First CSECTs are separated into text, data, and BSS sections and all TOC entries are placed at the end of the data section, preceded by any procedure descriptors. This concentrates most load-time relocation activity into a small part of the data section. Finally, code CSECTs are sorted and co-located near the routines which reference them to reduce paging.

In addition to tracking elapsed throughput performance, other performance parameters, and functions, pro- vided by the linker deserve consideration.

- Elimination of un-referenced modules and data

   The linker should not include modules or data (from either the run-time or application) which are not referenced by the application. This feature means that modules within a package that are not referenced are not included in the load image.

- Object Code Organization

   The linker should allow the user to specify the entry point of the executable module. The linker should provide options to specify the starting address for code and data and the alignment of code and data within the object file.

- Linker Controls

   The linker should provide options to allow the user to specify the maximum size the user stack is allowed to grow. The linker should provide options to strip out line number information and symbol table information to reduce the size of an executable module.

- Linker Reports

   The linker should produce a link map defining the layout of the load module developed by the linker. The report should include:

   − A list of the start and stop addresses, and module sizes, sorted by address.

   − Lists of all names of all files used to create the executable module.

   − A list of data objects and their associated memory requirements.

   − A notation indicating whether a CSECT belongs to code, data, read-only data, read-write data, or an exception handler.

---

[2] UNIX is a registered trademark of AT&T Bell Laboratories.

Table 3. Disk Utilization CPMs		
Description	Require-ments	Measured Results
Primary CPMs		
Bytes Per Ada Statement No Debug Information	800 Bytes	309
Bytes Per Ada Statement Including Debug Information	1950 Bytes	1573
Secondary CPMs		
Source code (number of lines of code to be developed)		
Listings (storage for maintaining listing of successful compilations)		
Cross reference listing storage requirements		
Object code storage requirements		
Executable code storage requirements		
Inter-record gap information required by operating system access methods		

4.4 Disk Storage Utilization CPMs

Ada software development is characterized by high demands placed on disk utilization. These high demands, if not properly understood and planned for, could result in the need to add additional disk resources to support the development and maintenance process and impact cost and schedules.

Ada Compilation Libraries: With Ada, the largest single factor contributing to the utilization of disk storage is the Ada library. The Ada library describes the compilation units and there relationships with one another. As an application is developed, a set of libraries is generated by the compiler. These libraries are one key reason for the high reliability of Ada programs. For example, with Ada it is impossible to call a separately-compiled subprogram with the wrong number or wrong type of parameters. The types and parameters of compiled routines are stored in the library and checked when these routines are used. An overview of the IBM Ada compilation library is shown in Figure 3. It is a hierarchical structure consisting of a library file and one or more sublibrary files. The library file contains an ordered list of the names of sublibrary files. When the compiler needs to resolve inter-compilation unit references, it searches each sublibrary in the library file in order, until a version of the referenced compilation unit is found. The first sublibrary in the library file is called the working sublibrary. It is the only sublibrary that is written to during a compilation. The last sublibrary is usually the system sublibrary that contains the run-time and other support code (e.g., predefined I/O).

Sublibraries contain all compiler-required information about compilation units, including:

1. Sublibrary Data Base - a relational data base containing information such as unit type, dependency information and compilation time stamps for each compilation unit.

2. High Form - a DIANA-like, tree-structured representation of the program source produced by the front end of the compiler and used by the front end to verify static semantics of inter-compilation unit references. Also serves as input to the middle pass.

3. Low Form - a low-level representation of the source produced by the middle pass, suitable for translation to object by the code generator. Low form can be thought of as instructions for a generic computer. Additional information is also provided in low form to aid in code generator optimizations ■ .

4. Object Form - this is object code produced by the code generator. Object form in sublibraries is optional - a compiler may produce assembly source or object code and place it in normal files outside of the sublibrary. The S/370 compilers place object code in the sublibraries, the Ada/6000 compiler places object code into a separate AIX archive library.

5. Debug Form - this is information produced by the code generator for use by the symbolic debugger.

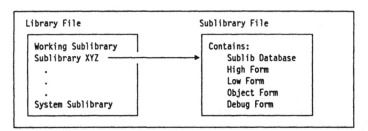

Figure 3. IBM Compilation Library Overview

From the perspective of the Ada library manager utility (a tool packaged with the Ada compiler that provides an interface to the Ada sublibraries), sublibraries consist of direct-I/O files. Externally a sublibrary is implemented a direct access file of 2 K records. Internally a sublibrary is a self-contained file system consisting of a directory and varying length subfiles. These subfiles contain the high form, low form, object form and debugger information for each compilation unit. In addition to the pages required for the subfiles, additional pages are used for library space management and temporary storage for files created during the compilation process.

Monitoring Disk Utilization CPMs: To measure the disk utilization CPMs, AAS applications were successively compiled into an empty sublibrary and the increase in the number of disk blocks used was captured between each compilation. The increase in blocks was multiplied by the block size to obtain the number of bytes. This number was divided by the number of statements (semi-colons) for each benchmark to obtain average bytes of disk storage per Ada statement.

When measuring disk utilization, the structure and implementation of the Ada library, as well as the operating system used to host the library, must be considered. For example, on the S/370, under MVS/XA, records are organized on disk in user-specifiable block sizes; the default block size for Ada sublibraries is 22 K Bytes. An Ada library may use only a small portion of the space allocated to it, however, that space is none-the-less allocated and no longer available to the rest of the system. The tests used to measure disk utilization must be large enough to ensure that results are not skewed by blocking factors or library management services.

As expected, bytes per Ada statement vary according to the type of code in a benchmark. For example:

- Benchmarks including tasking require more disk storage, due to compiler-inserted calls to the tasking run-time support packages necessary to support tasking semantics.

- Benchmarks containing a large proportion of numeric expressions, also require more disk storage. Expression evaluation results in more operations (machine instructions) than simple assignments or control flow constructs.

- Benchmarks containing a large proportion of control flow constructs and simple scalar operations require less disk storage. Constructs of this type require less low form because they are implemented with very few operations.

4.5 Compilation System Capacities

Ada compilation system capacities were measured to ensure that the size and complexity of the AAS system would be supported by the chosen Ada development environment. The CPMs listed in Table 4 were selected to reflect the capacity requirements critical to the AAS system.

Support Required by AAS Applications: The requirements for compilation system capacities were derived from the AAS design. As with all CPMs, the requirements listed in Table 4 are not necessarily the maximum capacities supported by the Ada compiler, but rather the capacities required for the AAS system. For example, the AAS requirement of 5000 source lines per compilation unit is less than the IBM corporate standard of 10,000. The IBM compiler will support 10,000 source lines per compilation unit, however, a compilation unit of this size would be a unique occurrence, because the average size of an AAS compilation unit is well under 200 source lines.

Some of the capacities are specific to the Ada compiler (e.g., the number of operands in an expression, length of conditional logic, number of formal parameters in a subprogram). Other capacities are related to both the compiler and configuration management system. For example, the configuration management system dynamically generates the Ada library file (refer to Figure 3) by examining the dependencies of the unit being compiled. The scope of the dependencies and the spread of the sublibraries throughout the various library levels (the AAS uses a hierarchical library structure) will determine the size of the Ada library file.

The capacities were measured with specific benchmarks, that were written to test for the required capacity. The Benchmark Generation Tool (BGT) from Mitre [5] was used to generate synthetic capacity tests. The BGT is an Ada program that creates Ada source files to stress test compilers. With BGT the user can create Ada library, generic, and subunit capacity tests.

All of the tests listed in Table 4 and Table 5 were compiled and measured on a pass/fail basis.

In addition to the capacity tests defined in Table 4 and Table 5 the fact that the IBM Ada compiler is written in Ada (approximately 300,000 source lines of code (SLOC)) and is a self-bootstrapped compiler (the compiler is used to compile itself) was another test of the compiler's ability to compile large applications.

Table 4. IBM Development Environment Capacity Primary CPMs				
	Requirements		Measured Results	
Description	S/370 Host S/370 Target	S/370 Host RS/6000 Target	S/370 Host S/370 Target	S/370 Host RS/6000 Target
Primary CPMs				
Number of elements in an enumeration type	5000	5000	pass	pass
Number of 'with's in a compilation unit	955	955	pass	pass
Formal parameters in an entry or subprogram	64	64	pass	pass
Number of source lines per compilation unit	5000	5000	pass	pass
Number of 'when' clauses in a case statement	255	255	pass	pass
Number of operands in an expression	64	64	pass	pass
Number of compilation units per sublibrary	2000	2000	pass	pass
Number of sublibraries per library	24	24	pass	pass
Number of compilation units per program	2500	2500	pass	pass

Table 5. IBM Development Environment Capacity Secondary CPMs	Measured Results	
Description	S/370 Host S/370 Target	S/370 Host RS/6000 Target
Secondary CPMs		
Width of source line	120	120
Length of identifier	120	120
Library units in a single context clause	54	54
Identifiers (including 'with'ed units)	4096	4096
External names	4096	4096
Declarations in a compilation unit	4096	4096
Declarations in a declarative part	1000	1000
Subtype declarations of single type	1024	1024
Literals in a compilation unit	500	500
Visible declarations	1000	1000
Private declarations	1000	1000
Declarations in a block	1000	1000
Depth of nesting program units	64	64
Depth of nesting blocks	20	20
Depth of nesting 'case' statements	20	20
Depth of nesting 'loop' statements	20	20
Depth of nesting 'if' statements	20	20
'elsif' alternatives	30	30
Exception declarations in a frame	50	50
Exception handlers in a frame	50	50
Frames an exception can propagate	64	64
Dimensions in an array	12	12
Elements in an array	65535	65535
Components in a record type	256	256
Discriminants in a record type	64	64
Variant parts in a record type	64	64
Size of any object in bits	65535	65535
Characters in type of 'string'	65535	65535
Operators in an expression	128	128
Levels in a call chain	64	64
Function calls in an expression	128	128
Depth of parenthesis nesting	64	64

5.0 TARGET ENVIRONMENT CPMS

Target Environment CPMs provide a set of metrics to characterize AAS hardware (S/390 and RS/6000s) and project AAS software performance. IBM considered execution performance requirements, machine architecture, hardware limitations (real memory), operating system, and Ada run-time implications and capacities.

5.1 Execution Performance

Execution performance CPMs were established to ensure that Ada compilers would be capable of generating the highly efficient code required to meet the demands of the AAS real-time applications. CPMs were defined to measure Ada executable statement expansion factors for use in pathlength estimation, execution performance for critical fixed and floating point algorithms, and Ada tasking performance.

Software Pathlength Estimation: One of the early concerns on the AAS program was the ability to accurately estimate the performance and CPU utilization of software early in its development. To accomplish this, a system model was developed to determine the performance requirements for critical AAS functions. The modeling constructs include a representation of the hardware and software architecture, methods for modeling thread processing, common system services, and response time performance. The model uses both measured and estimated pathlengths and processor instruction rates to derive performance budgets in terms of execution time.

To aid software development in providing pathlength estimates, based on source lines of code, to the systems engineering modeling group, CPMs were established for Ada executable statement expansion. IBM's goals were to provide a conservative estimation technique and to determine whether the use of Ada contributed significantly to pathlength. To accomplish these goals the following approach was used:

- Compare common primitive constructs

- Analyze Ada features that are not built into other high order languages (e.g., predefined attributes, run-time checks)

- Define a very small set of metrics for use in estimation.

Ada Executable Statement Expansion: Before establishing a CPM for executable statement expansion, IBM looked at language features that were common in Ada, FORTRAN, and C, as well as those language features unique to Ada.

Measuring the performance of individual language features through benchmarks involves isolating the feature to be measured. In order to isolate a specific feature from other features of the language, for measurement purposes, the basic technique uses a pair of procedures: a test version and a control version. The test version makes use of the feature under evaluation. The control version must have exactly the same execution time requirements except for the use of the specific language feature [6]. Theoretically, a difference of execution times between the control version and the test version yields the time of the feature being measured. Code optimization, however, can distort benchmark results by removing code from test loops, eliminating unreferenced variables, or eliminating subprogram calls. The benchmark programs must, therefore, use techniques to thwart code optimizers.

The key to avoiding these problems is keep the compiler from optimizing away constants or expressions in loops whose times are being measured. To ensure that these problems do not arise, control functions are inserted into both the control and test loops, and the feature being measured is placed in a subprogram called a library unit. If the bodies of these subprograms are compiled separately, after the benchmark itself, the compiler is unable to determine enough information to perform optimization and remove anything from either the control or test loops.

Primitive Construct Analysis: Using the approach described above, a set of tests were written that isolated those language features that could be found in FORTRAN, C and Ada. These tests were designed to measure very basic primitive constructs, such as conditionals (if-then-else, elsif, and-then, or-else, and Boolean operations), case statements, loop constructs (for, while, until), simple arithmetical expressions on different data types, and subprograms with varying numbers and types of parameters.

These tests were coded in Ada, FORTRAN and C, with care taken to ensure that they were identical. Once coded they were compiled and assembly code was generated. The assembly code was analyzed and the number of instructions required to implement the construct counted. IBM found that for very basic constructs there were no significant differences between FORTRAN, C and Ada, except for a slight difference in the area of subprograms. With Ada, subprograms generated more instructions due to run-time checks for stack overflow and elaboration checks.

When comparing Ada to other languages, one must be careful to make adjustments for code required by the Ada Language Reference Manual (LRM) [7] to perform run-time checks. For example, the LRM requires that Ada compilers generate checks to ensure that there is enough storage available during the elaboration of a declarative or execution of a subprogram. Checks are also required to ensure proper program elaboration, violation of range constraints, and various types of numeric errors. These checks can create longer pathlengths for even very primitive constructs found in Ada programs.

Complex Language Features Analysis: For the very primitive constructs it was sufficient to manually count the limited number of instructions required to implement the tests; however, for more complex features (e.g., Ada predefined attributes, tasking, or manipulations of large or arbitrarily complex data structures), this technique will not suffice.

There are a two basic techniques that can be used to measure these more complex features. The first is to isolate the operation and make time measurements before and after performing the operation. However, for this to be adequate, the time resolution of an individual measurement must be considerably less than the time required by the operation being measured. Clapp, et al. [8] have published methods for insuring timing accuracy. The second technique involves executing the operation a large number of times, collecting time readings only at the beginning and end, and then deriving an average by taking the difference between the two times and dividing by the number of times the test was executed.

These techniques are useful in determining the time and space requirements for a language feature; however, they can't provide instruction counts needed for pathlength estimation.

The approach IBM selected required the development of a hardware monitor for the RS/6000. This hardware monitor was built with special hardware that provides the capability to count machine clock cycles, single precision floating point operations, double precision floating point operations, fixed point instructions, branches taken, branches through, cache and Translate Look-a-side Buffer (TLB) misses. The hardware monitor can be started and stopped by software imbedded within the benchmark similar to a call to a clock function. One unique feature of the hardware monitor is its ability to separate operating system overhead from application code.

For the S/370 measurements, a software tool that counted assembly instructions during the execution of the program under test was used to measure pathlengths.

Once these tools were in place, tests were developed to measure Ada predefined attributes (LRM Appendix A) using various scalar and composite types, where appropriate, subprograms with varying numbers and types of parameters, dynamic allocation and deallocation of various sized objects on the heap using allocators, and the movement of data in sizes from 4 bytes to 8 kilobytes. The tests were constructed in the same manner as the tests for primitive constructs (isolation of features) and, in the case of tests run on the RS/6000, the source code was instrumented to allow the starting and stopping of instruction counts around the test and control loops.

The results for the predefined attributes were somewhat surprising: the instructions executed ranged from single instructions to hundreds of instructions, the most costly attributes being 'image, 'value and 'width. The data types used with the attributes had a profound effect on their overall pathlength.

When data moves were measured, the cost was linear with respect to the size of the object moved. This was as expected due to the bandwidth between memory and the fixed point processor. The bandwidth on the RS/6000 is one word between memory and the fixed point processor. A data move consists of a load from memory into the fixed point processor, and then a store back to memory from the fixed point processor.

Ada Executable Statement Expansion CPMs: Because Ada provides a vast array of language features, and the individual abstract features have numerous variations, it would not be feasible to measure every feature. IBM decided that, for the purposes of estimation, the variables would be limited to two. The two variables selected were subprogram calls and all other Ada executable statements. By selecting these two, software developers were freed from the task of trying to precisely estimate pathlengths from code which, in many cases, may still be in the design phase. IBM established a CPM of 10 instructions per executable statement and 30 instructions per subprogram call. (This is based on measurements for non-optimized subprograms which calls another subprogram within its execution frame.)

To test these CPMs, various fixed and floating point algorithms were analyzed. The domain of the data to be processed was known in advance (e.g., the worst case binary search of a fixed size array or the number of tracks and data processed by a tracking algorithm). In analyzing these algorithms, the execution flow was traced (at the source level), and a weighting factor of 10 instructions per executable statement and 30 instructions per subprogram invocation was applied. The tests were compiled (non-optimized) and executed using the hardware monitor. The results showed that the expansion factors of 10 instructions per executable statement and 30 instructions per subprogram invocation provided a conservative estimation technique.

Execution Performance Benchmarks: To evaluate execution performance key algorithms were selected because of their computation intensive nature, or because of the frequency at which they would be required to execute, based on the modeled and projected workloads.

To monitor floating point performance, CPMs were established for AAS specific algorithms known as Coordinate Conversion, Kalman Filter, Tab-G Tracker and Display Orientated tracking. To monitor fixed point performance, CPMs were established for binary search and various sorting algorithms. The target requirements for these CPMs are not shown because the algorithms are specific to the AAS.

Ada tasking performance was closely monitored. Ada tasking analysis requires a thorough understanding of the target independent, and target dependent portions of the run-time, as well as the target operating system. The following CPMs (shown in Table 6) were established for various Ada tasking paradigms.

Table 6. IBM Ada Tasking CPMs				
	Requirements		Measured Results	
Description	S/370 Host S/370 Target (insts.)	S/370 Host RS/6000 Target (time)	S/370 Host S/370 Target (insts.)	S/370 Host RS/6000 Target (time)
Primary CPM				
Complete Ada Rendezvous	1500	250 us	1244	95 us
Secondary CPMs				
Task Switch			707	64
Complete Rendezvous with Priority			1246	94
Complete Rendezvous with Selective wait (no Delay)			1625	187
Complete Rendezvous with Selective wait and a Delay			2289	188
Complete Rendezvous Across Operating System Processes			8273	2002

Note: Execution time reported for RS/6000 in micro-seconds.
   Results for System/370 reported in instructions.

The tests for the Primary CPM, Complete Ada Rendezvous, required measuring the time needed for a complete rendezvous between two tasks of equal priority (nothing on the delay queue), with one task incrementing an integer within its accept block.

The IBM Ada compilers support the mapping of Ada tasks directly onto operating system processes. (Ada tasks can be mapped one for one, or many to one, onto an operating system process.) This feature makes non-blocking I/O and interrupts possible. In addition, the RS/6000 compiler supports preemptive delays. Support for these features add overhead to Ada tasking performance.

Analysis of the tasking portion of the run-time has led to significant performance improvements. Through this analysis, the S/370 pathlength for a complete rendezvous was reduced from 4640 to 1244 instructions, and the execution time reduced from 1103 to 95 micro-seconds on the RS/6000. The most significant improvements came from the optimization and inlining of two small, frequently called subprograms, the elimination of some subprogram calls by adding a single parameter to other subprograms, and the replacement of two general purpose operating system supervisor calls with short assembly code sequences.

These improvements underscore the importance of a close working relationship with the compiler vendors. IBM's Ada compiler vendors have been extremely helpful in providing details regarding compiler internals, turning around problems, and implementing performance related changes.

Monitoring Execution Performance: The CPMs for execution performance on the RS/6000 were defined in terms of processing time required to perform their function. For the System/390, they were defined in terms of pathlength, to allow benchmarking to proceed on a S/370 until the S/390 was announced. (Processing times can be derived by dividing the pathlength by the instruction rate for the machine.)

The execution performance tests were measured using the dual loop approach described previously. The algorithms and tasking tests were iterated a number of times for normalization, and measured by using a timing function and the hardware monitor.

In addition to the execution performance CPMs listed above, IBM also measured some popular benchmarks from the public domain (e.g., Ada and C versions of the Dhrystone benchmark [9], and Ada, C and FORTRAN versions of the Whetstone benchmark). These benchmarks were used to determine differences in execution performance between different languages. Results for these benchmarks revealed that when checks were suppressed, Ada execution was comparable to that of FORTRAN and C.

Code and Optimization Analysis: To ensure that the compilers were generating the best possible code, and to find ways to improve upon IBM's use of Ada, significant code analysis was performed. Some of the features analyzed were access types, functions which returned large constrained types, the effects of inlining, short circuit operators, renames clause, variant record layout, generic instantiations, and the storage requirements of unconstrained array types.

To ensure that the compiler optimizers were taking advantage of various optimization techniques, a set of compiler optimization tests (shown in Table 7 on page 18) were written. These optimization analysis tests were based on the "Ada Europe Guidelines for Ada Compiler Specification and Selection" report. This report was produced by Nission, et al., and appeared in the October 1982 issue of Ada Letters. The tests were based on the items found in the "Target Code Performance" checklist. Some additional tests were implemented to improve the coverage of language features.

Table 7. Compiler Optimization Tests	
Test Name	Description
Static expression evaluation	Static expressions may be evaluated at compile time to eliminate unnecessary code generation.
Unused variable elimination	These tests indicate whether space is allocated for variables which are declared but not used.
Unused subprogram elimination	Subprograms declared but not referenced need not be loaded at link time and should not have code generated for them.
In-line code support	These tests evaluate optimizations involving the insertion of generated code for procedures in line, replacing the procedure call and eliminating the associated overhead.
Dead code elimination	These verify that dead (unreachable) code resulting from the static evaluation of control constructs is eliminated at compile time.
Static expression elimination	These tests combine both static expression evaluation and dead code elimination for statements which have no effect.
Minimizing constraint checking	These tests are used to check target optimizations of constraint checking. In many situations constraint checking is not required or just partially required because the constraints can be checked at compile time.
Array element references	These tests verify that the compiler takes advantage of optimizations involving address computations.
Special target instructions	These tests check for the use of available target specific instructions.
Register allocation	This test area evaluates optimizations involving the reuse of values previously loaded into registers.
Stack space/operations	This test area evaluates optimizations involving stack space and stack operations.

Cycles Per Instruction: In addition to knowing the pathlength for various language constructs, it is equally important to know the number of machine cycles per instruction (CPI) required to execute those constructs. Understanding CPI is especially important on a RISC architecture like the RS/6000, which is capable of executing multiple instructions per cycle. (The RISC System/6000 has separate fixed point, floating point, and branch processors that are capable of simultaneous execution.)

Measuring CPI provides valuable insight into instruction scheduling heuristics. The hardware monitor was used to measure CPI. The hardware monitor provides details on the number of fixed point, floating point, and branch processor instructions, as well as the number of instruction and data cache misses, and the number of cycles required to perform these operations. Using this information, we were able to derive CPI for various algorithms used in the AAS.

5.2 Memory Utilization

The primary motivation for establishing memory utilization CPMs was to provide an estimator for use in projecting the memory requirements for AAS applications.

Both the S/390 and RS/6000 processors used in the AAS support virtual memory; therefore, the concern about software size was not handling the size of the AAS applications, but keeping the working set of the application in real memory, to minimize or eliminate paging.

Estimating Code Size and AAS Memory Requirements: To estimate the real memory requirements for AAS software, IBM defined a model which consisted of separate allocations for the following:

- Executable code expansion

- Application static data

- Run-time support

- Dynamic memory allocations.

Executable Code Expansion: The expansion factors used for executable statement expansion were based on the assembly statement expansion factors for Ada executable statements. As discussed above, the Ada-to-executable-statement expansion factors are 10 instructions per executable statement. An expansion factor of 40 bytes per executable statement was established for the RS/6000 (each RISC System/6000 instruction is 4 bytes). For the S/370, where the instructions range from 2 to 6 bytes, we used an expansion factor of 40 bytes per executable statement. These expansion factors were used to estimate code size for large programs, where there is a mix of many different language features. The size of the programs tend to normalize the number of instructions.

Application Static Data: The AAS memory model considers data as a separate allocation. The allocation for data is derived by examining the amount and types of data required by a particular function. We gave consideration to the static data (data declared in packages), and buffer areas declared as static sized objects.

Run-time Support: With Ada, the run-time support system (RTS) has different memory requirements depending on the functions/support required of the run-time. To determine the total size of the run-time, in the event that every routine in the run-time would be used, we wrote a benchmark that explicitly referenced every routine in the run-time (e.g., support routines for various tasking paradigms, Direct, Sequential and Text I/O, etc.). Next, we examined the requirements of each application. It was determined that no application would require all of the RTS. Further, we analyzed the link maps and object code for various applications.

After this analysis, the CPM for RTS size was set to 400 K Bytes. It was further required that the RTS be sharable on the RS/6000. (AIX supports code sharing through the use of a special read-only segment **3**).

Dynamic Memory Allocations: Dynamic memory allocations are dependent on the application; therefore, dynamic memory allocation requirements were established on a case by case basis. To assist in determining the amount of heap space required by an application, AIX Trace hooks **2** were provided in the run-time. When AIX trace is turned on, these trace hooks cause data to be written to a log file. The hooks were implemented such that every time an application requests heap space, that increases the current amount of heap space used, a record will be written to a log file (buffer in memory and or hard file). The log file can then be analyzed at a later date to determine a high-water mark for an application's heap utilization.

Monitoring Static Memory Utilization: To monitor the use of static data, we developed tools to perform data reduction and analysis on link maps and object code. These tools summarize the size of each object in terms of text (code), initialized data (constants, literals, etc.), and uninitialized data. They have been an extremely effective technique for locating unnecessarily large data structures.

5.3 Run-time Support System Capacities

The final area IBM explored was Ada run-time system capacities. The run-time capacity category of CPMs provides a means to ensure that the size and complexity of the AAS system will be supported by the Ada run-time environment.

Support Required by the AAS Real Time Applications: In determining the Run-time System (RTS) requirements of the AAS application code, the software architecture of AAS applications was analyzed. This analysis led to the establishment of the tasking capacity related parameters shown in Table 8.

Table 8. IBM Ada Run-time Capacity CPMs

Description	Requirements		Measured Results	
	S/370 Host S/370 Target	S/370 Host RS/6000 Target	S/370 Host S/370 Target	S/370 Host RS/6000 Target
Primary CPM				
Simultaneously active tasks in program	50	50	1000	785
Secondary CPMs				
Values in subtype SYSTEM.PRIORITY			255	255
'accept' statements in a task			50	50
'entry' declarations in a task			25	25
Formal parameters in an 'entry' declaration			50	50
Formal parameters in an 'accept' statement			50	50
Delay statements in a task			25	25
Alternatives in a select statement			255	255

Techniques Used to Measure Run-time Capacities: To measure the capacity tests, a program was developed to dynamically create Ada tasks and rendezvous with the tasks. The tests were performed using both non-OS tasking and OS tasking. The number of tasks that can be dynamically created depends on the task stack size and the amount of real memory available to a given process. On the RS/6000 with 16 megabytes of real memory, 785 tasks were created. On MVS/XA, the testing was stopped after 1000 tasks had been activated.

6.0 CONCLUSION

Over the past two years IBM has held numerous informal meetings and six formal demonstrations with the FAA to discuss compiler performance. In addition to these meetings IBM has delivered a significant amount of documentation, nine formal documents totaling over 2000 pages of text. These documents provide detailed information about the compiler and operating system internals; plans and schedules relating to future compiler deliveries; CPM results, including environmental data such as CPU utilization and hardware configurations, measurement techniques and tools, results from code analysis, and data for historical trend analysis.

Benchmarking and CPMs have proven to be an effective technique for the reduction of risk and the identification of methods to improve the software development process. Many improvements to the compiler were identified and implemented.

In December 1990, the final scheduled benchmarking demonstration was held with the FAA. Results from this meeting were the acknowledgement from the FAA that all CPMs had been successfully met to their satisfaction, and that the Ada Compilation System was capable of generating efficient production quality code.

The most important aspect of this activity has been the transfer of information from benchmarking and CPM analysis to the software development community. Ada is an efficient programming language that, if not used proficiently, can be used to write inefficient programs.

The successful use of Ada for the development of real-time applications demands educated software engineers. On AAS many vehicles are used to accomplish this such as, (a) formal Ada training (b) software forums, where the performance characteristics of various language features and coding techniques are discussed, (c) electronic bulletin boards, where there is open discussion about the trade-offs associated with various coding techniques, and free form questions and answers, (d) Software Technical Notes, that formally document coding techniques and performance implications.

Further, early prototyping of design is very important. The best compiler optimizer has no appreciable effect on poorly designed software. Through early prototyping, design decisions can be evaluated before a design commitment is made. Establishing performance requirements as early as possible, keeping software developers fully aware of their performance constraints, and keeping them actively involved in the measurement of the components they are developing greatly reduces the risk of performance problems later in the life cycle.

7.0 ACKNOWLEDGMENTS

The author owes special thanks to the team performing the AAS benchmarking and compiler analysis; Ramsey Billups, Mike Glasgow, Steve Nelson, Andrea Marra, Karl Van Neste, Shuang Wei, and James Williamson. The author would also like to thank Robert Britcher for all of his helpful suggestions and editorial assistance.

8.0 REFERENCES

1. "User's Manual For the Prototype Ada Compiler Evaluation Capability (ACEC)", Institute For Defense Analysis, October, 1985.

2. AIX Commands Reference for IBM RISC System/6000, Version 3.

3. Auslander M., Chibib A., Hoagland C., and Kravetz M., "Dynamic Linking and Loading in the AIX System", IBM RISC System/6000 Technology, SA23-2619, IBM Corporation, 1990, p 150.

4. Aho, A., Sethi, R. and Ullman, J. (1988). Compilers Principles, Techniques and Tools. Addison Wesley, Reading, Massachusetts.

5. Rainier, S., Reagan, T., Salwin, A., "The Benchmark Generation Tool : Measuring Ada Compilation System Performance", 3rd International Ada, IEEE Conference on Ada Application and Environments, , May 1988.

6. Bassman, M.J., Fisher, G.A, and Gargaro, A. "An Approach For Evaluating The Performance Efficiency Of Ada Compilers". Ada in Use, Proceedings of the Ada International Conference (Paris, France,

14-16 May). ACM, New York, 1985, pp 72-84. Presents techniques for measuring Ada features and inhibiting code optimizers.

7. Ada Joint Program Office. Ada programming language (ANSI/MIL-STD-1815). OUSD(R&D), Dept.of Defense. Ada Joint Program Office, Washington, D.C., Jan.1983. The official reference manual for the Ada programming language.

8. Clapp, R. Duchesneau, L., Volz, R. Mudge, T. Schultze T. "Toward Real-Time Performance Benchmarks for Ada". Communications of the ACM Volume 29, 1986, pp 760-778. Presents techniques for benchmarking Ada language features and reports on results for specific features tested.

9. Weicker, R. (1984). Dhrystone: A Synthetic Systems Programming Benchmark, Communications ACM, 21 6, pp. 1013-1030. A synthetic benchmark program, emphasizing use of records and pointer data types, based on statement frequency, number of operands and operand locality from a large set of programs written in various high-level languages.

Part III: Concurrency and Parallelism in Ada

Modelling SIMD - Type Parallel Arithmetic Operations in Ada

J. WOLFF VON GUDENBERG

Lehrstuhl für Informatik II
Universität Würzburg
Am Hubland
D-8700 Würzburg

1 INTRODUCTION

1.1 Basic Linear Algebra Subroutines

Arithmetic operations for array types, i. e. matrices and vectors play a vital role in the basic building blocks for numeric software. Therefore Basic Linear Algebra Subroutines (BLAS) have been defined for many languages especially FORTRAN[3]. The construction of efficient, portable software is heavily supported by using these routines. The BLAS routines in FORTRAN are split into three levels, concerning vector/vector, matrix/vector or matrix/matrix operations, respectively. A task committee of the Ada-Europe Numerics WG is developing specifications for Ada-BLAS routines[1]. These specifications shall act as a secondary standard for all Ada users.

1.2 Parallel Computer Model

On the other hand vector and parallel computers become popular more and more and are used for large scale numerical problems. For these computers new arithmetic environments are to be formulated, where now the matrix/vector and matrix/matrix routines gain importance. As a parallel computer we consider a loosely coupled network of processors with local memory. The parallel computer or processing network is driven by a host computer which distributes the data and controls the communication between the various processors. A fixed network topology, e.g. a grid, a tree or a hypercube, is assumed. All processing elements execute the same code on different data, communication is by message passing and not by access to common memory. This concept is sometimes called SIMD or SCMD (single code - multiple data) even if the code must be replicated to every processing element [2].

1.3 Accurate Reliable Arithmetic

We do not only want to increase efficiency but also accuracy. As we consider the BLAS routines as a (secondary) standard we require that they shall be as accurate as usual standard functions. In other words our matrix multiplication, e.g. is as accurate as usual real multiplication, i.e. the error is less than 1 ulp (*unit* in *last place*) for every matrix component. For those matrix and vector operations which work componentwise this accuracy requirement is easy to fulfill, therefore we concentrate on scalar product and generalized axpy operations. In particular we consider the operations

$x^T \cdot y, A \cdot x, A \cdot x + y, \sum_{\nu=1}^{r} A_\nu \cdot \sum_{\mu=1}^{s} x_\mu, A \cdot B, A - B \cdot C$

for vectors x,y and matrices A,B,C.

These operations are implemented in a way that their results are guaranteed to have 1 ulp accuracy [6]. Therefore they may be used for the construction of E-methods [4,8]. Those are methods which compute a sharp *E*nclosure of the true result thus proving its *E*xistence by application of the algorithm.

For most of our BLAS routines it turns out that parallelizing scalar product computations is not helpful. Optimally rounded sequential scalar product routines can be formulated in various manners [7]. One of these algorithms uses a very long fixed point "accumulator" to store intermediate results. Ada implementations of this algorithm have been carried out [5].

2 PARALLELISM AND ADA

It is our goal to support the production of efficient, portable, reliable, parallel programs by providing high level Ada BLAS routines for parallel computers which exploit the parallelism inherent in matrix computations in a way that the application programmer does not need to know the target machine architecture.

We deal with fine grain parallelism here which means that we parallelize on the instruction level. Nevertheless we chose Ada tasks as units of distribution. We have to make sure that these tasks do not access any global data. One way to achieve this is to restrict to tasks which are declared in a library package or have their types declared in a library package [2]. This means that nested tasks may not be distributed over different processors. In our applications nested tasks do not occur at all. We make use of the task type concept which is the main tool for the parallelisation of SIMD algorithms.

Three approaches of the organisation of the system are possible.

1. Implement the BLAS routines for each topology separately but with identical specification. A fixed mapping of Ada tasks to processing nodes is assumed. Each routine performs its own distribution of data and communication. In the worst case this means that a large amount of data are copied from the host to the processing network and vice versa without being processed. The benefit is that application programs are portable across different architectures.

2. A generic specification of the BLAS routines allows to enter the network topology, adjacency relation or routing functions as generic parameters, so that the programmer may perform his own instantiations or use standard instantiations of the BLAS package. This approach will produce a lot of overhead because of the limited facilities of generic functions in Ada.

3. The specification of the BLAS routines makes use of several primitive communication functions which are implemented for each topology. In this approach the distribution of the data for the overall algorithm can be managed by the user and so useless transfers can be avoided. The problem of static permanent data in each local memory arises, however, and must be managed by suitable runtime system routines.

In this paper we outline item 1. by constructing some BLAS routines for array (grid) or tree computers, respectively. For all routines we discuss several variants, where we always calculate the execution time depending on the time needed for an arithmetic operation and the time used for transport of a real number from one processor to another. We therefore not only decrease the computation time, but also try to minimize communication. Together with our accuracy requirements this may increase the necessary local memory, since it is helpful, if all information about one scalar product is available on one processor. In [10] slightly different algorithms are proposed which are better suited for an environment described under variant 3.

3 IMPLEMENTATION ON GRID AND TREE COMPUTERS

3.1 Grids
Parallel algorithms using matrices conform to the following pattern:

- Distribute matrices or vectors to the grid processors.(Partition into rows, columns, blocks, or grids(non-contiguous blocks) may be considered)

Distribution of the full matrix sometimes may cause overflow of local memories, then several repetitions with different data are neccessary.

- Loop until ready

    - Perform arithmetic operations simultaneously.
    - Exchange data if neccessary

- Collect result

For the Ada implementation we assign a task to each processor. There will be a different task for each operation (BLAS routine) These tasks communicate via entries with neighbouring processors in the same row or column. Another entry is provided for communication with the host. If the network allows to broadcast data to a whole row or column this can be used to speed up the algorithms. Appropriate slicing and trimming methods are applied to transport the submatrices [1].

Three variants differing mainly in the scalar product calculation are considered.

sp *sequential scalar product:* All elements which contribute to a scalar product are located on the same processor. This may cause additional data copies and requires much local memory.

ac *accu concept:* Operations for the long accumulator are explicitely available on each processing element. Long accumulators are not exchanged between processors.

at *accu transport:* Operations for the long accumulator are explicitely available on each processing element. Long accumulators are exchanged between processors. This method achieves the highest degree of (operational) parallelism.

If the local memories are large enough we can perform the proper distribution of data in one step and need no communication during the operation.

We consider a $p \times p$ grid of processors $P(i,j)$ with $0 \le i, j \le p - 1$.

Matrices are assumed to be of shape $n \times n$, with $n = k \cdot p$, otherwise they are filled with zeros. The algorithms also work for rectangular matrices.

We declare an array(grid_dim,grid_dim) of tasks where grid_dim is $0..p-1$. We sketch the algorithms in an Ada like syntax where all actions which are performed in parallel are denoted by the for all parallel loop designator. These operations are programmed inside the task body.

We give detailed algorithms for the scalar product, matrix-vector product, and matrix product. The other algorithms are obvious extensions of the latter two.

We use the following notation for the timing characteristics:

Θ_A denote the time for addition of two accumulators

Θ_{TR}, Θ_{TA} the time for transport of one real or one accumulator, respectively

$\Theta_S(n)$ the time for a sequential scalar product with n terms

$$x^T \cdot y = a$$

The two vectors are distributed in slices of length k/p. Each processor further contains two long accumulators. Partial scalar products are computed in parallel and stored in a long accumulator. Their sum is collected in the first column and then in the top-left processor.

A task type with the following entries is declared
```
entry main_vec_con (x:  in out vector_type);
-- link to the host
entry accu_con (d:  in long_accu_type);
-- link to neighbour for accumulator transport
entry main_real_con (s:  out float_type);
-- link to the host
```

```
for i in grid_dim loop
   for j in grid_dim loop
      grid(i,j).main_vec_con(x(i*k+j*k/p..i*k+(j+1)k/p-1) )
      grid(i,j).main_vec_con(y(i*k+j*k/p..i*k+(j+1)k/p-1) )
   end loop --j
end loop --i
for all grid(i,j) compute partial scalar products
```

```
for m in 1..p-1 loop
  for all grid(i,j) where i > 0 transport long accu to left neighbour
  for all grid(i,j) add accumulators
end loop --m
for m in 1..p-1 loop
  for all grid(i,j) where j > 0 transport long accu to upper neighbou
  for all grid(i,j) add accumulators
end loop --m
grid(0,0).main_real_con(scalar_product)
```

Time estimate:

distribution of vectors	$2kp\Theta_{TR}$
k/p-long scalar product	$\Theta_S(k/p)$
addition	$2(p-1)(\Theta_{TA} + \Theta_A)$
collection of result	Θ_{TR}

This parallelisation only pays if the transport times are faster than computation times. This is not realistic for existing parallel computers.

$$A \cdot x = y$$

Only the processors of the first column are active. Each receives a $k \times n$ submatrix of A and the vector x. Then p matrix-vector products are performed in parallel and the slices of the result are collected. This parallelisation yields a speed-up of at most p if $(k+1)(p+2)\Theta_{TR} < \Theta_S(n)$.

A task type with the following entries is declared
```
entry main_mat_con (x:  in matrix_type);
-- link to the host
entry main_vec_con (x:  in out vector_type);
-- link to the host
```

```
for j in grid_dim loop
  grid(0,j).main_mat_con(A(j*k..(j+1)*k-1),0..n-1 )
  grid(0,j).main_vec_con(x)
end loop --j
```

```
for all grid(0,j) compute matrix vector products
for j in grid_dim loop
  grid(0,j).main_mat_con(A(j*k..(j+1)*k-1),0..n-1 )
  grid(0,j).main_vec_con(x)
end loop --j
for j in grid_dim loop
  grid(0,j).main_vec_con(y(j*k..(j+1)*k-1))
end loop --j
```

If broadcasting is possible the matrix may be distributed over the whole processor array yielding a speed-up of at most p^2 for $(n + 1)\Theta_{TR} < (1 - 1/p^2)\Theta_S(n)$.

Transportation time has to be in the order of computation time to obtain a speed-up.

$$A \cdot B = C$$

At first we consider the variant sp (sequential scalar product).

Each processor $grid(i,j)$ obtains the submatrices $A[ik..(i+1)k-1, 0..n-1]$ and $B[0..n-1, jk..(j+1)k-1]$ so that it can compute the block $C[ik..(i+1)k-1, jk..(j+1)k-1]$ of the result matrix. Here the maximal speed-up of p^2 can already be achieved, if $\Theta_{TR} < 0.25\Theta_S(n)$ in the case of broadcasting, or $\Theta_{TR} < 0.15\Theta_S(n)$ otherwise.

So this parallelisation shall be applied when the local memory is sufficiently large.

The task type for matrix multiplication needs the entry:
```
entry main_mat_con (x:  in out matrix_type);
-- link to the host
```

```
for i in grid_dim loop
  for j in grid_dim loop
    grid(i,j).main_mat_con(A(ik..(i+1)k-1,0..n-1)
    grid(i,j).main_mat_con(B(0..n-1,jk..(j+1)k-1)
  end loop --j
```

```
end loop --i
for all grid(i,j) compute submatrix products
for i in grid_dim loop
   for j in grid_dim loop
      grid(i,j).main_mat_con( C(ik..(i+1)k-1,jk..(j+1)k-1)
   end loop --j
end loop --i
```

We now describe variant ac (accumulator concept)

Here each processor contains a $k \times k$ submatrix and k^2 long accumulators. The matrices A and B are staggered in such a way that k^2 partial scalar products can be calculated on each processor. This may be obtained by the following algorithm :

1. Distribute A and B blockwise so that processor $grid(i,j)$ contains block (i,j).

2. Rotate blocks of A to the left; i times for processor row i.

3. Rotate blocks of B to the top; j times for processor column j.

This rotation is precalculated before the actual distribution.
After the computation of the scalar products A rotates blockwise one step to the left and B to the top. Now the next part of the scalar products may be computed. This procedure is repeated $p - 1$ times. Then processor grid(i,j) rounds its accumulators to obtain the block $C(i,j)$ of the result matrix.

The task type now needs two entries:

```
entry main_mat_con (x:  in out matrix_type);
-- link to the host
entry mat_con (x:  in matrix_type);
-- link to the neighbour
```

```
for i in grid_dim loop
   for j in grid_dim loop
      grid(i,j).main_mat_con(A(ik..(i+1)k-1,((j+i)mod p)k..((j+i)mod p+1)k-1)
```

```
      grid(i,j).main_mat_con(B(((j+i)mod p)k..((j+i)mod p+1)k-1,jk..(j+1)k-1)
    end loop --j
end loop --i
for m in 1..p-1 loop
    for all grid(i,j) accumulate k² scalar products
    for all i,j          --rotate A and B
      grid((i-1)mod p,j).mat_con(A)
      grid(i,(j-1)mod p).mat_con(B)
end loop --m
for i in grid_dim loop
    for j in grid_dim loop
      grid(i,j).main_mat_con( C(ik..(i+1)k-1,jk..(j+1)k-1)
    end loop --j
end loop --i
```

The rotation must be divided into two steps, so that no deadlock occurs.

This algorithm also needs quite a lot of local memory (2 $k \times k$ submatrices and k^2 long accumulators. It can, however, be reformulated in such a way, that each processor only contains 2 k- vectors and one accumulator. Only one row of A or column of B of the corresponding block is sent to the processors. The p^2 scalar products of these rows and columns are computed. The result is sent back to the host and the next row or column is read.

Now only vectors have to be communicated:
```
entry main_vec_con (x:  in out vector_type);
-- link to the host
entry vec_con (x:  in vector_type);
-- link to the neighbour
entry main_res_con (x:  out float_type);
-- link to the host for the result
```

```
for r in 0..k-1 loop
    for i in grid_dim loop
      for j in grid_dim loop
        grid(i,j).main_vec_con(A(i+r,((j+i)mod p)k..((j+i)mod p+1)k-1)
    for s in 0..k-1 loop
      for i in grid_dim loop
```

```
      for j in grid_dim loop
        grid(i,j).main_vec_con(B(((j+i)mod p)k..((j+i)mod p+1)k-1,j+s)
      end loop --j
    end loop --i
    for m in 1..p-1 loop
      for all grid(i,j) accumulate scalar product
      for all i,j          --rotate A and B
        grid((i-1)mod p,j).vec_con(A)
        grid(i,(j-1)mod p).vec_con(B)
    end loop --m
    for i in grid_dim loop
      for j in grid_dim loop
        grid(i,j).main_res_con( C(i+r,j+s)
      end loop --j
    end loop --i
    for all i,j          --rotate A
      grid((i-1)mod p,j).vec_con(A)
  end loop --s
end loop -- r
```

The time for the arithmetic operations is identical to the previous algorithm. More data are transported, however, since each matrix element visits each processor more often. The amount of data exchanged per communication step is smaller, so rendezvous time produces an additional overhead.

This parallelisation pays if $(3p + 2k)\Theta_{TR} + \Theta_A < p\Theta_S(n)$

Table 1 displays the results for all considered BLAS operations where we always assume that matrix size $n = k \cdot p$.

Operation	Alg	time
$x^T \cdot y$	seq	$\Theta_S(n)$
	at	$\Theta_S(k) + (p-1)(\Theta_{TA} + \Theta_A) + (2n+1)\Theta_{TR}$
$A \cdot x$	seq	$n\Theta_S(n)$
	sp	$k\Theta_S(n) + (n^2 + 2n)\Theta_{TR}$
$A \cdot x + y$	seq	$n\Theta_S(n+1)$
	sp	$k\Theta_S(n+1) + (n^2 + 3n)\Theta_{TR}$
$\sum_{\nu=1}^{r} A_\nu \cdot \sum_{\mu=1}^{s} x_\mu$	seq	$n\Theta_S(rsn)$
	ac	$n\Theta_S(rsk) + k(p-1)\Theta_A + k((p^2 + p - 1)(rk + s) + p)\Theta_{TR}$
$A \cdot B$	seq	$n^2\Theta_S(n)$
	sp	$k^2\Theta_S(n) + n^2(2p+1)\Theta_{TR}$
	ac	$nk\Theta_S(k) + k^2(p-1)\Theta_A + n^2(2p+1)\Theta_{TR}$
	ac	$nk\Theta_S(k) + k^2(p-1)\Theta_A + (3n^2 + 2k^3 p)\Theta_{TR}$
$A - B \cdot C$	seq	$n^2\Theta_S(n+1)$
	sp	$k^2\Theta_S(n+1) + n^2(2p+2)\Theta_{TR}$

Table 1: Grid algorithms

The algorithms can be improved if broadcasting is possible.

Trees
For tree computers data are split at each level of the tree and distributed to the "sons" of each processor. Arithmetic operations are only performed in the logical leaves of the tree. Then the results are sent back to the root which is the only processor with a link to the host.

This wave-like algorithm [11] is mirrored in Ada by one entry each for communication with "father" and "sons". We now may consider the following two approaches.

1. Tasks are distributed to all processors statically and are activated at elaboration time of the package.

2. Two son tasks are created dynamically for each task and activated on the physical sons of the father task.

Whereas the operation and transportation times are identical for both variants, the run time system overhead for mapping tasks to processors seems to be smaller for approach 2. which also does not reserve a lot of idle processors in the beginning of the algorithm.

Due to the recursive structure of the tree each node may act as root of a new wave. This means that matrix multiplication may call the matrix-vector multiplication which in turn starts the scalar product wave, if the physical height of the tree is high enough.

We consider a tree of height h which has 2^h leaves. The matrix dimension is assumed to be $n = 2^q$ where we usually have $n \leq q$. Since all leaves are executing in parallel, matrices filled with zeros do not slow down the performance.

$$x^T \cdot y = a$$

The only chance to obtain a speed-up for the scalar product is to use the concept of long accumulators. The two vectors are successively halved until the leaves are reached or each node only contains one element of each vector. Each processor further contains two long accumulators. Partial scalar products are computed in parallel and stored in a long accumulator. Their sum is computed during the transport to the root using the well known log-sum algorithm. Note that no rounding error is made, since long accumulators are added.

A task type with the following entries is declared

```
entry cut (x:  in vector_type);
-- link to the father for distribution
entry accu_sons (d:  out long_accu_type);
-- link to collect accumulators from sons
entry retrieve (d:  out long_accu_type);
-- link to root
```

As in the case of grids this parallelisation only pays if the transport times are faster than computation times. This is not realistic for existing parallel computers.

$$A \cdot x = y$$

The matrix A is split row-wise on the way down to the leaves, the vector x is replicated to each node. Then scalar products or submatrix-vector products are performed in the leaves, and the result vector is concatenated on the way back to the root.

A task type with the following entries is declared

```
entry cut (x:  in matrix_type);
-- link to get submatrix from father
entry sons (x:  in vector_type);
-- link to get vector form father
entry glue (x:  out vector_type);
-- send result to father
entry retrieve (x:  out vector_type);
-- send result to root
```

The time used for this algorithm is split into three parts

1. distribution: Here we assume parallel transport of all processors.

$$(n^2 + n + h - 1)\Theta_{TR}$$

2. computation:

$$2^{q-h}\Theta_S(n)$$

3. transport and composition of result vector:

$$(n + h - 1)\Theta_{TR}$$

The actual height h of the tree is assumed to be less than q the logarithm of the matrix dimension.

Again transport time has to be in the order of computation time to yield a speed-up.

$$A \cdot B = C$$

Matrix A is copied to the sons whereas matrix B is split column-wise q-times. Now each node has the complete matrix A and one column of B. The matrix-vector product may be called which splits the matrix A row-wise. After q further steps each node contains two vectors and performs a sequential scalar product or calls the corresponding tree operation, if this is faster.

Usually the physical height of the tree h will be less than q which means that matrix-submatrix products are computed, or at least less than $2q$ where now submatrix-vector products are computed sequentially.

A speed-up is achieved, if $3.0625\Theta_{TR} < (1 - 2^{-h})\Theta_S(n)$ which is certainly true for large n. Note, however, that much local memory is required.

A task type with the following entries is declared

```
entry cut (B: in matrix_type);
-- link to get submatrix from father
entry sons (A: in matrix_type);
-- link to get full matrix from father
entry glue (x:  out matrix_type);
-- send result to father
entry retrieve (x:  out matrix_type);
-- send result to root
```

Table 2 comprises the results for tree algorithms.

Operation	Alg.	seq.time	par.time
$x^T \cdot y$	T	$\Theta_S(n)$	$\Theta_M + q(\Theta_A + 2\Theta_{TA}) + (2n + q - 1)\Theta_{TR}$
$A \cdot x$	T	$n\Theta_S(n)$	$2^{q-h}\Theta_S(n) + (n^2 + 2(n + h - 1))\Theta_{TR}$
$A \cdot x + y$	T	$n\Theta_S(n+1)$	$2^{q-h}\Theta_S(n+1) + (n^2 + 3n + 2(h-1))\Theta_{TR}$
$\sum_{\nu=1}^r A_\nu \cdot \sum_{\mu=1}^s x_\mu$	T	$n\Theta_S(rsn)$	$2^{q-h}\Theta_S(rsn) + (rn^2 + (s+1)n + 2(h-1))\Theta_{TR}$
$A \cdot B$	T	$n^2\Theta_S(n)$	$2^{2q-h}\Theta_S(n) + (3n^2 + 2(2h-1))\Theta_{TR}$
$A - B \cdot C$	T	$n^2\Theta_S(n+1)$	$2^{2q-h}\Theta_S(n+1) + (4n^2 + 2(2h-1))\Theta_{TR}$

Table 2: Tree algorithms

References

[1] Ada-Europe Numerics Working Group meeting papers A-ENWG/19.3, A-ENWG/BLAS/x.x

[2] R.M. Clapp,T. Mudge: *Ada on a Hypercube*,Ada Letters,Vol.IX,No.2,1989,pp. 118-128

[3] J.Dongarra,J. du Croz, S. Hammarling,R.Hanson: *An Extended Set of FOR-TRAN Basic Linear Algebra Subprograms*,acm Trans. on Math.Software,Vol 14,No.1, 1988,pp. 1-17

[4] E.Kaucher,S.M.Rump: *E-Methods for Fixed-Point Equations $f(x) = x$*, Computing 28,p31-42,1982

[5] J.Kok: *The Embedding of Accurate Arithmetic in Ada*,in [9],pp99-120

[6] Kulisch, U., Miranker, W. L.: *Computer Arithmetic in Theory and Practice*. Academic Press, New York, 1981.

[7] Kulisch, U., Miranker, W. L.: *The Arithmetic of the Digital Computer: A New Approach*. SIAM Review, Vol. 28, No. 1, March 1986 (pp. 1-40)

[8] G. Schumacher, J. Wolff v. Gudenberg: *E- Methods for Improving Accuracy*, in [9], pp. 169-176

[9] P.J.L. Wallis(ed.): *Improving Floating-Point Processing*,Wiley,Chichester, 1990

[10] A. Weckherlin: Untersuchung und Implementierung paralleler, genauer Grundroutinen der Linearen Algebra, Diplomarbeit, Universität Karlsruhe, 1990

[11] W.Wöst: *Wie funktioniert der TX3?* ,c't, 1988/6

Analyzing Ada Tasking Deadlocks and Livelocks Using Extended Petri Nets

Jingde CHENG and Kazuo USHIJIMA

Department of Computer Science and Communication Engineering
Kyushu University
6-10-1 Hakozaki, Fukuoka 812, Japan

Abstract

This paper presents a static analysis method based on extended Petri nets to detect tasking deadlocks and livelocks in a class of concurrent Ada programs. We model the tasking behavior of concurrent Ada programs using extended Petri nets and analyze the Petri net model of an Ada program using an algebraic method. We show that detection of a tasking deadlock or livelock in a concurrent Ada program can be reduced to getting a positive integer solution for a matrix equation concerning the Petri net model of the program. The method is effective for those concurrent Ada programs that include no dynamic creation of tasks, no abort statement, and no exception handler.

1. Introduction

Deadlock and livelock are two kinds of typical synchronization errors in concurrent systems and may occur in applications with Ada tasking. A *tasking deadlock* in a concurrent Ada program is a situation where some tasks form a circular waiting relation at some synchronization and/or communication points and hence can never proceed with their computation. The tasks involved in the circular waiting relation are said to be *deadlocked*. A task that is waiting for synchronization and/or communication with a deadlocked task and is outside the circular waiting relation is said to be *deadlock-blocked*. A *tasking livelock* in a concurrent Ada program is a situation where each member of a group of tasks communicates infinitely forever with only tasks in this group, and hence can never respond to a request from the external world outside the group. The tasks involved in the group are said to be *livelocked*. A task that is waiting for synchronization and/or communication with a livelocked task and is outside the group is said to be *livelock-blocked* or *starving*. Note that a local tasking deadlock and a local tasking livelock may exist simultaneously during an execution of a concurrent Ada program.

In order for tasking objects to synchronize and communicate with each other, Ada defines five types of waiting relations between tasking objects. They are activation, acceptance, entry call, subprogram and/or block termination, and task termination waiting [DoD-83]. Since different combinations of the waiting relations form different tasking deadlocks, many types of tasking deadlocks may occur in concurrent Ada programs. By a complete classification, we know that there are 18 types of tasking deadlocks [Cheng-90a]. The major cause of tasking livelocks are infinite loops in tasks. We know a little about characters of tasking livelocks. No classification of tasking livelocks is given until now.

Since both tasking deadlocks and tasking livelocks are serious for any application with Ada tasking, how to handle the tasking deadlocks and livelocks is an inevitable issue in the development of the applications. Over the last ten years, a number of papers have dealt with the tasking deadlock problem and proposed various methods and tools to detect tasking deadlocks. However, none of the proposed detection methods and tools can handle all types of tasking deadlocks in any arbitrary Ada program [Cheng-91]. On the other hand, the tasking livelock problem has received little attention. Therefore, how to handle tasking deadlocks and livelocks in any arbitrary Ada program is still an open problem until now, though the issue is very important for practical applications of the Ada tasking.

As a powerful tool, Petri nets are used to model and analyze various concurrent systems [Murata-89a, Peterson-81]. In the recent years, several Petri net models for concurrent Ada programs have been proposed for various purposes [Cheng-88a,88b, Mandrioli-85, Murata-89b, Shatz-90, Stansifer-91].

This paper presents a static analysis method based on extended Petri nets to detect the tasking deadlocks and livelocks in a class of Ada programs. We model the tasking behavior of concurrent Ada programs using extended Petri nets and analyze the Petri net model of an Ada program using an algebraic method. We show that detection of a tasking deadlock or livelock in a concurrent Ada program can be reduced to getting a positive integer solution for a matrix equation concerning the Petri net model of the program. The method is effective for those concurrent Ada programs that include no dynamic creation of tasks, no abort statement, and no exception handler. The presented method is an extension of our earlier work [Cheng-88a,88b]. It can also be regarded as an extension of Murata, Shenker, and Shatz's work [Murata-89b] in the sense that our method can detect more types of tasking deadlocks than their method can do and can detect tasking livelocks that are not considered in their work.

2. Basic Definitions of Extended Petri Nets

A *bag* (or multiset) is a collection of elements from some domain D. Unlike a set, however, an element may occur in a bag more than once. A function #: $D \times D^\infty \to N$, where D^∞ denotes the set of all bags over D and N denotes the set of nonnegative integers, yields the number of occurrences of an element in a bag. Thus, $\#(x, B) = k$ $(k \geq 0)$ if and only if there are exactly k occurrences of element x in bag B.

An *extended Petri net* (EPN) is a 5-tuple (P, T, I, I_I, O). P is a finite nonempty set of *places*. T is a finite nonempty set of *transitions*. $P \cap T = \Phi$(the empty set). I: $T \to P^\infty$ is a mapping called *input function*. Place p is called an *input place* of a transition t if $p \in I(t)$. I_I: $T \to P$ is a mapping called *inhibitor input function*. Place p is called an *inhibitor input place* of a transition t if $p \in I_I(t)$. O: $T \to P^\infty$ is a mapping called *output function*. Place p is called an *output place* of a transition t if $p \in O(t)$. A *marking* M of an EPN is a mapping M: $P \to N$, which assigns *tokens* to each place in the EPN. A marking M of an EPN with n places can also be represented an $1 \times n$ vector of nonnegative integers. An EPN with marking M is called a *marked extended Petri net* and denoted by (P, T, I, I_I, O, M).

An EPN (P, T, I, I_I, O) can also be represented by an arc-labeled bipartite directed multigraph, where P is the set of place nodes, T is the set of transition nodes, a node $p \in P$ and a node $t \in T$ are joined by an arc from p to t, called *input arc*, if and only if $p \in I(t)$, a node $p \in P$ and a node $t \in T$ are joined by an arc from p to t, called *inhibitor input arc*, if and only if $p \in I_I(t)$, and a node $t \in T$ and a node $p \in P$ are joined by an arc from t to p, called *output arc*, if and only if $p \in O(t)$. Graphically, places are represented by circles, transitions by bars, arcs by arrows, inhibitor arcs by arrows with small circles, and tokens by small black dots inside places. Fig. 1 shows a marked EPN. We will give a tasking behavioral interpretation for the EPN in Section 3.

A transition t in a marked EPN (P, T, I, I_I, O, M) is said to be *enabled* or *firable* if and only if $M(p) \geqq \#(p, I(t))$ for all $p \in I(t)$ and $M(p) = 0$ for all $p \in I_I(t)$. A transition t can *fire* if and only if it is enabled. The firing results in a new marking M' such that $M'(p) = M(p) - \#(p, I(t)) + \#(p, O(t))$ for all $p \in P$. Firing of transitions is mutually exclusive, i.e., only one transition can fire at a moment. Except for this restriction, firing of transitions can proceed in an asynchronous manner.

The *state space* of an EPN (P, T, I, I_I, O) with n places, denoted by N^n, is a set of all possible markings of the EPN. A *next-state function* δ of the EPN is a partial function $\delta: N^n \times T \rightarrow N^n$. For a marking M and a transition t in the EPN, $\delta(M, t)$ is defined as $\delta(M, t) = M'$ if and only if t is enabled in M, where M' is the result of the firing of t. For a marked EPN (P, T, I, I_I, O, M_0), a sequence of its transitions $\sigma = t_1, t_2, ..., t_k$ is called a *firing sequence* for M_0 if and only if there exists a sequence of markings $M_1, M_2, ..., M_k$ such that $\delta(M_{i-1}, t_i) = M_i$, $i = 1, 2, ..., k$. An *extended next-state function* δ of an EPN (P, T, I, I_I, O) with n places is a partial function $\delta: N^n \times T^* \rightarrow N^n$, where T^* is the set of all possible transition sequences over T. For a marked EPN (P, T, I, I_I, O, M) and a sequence of its transitions $\sigma = t_1, t_2, ..., t_k$, $\delta(M, \sigma)$ is defined as $\delta(M, \sigma) = M'$ if and only if σ is a firing sequence for M, where M' is the result of the firing of t_k.

For a marked EPN (P, T, I, I_I, O, M), a marking M' is said to be *immediately reachable* from M if and only if next-state function $\delta(M, t) = M'$ is defined. M' is said to be *reachable* from M if and only if extended next-state function $\delta(M, \sigma) = M'$ is defined. The *reachability set* of the marked EPN, denoted by R(M), is the set of all markings reachable from M.

A place in a marked EPN (P, T, I, I_I, O, M) is said to be *k-bounded* if and only if there exists a fixed k $(k \geqq 1)$ such that $M'(p) \leqq k$ for all $M' \in R(M)$. The marked EPN is said to be *k-bounded* if each place is k-

p_1 : Elaborated

t_1 : Activation-start

p_2 : Activating

t_2 : Activation-completion

p_3 : Execution-waiting

t_3 : Execution-start
(Acceptance)

p_4 : Accepting

t_4 : Rendezvous-start
(Continuation,
Completion)

p_5 : Completed

t_5 : Termination

p_6 : Terminated

t_6 : Elaboration-start

p_7 : Elaborating

t_7 : Elaboration-completion

p_8 : Elaborated

t_8 : Activation-start
(Simple-entry-call)

p_9 : Simple-entry-calling

p_{10} : Activating

t_9 : Activation-completion
(Execution-start,
Completion,
Termination)

p_{11} : Working-for-internal-affairs

p_{12} : Terminated

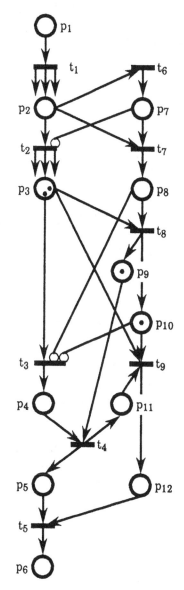

$$M = (0, 0, 2, 0, 0, 0, 0, 0, 1, 1, 0, 0)$$

Fig. 1 A marked extended Petri net

bounded for some fixed k (k≧1). In particular, a place is said to be *safe* if and only if it is 1-bounded. A marked EPN is said to be *safe* if it is 1-bounded.

The *input function matrix* D^- of an EPN (P, T, I, I_I, O) is a $|T| \times |P|$ matrix $D^-: T \times P \to N$ such that

$$D^-(i, j) = \#(p_j, I(t_i));$$

the *inhibitor input function matrix* D^I of the EPN is a $|T| \times |P|$ matrix $D^I: T \times P \to \{0, 1\}$ such that

$$D^I(i, j) = \begin{cases} 1 & \text{if } p_j \in I_I(t_i) \\ 0 & \text{if } p_j \notin I_I(t_i); \end{cases}$$

the *output function matrix* D^+ of the EPN is a $|T| \times |P|$ matrix $D^+: T \times P \to N$ such that

$$D^+(i, j) = \#(p_j, O(t_i));$$

the *incidence matrix* D of the EPN is defined as

$$D = D^+ - D^-.$$

For an EPN (P, T, I, I_I, O), a transition $t_i \in T$ may be represented by a $|T|$-ary unit vector $e(i)$ where ith element of $e(i)$ is 1 and all other elements are 0. For a marked EPN (P, T, I, I_I, O, M), a transition t_i can fire if and only if $M \geqq e(i) \cdot D^-$ and $(e(i) \cdot D^I) \cdot M^T = 0$, where M^T is the transpose of M. The result of the firing of t_i can be represented as follows :

$$\delta(M, t_i) = M - e(i) \cdot D^- + e(i) \cdot D^+ = M + e(i) \cdot D.$$

For a marked EPN = (P, T, I, I_I, O, M) and a firing sequence $\sigma = t_1, t_2, ..., t_k$, the result of the firings of σ can be represented as follows:

$$\delta(M, \sigma) = M + e(i_1) \cdot D + e(i_2) \cdot D + \cdots + e(i_k) \cdot D = M + f(\sigma) \cdot D,$$

where $f(\sigma) = e(i_1) + e(i_2) + \cdots + e(i_k)$ is called the *firing vector* of σ. The ith element of $f(\sigma)$ is the times of firing of t_i.

3. Modeling the Ada Tasking Using Extended Petri Nets

In detection of tasking deadlocks and livelocks using a static analysis method, the most important issue is that the abstract model of concurrent Ada programs used in the analysis must correctly represent tasking behavior of the programs. In particular, in order to detect tasking deadlocks as many types as possible, the model must correctly represent all the five types of waiting relations between tasking objects in the programs. Unfortunately, none of static analysis methods proposed in the recent years represents all the five types of waiting relations correctly [Cheng-91]. For example, the activation, subprogram and/or block termination, and termination waiting relations have not been considered in any proposed static analysis method. As a result, many types of tasking deadlocks cannot be detected using those methods [Cheng-91].

Now, we model the Ada tasking using extended Petri nets. Unlike various statement-based modeling methods proposed previously, our modeling method is based on tasking events.

We assume that the concurrent Ada programs discussed in this paper include no dynamic creation of tasks, no abort statement, and no exception handler.

A *tasking event* is an atomic tasking action that has a semantic interpretation at Ada language level. Below are 24 kinds of tasking events that may occur in the lifetime of a task. We specify each kind of tasking event by a *tasking event name* and describe its semantics informally.

(1) *Elaboration-start*: The elaboration of object declaration of the task is started.

(2) *Elaboration-completion*: The elaboration of object declaration of the task is completed. The task can be referred to by other tasks after this time.

(3) *Activation-start*: The elaboration of the task's declarative part is started.

(4) *Activation-completion*: The elaboration of the task's declarative part is completed.

(5) *Execution-start*: The first statement of the task's body is executed.

(6) *Simple-entry-call*: The task issues a simple entry call to another task.

(7) *Conditional-entry-call*: The task issues a conditional entry call to another task.

(8) *Timed-entry-call*: The task issues a timed entry call to another task.

(9) *Entry-call-cancellation*: A conditional or timed entry call issued by the task is canceled because the corresponding rendezvous cannot be started immediately or within the specified duration.

(10) *Acceptance*: The task is ready at an accept statement for accepting any corresponding entry call.

(11) *Simple-selection*: The task is ready at a selective wait statement with no else part, no delay alternatives, and no terminate alternative for selecting any of its open select alternatives.

(12) *Conditional-selection*: The task is ready at a selective wait statement with an else part for selecting any of its open select alternatives or for canceling the selection.

(13) *Timed-selection*: The task is ready at a selective wait statement with some delay alternative(s) for selecting any of its open select alternatives.

(14) *Termination-selection*: The task is ready at a selective wait statement with a terminate alternative for selecting any of its open select alternatives.

(15) *Selection-cancellation*: A selective wait of the task is canceled because the corresponding rendezvous cannot be started immediately or within the specified duration.

(16) *Rendezvous-start*: The task is calling an entry of another task, which has been ready to accept this entry call, or the task is waiting for accepting an entry call, which has been issued by another task.

(17) *Continuation*: The task, which has issued an entry call, resumes its execution as a result of the completion of the corresponding rendezvous, or the task has completed the execution of an accept statement and continues its execution.

(18) *Block-activation-start*: The elaboration of the declarative part of a block statement in the task's body is started, or the elaboration of the declarative part of a subprogram called by the task is started.

(19) *Block-activation-completion*: The elaboration of the declarative part of a block statement in the task's body is completed, or the elaboration of the declarative part of a subprogram called by the task is completed.

(20) *Block-execution-start*: The first statement of a block statement in the task's body is executed, or the first statement of a subprogram called by the task is executed.

(21) *Block-execution-completion*: The execution of a block statement in the task's body is completed, or the execution of a subprogram called by the task is completed.

(22) *Block-termination*: The execution of a block statement in the task's body terminates, or the execution of a subprogram called by the task terminates.

(23) *Completion*: The execution of the task's body is completed.

(24) *Termination*: The task terminates.

A *tasking state* of a task, which describes what that task is doing, can be defined by two contiguous tasking events. Below, we specify each kind of tasking state briefly. The semantics of these tasking states are easy to consider according to the semantics of the two tasking events.

(1) *Elaborating*: <Elaboration-start, Elaboration-completion>,

(2) *Elaborated*: <Elaboration-completion, Activation-start>,

(3) *Activating*: <Activation-start, Activation-completion>, or
     <Activation-start, Elaboration-start(subtask)>, or
     <Activation-start, Elaboration-completion(subtask)>, or
     <Activation-start, Block-activation-start>, or
     <Block-termination, Activation-completion>,

(4) *Execution-waiting*: <Activation-completion, Execution-start>, or
     <Activation-completion, Activation-start(subtask)>, or
     <Activation-completion, Activation-completion(subtask)>,

(5) *Simple-entry-calling*: <Simple-entry-call, Rendezvous-start>,

(6) *Conditional-entry-calling*:
     <Conditional-entry-call, Entry-call-cancellation>, or
     <Conditional-entry-call, Rendezvous-start>,

(7) *Timed-entry-calling*: <Timed-entry-call, Entry-call-cancellation>, or
     <Timed-entry-call, Rendezvous-start>,

(8) *Accepting*: <Acceptance, Rendezvous-start>,

(9) *Simple-selecting*: <Simple-selection, Rendezvous-start>,

(10) *Conditional-selecting*:
<Conditional-selection, Selection-cancellation>, or
<Conditional-selection, Rendezvous-start>,

(11) *Timed-selecting*: <Timed-selection, Selection-cancellation>, or
<Timed-selection, Rendezvous-start>,

(12) *Termination-selecting*: <Termination-selection, Rendezvous-start>,
or <Termination-selection, Termination>,

(13) *Suspended-by-rendezvous*: <Rendezvous-start, Continuation>,

(14) *Block-activating*:
<Block-activation-start, Block-activation-completion>,

(15) *Block-execution-waiting*:
<Block-activation-completion, Block-execution-start>,

(16) *Block-completed*: <Block-execution-completion, Block-termination>,

(17) *Completed*: <Completion, Termination>,

(18) *Terminated*: <Termination, *undefined*>,

(19) *Working-for-internal-affairs*: otherwise.

When we model the tasking behavior of concurrent Ada programs using extended Petri nets, we represent tasking events by transitions labeled with tasking event names, and tasking states by places labeled with tasking state names. Thus, enabling conditions of an transition correspond to conditions for occurrence of a tasking event, firing of transitions correspond to occurrences of tasking events, and moves of tokens correspond to sequential control transfer.

Below, we present our EPN model for the Ada tasking briefly by graphical representations of the model.

Fig. 2 shows the EPN model of the lifetime of a task. Note that there is a place labeled by *"Executing"*, which is not defined as a tasking state above. This means that the place should be refined into a subnet, which provides more detailed modeling according to the body of the task.

In Ada, a subprogram that is a library unit can be used as a main program in the usual sense. The main program of an Ada program acts as if called by some environment task [DoD-83]. In the following discussion, we call such an environment task *main task*. We assume that the execution of the main task stars from tasking event "Execution-start" and terminates at tasking event "Completion".

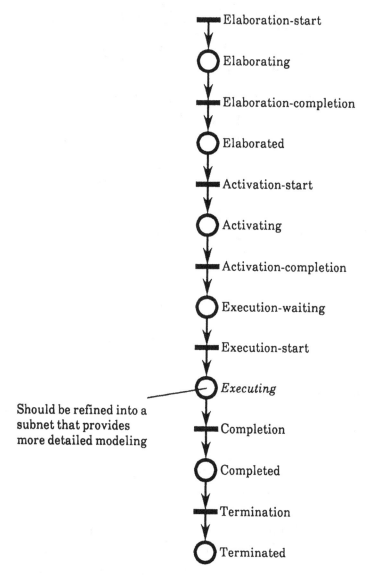

Fig. 2 The EPN model of the lifetime of a task

Fig. 3 shows the EPN model of the dependence relation between a task and its direct master. Note that the transitions labeled by "Activation-start" and "Activation-completion" have m output arcs respectively.

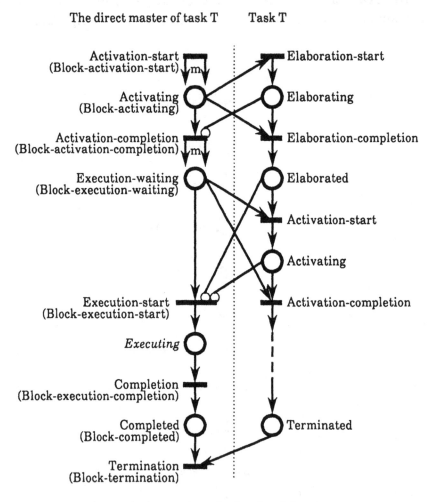

m = 2n + 1 where n is the number of subtasks of the master

Fig. 3   The EPN model of the dependence relation between a task and its direct master

Fig. 4 shows the EPN model of the most simple form of rendezvous between two tasks. Note that there is a place labeled by *"Executing"* that should be refined into a subnet, which provides more detailed modeling according to the body of the accept statement. If the accept statement has no body, then place "Executing" and place "Suspended-by-rendezvous" can be deleted from the model and transition "Rendezvous-start" and transition "Continuation" can be united into one transition.

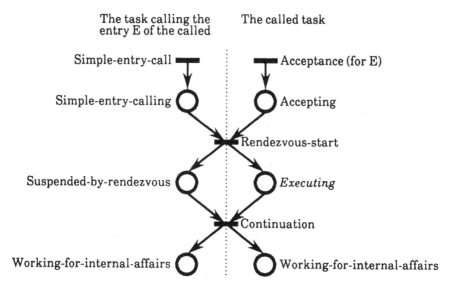

Fig. 4 The EPN model of rendezvous between tasks

Fig. 5 shows the EPN model of conditional and timed entry calls.

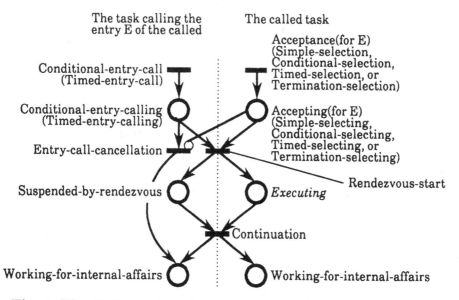

Fig. 5 The EPN model of conditional and timed entry calls

In Ada, during an object initialization invoking a function subprogram, an entry call can be issued by the execution of function subprogram. Therefore, an entry call can be issued during the activation of a task. Fig. 6 shows the EPN model of simple entry calls issued during the activation of a task. The EPN model of conditional and timed entry calls issued during the activation of a task are easy to consider based on the models presented in Fig. 5 and Fig. 6.

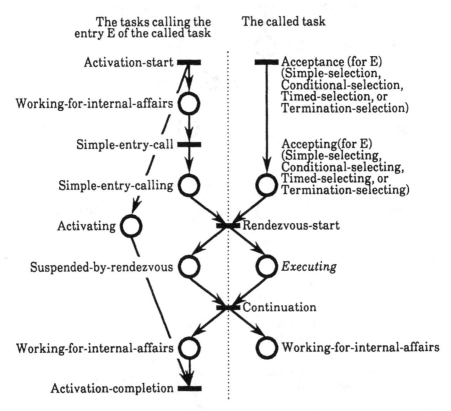

Fig. 6   The EPN model of simple entry calls
issued during task activation

In this paper, for the purpose of simplicity, we only consider the case of a selective wait whose each alternative does not start with the reserved word **when** and a condition. Fig. 7 shows the EPN model of simple, conditional, and timed selective waits. Fig. 8 shows the EPN model of selective waits with a terminate alternative. In the models, the modeling about the situation during or after the rendezvous is omitted because it is the same as the model represented in Fig. 4 and Fig. 5.

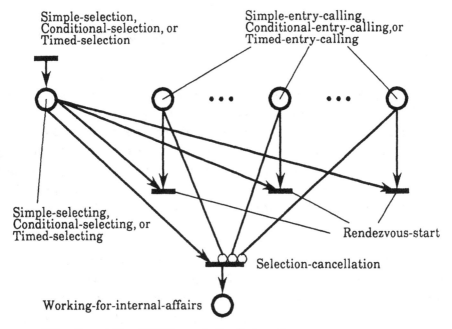

Fig. 7 The EPN model of simple,
conditional, and timed selective waits

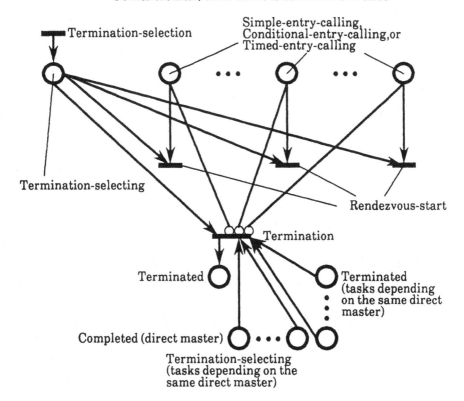

Fig. 8 The EPN model of termination selective waits

Our EPN model for the Ada tasking has four features. First, the model correctly represents all the five types of waiting relations between tasking objects in Ada programs. This provides a theoretical basis for our static analysis method to detect more types of tasking deadlocks. Second, no place in the model is shared by two different tasks. This provides some conveniences for identification of tasks in tasking deadlock and livelock analysis. Third, the model has no place serving as a "cycle place" [Murata-89b] and therefore is not strongly connected. This provides some conveniences for tasking livelock analysis. Finally, the model is non-reflexive, i.e., "self-loop-free" or "pure". This can avoid ambiguity in analyzing an EPN of the model using its incidence matrix.

The extended Petri net model of a given concurrent Ada program can be obtained by applying a series of transformation rules based on the above EPN model of the Ada tasking. During the transformation, some statements of the program should be ignored if they do not affect the tasking behavior of the program from a static analysis viewpoint. Such statements, for example, are: any assignment statement unless it includes a function subprogram whose execution issues an entry call or creates some subtasks, any compound statement unless it includes an entry call or accept statement or (in the case of a block statement) creates some subtasks, any subprogram unless it creates some subtasks or includes entry call statements, and all exit, return and goto statements. An in-depth discussion about the transformation is beyond the scope of this paper.

As an example, Fig. 9 shows a simple Ada program involving a tasking deadlock named "activation-and-entry-call-blocking" [Cheng-90a]. Fig. 1 shows a reduced EPN model of task T1 in the program. Places p_1, p_2, p_3, p_4, p_5, and p_6 and transitions t_1, t_2, t_3, and t_5 are used to represent task T1's tasking states and events. Places p_7, p_8, p_9, p_{10}, p_{11}, and p_{12} and transitions t_6, t_7, t_8, and t_9 are used to represent task T2's tasking states and events. Transition t_4 is shared by task T1 and task T2. In the model, some transitions are labeled by more than one tasking event names. This is a result of reducing the original EPN model of the program. The motivation of reduction is to simplify the original EPN model under condition of preserving various properties of the net. Fig. 1 shows that the EPN has reached a marking M such that no transition in the net can fire and therefore fallen into the deadlock.

```
procedure ACTECB is
  task T1 is
    entry E1;
  end T1;
  function GET return INTEGER is
  begin
    T1 . E1;
    return 0;
  end GET;
  task body T1 is
    task T2;
    task body T2 is
      I : INTEGER := GET;
    begin
      null;
    end T2;
    begin
      accept E1;
    end T1;
  begin
    null;
end ACTECB;
```

Fig. 9 An example of activation-and-entry-call-blocking

4. Analyzing Tasking Deadlocks and Livelocks

Based on the EPN model of a concurrent Ada program, we can analyze tasking deadlocks and livelocks in the program using various analysis methods established in Petri net theory. We adopt an algebraic method to analyze the EPN models of Ada programs in order to detect tasking deadlocks and livelocks.

For the EPN model of a given program P, we name a marking, denoted by M_0, *initial marking* of the EPN if it assigns only one token to the place labeled "Block-activating" of the main task and no token to other places; we also name a marking, denoted by M_t, *terminal marking* of the EPN if it assigns only one token to the place labeled "Completed" of the main task and no token to other places.

Lemma 4.1 For any given program P and its EPN model with incidence matrix D, if there is a firing sequence σ such that $\delta(M_0, \sigma) = M'$, then matrix equation $M' = M_0 + X \cdot D$ has a positive integer solution X (i.e., each element of X is nonnegative but at least one element is positive) as the firing vector of σ. □

Lemma 4.2 For any given program P and its EPN model with incidence matrix D, if P has an execution that can terminate, then matrix equation $M_t = M_0 + X \cdot D$ has at least one positive integer solution X as the firing vector of σ. □

For the EPN model of any given program P, we call a set of all places corresponding to a task *identifiable place set* of that task. Since no place in the model is shared by two different tasks, the identifiable place set of a task can be used to identify that task.

We say that a transition t in an EPN marked by marking M is to be *potentially firable* at M if and only if there exists a marking $M' \in R(M)$ in which t is enabled, a transition t in the marked EPN is to be *dead* at M if and only if t is nonfirable for any $M' \in R(M)$.

Lemma 4.3 A *static tasking dead-state* exists in a program P if and only if there exists a marking $M \in R(M_0)$ of the EPN model of P such that M satisfies the following conditions:

(1)   for the identifiable place set of each in a task group, there is at least one place p such that $M(p) > 0$, and

(2)   for every place p in the condition (1), any transition $t \in \{t' | p \in I(t')\}$ is dead at M. □

We say that there exists a *firing request cycle* among some transitions $t_1, t_2, t_3, ..., t_{k-1}, t_k$ $(k > 1)$ in an EPN marked by marking M if the transitions satisfy the following conditions at M: t_1 become firable only if t_2 fires, t_2 become firable only if t_3 fires, ..., t_{k-1} become firable only if t_k fires, t_k become firable only if t_1 fires. For example, there exists a firing request cycle among transitions t_3, t_4, and t_9 in the EPN shown by Fig. 1.

Lemma 4.4 A *static tasking deadlock* exists in a program P if and only if there exists a marking $M \in R(M_0)$ of the EPN model of P such that at M there exists a firing request cycle among some transitions t_1, $t_2, t_3, ..., t_{k-1}, t_k$ $(k > 1)$, where $t_i \in \{t |$ there is a place p such that $M(p) > 0$ and $p \in I(t)\}$, $i = 1, ..., k$. □

Lemma 4.5 A *static tasking livelock* exists in a program P if and only if for a marking $M \in R(M_0)$ of the EPN model of P there exists an infinite firing sequence σ in which a subsequence σ' including some transitions labeled "Rendezvous-start" and "Continuation", repeats infinite times. $\square$

Lemmas 4.3 ~ 4.5 can be regarded as a definition for static tasking dead-states, static tasking deadlocks, and static tasking livelocks, respectively.

Lemma 4.6 Any static tasking deadlock must be a static tasking dead-state. $\square$

Note that the converse of Lemma 4.6 is not necessarily true. A static tasking deadlock contains only deadlocked tasks, but a static tasking dead-state may include deadlocked tasks, deadlock-blocked tasks, livelock-blocked tasks, and "indefinite postponement" tasks (e.g., a task T is waiting at an accept statement for entry E, but there is no entry call statement to E in the program in question, and some other tasks are waiting for synchronization and/or communication with T). Distinguishing various types of "dead" tasks explicitly is very important for resolution of tasking dead-states and deadlocks.

According to the semantics of termination of an Ada program and Lemmas 4.1 ~ 4.6, we have the following theorems.

Theorem 4.1 For any given program P and its EPN model with incidence matrix D, if matrix equation $M_t = M_0 + X \cdot D$ has no positive integer solution, then a static tasking dead-state, a static tasking deadlock, or a static tasking livelock exists in P. $\square$

Theorem 4.2 For any given program P and its EPN model with incidence matrix D, if (1) there exists a marking M such that a transition $t \in \{t' | \text{ there is a place p such that } M(p) > 0 \text{ and } p \in I(t')\}$ is dead at M, and (2) matrix equation $M = M_0 + X \cdot D$ has a positive integer solution X as a firing vector for M_0, then a static tasking dead-state exists in P. $\square$

Note that a positive integer solution X for matrix equation $M = M_0 + X \cdot D$ is not necessarily a firing vector for M_0. [Peterson-81] discussed methods to check whether a positive integer solution X for matrix equation $M = M_0 + X \cdot D$ is a firing vector for M_0 or not.

Lemma 4.7   If a bounded marked EPN with incidence matrix D always has at least one firable transition, then there exists a firing vector $f(\sigma)$ such that $f(\sigma) \cdot D = 0$, where 0 is the zero vector. □

Lemma 4.8 Any marked EPN of any program P is bounded. □

According to Lemmas 4.5, 4.7, and 4.8, we have the following theorems.

Theorem 4.3   For any given program P and its EPN model with incidence matrix D, if a static tasking livelock exists in P, then matrix equation $X \cdot D = 0$, where 0 is the zero vector, has a positive integer solution X. □

Theorem 4.4   For any given program P and its EPN model with incidence matrix D, if matrix equation $X \cdot D = 0$, where 0 is the zero vector, has no positive integer solution X, then P is free of static tasking livelocks. □

The analysis results presented above are primary. In particular, the analysis results can only be used to detect the effect of a static tasking dead-state, deadlock, or livelock rather than its cause. Many work remains to do in order to establish a practical static analysis approach to detect real tasking dead-states, deadlocks, and livelocks in concurrent Ada programs.

5. Concluding Remarks

We have modeled the Ada tasking using extended Petri nets and proposed an algebraic analysis method to detect tasking dead-states, deadlocks, and livelocks in concurrent Ada programs.

As a static analysis method, our method has the same major advantage as that other proposed static analysis methods have, i.e., the method can guarantee the absence of some tasking dead-state, deadlocks, and livelocks, and the analysis result is independent of run-time environment [Cheng-91]. Indeed, static analysis is the only way that can have such a guarantee. This fact, however, may also be a disadvantage in the sense that it may detect some spurious tasking dead-states, deadlocks, and livelocks. This is because any static analysis has to assume that each execution path in the analyzed program is executable in order to cover all possible situations, and therefore, has to introduce some spurious executions in the program. For example, a tasking dead-state, deadlock, or livelock may be "data-dependent" (or "value-dependent"), i.e., under conditions of some input data of a program, the tasking dead-state, deadlock, or livelock can never occur in the program because the execution path, in which the tasking dead-state, deadlock, or livelock occurs, cannot be performed. However, since the static analysis is "data-independent" (or "value-independent"), such a tasking dead-state, deadlock, or livelock is detected as a static tasking dead-state, deadlock, or livelock. This is the reason why we say the tasking dead-states, deadlocks, or livelocks detected by using our method are to be "static".

As compared with other previously proposed static detection methods, our method has two important features. First, our method can be used to detect many types of tasking deadlocks, such as those deadlocks concerning activation, acceptance, and termination waiting relations, which cannot be detected using those previously proposed methods. This is because our extended Petri net model for the Ada tasking correctly represent all the five different types of waiting relations between tasking objects in the programs. Second, our method can be used to detect tasking dead-states and livelocks, which are not considered in those previously proposed static analysis methods.

We are continually investigating analysis techniques of our extended Petri net model of the Ada tasking, extending the model in order to include abort statements and exception handlers in concurrent Ada programs, and developing an automatic analysis tool to support the analysis of tasking dead-states, deadlocks, and livelocks in concurrent Ada programs.

References

[Cheng-88a] J. Cheng and K. Ushijima: Modeling the Ada Tasking Using Extended Petri Nets, Memoirs of the Faculty of Engineering, Kyushu University, Vol. 48, No. 1, pp. 17-30, 1988.

[Cheng-88b] J. Cheng and K. Ushijima: Analyzing Deadlocks and Livelocks in Concurrent Ada Programs Using Extended Petri Nets, Memoirs of the Faculty of Engineering, Kyushu University, Vol. 48, No. 2, pp. 153-165, 1988.

[Cheng-90a] J. Cheng: A Classification of Tasking Deadlocks, ACM Ada Letters, Vol. 10, No. 5, pp. 110-127, 1990.

[Cheng-90b] J. Cheng: Task-Wait-For Graphs and Their Application to Handling Tasking Deadlocks, Proc. of the ACM Third Annual TRI-Ada Conference, pp. 376-390, Baltimore, USA, December 1990.

[Cheng-91] J. Cheng: A Survey of Tasking Deadlock Detection Methods, ACM Ada Letters, Vol. 11, No. 1, pp. 82-91, 1991.

[DoD-83] United States Department of Defense: Reference Manual for the Ada Programming Language (ANSI/MIL-STD-1815A), 1983.

[Mandrioli-85] D. Mandrioli, R. Zicari, C. Ghezzi, and F. Tisato: Modeling the Ada Task System by Petri Nets, Computer Languages, Vol. 10, No. 1, pp. 43-61, 1985.

[Murata-89a] T. Murata: Petri Nets: Properties, Analysis, and Applications, Proceedings of the IEEE, Vol. 77, No. 4, pp. 541-580, 1989.

[Murata-89b] T. Murata, B. Shenker, and S. M. Shatz: Detection of Ada Static Deadlocks Using Petri Net Invariants, IEEE Transactions on Software Engineering, Vol. 15, No. 3, pp. 314-326, 1989.

[Peterson-81] J. L. Peterson: Petri Nets Theory and the Modeling of Systems, Prentice-Hall, 1981.

[Shatz-90] S. M. Shatz, K. Mai, C. Black, and S. Tu: Design and Implementation of a Petri Net-Based Toolkit for Ada Tasking Analysis, IEEE Transactions on Parallel and Distributed Systems, Vol. 1, No. 4, pp. 424-441, 1990.

[Stansifer-91] R. Stansifer and D. Marinescu: Petri Net Models of Concurrent Ada Programs, Microelectronics and Reliability, to appear, 1991.

A Coprocessor for High Performance Multiprocessor Ada Tasking

Lars Lundberg

Department of Computer Engineering
Lund University
P. O. Box 118, S-22100 Lund, Sweden

Abstract: The complex semantics of Ada tasking cause excessive run-time overhead that cannot be avoided even when using the best compiler technology available. It has been demonstrated that special-purpose hardware can reduce the rendezvous latency with 90-99 % depending on the case [Roo89]. All the necessary extra hardware is contained in a single chip coprocessor which easily can be integrated into standard computer hardware. Multiprocessor tasking involves the additional problem of latency and limited bandwidth of the interprocessor communication system. By restructuring the run-time system the communication overhead can be reduced by 90-95 %, which has been demonstrated in a previous project [Lun90]. The success of both these projects has been due to a set of operations or a protocol cleverly tuned to the specific requirements in each case. In the present paper the coprocessor approach will be used and it will be extended to cover also the distributed tasking protocol developed in the previous project.

1 INTRODUCTION

A widely accepted way to program real-time systems is to structure them into parallel activities. The tasking constructions in Ada [Dep83] make it convenient to program the real-time application as one Ada program consisting of a number of cooperating tasks. Moreover, Ada tasking makes it possible to use the computing power of multiprocessor computers, which some tough real-time applications require.

Ada tasking requires a shared address space because different tasks, which may be allocated to different processors, can share the same global variables. Most parallel Ada systems take advantage of the shared address space in the implementation of the tasking mechanisms, i.e. inter processor tasking is performed by remote updating of shared data structures [Lun89a, Ard84, Hum88]. The indivisibility is usually provided by some atomic test-and-set primitive and global spin locks. Unfortunately, using this approach multiprocessor Ada tasking generates excessive communication and processor overhead. However, even synchronization between tasks allocated to the same processing unit, i.e. single-processor tasking, is very expensive in terms of processor overhead. Designers of Ada compilers have attacked this problem by trying to isolate simple synchronization situations which could be implemented more efficiently. This introduces large variations in the synchronization times and makes it hard for the programmer to predict the performance of the Ada program.

A previous study has shown that global communication due to inter processor tasking can be dramatically reduced by using a special protocol for inter processor tasking instead of remote updating of shared data structures. However, the processing overhead caused by tasking still remains. One way of attacking this problem is to introduce a special support processor, i.e. a tasking chip. This approach has shown to be successful in single-processor systems [Roo89].

Here, we will present a schema which uses the protocol for inter processor tasking together with distributed hardware support for Ada tasking, thus dramatically reducing both communication and processor overhead in all tasking operations.

2 CONCEPT OVERVIEW

Two previous projects, one concerning single-processor hardware support for Ada tasking [Roo89] and the other concerning a protocol for distributed Ada tasking [Lun90], form the foundation for this work. Here, it will be demonstrated how experiences from these two projects can be joined together to a concept for distributed hardware support for Ada tasking.

In the single-processor tasking chip project a set of primitive operations was defined. These operations are complex enough to replace a considerable amount of code in the Ada run-time system. Never the less it was demonstrated that the operations could be efficiently implemented using modern VLSI technology. The semantics of these operations are similar to the operations suggested by the Ada runtime environment working group [AREWG89]. However, the operations used by the coprocessor chip are designed to require minimal communication between the chip and the processor, i.e. these operations are on a somewhat higher semantic level than those suggested by the runtime working group.

Task scheduling is handled by the chip, i.e. it manages the ready queue and the delay queue. All operations are self contained in the sense that only

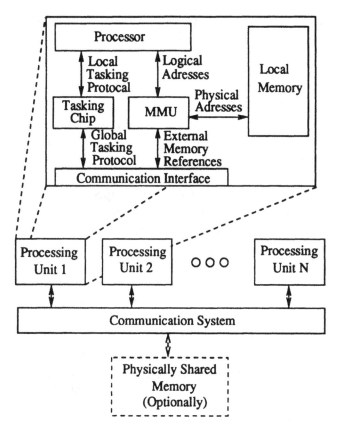

Figure 1: A multiprocessor system with N processing units. Each processing unit has distributed hardware support for Ada tasking.

results and parameters are communicated. As a consequence a significant amount of storage holding all necessary state information is contained on the chip.

For each task in the system there is one internal task control block (with the identity ITID). The internal task control block is stored on the chip and it contains information needed for tasking. However, CPU context and data structures for memory management is stored in an external (normal) task control block (with the identity ETID). The external task control block is stored in the ordinary memory outside the chip.

Parameter passing is based on these two duals (ITID and ETID). Arguments and results are often context variables referring to a specific task. To avoid table lookup schemes, each internal task control block contains the corresponding ETID, and each external task control block contains the corresponding ITID.

The protocol for distributed Ada tasking is based on a set of messages, here called global operations, with associated semantics. There is a clear correspondence between these global operations and the semantics of the Ada tasking primitives.

The protocol eliminates all remote updating of tasking related data structures, because the information is communicated explicitly through messages. Moreover, the need for global spin locks is eliminated. Consequently, this protocol minimizes global communication due to tasking.

When implementing the protocol in software, a special system process (Agent Process) and surrogate tasks (Ghost Tasks) were used to mimic the calling task locally in inter processor rendezvous, thus making the physical location of the caller transparent in the tasking algorithms.

Although inter processor tasking is handled through messages, global memory references are still needed for shared variables and passing of rendezvous parameters. A shared address space is therefore required and it could be provided either through physically shared memory or by uniquely mapping different parts of the address space onto different processing units. This is a logically shared and physically distributed memory organization and it has been used in many multiprocessor projects [AP84, BMW85, SP87].

Figure 1 shows a multiprocessor system including distributed hardware support for Ada tasking. The coprocessor chip handles one local protocol towards the processor and one global protocol towards the communication system, which could be a common bus. As will be demonstrated later the local protocol is almost identical to the one used by the single-processor Ada chip. Similarly, the global protocol is almost identical to the previously developed protocol for distributed Ada tasking.

Table 1 shows the the local tasking operations. the table includes some operations which were not implemented in the single-processor version. The only new operation which is related to multiprocessor tasking is *GetMyId* which is used by newly created tasks to get their ITID. In the single-processor version the ITID was returned to the creator by the *CreateTask* operation. All other new operations concern abort and exception management which was omitted in the first version of the single-processor Ada chip. However, operations corresponding to these will be implemented in the next version of the single-processor chip, which thus will support full Ada tasking.

If an ETID is retuned from a local tasking operation then that operation has resulted in a context switch. The ETID is the pointer to the external task control block where CPU status is stored. Figure 2 shows the code the

Local tasking operations

CreateTask(ProcessingUnit, CreatedTask'ETID, NrEntries,
                     Priority, Master, Block, ActLevel) **return** ETID
ActTasks(ActLevel) **return** ETID
Elaborateed(Status)
EnterTaskBlock
ExitTaskBlock **return** ETID
EntryCall(CalledTask, Entry) **return** ETID
TimedEntryCall(CalledTask, Entry, Time) **return** ETID
SelectArg(Entry, Number, Type)
SelectRes **return** ETID
WhichAlt **return** Number
GetAccepted **return** ETID
RenedezvousCompleted **return** ETID
Delay(Time) **return** ETID
QueueCount(EntryQueue) **return** Number
IsTerminated(Task) **return** boolean
IsCallable(Task) **return** boolean
Switch **return** ETID

Operation not included in the single-processor project
GetMyId **return** ITID
PropagateException(Exception)
Deallocate(ActLvl)
GetException **return** Exception
Abort(Task) **return** ETID
ReturnMem(Task) **return** ETID

Table 1: The local tasking requests and the parameters associated with each request.

processor executes in order to do a context switch.

In addition to the request issued by the local processor the chip must also be able to handle requests issued by coprocessor chips on other processing units (see table 2). One fundamental difference between these operations and the local requests is that in the global operations the identity of the requesting task must be explicit, whereas it was implicit in the local requests. The reason for this is that the identity of the currently executing task is always known to the coprocessor chip, because scheduling is handled by the chip. All new operations concern exception and abort management.

All names of global operations starts with a "G", thus making it easy to distinguish between local and global operations in the text.

Global tasking operations

GCreateTask(ProcessingUnit, CreatedTask'ETID,
                   NrEntries, Priority, Creator, Master, Block)
GEntryCall(CalledTask, Entry, Caller, Caller'ETID, Caller'Prio)
GTimedEntryCall(CalledTask, Entry, Caller, Caller'ETID, Caller'Prio, Time)
GTaskCreated(Creator, CreatedTask, Status)
GElaborated(Creator, ElabTask, Status)
GCreated(Master, Block, CreatedTask)
GTerminated(Master, Block, TerminatedTask)
GWillingToTerminate(Master, Block)
GNotWillingToTerminate(Master, Block)
GAnswer(Task, Information)
GRemoveCall(CallingTask, CalledTask, Entry)
GIsTerminated(Task, AskingTask)
GIsCallable(Task, AskingTask)

Operations not included in the original multiprocessor protocol
GAbort(Task, AbortingTask)
GAborted(AbortingTask, AbortedTask)
GPropagateException(Task, Exception)
GDeallocate(Task)
GRemoveCall(CalledTask, Entry, Caller)

Table 2: The global tasking requests and the parameters associated with each request.

The coprocessor chip can only distinguish between tasks allocated locally and tasks allocated on other processing units, i.e. a coprocessor chip does not know where a remote task is allocated. The global operations are therefore broadcasted on the communication system and the coprocessors will then decide if the operation is relevant for them. The first parameter in each operation is the identity of the task affected by the operation (except for *GCreateTask* where the identity of the processing unit is explicit). A coprocessor can thus determine if a global operation is intended for a task allocated on its processing unit by looking at the first parameter.

3 THE TASKING PROTOCOL

This section will demonstrate and discuss how the protocol works for normal tasking. Exception and abort management were not included in neither the single-processor Ada chip nor the distributed tasking protocol. These issues are therefore discussed separately in section 5.

Figure 3 shows the local and global operations issued in a rendezvous between

```
(* SaveContext( Current ) *)
Push(After)              ; Save return address on the stack
PushReisters             ; Save registers on the stack
SaveSP(Current)          ; Save stack pointer in the task control block
Current := Switch;       ; Get the next task from the chip
(* RestoreContext( Current ) *)
ResoreSP(Current)        ; Get stack pointer for new task
PopRegisters             ; Get registers from the stack
Ret                      ; Jump to the the code of this task
```
After: ...

Figure 2: A context switch on a processing unit with an Ada coprocessor chip. "Current" is a pointer to the currently executing task.

task A and task B allocated to different processing units. In this case, task B reaches the synchronization point before task A.

When the accepting task (task B) reaches the select statement, it opens the entry queues by issuing one *SelectArg* operation for each alternative in the select statement. The last parameter *Ent* indicates that this is an entry alternative as opposed to a terminate or delay alternative, i.e. the third parameter may have one of the three values *Ent*, *Delay* or *Term*. In the case of a delay alternative the parameter indicating the identity of the entry is replaced with the delay time. A *SelectRes* operation is used to indicate the end of the list of select alternatives. Task B is now blocked because no task has made an entry call to any of the select alternatives, i.e. a TaskId other than task B is returned by the *SelectRes* operation.

When task A reaches the entry call it issues a local entry call operation, i.e. task A does not know that task B is allocated on another processing unit. However, the coprocessor chip on processor unit 1 knows that task B is not allocated on this processing unit. Therefore, the chip broadcasts a global entry call operation.

This global entry call includes both A's ITID and A's ETID. The coprocessor chip on processing unit 2 needs the ITID in order to identify the calling task when it issues a reply at the end of the rendezvous. If any parameters are passed in the rendezvous then these parameters are stored in the caller's task control block, i.e. the accepting task must know the caller's ETID in order to access these parameters. Therefore, before the accepting task can access any rendezvous parameters it issues the local operation *GetAccepted* which

154

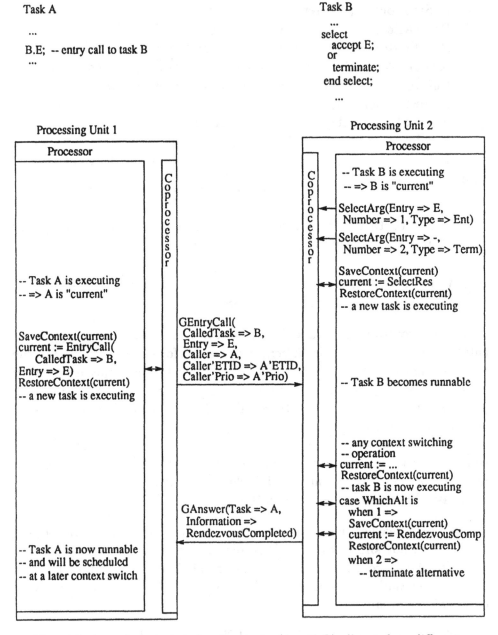

Figure 3: A rendezvous between two tasks (A and B) allocated on different processing units.

returns the ETID of the calling task. This is the reason why the ETID of the calling task is needed in the global entry call operation.

The coprocessor on processing unit 2 knows that task B is allocated on unit 2, consequently it accepts the global operation *GEntryCall* thus making task B runnable. At some later context switching operation task B will be scheduled for execution by the coprocessor on processing unit 2. When this happens depends on the number of runnable tasks on processing unit 2 and on their priorities.

By issuing the local operation *WhichAlt* task B decided which alternative in the select statement to execute. Here, *WhichAlt* returns the value 1 because the first alternative in the select statement was chosen.

In this case there are no rendezvous parameters and task B never has to know the identity of the caller, i.e. it never issues the *GetAccepted* operation. When task B reaches the end of the rendezvous it issues the local operation *RendezvousCompleted*, i.e. task B does not know that it has accepted a remote task. However, the coprocessor chip on processing unit 2 knows that the caller (task A) is not allocated locally. Therefore, the chip issues a *GAnswer* operation thus notifying the remote task that the rendezvous is completed.

The coprocessor on processing unit 1 knows that task A is allocated on its processing unit. Therefore, it accepts the *GAnswer* operation thus making task A runnable. This completes the inter processor rendezvous.

In a timed entry call to a task allocated on another processing unit, the time until time-out is measured on the processing unit of the called task. If the delay expires before the call has been accepted then the coprocessor chip of the called task removes the call and issues the operation *GAnswer(Caller, Time-Out)*, otherwise it sends *GAnswer(Caller, RendezvousCompleted)* when the rendezvous is completed. The caller uses the operation *WhichAlt* to determine if the call was accepted or if the call timed out. A conditional entry call is treated as a timed entry call with zero delay.

This rendezvous example demonstrates how the local and global operations can be used to implement Ada tasking in a multiprocessor environment. Most of the other tasking situations, e.g. task creation and task termination, are also straight forward combinations of the two protocols reported previously [Lun90, Roo89]. However, exception and abort handling was disregarded in these projects, and these issues are therefore discussed in section 5.

Processor

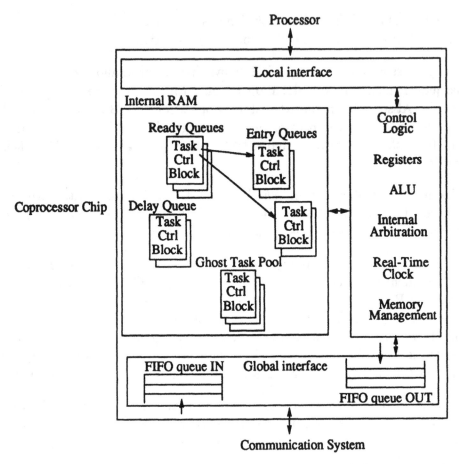

Figure 4: An overview of the internal data structures and the computational units of the coprocessor chip.

4 COPROCESSOR CHIP ARCHITECTURE

Figure 4 shows the major units of the coprocessor chip. The semantics of Ada tasking is encoded in the control unit. The registers contain information about the currently executing task, e.g. the external and internal identity of the task. Besides the ALU the chip must provide hardware mechanisms for internal arbitration, because on-chip data structures may be updated by both local and global operations. The arbitration mechanisms protect the internal data structures against concurrent updating, thus guaranteeing a consistent internal state. In order to handle the delay queue the chip contains a real-time clock. The local memory management unit will keep track of free internal memory space.

The global interface contains one FIFO queue for global operations going out to the communication system, and one FIFO queue for operations coming in

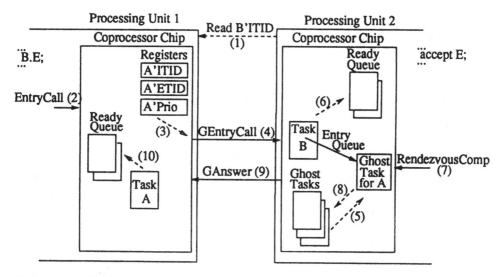

Figure 5: Manipulation of the on-chip data structures during a rendezvous between two tasks (A and B) allocated on different processing units. This is the same scenario as in figure 3.

from the communication system. The FIFO queue for operations going out makes it possible for the chip to continue even if the communication system is temporary congested, without this queue the chip would be blocked until it was able to transmit the global operation. The other FIFO queue makes it possible to run the communication system at high speed, i.e. the communication system does not become blocked if the receiving chip is temporarily busy. Moreover, the global interface decides if an operation is intended for a task allocated on this chip, i.e. only operations intended for local tasks are put into the queue for incomming operations. The most significant bits of the ITID is the processing unit number, and the first parameter in all global operations (except *GCreateTask*) is the ITID of the affected task. Therefore, the global interface can decide if the global operation is intended for its processing unit by looking at the most significant bits in the first parameter of each message. In order not to lose any global operations, an acknowledge protocol between the global interface of the receiving chip and the global interface of the sending chip is needed.

Besides one TCB for each task allocated locally, the internal RAM also contains a ready queue (with several priority levels) and a delay queue. These data structures are identical to the ones used in the single-processor version. However, the multiprocessor environment makes it necessary to introduce additional task control blocks (Ghost Tasks), which are used in inter processor rendezvous.

Figure 5 demonstrates how Ghost Tasks are used in the inter processor rendezvous showed in figure 3. The actions have been divided into ten steps:

1. Before task A can make an entry call to task B it must know B's ITID. Therefore, task A reads the ITID of task B. This is an ordinary shared memory read to the external task control block of task B. If a physically distributed and logically shared memory organization is used then the task control block of task B should be stored in the memory on processing unit 2. If the external task control blocks are stored in physically shared memory then this is a read operation to the module containing the shared memory.

2. Task A then makes a local entry call to task B.

3. The chip uses the ITID to determine that task B is not allocated locally, therefore a global entry call operation must be issued. However, in a global entry call operation the internal and external task identity and the priority of the currently executing task (task A) are needed. These values are stored in the internal registers.

4. The chip reads the priority, ETID and ITID from the the internal registers and issues the global entry call operation, i.e. the operation is put into the queue for outgoing operations in the global interface.

5. When the global entry call operation is being transmitted the chip on processing unit 2 uses the ITID to determine that task B is allocated on processing unit 2. This causes the chip to take a Ghost Task from the pool and instantiate it with the parameters in the global entry call operation. This instantiated Ghost Task is put into the entry queue, exactly as the internal task control block would if the entry call had been issued by a task allocated on processing unit 2.

6. Task B was waiting for an entry call. Therefore, it becomes runnable, i.e. it is put into the local ready queue.

7. When Task B has executed the code in the accept statement it issues the local operation *RendezvousCompleted*.

8. When the coprocessor chip receives *RendezvousCompleted* it uses the ITID to determine that task A is not allocated locally. Therefore, the Ghost Task used to mimic task A is returned to the pool.

9. After returning the Ghost Task to the pool the chip issues the the global operation *GAnswer*, thus notifying task A that the rendezvous is completed.

10. On processing unit 1 the *GAnswer* operation makes task A runnable, i.e. task A is inserted into the local ready queue.

This strategy using Ghost Tasks for remote rendezvous was used in the software implementation of the distributed Ada tasking protocol [Lun90].

Ghost Tasks are also used to handle task dependencies, i.e. the master of a remote task has a local Ghost Task in its list of dependent tasks. During task creation a chain of tasks to be activated is used. Therefore, if a task is created on a remote processing unit then a Ghost Task is used temporarily on the processing unit of the creator. This Ghost Task is returned to the pool when the remote task has been activated.

If the Ghost Task pool is empty when a global entry call arrives, then the coprocessor issues a *GPropagateException* to the calling task, thus raising the exception TASKING_ERROR. Should the Ghost Task pool be empty during remote task creation then the exception STORAGE_ERROR is raised. However, using a modern CMOS process there should be room for several hundred task control blocks on each chip. This will make it possible to use large Ghost Task pools, thus minimizing the risk of running out of free Ghost Tasks.

5 ABORTS AND EXCEPTIONS

Exceptions and aborts are handled by special exception handler processes. There is one exception handler for each task, and a reference to the context of the exception handler is stored in the internal TCB (see figure 6). The context of the exception handler is stored in a part of the external TCB. When an exception has been raised in a task synchronization then the exception handler becomes runnable, i.e. when scheduling the task affected by the exception the chip will return a pointer to the exception handler context instead of a pointer to the task context (see figures 2 and 6).

If an exception is raised during a rendezvous and there is no exception handler within the accept statement then the rendezvous becomes abnormally completed and the exception is propagated to the calling task. In order to propagate the exception the accepting task issues the local operation *PropagateException* thus notifying the local coprocessor that an exception should be raised in the caller. If the caller is allocated on another processing unit then the coprocessor chip will issue the global operation *GPropagateException*. If a rendezvous becomes abnormally completed due to an exception then a reference to the caller's exception handler is returned by the chip instead of a reference to the caller itself. The exception handler starts by issuing the operation *GetException*, thus determining the type of exception, after that it executes the corresponding exception code.

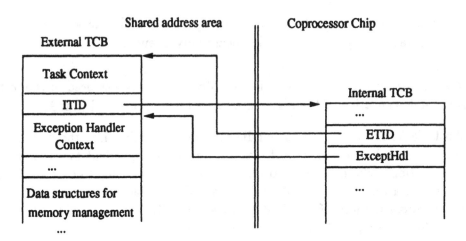

Figure 6: Implementation of the exception handler.

If the rendezvous with a remote task fails, e.g. because the called task has terminated, or if the called task has been aborted then the global operation *GAnswer(Caller, RendezvousFailure)* is sent to the processing unit of the caller, thus raising the exception TASKING_ERROR and activating the exception handler of the calling task.

Figure 7 demonstrates how the protocol works when task A allocated on processing unit 1 aborts task B allocated on processing unit 2. First, task A issues the local operation *Abort*. Since task B is not allocated locally, the coprocessor on processing unit 1 issues the global operation *GAbort*. Task A may not proceed until the abort has been propagated to task B and all of B's dependent tasks, i.e. task A is blocked until it has received the global operation *GAborted*, which is an acknowledge that the abort has been propagated to task B and all of B's dependent tasks.

On processing unit 2 task B is being marked as aborted when the global operation *GAbort* arrives, i.e. a special abort flag in B's internal task control block is set. Before the coprocessor on processing unit 2 can issue a *GAborted* to task A it must propagate the abort to all of B's dependent tasks. If these are allocated remotely then the global operations *GAbort* and *GAborted* are used to propagate and acknowledge the aborts. However, in this example task B has no dependent tasks and the global abort operation can be acknowledged directly.

The chip tests the abort flag when a task reaches a synchronization point. When the chip sees that a task has been aborted it performs the necessary actions according to the semantics for abort, e.g. if the task is waiting at an entry call, and is not yet in the corresponding rendezvous then the chip re-

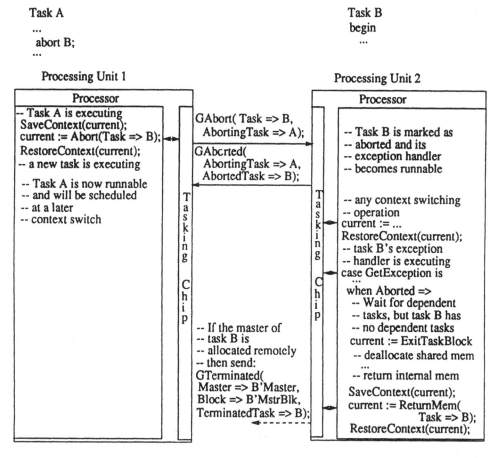

Figure 7: Task A allocated on processing unit 1 aborts task B allocated on processing unit 2.

moves the task from the entry queue, if it is a remote entry call then the global operation *GRemoveCall* is used. When this is taken care of, the exception handler of the aborted task is activated.

In order to be able to perform the appropriate actions the exception handler issues the operation *GetException*. In the case of abort, the exception handler handles deallocation of shared and on-chip memory. Before, the exception handler can deallocate any memory it must wait until all dependent tasks has terminated, this is handled as an ordinary termination of a tree of dependent tasks. In order to wait for dependent tasks the exception handler issues the the local operation *ExitTaskBlock*, which blocks the exception handler until all dependent tasks have terminated. However, task B has no dependent tasks and the *ExitTaskBlock* operation is therefore not necessary in this case.

The *ReturnMem* operation deallocates the internal data structures of task B. Finally, the master of task B is notified that task B has terminated, should the master be allocated remotely then the global operation *GTerminated* is issued. The termination algorithm used by the protocol has been reported separately [FSS87].

If an exception is raised during a task elaboration then tasks which have been created during that elaboration and that have not yet been activated should become terminated. Such tasks are removed by through the *Deallocate* and *GDeallocate* operations.

6 DISCUSSION

This chip has not been implemented but experiences from the single-processor Ada chip and from other advanced VLSI projects indicate that it would be quit feasible to build. Modern VLSI design tools and design techniques make it possible to design and implement chips at this level of complexity at a reasonable cost.

The single-processor Ada chip was implemented with a silicon compiler [Joh84] using a 2 μm CMOS process. Today, it is possible to use 1 μm CMOS processes which will increase the number of available transistors dramatically, thus making it possible to put more functionality on the same chip. Arbitration between two streams of operations, which is new compared to the single-processor chip, was successfully implemented in a multiprocessor cache controller [SDL91]. FIFO queues almost identical to the ones used in the global interface of this chip were also successfully implemented in that project.

Introducing this kind of hardware support for Ada tasking will no doubt dramatically reduce both the communication and the execution overhead due to tasking. Experiments using systems with logically shared and physically distributed memory has shown that the global tasking protocol will reduce the communication overhead due to tasking with 95 percent, compared to implementations using shared data structures in inter processor tasking. The total reduction of global communication depends on the application program. However, experiments using three parallel Ada programs showed that replacing accesses to shared data structures with these global operations in inter processor tasking led to a considerable reduction of the total amount of global communication [Lun90] (the total amount of global communication was reduced with more than 50 percent for all three Ada programs). Also, the global tasking operations eliminate the use of global spin locks, which are often used to provide indivisibility in multiprocessor systems. Therefore, most multiprocessor systems, e.g. bus-based systems, adopting this approach should be able to scale up without risking severe communication system contention.

The single-processor version of the tasking chip cut the execution overhead due to tasking by two orders of magnitude [Roo90], and for local tasking we expect the same improvement for the multiprocessor version. The reduction of overhead in inter processor tasking will however depend on the capacity of the global communication system. In systems with very long inter processor communication delays the time required for transmitting a global operation will dominate the total synchronization cost. This will limit the benefit of the distributed tasking support compared to implementing the global tasking operations in software, because the coprocessor chip only reduces the processor overhead. However, if a fast communication system, e.g. a common bus, is used then the time for transmitting a global tasking operation is small and the coprocessor will reduce the time required for inter processor task synchronizations with approximately two orders of magnitude.

The proposed concept does not permit task migration, i.e. a task cannot be moved from one processing unit to another. Tasks can, however, be created on any processing unit in the system. In order to facilitate task migration the protocol would have to be extended with operations which make it possible to move the internal data structures of a task from one coprocessor to another. A number of difficult problems must be solved in order to manage task migration in this type of environment, e.g. how should all data structures including Ghost Tasks be kept consistent during task migration, i.e. some Ghost Tasks may have to be replaced by real task control blocks after the migration and new Ghost Task may have to be used. Moreover, the ITID stored in the external task control block must be updated because the most significant bits of the ITID indicate the processing unit number. Consequently, task migration would require a substantial revision of the tasking protocol and would make the control logic more complex. Due to the communication overhead task migration tend to be very expensive in systems with logically shared and physically distributed memory [Lun89b]. Most systems with physically shared memory contain some kind of local cache, and task migration will probably reduce the hit ratio in these caches. Therefore, task migration is not always wanted in parallel Ada systems.

The tasking constructs of Ada are well suited for building real-time systems using multiprocessor computers. One of the prohibiting factors with the tasking concept has been the untolerable cost for making a rendezvous, thus creating different kinds of work-arounds. For instance, avoiding tasking or using synchronization mechanism outside the Ada language. All these work-arounds have a bad influence on software engineering and portability; two corner-stones in the Ada philosophy. Using hardware support like the one described here facilitates full use of Ada tasking without loss of performance.

Acknowledgements

The author is deeply indebted to Lars Philipsson for his advice and support. I would also like to thank Joachim Roos for valuable ideas and comments. This project was sponsored by the Swedish National Board for Technical Development (STU) under contract numbers 83-3647, 85-3899 and 87-2427.

References

[AP84]   A. Ardö and L. Philipson. Implementation of a Pascal Based Parallel Language for a Multiprocessor Computer. *Software - Practice and Experience*, 14(7):643–657, July 1984.

[Ard84]   A. Ardö. Experimental implementation of an Ada tasking run time system on the multiprocessor computer Cm*. In *Proceedings of the Washington Ada Symposium*, pages 145–153, March 1984.

[AREWG89]   MRTSI Task Force Ada Runtime Environment Working Group. A Model Runtime System Interface for Ada. *ACM, Ada Letters*, Vol. 9 No. 1:84–132, January 1989.

[BMW85]   W. C. Brantley, K. P. McAuliffe, and J. Weiss. RP3 Processor-Memory Element. In *Proc of the 1985 International Conference on Parallel Processing*, pages 782–789, Oct 1985.

[Dep83]   Department of Defense, USA. *Ada reference manual*, February 1983. ANSI/MIL-STD-1815A.

[FSS87]   Susan Flynn, Edith Schonberg, and Edmond Schonberg. The Efficient Termination of Ada Tasks in a Distributed Environment. *ACM, Ada Letters, Vol 7*, November 1987.

[Hum88]   Susan Flynn Hummel. *SMARTS - Shared-memory Multiprocessor Ada Run Time Supervisor*. PhD thesis, New York University, December 1988.

[Joh84]   S.C. Johnson. Silicon compiler lets system makers design their own chips. *Electronic Design*, pages 167–181, October 1984.

[Lun89a]   L. Lundberg. A Parallel Ada System on an Experimental Multiprocessor. *Software Practice and Experience*, 19(8):787–800, August 1989.

[Lun89b]   L. Lundberg. Performance evaluation of parallel Ada programs using an experimental multiprocessor. Technical report, Department of Computer Engineering, Lund University, July 1989.

[Lun90]   L. Lundberg. A Protocol to Reduce Global Communication in Dis-
           tributed Ada Tasking. *Journal of Parallel and Distributing Comput-
           ing*, 10(3):261–264, November 1990.

[Roo89]   J. Roos. A Real-Time Support Processor for Ada Tasking. In *Pro-
           ceedings of the ACM conference ASPLOS-III*, pages 162–171, April
           1989.

[Roo90]   J. Roos. The Performance of a Prototype Coprocessor for Ada Task-
           ing. In *Proceedings of TRI-Ada*, December 1990.

[SDL91]   P. Stenström, F. Dahlgren, and L. Lundberg. A Lockup-free Multi-
           processor Cache Design. Technical report, Department of Computer
           Engineering, Lund University, January 1991.

[SP87]   P. Stenström and L. Philipson. A layered emulator for design eval-
           uation of MIMD multiprocessors with shared memory. In *Proceed-
           ings of Parallel Architectures and Languages, Europe*, pages 329–341.
           Springer Verlag, June 1987.

Part IV: Continuous Systems

Software Project Activity Network for Managing the Development and Testing Process

Kurt M. Gutzmann, David L. Remkes, and Jeffrey L. Ragsdale

SofTech, Inc.
1300 Hercules Drive, Suite 105
Houston, Texas 77058-2747   USA

ABSTRACT

The software project activity network (SPAN), similar to a PERT network, is developed for the effective and correct management of the software development and testing process. The software project activity network follows naturally from the structural dependency properties of the system under development and the strategy and plan for its testing and integration. The software project activity network supports development and testing of systems developed in structured languages, and is very appropriate for systems written in Ada due to the explicit and formal definitions of dependencies in the Ada language. The software project activity network semantics accommodate the various possibilities for the outcome of testing activities and potential subsequent repetition of those activities (e.g. regression testing and software rework). The concept of testing configuration management is introduced, as each test identifies a particular sub-configuration or version of the ultimate system, augmented with test procedures. Change control points are rigorously identified in the software project activity network, providing complete test reproducibility and testing configuration management. Rigorous models of the coupled state transitions of the three object types minimally necessary for software development and testing models are presented. Since the software project activity network management model readily integrates its state transition models with commercial configuration control tools, implementations of it will be a key element in software development environments (SDE). The prototype implementation in Ada of the SPAN model and its integration with a commercial off-the-shelf (COTS) configuration management tool is discussed.

1. INTRODUCTION

The software project activity network (SPAN), similar to a PERT network, is developed for the effective and correct management of the software development and testing process We discuss the need for effective management models in this area first. The development of the SPAN from program dependency graphs and the associated code analysis tools that complement SPAN development are presented. The three object types of the SPAN model and their state transitions are next discussed. The necessary conditions for network consistency and coherency are introduced next. The derivation and collection of project management metrics and methods for software cost estimation using the SPAN are presented. Finally, the integration of SPAN management software with commercial configuration management tools and the prototype implementation experience in Ada completes this paper.

While many software projects use the waterfall life cycle model to manage its development activities, this approach presents problems when previous phase product rework and testing is required. Conventional methods of project management (i.e., PERT and CPM) do not directly accommodate this type of rework and the related regression testing activities. Having been structured with these problems in consideration, the software project activity network provides direct support for these tasks (see Section II. The Software Project Activity Network).

The SPAN model for software test management directly promotes test repeatability and reproducibility, two critical elements of the testing process often not supported by life cycle development methods. Positive control of versions (including tests) is required for proper software management [Babich]. The ability to reproduce any task and the testbed data captured in the test version description report provide absolute test repeatability. This is accomplished by integration of the SPAN with commercial off-the-shelf (COTS) configuration managements tools (in the prototypes, Polytron PVCS [Polytron85] and SofTool CCC [Bryan89,SofTool88,SofTool89,Bersoff84] were used).

2. THE SOFTWARE PROJECT ACTIVITY NETWORK

The *software project activity network (SPAN)* concept is introduced to accommodate the unique requirements for managing the development and testing phase of software projects. The usual project management networks, Project Evaluation and Review Technique (PERT) networks, and Critical Path Method (CPM) networks have been in use for many years. The SPAN augments the

PERT network to accommodate software structural dependencies and the unique aspects of software testing activities.

The PERT network represents activities with vertices, whereas CPM represents activities with edges. The PERT and CPM methods structure a set of tasks (often represented in an outline form known as the work breakdown structure (WBS)) and their dependencies into a network [Rosenau84]. Tasks are characterized by start and finish dates (planned and actual, 'must' or ASAP, and so on) and durations. The critical path of tasks (i.e. tasks that may suffer no schedule slippage if the project is to remain on schedule) is identified from this information. The precedence relationships in the network attempt to model the start and finish dependencies among tasks. Actual dates may be tracked against planned dates with automated project management tools. Figure 1 illustrates a PERT network produced by a commercially available project management tool.

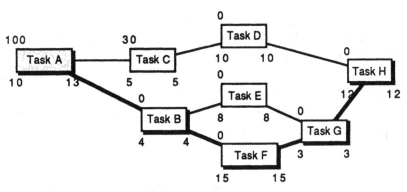

Legend: Upper Left = % Complete
Lower Left = Planned Duration
Lower Right = Actual Duration

Figure 1. Example of a PERT Network

Unfortunately, both PERT and CPM require that once an activity is designated complete, it must not be revisited (unless a replan of the project is undertaken). In the case of testing activities, they are assumed to always complete successfully. Naturally, tests fail, and the possibility of various activity *outcomes* is not accounted for in PERT and CPM. This poses a problem in software projects, since testing activities may be completed successfully, only to be repeated in regression testing required by downstream test failures. A testing task that has been designated complete, since it has been passed, may have to be repeated later. Hence, tracking the actual start and apparent stop dates (and associated WBS element opening and closing) of testing activities is not highly meaningful to a project manager.

The software project activity network is structured in much the same manner as a PERT network, where activities occur in the vertices of the graph and the edges represent activity dependencies. Unlike the PERT network, the software project activity network allows for the potential repetition of activities caused by the outcome of tests further along in the network. The semantics for managing the network are based on the coupled state transitions (discussed further in Section 4) of three object types common to all software projects. Briefly, the object types are: code units, tests, and test resources. These object types and their state transitions are discussed at greater length in Section 3.

The actual topology of the software project activity network is best derived from the dependency graph of the system under development. While this approach is not strictly required, is does provide some benefits in library currency. For projects implemented in the Ada [ANSI83] language, rules on compilation order must be followed to obtain current and consistent Ada object libraries. Ada object libraries have two types of currency, compilation and execution [Bryan89,Thall83]. Compilation currency exists for Ada libraries when package and procedures specifications are current. Execution currency exists for Ada libraries when compilation currency is present, and the bodies of packages and procedures are also current and may be linked to form an executable program.

The software project activity network was developed particularly with Ada in mind, but is equally applicable to any other language, since library currency (or obsolescence) and intermodule dependencies are not unique to any particular language. This problem has been attacked in the past through the use of MAKE utilities that analyze object file dates with user-supplied dependency definitions (or default rules) [Feldman79], but MAKEs are really only needed when the testing and code modification process is incorrectly structured or sequenced. Tools that support the definition of a SPAN are compilation order generators and dependency analyzers.

The testing process incrementally constructs an approved object library from which the programs comprising the final system are built. Successful testing of a module at the unit level (or perhaps in integration testing) should result in the entry of that module's object code into the approved library. If activity network of testing activities with subsequent object code entries is a morphism of the dependency graph of the system under development, then the approved object library will require no recompilations and it will be constructed in such a manner that its currency is guaranteed.

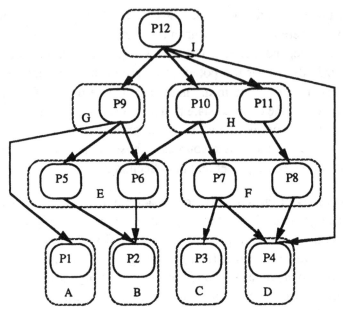

Figure 2. Bottom Up Integration Test Groupings
(test activities shown in dashed boxes)

The software project activity network naturally accommodates the various testing and integration strategies of bottom-up, top-down, middle-out, and various hybrids [Ould86]. Figure 2 shows a compilation unit dependency graph for a small Ada program and its groupings for bottom-up integration testing. The dependency graph is transformed into a SPAN in the sequences shown in Figures 2, 3(a), and 3(b). The bottom-up testing strategy requires the development of drivers for the execution closure of the test. Immediately it is apparent that the dependencies among the test activities have been defined by the program structure. Figure 3(b) shows the testing activity network (the program dependencies are embedded in the graph as a homomorphism).[1]

3. TYPES OF OBJECTS IN THE SPAN

Three types of objects are minimally necessary for the software project activity network approach to managing the development and testing of software systems.

---

[1]The top down integration strategy will result in a software project activity network with an additional test for each compilation unit (or compilation unit group) with a non-empty closure. The additional test provides the stub-based testing of the unit, and then advances to the driver-based testing.

Naturally, many more types of objects are generated in software projects, but again, our focus here is on the management of the development and testing activities. The three types of objects managed with the software project activity network are:

- Code Units
- Testing Resources
- Tests

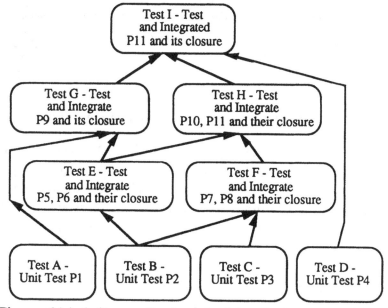

Figure 3(a) 3oftware Project Activity Dependency Graph

In addition to these, the usual software project has a large number of documents of varying types, such as requirements, design documents, user's guides, installation guides, concept definitions, interface control specifications, and many more (MIL-STD-2167 provides an extensive set of documents for software projects). Ordinarily these documents are the distillation of project knowledge which resides in other forms in the project object base. For example, a design document may have graphical representations of the system structure generated initially by a CASE (Computer Aided Software Engineering) tool. The file created by the CASE tool may be considered a design type of object. Clearly, a project object manager must be able to permit a wide variety of user defined object types.

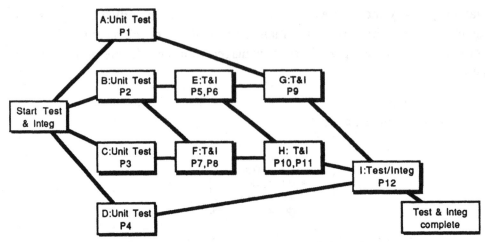

Figure 3(b). Software Project Activity Network
(test preparation and code development excluded)

An information metamodel for the object types of the SPAN is presented in Figure 4, providing the attributes and relationships among the various object types. The required attributes are shown in bold face, while additional attributes of instances of these objects are in plain font. The additional attributes are suggested for project status reporting requirements, but are not used explicitly for the process management of the SPAN.

3.1. The Code Object

The code object undergoes the state transitions defined in Figure 5. The change control points are identified by the *check_in* and *check_out* actions between states. The state transition model for the code object permits modification of code units only when they are not undergoing testing. The code object must naturally have a reason for modification, usually the discovery of a bug during testing (the *failed_test* state).

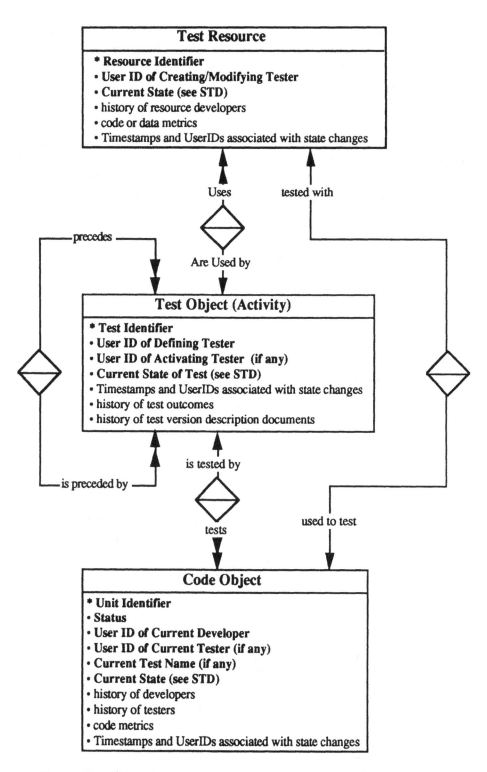

Figure 4. Information Metamodel of Object Types in SPAN

The attributes of the code object allow the tracking of its state and the accountability for the state to user names in the project. Figure 4 lists the attributes required for the management of the code object. The additional information of history and metrics may be useful to project managers also.

A test has a *pass action*, which prescribes actions to be taken upon the successful outcome of a testing activity. Ordinarily, the pass action may be specify compilation of code to the approved object library. The *pass action* may be null, of course, or it may specify other actions such as release of documentation. The *pass action* provides the means to properly manage the entry of object code into the approved object library of the project .

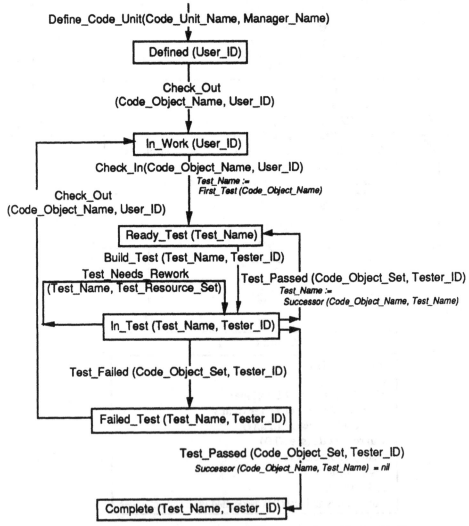

Figure 5. State Transition Diagram for Code Unit

3.2. The Test Resource Object

Resources are used to carry out a testing activity. Examples of test resources are:

- test data
- test driver code
- test stub code
- test instructions
- design data
- software requirements statements
- test requirements statements
- command procedures

The test resources are uniquely associated with a particular test. The notion of shared test resources, such as tools or common data are not explicitly defined for the SPAN (however, current work on the SPAN is investigating the management of shared resources among a set of tests). The test resources undergo the state transitions shown in Figure 6.

Test resources are defined through a test definition function and enter the *ready* state. A test resource may be discovered to be faulty during the course of carrying out the testing activity with which it is associated. The resource is designated *needs_rework* through the reporting of test results for the test (the test itself enters the *rework* state, discussed further below). The *check_in* and *check_out* operations are the change control points for the resource. Once a resource has been reworked (e.g. fixing a bug in test driver) it is ready to be redefined along with the test to which it belongs.

3.3. The Test Object

The test object is a collection of code objects and test resources (an *assembly structure* as in Coad and Yourdan [Coad90]). A *testbed* is a copy of the objects (code and resources) created for the purpose of executing the test. A testbed is built by retrieving the current revisions of all objects from the object management system and placing them in a directory. The testbed construction process also creates a test version description report (TVDR) of revision numbers of the contents of the testbed, and stores the TVDR in the history of the test.

A test is *ready* after it has been properly defined. The definition of a test comprises the following:

- test name
- direct predecessor tests that must be passed prior to beginning this test

- the execution or compilation closure of code objects required by the test (compilation closure for static tests, and execution closure for dynamic tests)

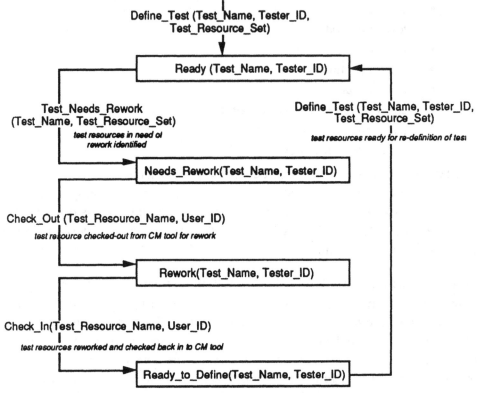

Define_Test (Test_Name, Tester_ID, Test_Resource_Set)

Ready (Test_Name, Tester_ID)

Test_Needs_Rework (Test_Name, Test_Resource_Set)
test resources in need of rework identified

Define_Test (Test_Name, Tester_ID, Test_Resource_Set)
test resources ready for re-definition of test

Needs_Rework(Test_Name, Tester_ID)

Check_Out (Test_Resource_Name, User_ID)
test resource checked-out from CM tool for rework

Rework(Test_Name, Tester_ID)

Check_In(Test_Resource_Name, User_ID)
test resources reworked and checked back in to CM tool

Ready_to_Define(Test_Name, Tester_ID)

Figure 6. State Transition Diagram for Test Resource

- the set of unique test resources required for the test, such as data files, command procedures, test drivers, test stubs, test instructions

Other information associated with a test is:

- the user_id of the tester creating the current definition of the test
- the current state of the test (see the STD)
- the user_id of the tester causing the most recent state transition of the test
- the state transition history of the test
- the version description documents (object revision numbers of the test definition) for each configuration of the test
- a *pass action* that prescribes action to be taken upon the successful completion of the test. The *pass action* is the mechanism for the orderly and correct construction of the system's object library.

The test is defined initially with the information described above. Upon definition it assumes the *ready* state. This does not mean that the testing activity may be initiated however. Initiation of testing activity requires that the following conditions be met:

- the test is in the *ready* state
- all resources of the test are in the *ready* state
- all code objects in the test closure are in one of the following states:
    ready_test, for this particular test
    complete, or
    in_test, for this particular test
- all direct predecessors of this test are in the *passed* state

The states of a test activity are shown in Figure 7. The state transition diagram models testing activities in a manner similar to a process manager in an operating system. The test is activated by the testbed construction function. Immediate subsequent reconstructions of a testbed do not cause a distinct change in state, solely an autotransition. The *active* test may have one of three results posted for it: *passed, failed*, or *rework*. The test is passed if no errors are detected in the code objects. The test fails if errors are detected, and the faulty code objects are identified in the result posting process. The test needs rework if an error is detected in the test resources rather than in the code objects.

The reasoning for the code object state requirements is based on the orderly activation of testing activities according to the precedence conditions of the test. Code objects that are *complete* are available to the testbed in source code and are also available in object code form from the approved object library.

4.   INTEGRATED STATE TRANSITIONS IN THE SPAN

The three object types undergo coordinated state transitions. Changes in one object necessarily cause changes in other objects. The principal operations that that create state changes are identified in Figure 7, since from the viewpoint of the software test engineer, those are the functions invoked to test and rework code. The check-in and check-out operations of the code and test resource objects create change in *content* as well as change in state. The ten coupled state transitions of the SPAN are described below. The notation is as follows:

4.1. Notation

T is the set of vertices in the directed graph constituting the test network

C is the set of code units of the software system under development and test.

R is the set of testing resources required by the test activities designated at the vertices of the test network.

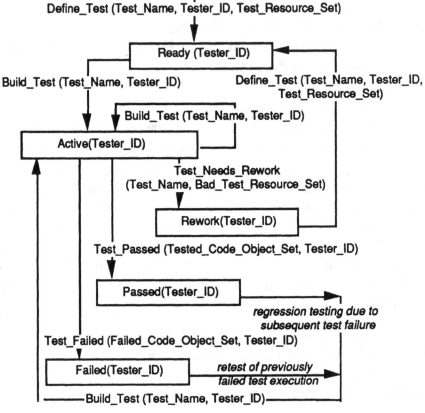

Figure 7. State Transition Diagram for Test

U is the set of user_ids (to associate with objects)

Subscripts of the above sets indicate a particular element of the set.

One-to-one mapping functions
X_c (**C**$_i$) maps a code unit to an element of **U**, the set of user_ids. The mapping from **C**$_i$ to **U**$_j$ is one to one.

X_t (**T**$_i$) maps a test definition (vertex of the test network) to a user_id, **U**$_j$. The purpose of the function is to designate the tester responsible for the current state of the test. The mapping from **T**$_i$ to **U**$_j$ is one to one.

X_r (**R**$_i$) maps a test resource to a user_id, **U**$_j$. The purpose of the function is to designate the user_id responsible for the current state of the test resource.

Q_c (C_i) maps a code unit to an element of T, T_j. The purpose of the function is to qualify the state of the code unit to a node in the test network. For example, a code unit state of *ready_test* is qualified by TEST_1, to indicate that the unit is ready for testing in the testbed designated TEST_1. The mapping from C_i to T_i is one to one Q_c is meaningful only when $S_c(C_i) \in$ {*ready_test, in_test, failed_test, complete*}, i.e. when the code unit is in test rather than in development.

Q_t (T_i) maps a test definition (vertex of the test network) to a user_id, U_j. The purpose of the function is to designate the tester responsible for the current state of the test. The mapping from T_i to U_j is many to one.

Q_r (R_i) maps a test resource to a user_id, U_j. The purpose of the function is to designate the user_id responsible for the current state of the test resource.

$S_t(T_i)$ maps a test to a state, and returns an element of {*ready, active, passed, failed, rework*}.

$S_c(C_i)$ maps a code object to a state , and returns an element of {*defined, in_work, ready_test, in_test, failed_test, complete*}.

$S_r(R_i)$ maps a test resources to a state, and returns an element of {*ready, rework*}. This reduced state transition set is sufficient for managing test resources. Figure 8 illustrates the transitions. For convenience, we shall define the function as returning the current state of R_i.

One-to-many mapping functions
T_r (T_i) maps a set of test resources to a test definition, T_i. The purpose of the function is to designate the test to which the test resources belong.

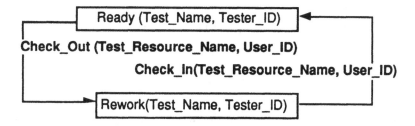

Figure 8.   Simplified Test Resource State Transitions

$T_c(T_i)$ maps a set of code units to a test definition, T_i. The purpose of the function is to designate the code units that are tested as a group by a particular test, T_i.

Succ(C_k, T_i) generates the set of tests for code unit C_k that are direct successors to T_i in the network.

Pred (T_i) generates the set of tests that are direct predecessors to T_i in the network.

4.2. State Transition Definitions

Coupled Transition 1 - New Build of a Test
The test moves from the *ready* state to *active* while the code objects tested by it move from *ready_test* to *in_test*. This occurs at the first build of a testbed for a code unit as it moves through the testing network.

Precondition:

$$S_t (T_i) \in \{ready\} \wedge \tag{1}$$
$$\forall\ R_j \in T_r (T_i),\ S_r (R_j) \in \{ready\} \wedge \tag{2}$$
$$\forall\ T_k \in Pred (T_i),\ S_t (T_k) \in \{passed\} \wedge \tag{3}$$
$$\forall\ C_l \in T_c (T_i),\ S_c (C_l) \in \{ready\_test, complete\} \wedge \tag{4}$$
$$\forall\ C_l \in T_c (T_i),\ Q_c (C_l) = T_i \tag{5}$$

Coupled Transition 2 - Rebuild of a Currently Active Test
The *build_test* function has been applied to an already *active* test. This indicates a reconstruction of the testbed by the tester. This situation may occur when a tester has built a testbed previously, has not posted results on it yet, and wished to generate another copy of the testbed. It is possible that the execution of the testing activities has required a fresh start in order to diagnose the faults observed.

Precondition:

$$S_t (T_i) \in \{active\} \wedge \tag{6}$$
$$\forall\ R_j \in T_r (T_i),\ S_r (R_j) \in \{ready\} \wedge \tag{7}$$
$$\forall\ T_k \in Pred (T_i),\ S_t (T_k) \in \{passed\} \wedge \tag{8}$$
$$\forall\ C_l \in T_c (T_i),\ S_c (C_l) \in \{in\_test\} \wedge \tag{9}$$
$$\forall\ C_l \in T_c (T_i),\ Q_c (C_l) = T_i \tag{10}$$

Coupled Transition 3 - Rework of Test Resources Required
The testing activities have indicated that a problem exists in the resources used in the testbed. Perhaps a test data file is incorrect, or a stub or driver does not function correctly. The faulty test resource needs rework, and so one or more test resources are placed in the *needs_rework*(Test_Name, tester_id) state. The tester_id attribute serves to identify the tester who has posted these results. The

test resources are checked out from the CM system, reworked, and checked back in. The testbed will be redefined (Transition 9) and then rebuilt (Transition 10).

Precondition:

$$S_t (T_i) \in \{active\} \wedge \tag{11}$$

$$\forall \, R_j \in \, T_r (T_i), \, S_r (R_j) \in \, \{ready\} \wedge \tag{12}$$

$$\forall \, T_k \in \, Pred (T_i), \, S_t (T_k) \in \{passed\} \wedge \tag{13}$$

$$\forall \, C_l \in \, T_c (T_i), \, S_c (C_l) \in \{in\_test\} \wedge \tag{14}$$

$$\forall \, C_l \in \, T_c (T_i), \, Q_c (C_l) = T_i \tag{15}$$

Postcondition:

$$\exists \, R_k \in \, T_r (T_i) \ni S_r (R_k) \in \, \{needs\_rework\} \wedge \tag{16}$$

$$Q_r (R_k) = T_i \, \wedge \tag{17}$$

$$X_r (R_k) = U_j \tag{18}$$

Coupled Transition 4 - Test Passed and Other Tests Follow

This transition indicates successful completion of the test. The code objects individually advance to a ready_test state with the Test_Name attribute set to that of the next test in their respective test paths. The test is set to *passed*(tester_id), and the *pass_action* for the test is executed. An example of the *pass_action* for a test is the compilation of object code of the successfully tested code to an approved testing library. This provides a mechanism for the controlled and properly sequenced entry of object code to an library. For Ada systems, the testing activity network should be an isomorph of the system dependency graph, *thus guaranteeing that no recompilations of the approved Ada object library are required..*

Precondition:

$$S_t (T_i) \in \{active\} \wedge \tag{19}$$

$$\forall \, R_j \, \times \, T_r (T_i), \, S_r (R_j) \, \times \, \{ready\} \, L \tag{20}$$

$$\forall \, T_k \in \, Pred (T_i), \, S_t (T_k) \in \, \{passed\} \wedge \tag{21}$$

$$\forall \, C_l \in \, T_c (T_i), \, S_c (C_l) \in \, \{in\_test\} \wedge \tag{22}$$

$$\forall \, C_l \in \, T_c (T_i), \, Q_c (C_l) = T_i \tag{23}$$

Postcondition:

$$\forall \, C_k \in T_c (T_i) \ni (S_c (C_k) = ready\_test \, \wedge \, Q_c (C_k) \in \, Succ(C_k, T_i)) \tag{24}$$

Coupled Transition 5 - Regression Testing

The test moves from *failed*(tester_id) or *passed*(tester_id) to *active*(tester_id) while the code object moves from ready_test to in_test. This situation occurs in regression testing for the code object, since it was previously tested and failed by this test. The code object has previously moved *in_test* (This_test, tester_id) $\Rightarrow$ *failed_test*(This_test,tester_id) $\Rightarrow$ *in_work*(Developer_Id).

Precondition:

$$S_t (T_i) \in \{passed, failed\} \tag{25}$$
$$\forall\; R_j \in T_r (T_i), S_r (R_j) \in \{ready\} \land \tag{26}$$
$$\forall\; T_k \in Pred (T_i), S_t (T_k) \in \{passed\} \land \tag{27}$$
$$\forall\; C_l \in T_c (T_i), S_c (C_l) \in \{in\_test, ready\_test\} \land \tag{28}$$
$$Q_c (C_l) = T_i \tag{29}$$

Coupled Transition 6 - Test Failed

This transition indicates the failure of the test. One or more code objects have been found faulty and must be reworked. The failed code objects move to the Failed_test(Test_Name, tester_id) state, from which they may be checked out by a developer from the CM system. The test moves to the Failed(tester_id) state, thus indicating its failure. The code objects will be reworked, checked back in, and undergo regression testing.

Precondition:

$$S_t (T_i) \in \{active\} \land \tag{30}$$
$$\forall\; R_j \in T_r (T_i), S_r (R_j) \in \{ready\} \land \tag{31}$$
$$\forall\; T_k \in Pred (T_i), S_t (T_k) \in \{passed\} \land \tag{32}$$
$$\forall\; C_l \in T_c (T_i), S_c (C_l) \in \{in\_test\} \tag{33}$$

Postcondition:

$$\exists\; C_k \in T_c (T_i) \ni S_c (C_k) \Rightarrow \{failed\_test\} \land Q_c (C_k) \Rightarrow T_i$$
$$\land \tag{34}$$
$$\forall\; C_j \notin T_c (T_i) \ni S_c (C_k) \Rightarrow \{in\_test\} \land Q_c (C_k) \Rightarrow T_i \tag{35}$$

Coupled Transition 7 - Test Passed and No Further Testing is Defined

This transition indicates successful completion of the final test for a code object. No successor for the current test exists for this code object, and so it is designated complete. In actual practice, 'completed' code may need rework, and so the system provides administrative functions to force the state of an object to *failed* so that rework and regression testing may commence on it.

Precondition:
$$St (Ti) \oe \{active\} L \tag{36}$$
$$\forall\; R_j \in Tr (Ti), S_r (R_j) \in \{ready\} \land \tag{37}$$
$$\forall\; T_k \in Pred (Ti), S_t (T_k) \in \{passed\} \land \tag{38}$$

$$\forall \; C_l \in \; T_C \, (T_i), \; S_c \, (C_l) \in \; \{in\_test\} \wedge \tag{39}$$

$$\forall \; C_l \in \; T_C \, (T_i), \; Q_c \, (C_l) = T_i \tag{40}$$

Postcondition:

$$\forall \; C_k \in T_c \, (T_i) \ni (S_c \, (C_k) \in \; \{complete\} \wedge Q_c \, (C_k) = T_i \tag{41}$$

Coupled Transition 8 - Definition of a New Test

This transition creates a test and its test resources. The testbed may not be built until all the code objects defined in its set of units tested are *ready_test*(This_test). There is some parallelism between test resources and code objects evident in their transition diagrams. Practical experience indicates that test resources do not require a regression testing network of their own, and so the transition model for them allows simple check out, rework, and check in functions. The reduced state transition diagram of Figure 9 also provides an acceptable model for managing test resources. T' designates the new test.

Precondition:

$$T' \notin T \wedge \forall \, R_i, \forall \, T_k \ni R_i \in T_r \, (T'), T_k \neq T', R_i \notin T_r \, (T_k) \tag{42}$$

Coupled Transition 9 - Rework a Test

This transition redefines a test that has been previously designated in need of rework. Some of the test resources have been checked out and reworked. All necessary new versions of the test resources have been checked in and the test is redefined. Resources may be added to or deleted from the test definition at this point. Test resources may be shared among several tests, and shared resources have their state attribute unbound, i.e. *ready*(tester_id). The tester_id attribute gives the identity of the tester defining these versions of the test resources.

Precondition:

$$S_t \, (T_i) \in \; \{rework\} \wedge \tag{43}$$

$$\exists \; R_k \in \; T_r \, (T_i) \ni S_r \, (R_k) = \{ready\_to\_define\} \tag{44}$$

Postcondition:

$$\forall \; R_i \in \; T_r \, (T_i), \; S_r \, (R_i) \in \; \{ready\} \wedge \tag{45}$$

$$S_t \, (T_i) \Rightarrow \{ready\} \tag{46}$$

Coupled Transition 10 - Rebuild of a Reworked or Redefined Test

This transition occurs when a test and its associated resources have been reworked while the code objects have waited in the *in_test*(Test_Name, tester_id) state. The test becomes *active* again, and testing activity resumes with the new versions of the test resources.

Precondition:

$$S_t (T_i) \in \{ready\} \wedge \tag{47}$$

$$\forall\ R_j \in T_r (T_i),\ S_r (R_j) \in \{ready\} \wedge \tag{48}$$

$$\forall\ T_k \in Pred (T_i),\ S_t (T_k) \in \{passed\} \wedge \tag{49}$$

$$\forall\ C_l \in T_c (T_i),\ S_c (C_l) \in \{in\_test\} \wedge \tag{50}$$

$$\forall\ C_l \in T_c (T_i),\ Q_c (C_l) = T_i \tag{51}$$

5. SPAN COHERENCY CONDITIONS

The graph of the SPAN must exhibit certain properties in order to make sense. Acyclicity is an obvious requirement. Changes to the SPAN must follow certain rules in order to maintain a property that we shall call *coherency*. It is natural in a software project that the SPAN will change over time as code and design changes result in testing process changes. The various types of changes in a SPAN are:

- Addition/Deletion of a tests, test resources, or code units
- Change in the sequence tests

All of these changes must be carefully managed in order to maintain coherency and sensibility of the SPAN.

Adding a new test means modifying the test paths of the code units tested by it as well. The test network must remain acyclic whenever a test is added. For each code unit in a test definition, we must also have a new test path which shows where the new test is inserted into the sequence of testing for the code units tested.

Definition of a code unit alone also requires a test path for it, and the convention we shall use here is that the tests in the test path must already exist. Test path modification is obtained by the addition and deletion of tests and the coordination of those changes in the affected code units.

A mechanism for establishing the identities of code units, tests, and resources, without requiring that they already be organized into a coherent network is needed in a practical implementation of the SPAN. Usually we will identify the code units before we identify what all the tests will be. We can add the tests later, or modify the pattern of testing for a particular code unit.

A SPAN will be coherent if:

1) Code units are defined with a test path; however, the tests in the test path do not have to exist *a priori*.

2) When a test is defined, impose a necessary condition for network coherency that the test already be defined in the test path of each of the code units that it tests (condition 1 above).

3) For all tests, the code units in the set *units_tested* exist.

4) Each test is an element of the *test_path* for each of the code units that it tests.

5) The test predecessor and successor relationships define an acyclic graph.

6) The test predecessor and successor relationships define a graph with at least one source and one sinks.

7) For each test in the predecessor set of a test, there exists at least one test path for a code unit such that this test succeeds the predecessor test.

It appears that the sink(s) of the test graph should be a final test and system build type of activity. A code unit may appear in several versions of a built system (e.g. unix, Mac, VMS versions), through ubiquity of object code. Many pieces of reused code undergo their unit tests and lower level integrations, whereupon they are assumed satisfactory and their testing activity is complete. They continue to be used in other higher level integration tests, but they are not the focus of those tests. When they have completed their tests, and even perhaps when they have completed their unit level tests, they are entered into an approved test object library. This approved test object library contains only acceptable, verified, and validated code units. When a code unit is in the approved test object library it becomes ubiquitous with respect to any tests having an execution closure of which the unit is a member. That is, it need not appear in the units_tested set of a test explicitly, but it does appear in the execution closure of the test.

Should testing proceed unless the test network abides by the above conditions? It is possible that partial coherency conditions are permissible, i.e. for a continuous sequence of tests in a code unit's test path (and the respective tests), that the conditions of network coherency are met for that subgraph of tests and code units. This appears reasonable, as it permits testing to proceed without requiring complete definition of all tests *a priori*. Another way that partial coherency of the test network is obtained is through incomplete test path definition for the code units. The test paths are modified as tests become defined, but for any test path of a code unit, the coherency conditions above are satisfied.

6. SOFTWARE PROJECT ACTIVITY NETWORK METRICS FOR PROJECT MANAGEMENT AND COST ESTIMATION

Implementations of the software project activity network model can provide useful metrics on the development and testing process. Instrumentation of management systems is common practice. The metrics of a SPAN may be used for project tracking, producing measures of completeness that are more precise. Historical data may used for cost modeling of new systems and for estimates to completion for current project. The cost modeling is based on either analytical queueing network analysis [Kleinrock75] or network simulation modeling [Pritsker84].

The two fundamental metrics collected in a SPAN are:

- pass/fail probabilities of the testing activities, and
- time between state changes of the objects, such as the time to complete a test.

These metric records should be attributed by user identifier, time stamps, and other attributes, minimally the set shown in the information model of Figure 4. Association of activities with the work breakdown structure of the project is essential for traditional cost and schedule tracking.

Measures of completeness of system testing are based on the fraction of nodes in the SPAN that are in a *passed* state. While this measure does increase monotonically to unity (testing completion), it provides one measure of testing completion. Another measure is the fraction of nodes in the SPAN that have at some point in their history attained a *passed* state. This measure does increase monotonically given a stationary network.

Simulation modeling of the network can produce estimates of cost and schedule for current projects and contemplated projects. Actual data for a current project supplies the parameters of the queueing network as above, but with the addition of resources. Resource in this context means people (developers, testers) and hardware (computers, networks, etc.). Utilization of resources and their costs per unit time are integrated into a cost and schedule estimates for the software project. Bottleneck analysis is beneficial, since resources may be reallocated to alleviate such conditions. Since these simulations are quickly executed on workstations, the software project manager may model many different strategies and resource allocations in order to optimize for quality, cost, or schedule.

This type of project activity modeling approaches the reality of the process much more closely than parametric models of estimation, such as COCOMO [Boehm81]. Management may have a higher degree of confidence in simulation estimates based on the historical experience of their organizations. We are developing simulation models and metrics collections for the SPAN prototypes described in Section 7.

7. SPAN IMPLEMENTATION PROTOTYPES

This section discusses the development of an operational specification of the SPAN model in Prolog and a protype system in Ada. Both of these were integrated with commercially available configuration management systems.

An implementation of a SPAN model can be integrated to operate with commercial-off-the-shelf (COTS) configuration management tools (e.g., CCC, RCS, PVCS, SCCS, CMS [SofTool89, Polytron85, SofTech84, Tichy82, Digital82, Rochkind75]). When used with existing configuration management products, the SPAN implementation software offers a layered approach to object management by acting as a pre-processor for that CM tool. Each change control point between the various state transitions of an object corresponds to one or more CM tool interfaces. The SPAN software that implements the change control can be made to externally call the appropriate CM function(s).

Two SPAN model prototype implementations have been developed to support configuration and process management activities for the CAIS-A Implementation Validation Capability (CIVC) project. The CIVC project comprises 14,000 source lines of Ada code developed by six people?. An operational prototype was implemented in Prolog on an IBM-PC compatible and another prototype was developed using DEC-Ada on a MicroVax II. Both implementations provide the following functional capabilities:

- change control functions (object check-in/check-out)
- test management functions (test definition, testbed builds, test results posting)
- report and query functions (state information for code units, tests, and test resources; object existence; test network topology)
- list management functions
- state change functions

The behavioral characteristics of the SPAN for these implementations was encoded in the system, however, the object types, their attributes, and their state information could be supplied in user-defined data files. The latitude provided by the latter approach permits the responsible manager to define the specific object data necessary for modeling a particular system. Allowing the user to define the state transitions would have necessitated the automatic verification of these state transitions.

7.1 Prolog Implementation

The Prolog implementation was developed expressing the state transition definitions in Section IV as predicates. This provided a formal verification mechanism for the correctness of the specification of the process model. This implementation combines the state transition model with the data base capabilities supported by the Prolog language. Only 400 SLOCs in size, this implementation contains 68 predicates, 40 non-predicate clauses, and 13 relational database files (data reduces to 12 files in third normal form). This operational specification guided the development of the Ada system.

7.2 Ada Prototype

The Ada prototype comprises fourteen Ada packages which yield 4800 SLOCs. Many of the packages are instantiations of generic I/O packages for each of the three object types managed on this project (source code modules, tests, and test resources). The Ada system was integrated with the commercial CM software system CCC from SofTool [Bryan89,SofTool88,SofTool89,Bersoff84]. CCC was used to store the different revisions of the three object types.

In response to user requests, the prototype would verify the preconditions necessary to perform any transitions or, if the request was simply a query, would provide the requested information. The interactions between CCC and the prototype were through VMS command scripts and data files. Once fully implemented, the CIVC project was able to easily define the SPAN for the CIVC (CAIS Implementation Validation Capability) [Gutzmann90] objects.

8. CONCLUSIONS

The software project activity network model provides the foundation for the implementation of software development and testing management systems. Since the software project activity network model is well-suited for the management of Ada systems development and testing, it is expected that software support environments such as STARS (Software Technology for Adaptable Reliable Systems) and NASA Software Support Environment will adopt the software project activity network model to implement test management systems. The rigorous and unambiguous definition of the underlying model of the SPAN and the operational specification in Prolog provide implementors with clear design direction.

The coordinated state transitions of various objects are an essential feature of any software development environment object management system. While the SPAN is directed towards code development and testing, current work on the SPAN is extending the object type definitions and state transition models to include requirements and design products, their associated verification processes, and the traceability relationships among the project objects.

The SPAN provides a logical framework for the collection and application of software project metrics to project management and cost estimation. Reliability of software cost and schedule estimates can be greatly enhanced by using network simulation models of a SPAN. Such models, driven by historical experience ideally, introduce more reality to project schedules.

Various software tools to support SPAN systems have been and will be developed, while the ability to integrate commercial configuration management tools with a SPAN implementation significantly reduces the costs and risks of implementation. Code dependency analyzers directly support the SPAN model in the generation of testing networks. Compilation order generators may be used to develop network topologies. Specialized tools have been developed by SofTech to analyze the dependency structure of an Ada system and produce the SPAN topology and all necessary test specifications. Network simulators that support cost and schedule estimation tools for the SPAN are currently in development.

Our experience with the SPAN prototypes at SofTech has been extremely rewarding in terms of orderly process management and test repeatability. The prototypes have provided a solid basis for further enhancement of development and test process management systems for our customers (USAF).

REFERENCES

[ANSI83]   United States, Department of Defense, *Reference Manual for the Ada Programming Language*, ANSI/MIL-STD-1815A-1983.

[Babich86]   Babich, Wayne, *Software Configuration Management - Coordination for Team Productivity*, Addison-Wesley Publishing Company, Reading, Massachusetts, 1986.

[Bersoff84]   Bersoff, Edward, "Elements of Software Configuration Management," *IEEE Trans. Software Engineering*, Vol SE-10, No. 1, Jan. 1984.

[Boehm81]   Boehm, Barry, *Software Engineering Economics*, Prentice-Hal, Englewood Cliffs, New Jersey, 1981.

[Bryan89]   Bryan, William, "Configuration Management with CCC in an Ada Environment",.Softool Users Group meeting, Santa Barbara, CA, March 1989.

[Coad90] Peter Coad, Edward Yourdon, *Object Oriented Analysis*, Yourdon Press, Prentice Hall, Englewood Cliffs, New Jersey, 1990.

[Digital82] Digital Equipment Corporation, *CMS/MMS: Code/Module Management System Manual*, Maynard, Mass., 1982.

[Feldman79] Feldman, S. I., "Make - A Program for Maintaining Programs," *Software Practice and Experience*, Vol. 9, No. 4 (April 1979).

[Gutzmann90] K.M.Gutzmann, D.L.Remkes, G. Woodcock, G.B. Young, J.L.Ragsdale, D.A. Auty, "CAIS Implementation Validation Capability (CIVC) Phase I Report", Report CIVC-FINL-021, SofTech, Houston, TX, 1990.

[Kleinrock75] Kleinrock, Leonard, *Queueing Systems, Volume I: Theory*, John Wiley and Sons, New York, 1975.

[Ould86] Ould, Martyn, and Unwin, Charles, *Testing in Software Development*, Cambridge University Press, London, 1986.

[Polytron85] Polytron Corporation, *Polytron Version Control System User's Manual*, Beaverton, OR, 1985.

[Pritsker84] Pritsker, A. Alan B., *Introduction to Simulation and SLAM II, 2nd edition*, Halsted Press, Joh Wiley and Sons, New York, 1984.

[Rochkind75] Rochkind, M. J., "The Source Code Control System (SCCS)," *IEEE Trans. Software Engineering*, Vol. SE-1, No. 4, December 1975.

[Rosenau84] Rosenau, Milton D. Jr., *Project Management for Engineers*, Lifetime Learning Publications, Belmont, CA, 1984.

[SofTech84] SofTech Inc., *Ada Language System Textbook*, Document 1102-9.2, Waltham, Mass, December 1984.

[SofTool88] Softool Corporation, "Configuration Management with CCC in an Ada Environment", Goleta, CA, November 1988.

[SofTool89] Softool Corporation, "Change and Configuration Control", Technical Note, July 27, 1989.

[Thall83] Thall, R., "Large Scale Software Development with the Ada Language System," *Proceedings of the 11th Annual Computer Science Conference*, ACM, February 1983.

[Tichy82] Tichy, W. F., "Design, Implementation, and Evaluation of a Revision Control System," *Proceedings of the 6th International Conference on Software Engineering*, September 1982.

Ada in Safety Critical Applications

A. Welz, LITEF GmbH, Lörracher Str. 18, 7800 Freiburg, FRG

1 INTRODUCTION

This paper reviews a LITEF internal study about the use of Ada in safety critical real time avionic systems. The study is part of the development of the Inertial Measurement Unit (IMU), a flight control subsystem of the European Fighter Aircraft (EFA). The study's goal was to establish programming rules and examine support tools and methods for the development of safe Ada programs for flight critical systems.

The study was divided into following parts:

1: Definition of safety related to Ada.

2: Derivation of Ada programming rules with the above definition and adjustment with already existing rules.

3: Classification of the Ada programming rules found in 2.

4: Examination of appropriate Ada test programs with the above Ada programming rules and confirmation of the rules.

5: Examination of tools and methods for safe Ada.

2 MOTIVATION

For the EFA project the Ada language is mandatorily required for the software implementation of all operational aircraft software. Currently assembly language is used most for such systems and typical assertions against the Ada language in safety critical applications are:

- Ada is unsafe because the language is too complex.

- Ada tasking is unsafe because Ada tasking is too complex.

- Ada tasking is not deterministic and therefore unsafe.

- In Ada there is an unsafe kind of "erroneous execution".

- The Ada exception mechanism is unsafe.

- The language Ada is extremely inefficient and Ada compilers have lots of bugs.

Therefore the EFA Joint Team ordered a study (called "Safe Ada Study" [1]) to investigate ways to apply Ada avoiding features of the language that are considered to be potentially "unsafe".

3 DEFINITION "ADA SAFETY"

A translation of the avionic term "safety" into the Ada terminology, in accordance with the current implementation practice of safety critical software, is ([1] Appendix A):

1: The program's memory requirements are known before runtime.

2: The program contains no action that has an unpredictable overhead in execution time.

3: The program and all its components have a deterministic behavior for every possible input of data. All branches in the program are explicit. The program is verifiable so that no error can occur at run time - no matter whether it is detectable or not.

4: The program is source level transparent. That means it is written in a consistent and readable way. The program does not make use of different features to express the same thing. All actions are visible.

4 ADA PROGRAMMING RULES

With the aid of the above-mentioned requirements, it is possible to extract Ada programming rules by identification of all "safety contradictions" in the ALRM. This method results in a lot of rules, which adapt the Ada syntax/semantics to the safety requirements. For example the following EFA rule 1:

> Access types shall not be used.

results from the static memory requirement.

During the LITEF study it was found that some of the EFA rules can be slightly modified without injuring any safety requirement. For example the following EFA rule 8:

> Actions shall not raise a predefined exception.

was changed to:

> All possible exceptions shall be handled with defined effects on the program execution.

This rule was modified, because it results in a very inefficient programming style with explicit range testing. Also the Ada tasking and machine code insertion restrictions where modified. The whole description of EFA rules and LITEF changes is beyond the scope of this paper ([1] Appendix A,[2]).

5 CLASSIFICATION ADA PROGRAMMING RULES

The resulting rules could be split into two classes:

(1) Rules which describe the sequential execution of the program ('sequence of statements' in the sense of Ada).

(2) Rules which describe the parallel execution of the program ('tasking' in the sense of Ada).

6 TEST PROGRAMS

The second step in defining and verifying Ada programming rules uses relevant parts of a typical Ada avionics program. The assembler output of this program is examined for implicit contradictions to the safety requirements which leads to a confirmation or to a modification of the above rules. It is natural that this method is only applicable if a stable version of the project Ada compiler has been defined.

A further improvement of this method is a more or less complete set of test programs with all possible Ada language elements. This was the method used in the LITEF study [2]. Only this method is able to find all possible safety risks of a specific project Ada compiler. The method has also the advantage that it delivers code-tables (Ada --> Assembler) which can be used in a later verification process. With an optimizing Ada compiler, however these tables should be handled with great care.

Another very useful outcome from analyzing these tables are rules for efficient Ada programs. In the LITEF study, it was found that these rules are, in part, the same as the safety rules (which is on the other hand a proof that safety need not be contradictory to efficiency).

7 TOOLS AND METHODS FOR SAFE ADA

Critical for the real safety of the developed software is the strict supervision of the adherence to the Ada programming rules. As mentioned above there are two classes of rules for supervision:

- Sequential rules

- Parallel rules

It is clear that each of these classes of rules needs to be applied differently:

7.1 Tools for Sequential Rules

This type of rules could be further subdivided into two groups:

(1.1)   Rules which describe the static behavior of the program (like a rule "All constraints shall be static").

(1.2)   Rules which describe the dynamic behavior of the program (like a rule "All program paths should be covered").

The first type of rule can easily be checked with a special Ada parser. This had already been developed by LITEF for a related project.

Also on the commercial market there are some tools for such sequential testing. For EFA the SPARK tool [4] has been selected. The disadvantage of this tools is that it only supports a very small subset of Ada. This kind of tool relies on formal test methods, which only works with a 'PASCAL' like subset of Ada, and needs additional special Ada comments (so called annotations) to help the tool in understanding the semantics of Ada.

The second type of rule needs dynamic testing, which means that the program is tested during execution. There are two major problems with this test method:

- Test input pattern and/or test strategies for the program must be generated.
- The program flow must be controlled by additional Ada control code or with the aid of a special trigger state analyzer.

There are some tools on the market which perform these functions but all tools are based on additional Ada control code which will destroy the real time behavior of the original program [5].

For this reason, LITEF has developed special trigger state hardware which can control an avionic target even during flight conditions. Studies for special pre- and postprocessing tools are currently under development.

7.2 Tools for Parallel Rules

Rules of this type are very difficult to control. The general case is investigated in the information studies ([6],[7],[8]).

Nevertheless, for "simple" avionic applications purposes, there are already sufficient methods to verify or control the above-mentioned rules. A typical avionic application consists of different tasks which are controlled by a scheduler mechanism. This scheduler can easily be implemented with the aid of an Ada rendezvous [3]. For this special kind of Ada tasking system the following methods where investigated:

- A method which uses a equivalence representation of Ada rendezvous and petri nets. This method has the advantage that a lot of commercial tools for petri nets already exist and the only problem is the conversion of Ada code to the appropriate net representation.

- A method which uses parallel-prolog which is a extension of prolog with parallel communication. With this language the above-mentioned scheduler mechanism can be verified without an extensive stochastic simulation as needed with the petri nets.

8 CONCLUSION

The language Ada is no less safe than other languages. Because of its strong typing, the predefined exception mechanism and the standardized tasking features, it has an even greater advantage compared to other languages. There are reasonable alternatives to restricting Ada to a 'PASCAL subset' as required in the EFA Safe Ada Study. With some precise rules, Ada fulfills all requirements of safety critical avionic applications. The adherence to these safety rules can be controlled with appropriate tools and methods.

9 REFERENCED DOCUMENTS

[1]   Flight Control System Safety Critical Software Study / EFJ-STY-EFA-020-0005 / Issue 1 / 30 October 87

[2]   Safe Ada & Compiler Study for EFA IMU / A. Welz / Internal LITEF Report / Revision 1.00-04.

[3]   Study LITEF Executive in Ada (LEA) / Phase 1-3 / A. Welz / Internal LITEF Report / 16.2.89.

[4]   SPARK - The SPADE Ada Kernel / Carre et al / July 1989 / HMSO London / Second Edition

[5]   LDRA TESTBED ADA / User Documentation & Technical Description / Liverpool Data Research Associates Ltd. / 1985

[6] Verifying General Safety Properties of Ada Tasking Programs / Laura K. Dillon / IEEE Transactions on Software Engineering / Vol 16. No. 1 / January 1990

[7] Critical Races in Ada Programs / Gerald M. Karam et al / IEEE Transactions on Software Engineering / Vol. 15 No. 11 / November 1989

[8] Starvation and Critical Race Analyzer for Ada / Gerald M. Karam et al / IEEE Transactions on Software Engineering / Vol. 16 No. 8 / August 1990

Real Time Electronic Funds Transfer and Ada

Jean Willain, Pierrot Baesens

Banksys S.C.
Chaussee de Haecht, 1442
B-1130 Brussels
Tel: 32-2-244.61.64
Fax: 32-2-245.50.26

Joël Sanzot, Stef van Vlierberghe

Offis S.A.
Weiveldlaan, 41 B.32
B-1930 Zaventem
Tel: 32-2-725.40.25
Fax: 32-2-725.40.12

1 BANKSYS AND ELECTRONIC FUNDS TRANSFER

Banksys is responsible for electronic funds transfer in Belgium and also has developed either complete systems or special purpose terminals for other countries.

Banksys terminal types are:

- automatic teller machines (cash dispensers),
- terminals for petrol stations,
- terminals for the large and small distribution sector.

The Banksys system in Belgium is based on TANDEM central computers, a private X25 network, concentrators and Banksys developed terminals.

The concentrators and terminals can be considered as embedded systems based on specific and standard hardware (8 or 16 bits micro-processors).

The current organization of the Banksys network is shown in figure 1.

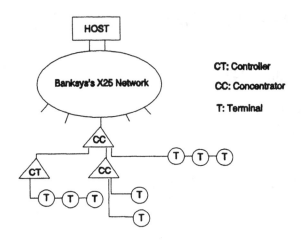

figure 1.

The present field of terminals and controllers reaches 29,000 units and is distributed in 10% for the petroleum sector, 12% for cash dispensers and 78% for the large and small retail sector. The number of concentrators is approximatively 500.

The development technology used by Banksys for embedded systems was based on assembler and C languages till 1989. At that time, Banksys decided to use Ada for new projects. At present, 4 Ada products (2 terminals, 1 concentrator and 1 controller) are operational.

The first part of the paper explains the motivation for this change of technology, the introduction of Ada and its implications.

The second part describes the four Ada projects with respect to reusability and maintenance.

2 ADA AT BANKSYS

Evolution in reliability and competitivity of the Banksys network has induced some studies for new products and new development methods.

At the end of 1988, the decision for the development in Ada of a new concentrator was taken. The selection of ARTK Alsys as operating system for embedded systems was based on the following criteria:

- size of the kernel,
- configurability of the kernel,
- ROMability,
- expansiveness of the kernel,
- existence of drivers.

Selection of Ada as a high-level language was based on these criteria:

- integration of real-time concepts in the language definition and thus reliability improvement,
- ease of maintenance and evolution capability and thus adequation for inherent evolutions and fluctuations of Banksys projects,
- high portability important for hardware redesign.

In addition, the following aspects also have been taken into account: widespread support, training and high-level debugging.

A first pilot project concerned a concentrator for the hierarchical part of the network, able to manage all terminal types and protocols used by Banksys. After the success of this first Ada development, three projects were developed with Ada technology:

- a terminal for electronic funds transfer for a foreign company accepting credit cards,
- a controller (concentrator for terminals of the same type) with special functionalities for the distribution sector,
- a terminal for electronic funds transfer accepting credit cards for the distribution sector.

3 ADA PROJECTS AT BANKSYS

3.1 The concentrator project

This product was developed to replace an older generation of concentrators written in assembler, to gain efficiency, add new functionalities and allow easier maintenance.

Its main goals are:

- transfer messages between terminals and the host system (and vice versa),
- report terminal activities and problems to the central system,
- execute supervision commands from the central system on specified terminals,
- provide man-machine interface for terminal supervision and tests.

The development of the concentrator was organized in several phases. It began with a basic concentrator for leased lines of the Public Telephone Network. The concentrator was then upgraded to allow connection with the central system through the Banksys X25 network. The last phase allows communications between third party terminals and host systems.

The concentrator is able to resist to message traffic peaks. Its communication part was designed to work with interrupt driven I/O.

3.2 The EFT-1 project

This product was developed for a foreign company.
Its capabilities are:

- handle electronic payments with credit cards for the small distribution sector,
- produce book-keeping documents,
- allow consultation of commercial information,
- ensure security on private information in messages like personal code, available amount,...

This payment system works autonomous and can establish connections with hosts via the Public Switched Telephone Network. It controls the man-machine interface for customers and merchant. It is able to withstand power and communication failures without loosing financial transactions.

3.3 The EFT-2 project

The EFT-2 project is like the EFT-1 project in its basic functionalities. The main differences are:

- other types of credit cards,
- communication with hosts through cash registers,
- another type of security management,
- another man-machine interface.

3.4 The controller project

This product includes, in addition to concentrator capabilities, the management of:

- security in communication with host,
- redundancy for communication with host through another controller,
- financial informations.

Figure 2 illustrates physical integration of the controller, EFT-2 terminals and other components of a distributed system.

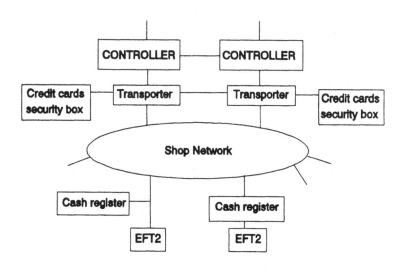

figure 2.

4 REUSABILITY

Reusability quickly appeared to be one of the most important objectives since Banksys projects are characterized by a high degree of functional similarities. For this kind of projects, design and code reusability are efficient means to improve reliability, development time, maintenance time and testing time so that it can significantly decrease project costs.

The Buhr methodology [BUH87] for real time system design with Ada appears well adapted to Banksys projects. This approach leads to modular design and allows reuse of parts kit of canonical architectures in design activity.

The notion of code reusability has two aspects, induced by the following questions:

- what can be reused ?
- what can be improved or completed ?

These two aspects are due to parallel development of projects with a close deadline.

The first one, named strong reusability [CSC87], consists in reuse of modules in libraries, whether from inner development or induced by published examples [BOO87] [TAF87]. Current organization of libraries is shown in figure 3 (an arrow from library A to library B represents a transitive relation meaning that A acquires packages from B).

The second one, called weak reusability [CSC87], consists in code extraction from existing projects and immediate evolution for quick availability.

Two guidelines for weak reusability ensure no wild widespread of code:

- users of extracted code must be aware of exact specifications of the present form of the code,
- modification, insertion or replacement of functionalities are referred and related to the new form of the code.

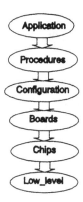

figure 3.

When a project is in maintenance phase, the code can migrate from weak reusable code to strong reusable code. If done so, feedback is applied to all projects using it.

Figure 4 represents the analysis of the two kinds of reusability through all Ada Banksys projects without distinguishing terminal and concentrator projects. The table shows the percentage of the number of code lines (number of semi-colons) of the category in respect with the total number of code lines of the project.

%	concentrator	EFT-1	EFT-2	controller
strong reuse	8.6	4.5	19.6	11.9
weak reuse	0	3.8	25.4	38.9
other code	91.4	91.7	55.0	49.2

figure 4.

The percentage of the strong reusable code of the concentrator is not null because some basic and project independent packages have been used or developed before.

Weak reusability takes obviously an important and increasing part of the whole reusability. Figure 5 illustrates its role comparing highly similar products (controller with concentrator, EFT-2 with EFT-1) and distinguishing weak reusable code not yet strong reusable code and weak reusable code already migrated at this time.

%	Code of controller from		Code of EFT-2 from	
	concentrator	all	EFT-1	all
weak reusable code not yet strong reusable code	12.0	17.6	14.6	15.2
weak reusable code already strong reusable code	14.7	21.3	9.6	10.2

figure 5.

5 MAINTENANCE: COMPARISONS BETWEEN TECHNOLOGIES

Maintenance requires a large part of the Banksys product resources. The marketing objectives are continuously re-specified and re-studied to improve competitivity and answer to new user requirements. Moreover, the wide distribution of the products implies an internal quality control which produces standardized problem reports.

The concept of maintenance is divided in two major categories:

- evolutive maintenance (modify or add fonctionalities),
- corrective maintenance (resolve problems).

The example of the concentrator in figure 6 illustrates the major role of evolutive maintenance and its impact on manpower, timing and code size. (Phase I includes all the life cycle of the first part of the project, other phases only concern evolutive maintenance).

concentrator	phase I	phase II	phase III
number of lines	3010	8133	9333
man-months	32	6.5	8
duration (months)	7	2	3

figure 6.

Comparison between the assembly written concentrator and the first phase of the Ada written concentrator in figure 7 illustrates implications of technology changes. The table shows that corrective maintenance of Ada projects significantly decreases and is due, in part, to modularity of Ada that allows to test packages and functionalities much before integration time. But, if Ada provides a lot of positive aspects, Ada also leads to increase the memory size of embedded systems in comparison with programs written in Assembler.

	assembler concentrator	ADA concentrator phase I
hardware used	dedicated on 6809	AT286 + dedicated boards
memory size	32 Kbytes	120 Kbytes
generated code	38 Kbytes	132 Kbytes
development of common basic part	12 man/months	7.5 man/months
development for new procedure	2 man/months	1 man/month
integration and corrective maintenance	8 man/months	0.5 man/month
number of versions before stability	8	2
number of problem reports	> 100	< 10

figure 7.

Some applications at Banksys are written in C but do not have their equivalent in Ada so that it is not possible to illustrate a comparison between these two technologies. However, all C applications consist of cash dispensers and have a high degree of common functionalities. Most of the differences correspond to card type acceptations, man-machine interfaces and communication protocols

Reuse of the common parts of these applications consists in code extraction and direct adaptation to present code not taking into account the guidelines leading to pure reusability that is not encouraged by the too weak abstraction mechanisms and modularity of C. Migration from this type of reusability to pure reusability would be very time expensive.

Impacts on corrective and evolutive maintenance are consequent because any modification (correction or new functionality) concerning a common part of code implies as many modifications as code duplications. This is also time expensive and, moreover, not safe.

6 CONCLUSIONS

All around Ada, new structures and organizations have evolved. Very early, the ease of team work due to the use of Ada has led to non-ambiguous repartition of the work and reusability has led to build libraries of packages and structures for design reuse.

Many fluctuations of specifications appeared during developments. They affected application structures but were always taken into account without much trouble due to the high flexibility of the modular Ada-based design.

From the Banksys experience can be deduced that Ada has improved a valuable number of aspects: reliability and reduction of development, integration and maintenance costs.

7 REFERENCES

[BOO87] - Booch G., Software Components with Ada, Benjamin/Cummings, 1987.

[BUH87] - Buhr R.J.A., System design with Ada, Prentice-Hall Software Series, 1987.

[CSC87] - Computer Sciences Corporation, Ada Reusability Handbook, Moorestown, NJ, Technical Report SP-IRD 11, December 1987.

[TAF87] - Tafvelin S., Ada Components: Libraries and Tools, Cambridge University Press, 1987.

Part V: Environments and Tools

Introducing HOOD into Software Process Modelling Based Environments[1]

J.R. LARRE, N. ALFARO, J.J. GALÁN and J. GARBAJOSA

Grupo de Mecánica del Vuelo, S.A.

Keywords: Ada, HOOD, methods, tools, CASE, MASP, ALF

Abstract

HOOD (Hierarchical Object Oriented Design) is the standard ESA (European Space Agency) method for the architectural design phase and essentially oriented towards Ada program development. The HOOD method can be described using the so called MASP — Model for Assisted Software Processes — model developed within the ALF project (ESPRIT Ref 1520) that allows the depiction of software development activities for a wide range of methods such that the knowledge encompassed in the method description can be exploited to assist the user leading to the production of more reliable software and a cost reduction. Therefore, a MASP description for the HOOD method could be used as basis for future HOOD toolset developments. Furthermore, representing the HOOD method using the MASP formalism can result in obtaining a greater stage of formalisation and understanding of its semantics. The MASP model has been envisaged as part of a third generation software engineering environment framework based on the interpretation of this software process model and developed within the project ALF [B*89], [GGGS89].

[1]This work is partially sponsored by the Commission of the European Communities under the ESPRIT programme (Project Ref. N. 1520).

1 Introduction

The software marketplace is demanding tools that provide a higher degree of assistance than those presently available as a means of improving productivity and software quality in costly, complex and critical applications such as those of the aerospace field [Som89], [OT88]. The incorporation of information concerning the software process description into tools to achieve the mentioned goal is one of the directions that is being widely investigated [SW88], [T*87], [KFP88], [TBC*88].

HOOD (Hierarchical Object Oriented Design) is the standard ESA (European Space Agency) method for the architectural design phase of the software development lifecycle. It is oriented towards Ada program development based on the principle of successive decomposition of objects representing the system to be designed.

The use of the ALF framework, developed within the project ALF (ES-PRIT Ref. 1520), applied to the HOOD method is expected to result in tools that provide the user with a higher degree of assistance than those presently commercialised. Furthermore, the description of HOOD using the MASP formalism, that we shall introduce, may help to obtain a greater stage of formalisation and understanding of the semantics of the method.

Within this paper we present our approach to describe HOOD using the MASP formalism and how this knowledge description concerning HOOD can be utilised to support tools. First, we do a quick presentation of the HOOD method and how tools can be incorporated into it. Following, we describe the ALF approach to 3th generation environment frameworks and process modelling. With this basis we shall present a MASP for HOOD and explain how the assistance, control, quality are increased through its use.

2 The HOOD Method

2.1 HOOD Description

HOOD [2] (*Hierarchical Object Oriented Design*) is an architectural design method oriented towards Ada program development. Following [Gro89b],

---

[2] The HOOD method was developed under ESA contract A0/1-1890/86/NL/MA by a consortium of CISI Ingenierie, CRI A/S and Matra Espace.

"HOOD is a method of hierarchical decomposition of the design in the solution domain based on identification of objects and operations in the problem domain, supported by abstract objects related to design entities". The HOOD method comprises textual definition of the solution, diagrams and formal refinement, in order to facilitate that, at the end of the design, a proper documentation exists; automated checking can also be performed and Ada source code can be generated. HOOD is essentially oriented towards Ada program development though its application to other programming languages is being currently studied [Gro89a].

A HOOD design is based on the principle of successive decomposition of the objects representing the system to be designed. This decomposition process starts at the top level parent object, called root object, and results in several lower level child objects. Each component object, in turn, may be decomposed into other lower level objects in following design steps until the bottom level or terminal object is reached. Terminal objects are designed in detail without any further decomposition, being transformed into code directly. The output of the HOOD method is a HOOD document, that completely describes the architecture of a software system.

A basic design step has as goals the identification of child objects of a given parent object and their individual relationships to other existing objects. In consequence there are two types of hierarchy between objects: the *parent-child* that reflects the decomposition of a parent object into one or several child objects, and the *senior-junior* one that shows the use relationship between objects.

Four steps must be repeated recursively for each object until no further decomposition be possible according to [Gro89c]:

1. Problem definition.

2. Elaboration of an informal strategy.

3. Formalisation of the strategy.

   3.1. Identification of objects.

   3.2. Identification of operations.

   3.3. Grouping of operations and objects.

   3.4. Graphical description.

   3.5. Justification of design decisions.

4. Formalisation of the solution (ODS[3]).

The output of a basic design step is a *HOOD chapter*. Each HOOD chapter is divided into four different subchapters that reflect the output for each of the four steps. In addition, we have a textual or a graphical output included into the chapter corresponding to each of the objects being described.

The philosophy followed to elaborate the chapters is top-down. Therefore in each basic design step, the decomposition of a given object into its child objects is performed together with the definition of, the *use* relationship with other objects. Although in theory the method is strictly top-down, practice has shown that once a new level has been defined, a bottom-up revision may be convenient. Further details on each step can be found in [Gro89b].

2.2 Considerations on the Method and Tools

The actual definition of the HOOD method provides a lot of information and constraints concerning object hierarchy, dependencies and so on. Nevertheless a lot of tips can be suggested for the Problem Definition, Elaboration of an Informal Strategy, Identification of Objects, and some other subjects where the method leaves place for the user creativity.

For the Problem Definition and Elaboration of an Informal Strategy actually not many of the available tools help in consistency checking, or ease the strategy elaboration task. The most common tool is not very far from a text editor.

Concerning the third step, Formalisation of the strategy, scarce help, except for the edit job (text & graphics) is provided by the current tools in the identification or object grouping, operations, etc. Nevertheless, a consistency checking is often done between the different descriptions —graphical&textual— of a given object.

The fourth step results in an Object Description Skeleton together with some basic Ada pseudocode. This Skeleton and the code can be partially generated automatically from the information obtained in the third step.

---

[3]When the Formalisation of the strategy has been completed, the designer can elaborate a formal model of the solution, describing for each parent object the child object properties, operations and the relationships between objects. This model is formally referred to as the Object Description Skeleton.

The formality of the HOOD method might be improved in the two first steps, as their result is just a mere text file whose semantics is ignored by the method. The method provides just a few tips on how to perform these two steps, and the user may feel lost when starting to design according the method. A tool that should provide assistance on these topics might be helpful.

Preceding experiences can be interesting whenever the method leaves place for user creativity, and these experiences are, probably, one the few sources to provide assistance. Taking previous works as a basis, a set of metrics can be prepared in order to formalise the gained knowledge. These metrics can be decisive for the objective of increasing the quality of the design and providing assistance if the design tasks are monitored.

3 The ALF Approach

The ALF project [B*89] aims to lay the foundations of a third generation software engineering environment framework. In order to fulfill its objective, a *Model for Assisted Software Process* (MASP) has been developed. The main idea of the MASP concept is to provide a formalism which can be used to describe software process models of various methods. A representation of a particular software process model written in the formalism of the MASP concept is called a MASP. Within this section we shall present the underlying ideas of the model and will explain its operation in section 4.

The knowledge concerning the tasks to be performed is exploited to assist the user using an *interpretation technique* [GGGS89]. The provided assistance ranges from explanation to control and guidance, owing to the ability of the system to act at user's request or at its own initiative. The interpretation of the MASP model allows user initiatives, certainly a quite usual feature in commercial environments, and system initiatives, a not so usual one. Initiatives are expressed by means of operator execution requests.

The MASP is a multimodel paradigm composed of an object, operator[4], expression, rule, ordering and a characteristic model [B*89]. The MASP object model defines the object structures by means of object properties and relationships among these objects. It is based on the ERA-model —Entities, Relationships and Attributes— [Che76] and supports multiple inheritance of

---

[4]These object and operator models have nothing to do with HOOD objects and operations. There is a clear distinction between HOOD objects and operations, and MASP objects and operators.

types. Actually, the object model of PCTE [ESL88], enhanced with multi-valued attributes, is the basis for the MASP object model.

The expression model describes particular states of the system. The basic elements in describing system states are objects and events resulting from the object manipulations and the operator executions. These expressions may thus include two parts: a logical part, that specifies properties of objects, and an event part that describes when the logical part has to be evaluated. An expression with an empty event-part is always available for evaluation. Empty logical parts are always true. The expression model thus allows the description of static situations of the system (current state of entities, relationships and attributes), when the event part is not used, and dynamic ones when concrete events are considered.

The operator model describes the potential sort of operations that may be performed either by user or system through initiatives. An operator description includes its name, conditions under which the operator is executable (precondition), conditions that must be held after its execution (postcondition), object types on which the operator is applicable (domain), and the type of objects created during the execution (range). Following the MASP model terminology, operators are classified as *non-elementary* and *elementary*, depending whether they can be further decomposed or are plain tools. The definition of an operator enables the linking of a tool to an operator type called elementary operator type. To enable a structured and thus easier description of a complete software process, the semantics of those operators which are not elementary can be described as MASPs. An additional feature is that an operator provides information about whether it may be processed by the system alone, or it needs user's cooperation. These operators are called, respectively, *non-interactive* or *interactive*.

The characteristic model defines assertions that characterise a correct state of the system. It represents a set of constraints that must be satisfied during the model interpretation. It could be considered as a set of integrity constraints. Characteristics are defined by a set of expressions whose truth must be guaranteed. A violation of any of the characteristic expressions will force to take some actions oriented to repair the abnormal situation.

The rule model describes specific reactions to specific situations arising during the software development. A rule is composed of a condition part represented by means of expressions, and an action part described by an operator. A rule describes what to do when an specific event, defined by a state, is raised. A rule is said to be firable when its condition part becomes true. When several rules are firable, the system will decide which rule must be fired according to a strategy and will guarantee that, at least, one is fired.

Ordering is a means of specifying policies for operator executions. It explicitly constrains the operator execution with respect to those already executed. Orderings are used to specify that particular operators must be executed concurrently, alternatively or sequentially or that an operator can be repeated or executed simultaneously. These constraints restrict potential operator activation sequences but do not define a preferred execution ordering.

Rules, operator ordering and characteristic models include control features to manage process and object evolution.

The operational view of MASPs is described by means of *Assisted Software Processes* (ASPs) that are representations of tasks being performed during the software development according to a given MASP. The needed instantiation produces the *Instantiated Model for Assisted Software Process* (IMASP) which binds actual data and the model. We can say that the interpretation consists of the instantiation of a MASP yielding an IMASP and the activation of the IMASP providing the ASP. The activation happens at the moment the operator is invoked. If necessary a lazy instantiation of a MASP may take place when an operator is invoked.

During the life of an ASP two basic kinds of actions are performed: initiative taking and evolvement control. Initiative taking includes user and system initiatives. Initiatives, both user and system, are expressed by means of operator execution requests. The system, making use of the MASP rule model, will take initiatives when rules conditions are satisfied. To be executed, an operator will have to be activatable, that is, its precondition will have to be true, its execution will be according to the orderings and characteristics will not be violated. These issues involve evolvement control. Evolvement control will guarantee the stability of the MASP interpretation by respecting the model constraints. If an operator is non activatable or a characteristic is not respected, the system, as a result of the interpretation, will take the initiative of trying to find operator sequences whose execution, fulfilling the activation condition, would enable the requested operator to be executed. This property corresponds to one of the several assistance mechanisms that the ALF system provides. The system will not request to execute a not activatable operator.

Additional assistance features are provided through utilization of the information contained in the operator pre- and postconditions, taking constraints into account. Other properties, such as *coordination and cooperation* based on powerful communication mechanisms, are also supported [GLS*90].

An *interpreter* is in charge of exploiting the various MASP model descriptions according to the model semantics and considering the instantiated data. It enables the system to take initiatives and control the consistency of the system according to the model constraints. Further details of the ALF system architecture can be found in [B*89].

The interpretation outcome is complemented with Observation, History Generation and Feedback. Observed data is processed afterwards by using metrics and the obtained information is used to improve the *quality* of the software process by either informing the user or project manager or even firing rules that may automatically —Feedback— correct the identified problems.

4   A MASP for HOOD

4.1   Object Model Description

The design of a system following HOOD proceeds according to the four phases defined by the HOOD Basic Design Steps. For each step the MASP for the HOOD method will provide support for textual and graphical forms, even pseudocode and final Ada code generation. Each HOOD design can support an arbitrary number of simultaneous HOOD Design Steps, each corresponding to design of some Object in the system, and also the whole system itself. Some of these documents directly correspond to those phases or are directly related to them, whilst others are supplementary documentation which could help the user to make the most efficient use of the HOOD method.

All the documents that make up a HOOD chapter would form our domain. The main object would be a HOOD design, that would have a HOOD document associated. A HOOD document could be divided into several chapters, each one dealing with one object.

Like the informal strategy, the problem definition and the code seem to be more related to the chapter than to the object itself, as there is not a formal semantical link between them and the object.

The ODS (Object description Skeleton) could be decomposed into its main components: the provided and required interfaces, its internal definitions, and its OPCS (Operation Control Structure) and OCS (Object Control Structure), if exists.

On the other hand, there are topics such as operations, exceptions, types, and data that seem to be more related to the object, as the method determines relations between them, and provides some restrictions that have to be followed.

The MASP object model provides mechanisms to support a schema which would take into account all those entities (objects) and relationships (links) previously defined. Figure 1 shows a first approach to a data model according to the formalism usually used to represent PCTE OMS data models. This first model only tries to reflect the simplest data structure needed to support a HOOD design.

The link numbers on figure 1 represent the following identifiers:

1- .has_chapter	10- .to_provide	19- .provided_constant
2- .to_define_problem	11- .to_require	20- .required_object
3- .to_elaborate_strategy	12- .internal	21- .required_operation
4- .to_formalize_strategy	13- .opcs	22- .required_exception
5- .coding	14- .ocs	23- .required_type
6- .formal_solution	15- .has_operation	24- .internal_object
7- .logical_object	16- .provided_operation	25- .internal_operation
8- .logical_operator	17- .provided_exception	26- .its_operation
9- .graphic	18- .provided_type	27- .object_design
		28- .designed_object

We shall not explain figure 1 in detail but just make some remarks to help understand how the object model works and is related to the rest of the MASP models. We see, for instance, that a *HOOD_Chapter* is composed of *Problem_Definition*, *Informal_Strategy*, *Formal_Strategy* and *Ada_Code_Generation*. When the OMS links *.to_formalize_strategy* exists it means that the phase *Formal_Strategy* has been performed. Obviously, a lower level of detail in the object model would allow to represent subphases of *Formal_Strategy*. Nevertheless we still have more information in our object model since the existence of reference link *.logical_object* and *.logical_operator* shows whether a given object or operation have *been involved* in the formal strategy and have been defined as *.logical_object* and *.logical_operation*. This kind of information can be used in the logical expressions as described in section 4.3.

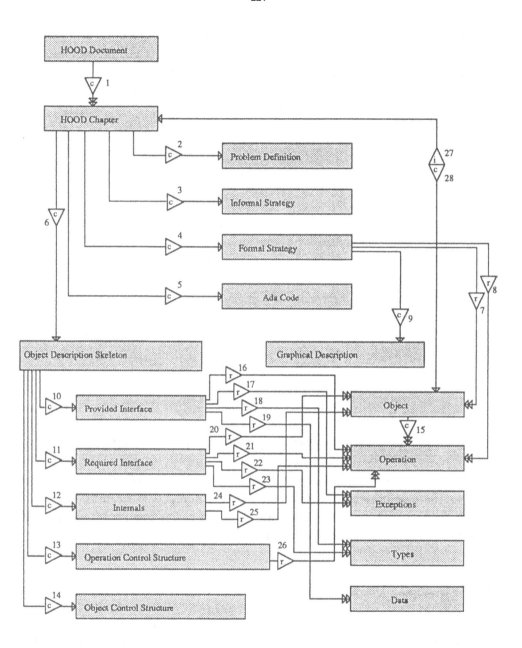

Figure 1: HOOD MASP Data Model

Besides, some other redundant relations (figure 2) have been also defined in order to reflect higher order relations between objects themselves and between objects and their components like operations, exceptions, types, and constants. These redundant links ease the data management and provides a better performance accessing the database.

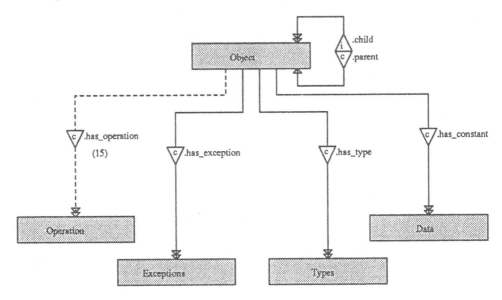

Figure 2: HOOD MASP Data Model: Redundant Links

We must note that some other OMS data models for HOOD already exist such as the one presented in [Sav89]. Furthermore, tools running on top of PCTE using a rich object model can be much easier incorporated into the ALF framework than those that do not use it.

4.2 Operator Model Description

As we have said before, the operations that have to be performed to carry out a software task, a HOOD design in our case, are represented using the MASP operator model. Operator model instances, termed operators, portray the design substeps — operations—. As we explained in section 3 operators are classified into elementary and non-elementary. Taking advantage of this feature we can establish several levels of abstraction to describe the subsequent steps, representing them through non-elementary operators that would be refined into others closer to plain tools. The MASP does not constrain either the set of used tools to implement the needed elementary operators or the granularity of such operators.

Some operators will be a straight mapping of design phases and sub-phases steps such as those that might be termed as *strategy_elaboration* or *solution_formalisation*. We can refine *solution_formalisation* according to the method into other operators that could be defined to help the user work such as *logical_operation_definition*, *grouping* or *graphical_definition* corresponding to the definition of the logical operations, grouping of objects operations and graphical description of the system.

Thus, there is a set of checking operators to verify the consistency of each step design and, finally, the whole system design. For instance, to verify the fact that an object represented as a child and as a parent must be consistent is an issue that cannot be described by using the defined object model[5]

The precondition and postcondition in MASP operators help clearly to achieve a friendly and easy to use system in which quality issues are not left apart. For example, after executing *grouping*, objects should be together with operations. That means that for a given HOOD operation, the link *has_operation* must exist and the object must be destination of *.child* link, as only childs can hold operations. Furthermore, *.logical_obj* must also exist if the HOOD object is a child. This summarizes the postcondition for *grouping* and the precondition for *graphical_definition*. If it is not true for a HOOD object that we want to include into a graphical definition, we can prevent the designer from introducing the alluded definition and suggest him to change his design. We can provide an explanation based on the reasoning trace as well.

The precondition for *grouping* will be the postcondition cooresponding to the MASP operators for the logical identification of objects and operators and similar examples might be presented.

4.3 Control Models Description

As we said above, the rest of the MASP models (characteristics, ordering and rules) are used to provide assistance ranging from explanation to control and guidance. This way, operator behaviour (tasks to be performed) are modeled by means of constraining, suggesting or forcing operator executions. Rules will be fired when their precondition is true and when a user request fails

---

[5]The models that make up a MASP can be complementary in order to reflect, for instance, all the restrictions of the object abstract model, or to assure semantic restrictions and coherence between parent and child HOOD objects [GLS*90].

the system will try to help the user proposing him the sequence of operators needed to solve his problem.

Furthermore, by means of the MASP ordering, rule and, also, the operator (pre- and post-conditions) models it is easy to be aware of the state of the HOOD design, and this information will be used to help the user to decide on the following task to perform.

The MASP will keep track of the state of each of chapter, and will have the knowledge concerning the ordering of the design subphases (modeled as non-elementary operators, that is, child MASPs). It will therefore propose the user one or many of the next available steps or the system itself will carry out non-interactive ones.

An example of the use of the MASP characteristic can be the following: It must be always decided whether an object is terminal or not. An OMS attribute can express this property. We can assert within a characteristic that the value of this attribute must be filled mandatorily. As soon as it is detected that the characteristic is false an action will be initiated to solve this inconsistency. One of the advantages of using a characteristic is that the user can be actively helped as soon as it is noticed that the characteristic is false —at any moment of the development— explaining what is happening and, in case the system cannot solve completely the problem, suggesting how to solve the incident. A traditional input menu can prevent from leaving a field blank but nothing else.

Finally, we shall describe how a rule can be used to improve the quality of the design. Though this is not the only purpose of a rule it is a helpful application. We know the problem that a high number of active objects can mean. If we define a metric to estimate a top value we can always observe whether the number of active objects is a proper one. If not, the system might warn the designer *a posteriori* on the potential danger of his design decision. To perform this task a MASP rule would be used. The precondition part of the rule should evaluate the final result of the metric, probably an OMS attribute. If the value is higher than the top value the rule would be fired providing a warning. This warn may become a prohibition according to a project manager decision. That is, MASPs can be generated to make them conform to local standards, for instance. This is another sign of flexibility.

5 Conclusions

This paper has presented a procedure to describe and support the HOOD method according to the ALF project approach. Presently, the implementation of the ideas described is being performed. The experience is being used to improve the model definition and to gain experience in order to enhance the general system operation. Problems concerning the way to provide the most suitable kind of assistance or control at any stage are coming up and being a source of useful information. A feedback consisting of guidelines that will allow to improve the degree of assistance provided by the current toolsets and, as important, a better understanding of the method is expected.

References

[B*89]   K. Benali et al. *Presentation of the ALF project*. In *Proc SDE&F*, Berlin, May 1989.

[Che76]   C.C. Chen. *The Entity-Relationship model: Toward an Unified View of Data. ACM-TODS 1,1, pages 9-36*, 1(1):9–36, March 1976.

[ESL88]   GIE Emeraude, Selenia, and Software Sciences Limited. *PCTE+ C Functionnal Specifications*. Issue 3, 660p, 08 1988.

[GGGS89]   J.J. Galán, J. Garbajosa, V. Gruhn, and W. Stulken. *Interpretation of Assisted Software Processes*. In *CASE 89 workshop*, London, July 1989.

[GLS*90]   J. Garbajosa, J.R. Larre, J. Sánchez, N. Alfaro, and J.J. Galán. *Implementing Cooperation and Coordination*. In *CASE 90 workshop*, Irvine, 1990.

[Gro89a]   HOOD Working Group. *HOOD Reference Manual, Issue 3.1 DRAFT 1*. ESA, August 1989.

[Gro89b]   HOOD Working Group. *HOOD Reference Manual, Version 3.0*. ESA, 1989.

[Gro89c]   HOOD Working Group. *HOOD User Manual, Version 3.0*. ESA, 1989.

[KFP88]   G.E. Kaiser, P.H. Feiler, and S. Popovich. *Intelligent Assistance for Software Development and Maintenance*. IEEE Software, 5 1988.

[OT88]   GC. Oddy and C. Tully. *Information Systems Factory study. Final Report*. Technical Report, Alvey Directorate, 1988.

[Sav89]   G. Savoia. *Porting AdaNice on PCTE*. Maffliers Workshop Documentation. Atmosphere Project, November 1989.

[Som89]   I. Sommerville. *Software Engineering*. Addison-Wesley, 1989.

[SW88]   W. Schäfer and H. Weber. *The ESF-Profile* . Handbook of Computer Software Engineering Van Nostrand, New York, 1 1988.

[T*87]   R. Taylor et al. *Next Generation Software Environments: Principles, Problems, and Research Directions* . Technical Report, University of California, Irvine, 1987.

[TBC*88] R. Taylor, F.C. Belz, L.A. Clarke, L. Osterweil, et al. *Foundations for the Arcadia Environment Architecture* . Proceedings of the ACM SIGSOFT/SIGPLAN Software Engineering Symposium on Practical Software Development Environments, 1988.

Acknowledgement

We are grateful to J. Sánchez, J. Romañach, J. Amador, and E. Risco for intensive discussions. Special thanks must be given to J. Campos, member of the HOOD User Group and the HOOD Technical Group, for his comments. We are also grateful to the referees for their helpful remarks. We are indebted to all the members of the ALF Consortium, for fruitful discussions and advice. The partners involved in the project ALF are GIE Emeraude (France), Computer Science Corporation (Belgium), Computer Technologies Co.-CTC (Greece), Grupo de Mecánica del Vuelo, S.A. (Spain), International Computers Limited (United Kingdom), University of Nancy-CRIN (France), University of Dortmund-Informatik X (Germany), Cerilor (France), Université Catholique de Louvain (Belgium) and University of Dijon-CRID (France). This work is partially sponsored by the Commission of the European Communities under the ESPRIT programme (Project Ref. N. 1520).

Design Assessment of Ada Systems Using Static Analysis

ALEXIOS DELIS and WILLIAM M. THOMAS

Department of Computer Science
University of Maryland
College Park, MD 20742 U.S.A.

A well structured design is an essential feature in the development of a software system. Assessment of the design throughout the development process is therefore an important task. However, it can be a difficult and highly subjective process. We present tools to assist in the evaluation of designs of Ada systems. These tools furnish two different abstract views of the system structure, one focusing on control flow and the other on data coupling. We identify the effect of three classes of design methodologies on these views, and discuss how to use the views to facilitate design assessment[1].

1 Introduction

During the last decade design techniques have been refined and heavily used in the realization of medium and large scale developments of software systems. Design represents an intermediate but still extremely essential part of any project [LMW79, JT79]. High level solutions are offered to a set of problems furnished by the requirements analysis phase. Programmers are expected to comply with the outlined design plans on their way to implementation. In an environment where a fair number of people work simultaneously to meet development goals and where changes of design are not rare, regular inspection and validation of the design blueprints are desired. Compatibility of the design with the released code could be observed as well.

There is a great deal of interest in using Ada as a design language, which provides the benefit of the analysis of design utilizing the numerous tools implemented for the analysis of Ada source code. While it is not expected that full elaboration of the source code is available at design time, the system

[1]This work was supported in part by the ITALSIEL S.p.A. and the U.S. Army Institute for Research in Management Information and Computer Science (AIRMICS) under grant AIRMICS-01-4-33267

architecture and interfaces between system components should be identified. Analysis of the architecture and inter-module information flows provides indication of product qualities such as reliability, maintainability and reusability. The purpose of this paper is to discuss a set of measurement tools that are useful in the assessment of design by performing static analysis on the produced code or design products (assuming that the design is carried out with some Ada PDL). More particularly, we examine the impact of three major techniques broadly used in development of Ada systems. The design techniques examined are: hierarchical decomposition, bottom–up composition, and object–oriented design. These techniques can be used either alone or in combination, yielding hybrid methodologies. The hypothesis of this study is that the three design methodologies reveal different characteristics in the output of the tools. This knowledge will allow software engineers to better assess design quality.

This paper presents two Ada based tools **dbt** (Data Binding Tool) and **ctt** (Call Tree Tool) and demonstrates how they can assist in system design assessment. The tools have been developed around the ideas of information and control flow. The **dbt** was developed to provide a data binding analysis of Ada systems. Data bindings [BT75] provide a measure of information flow among components (or modules). Cluster analysis of the data bindings is used to evaluate proximity of system components. Proximity is demonstrated in the format of a tree – called a dendrogram – that indicates element similarities based on information flow. On the other hand, **ctt** capitalizes on subprogram and task entry calls and outputs a tree that is solely based on potential control flows among system components. The call tree generated by **ctt** shows all potential calls in a system and can be analyzed to determine various measures of control flow. These tools work in synergy. Their roles are complimentary since one emphasizes control sequences and the other stresses data flows.

Using these tools in the analysis of a number of Ada systems has shown that indicators of quality factors vary according to the utilized design techniques. The implication of this result is that design assessment methodologies must be tailored according to the design technique utilized in the system under analysis.

The paper is organized as follows: Section 2 describes the essential ideas behind the examined design techniques. The third section discusses a model of Ada components with varying granularity, allowing for analysis of systems at various levels of detail. The fourth section gives a description of the functionality of the **dbt** and **ctt** tools, and section 5 discusses their implementation. Sections 6 and 7 identify some measures of design quality that can be obtained through the use of these tools, and discusses a method of analysis of the outputs. Test data and results of the assessment analysis are presented in section 8. The paper ends with conclusions and future plans.

2   Examined Design Techniques

Design involves a substantial effort to reduce complexity and facilitates the resolution of implementation problems in a system under development. The design process involves the transformation of requirements into a model of the software system upon which the implementation may be based. The design model may be analyzed for qualities such as functionality, performance, reliability and maintainability, among others, to provide an indication of problem areas. Based on these analyses, corrective action can be taken at an early stage.

Several design methodologies have been proposed over the years. Most of these techniques can be classified as either top–down decomposition (TDD) or bottom–up composition (BUC).

The essential theme in top–down decomposition methods is that systems are decomposed into a set of cooperating parts, with each part at the same level of abstraction. The design at each level hides the details of the design at lower levels, as only the data and control flow across the components of that level are depicted. If needed, this decomposition process is applied as many times as is appropriate. The details of the design of low level components are thus postponed until the last stages of design. Issues like implementation feasibility, ability to manage the components and component complexity decide the level of nesting.

Functional decomposition is an example of a top–down, hierarchical method. Here, the designer separates the system into its top level functions. Each of these functions is similarly decomposed until the appropriate level of decomposition has been reached. Breaking up the system according to functions is only one such method for decomposing a system. The Jackson System Development technique recommends a top–down decomposition of the system according to data structure [Cam89], and the Yourdon–Constantine Structured Design recommends a decomposition according to data flow [YC79]. The common idea in these methods is that the refinement is done in a top–down manner, which focuses attention on designing solutions to the whole of the problem before concentrating on solutions to the sub–problems.

On the other hand, bottom–up design techniques embrace the idea that primary designer's concern is the development of the elementary system units.

The designer determines the most critical units based on experience, intuition or a simple analysis. These parts are the focus of the design process, and the remainder of the design is tailored to accommodate the design of these critical parts [Sho83]. Hence, certain virtual machines and abstractions can be constructed. A rapid prototyping method often utilizes BUC, in that it allows for the development of the critical parts early, and for an early assessment of the feasibility of the design. These techniques are generally not recommended alone, rather if they are to be used, they should be only used to investigate the critical parts, followed by a top–down approach for the final design [Sho83]. BUC is appropriate where the elementary units are of primary concern, such as in the development of sets of utility packages. There seems to be a relationship between BUC and reuse–oriented design, in that the focus is on the elementary units, and how these units can be integrated to generate the desired system.

Another technique that has received a lot of attention recently is the paradigm of Object–Oriented Design (OOD). The main idea is that instead of trying to partition the system according to architectural, functional or informational boundaries, the system is structured around objects. Each system module stands for either an object or a group of objects along with their operations in a problem subspace. Objects are extracted from a model of the real world problem that needs to be automated. The application of Object–Oriented design is accompanied by the use of abstract data types. OOD has been influenced by the techniques used in Object–Oriented programming. Broadly speaking, a OOD system could be categorized as such if the following attributes are present[KM90]: (1) objects, (2) object classes, (3) inheritance of properties of one class to its subordinates (4) dynamic binding, or the association of the correct code to be executed at run time, and (5) polymorphism, or the ability of a reference to be bound to more than one class object instance over time.

We need to recognize that Ada is limited in terms of its support of these attributes. More specifically, objects and classes are directly supported by the language constructs and its design rationale. Objects are the run–time elements that depict the real–world entities. Classes are sets of possible objects. It can be advocated that generics offer support for classes. The rest of the properties are not directly or implicitly supported by the Ada rationale.

Ada is predominantly an "encapsulation language" but as was pointed out maintains a certain number of characteristics that enable pragmatic Object–Oriented design[Boo86]. In most cases, a set of fundamental system objects that model a problem are identified. Subsequently, their operations, interfaces, interactions and structures are designed.

In contrast with the previous two approaches, this methodology tends to be more "localized" as far as changes are concerned, since extensive use of abstract data types and state machines is advocated. Constructs such as the Ada package make this kind of design more feasible, as localized data structures, invisible types and their implementations are supplied. Generics are another means for facilitating OOD, by furnishing parameterized object templates.

Many design techniques borrow from several of the classes. The concepts that are borrowed and how they are combined distinguish the variants. For instance, incorporation of a reuse oriented process into an object–oriented design paradigm will also affect the resulting process model, as the designer will be concerned with both the objects that are modeled and with the objects that are stored within the repository. Therefore, when assessing design, one has to consider how the techniques are combined.

3   Model of Ada Components

Our analysis is performed on modules of varying granularity. The term module is overloaded in the literature. Myers in [Mye78] proposes that a system module (component) is a set of executable statements that should satisfy the following criteria:

- it is a closed subroutine

- it has the potential to be called from any other module in the program

- it has the potential of being independently compiled

The last two requirements are more suggestive than defining. Hammons in [HD84] defines Ada modules as non–nested subprograms. However, subprograms encapsulated in package bodies are not characterized as modules. The claim is that since such subprograms can not be called from any random point in the system (except the package body scope), they do not qualify as modules. Tasks do not qualify either.

Ada provides a wealth of programming constructs and it is generally difficult to identify one of them as the general modularization mechanism. Packages primarily accommodate the need for encapsulation and abstraction. The main routine that "drives" an Ada system is a subprogram.

A flexible scheme, called Ada data Binding and Call tree components, (*ABCs*) allowing entities ranging from subprograms to packages and subsystems to participate in the analysis is proposed here. At the first level, subprograms (functions and procedures), as well as task entry bodies, constitute the system components. A substantially different view of a system under analysis could be taken by recognizing there is no need for units within a package to be analyzed separately. That would change the formulation of the participating *ABC*s. There are occasions where packages implement abstract data types and are required to be seen as unique (integrated) components. The same applies in the case of nested functions, subprograms as well as tasking constructs encapsulated either in subprograms or packages. Thus, a mix of higher level components (packages) with elementary ones (procedures, functions) may be obtained, providing a more diversified view of the system.

In our scheme, at the second level certain components of the first level are viewed as integrated entities. For instance, one could view the subprograms encapsulated in a package as making up a unique and indivisible system component. On the other hand, one may view nested subprograms not as separate components, but rather as parts of their incorporated construct. This grouping can be continued at higher levels by combining the lower level *ABC*s to form subsystems and systems.

*ABC*s of the first level are the essential building blocks of the language and of our analysis. The ability to express second level *ABC*s (and higher) is supported by the tools. The default analysis is carried out on the first level components unless otherwise requested. Naturally, higher level *ABC*s build on knowledge acquired by the analysis performed at lower levels.

It should be noted that a package consisting of only declarations is not considered an *ABC*. The *ABC*s were chosen to be executable segments or groups of segments. Therefore, a package specification containing only declarations will not be depicted as a separate *ABC* interacting with other *ABC*s. However, the interaction of the *ABC*s through a common package specification will be included in the analysis.

4 Description of the Tools

4.1 Functionality

The Data Binding Tool (dbt) is based on the data binding family of metrics. Data bindings were used in [BT75] to determine data visibility. In this study, they are used to measure interaction among system components (*ABC*s). A data binding between two segments (where segment is a set of executable statements) is defined as follows:

- Let α and β be two program segments and variable γ global to α and β. If γ is assigned by segment α and accessed by β then there exists a data binding between these two program segments denoted by the triplet (α, γ, β).

This triplet indicates a flow of information from the first segment to the second. It is also possible, that another binding of the reverse type of flow exists (i.e. (β, γ', α) where γ' is a global assigned by the second segment and referenced (accessed) by the first). Intra–segment bindings are not considered to be of interest since they portray flow internal to the segment (i.e. (α, x, α) does not count as an extra data binding).

The definition of Data Bindings, in light of the ABC scheme, is modified. The following definitions are used to identify bindings in an Ada system.

Definition I:

There exists a Data Binding (abc_i,x,abc_j) between two ABCs abc_i, abc_j if:

- abc_i calls abc_j.

- object x is part of the abc_j interface (either an element of the formal parameter list or a returned function value).

- one of the abc_i,abc_j assigns x and the other references it.

Note that in Ada, the mode of the formal parameter x directs the binding. If it is an *IN* parameter type then the binding (abc_i,x,abc_j) is established. If it is an *OUT* then the reverse direction binding is set up (ie. (abc_j,x,abc_i)). In the case of *INOUT*, either binding depending of who assigns and who references could be established.

Definition II:

There exists a Data Binding (abc_i,x,abc_j) between two ABCs abc_i, abc_j if:

- Object's x scope extends to both abc_i and abc_j.

- abc_i assigns to x and abc_j references it.

Scope represents the set of system variables that are accessible by both ABCs. Some of these objects may be local to the ABCs library units. They may also be objects belonging in different library units than those of the ABCs, but are visible by being *WITH*ed.

The tool basically performs the following operations:

- Identification of Ada data Binding and Call Tree components (*ABCs*).

- Computation of Data Bindings among *ABCs*.

- Perform a Clustering Analysis Algorithm.

The first two functions are performed simultaneously while the source of an Ada system is being parsed. Their final output consists of a matrix (data binding matrix) whose size is equal to the number of identified *ABCs*. Every element in this matrix corresponds to the total number of unidirectional bindings that are established between any possible pairs of *ABCs*. The matrix is symmetric with elements in the diagonal equal to zero. A short discussion on how bindings are computed is presented in a subsequent section.

The last operation is computationally independent of the other two. After the derivation of the number of data binding among components, this data is fed into a clustering algorithm. The goal of the cluster algorithm is to group relevant components in terms of data flow. The clustering process works in a bottom–up fashion. It proceeds in a series of successive fusions of the n objects into clusters in order to reduce the size of the matrix. The grouped objects are those with the greatest number of bindings (those objects whose strength of coupling is the highest). In every iteration of the algorithm new clusters are created by fusing the groups and objects with the greatest amount of data binding between them. At the very end, all clusters coalesce into a single group that corresponds to the software system. A more detailed description of the process can be found in [DB90].

The Call Tree Tool (**ctt**) is designed to provide a graphical abstraction of the structure of an Ada system, as well as to provide mechanisms for studying the system's inter-module control flow. Call trees are a common mechanism for documenting a system, as they provide view of component interaction that hides the intra–module details. The **ctt** generated call tree shows all potential control flows among components in a system. The component of analysis is the *ABC* that was defined above. The call tree dependencies are defined as follows:

<u>Definition III:</u>

There exists an *invocation dependency* from **abc_i** to **abc_j** if either of the following is true:

- **abc_i** contains a call to a subprogram in **abc_j**

- **abc_i** contains an entry call to a task in **abc_j**

The call tree is defined from the invocation dependencies of the lowest (sub-program) level *ABC*s as follows:

- If abc_i has an invocation dependency to abc_j, then a branch containing abc_j is added to the call tree of abc_i, and the call tree of abc_j is appended to this branch.

- If abc_i is invoked recursively (either directly or indirectly), then the invocation of abc_i appears in its call tree with a recursive mark, and the recursive subtree is then pruned from the tree.

- Package level dependencies are determined by compressing the tree to depict only the inter–package invocations.

- Higher level dependencies are determined by compressing the tree according to user defined groupings.

Task entries are counted and depicted in the tree in the same manner as subprogram calls, although each is identified as an entry rather than a call. Similarly, tasks are depicted much like packages (i.e. as a collection of entries, identified as a task).

Once the tree has been generated, a variety of analyses can be performed on it, from analysis of the average depth of invocation to analysis of how this depth varies across several invocations of one component. The following measures are provided: (1) maximum depth of invocation, (2) average depth of invocation, (3) fan–in/fan–out. Counts of potential use of a component within a system are generated if a main procedure has been identified. A comparison of the call tree relationship between *ABC*s with the package structure relationship provides insight into the quality of the design.

The call tree as defined above can grow quite large and thus become difficult to analyze. An alternate representation is to provide a graph where each vertex represents an *ABC*, and each edge corresponds to a transfer of control between *ABC*s. With this representation the size is limited to the number of *ABC*s, as is the case with the **dbt**. If it is assumed that control will be returned to the invoking *ABC*, the edges can be considered to be bi-directional. This provides a representation of the control flow of a program by a symmetric matrix with a zero diagonal that can then be analyzed with the same clustering principles as are used by the dbt.

The **ctt** performs the following operations:

- generation of the call tree

- computation of counts of component usage

- control flow analyses

4.2   An Example

A small example is shown below. The package **EXAMPLE** contains 4 subprograms, **BAR**, **COO**, **FOO** and **ZOO**. **ZOO** is the entry point for the package.

```
package        EXAMPLE is
               procedure BAR(X : in INTEGER);
               function COO(Y : in INTEGER) return INTEGER;
               procedure FOO(Z : in INTEGER);
               procedure ZOO ;
        end EXAMPLE;
        package body EXAMPLE is
               A, B, D   : INTEGER;
               C         : INTEGER :=0;
               procedure BAR(X : in INTEGER) is
               begin
                          C := X + B;
               end BAR;
               function COO(Y : in INTEGER) return INTEGER is
                          TEMP : INTEGER := 0;
               begin
                          TEMP := Y + C;
                          return (TEMP);
               end COO;
               procedure FOO(Z : in INTEGER) is
               begin
                          D := Z;
                          A := COO(D) + C;
                          BAR(A);
               end FOO;
               procedure ZOO is
               begin
                          D := 1;
                          B := 2;
                          FOO(D);
               end ZOO;
        begin
        null;
        end EXAMPLE;
```

According to the definitions, the data bindings found in this piece of code are:
(ZOO,D,FOO), (ZOO,B,BAR), (FOO,A,BAR), (BAR,C,COO), (FOO,D,COO),
(BAR,C,FOO), (FOO,COO,COO). The last of the above bindings is due to a

returned function value. Figure 1 illustrates the clustering and the call tree of the package *ABCs*. COO and FOO are the most tigthly coupled and are clustered first. BAR is grouped next and finally, ZOO comes in to complete the system. The call tree shows COO and BAR as the leaf nodes, since they make no calls. FOO's call tree has two entries, for the COO function and BAR procedure. The call tree for ZOO will have one lower level entry for the FOO procedure, which in turn has entries for COO and BAR.

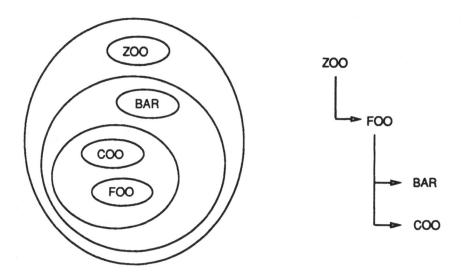

Figure 1: Clustering Structure and Call Tree

4.3 Description of Output

In this section we describe the output of the tools.

The **dbt** produced dendrogram is a tree structured representation of the clustering of system components (*ABCs*). A component in the dendrogram has three properties associated with it:

- its level in the tree

- the subtree to which it belongs

- the number associated with the cluster

The dendrogram produced for the system **String_Utilities_Package** is shown in figure 2. There are nineteen components, four levels, and six unique cluster numbers.

The numbers represent the passes at which components were clustered. The six unique cluster numbers indicate six iterations in the clustering process. The components with the smallest number were clustered during the first pass of the clustering. In general, the number (divided by 100) associated with a cluster at every pass represents the probability that a data binding chosen from the set of bindings that involve an element of the cluster, is not a binding among the components of the cluster. Thus, the components Leading_Nonblank_Position and String_End_Position represent the most tightly bound components in the system, with a .50 probability that a binding to or from either one is to the other.

The number 0 associated with a cluster means that there are no bindings among the elements of the cluster. Since this number occurs only at the highest level, it also means that there is no actual data binding to any other components in the system. In terms of data coupling, these components are completely independent of the system. Some of them may present potential data bindings [HB85]. ctt can isolate which of these *ABCs* are really called from the system (revealing so potential bindings).

At the next pass of the clustering process, two new clusters were created (at 66). At cluster number 71, one more cluster containing String_Equalities and Change_Character_Case_Lower was formulated. Until this point 9 of the 19 components have been clustered into 4 first level independent clusters as figure 2 shows. At 75, two already existing clusters were bound together and another group containing Substitute_Substring and Substitute_Character was created and bound with an existing group with cluster number 66 (note that components carrying out similar computations or performing operations on the same data are grouped in the same cluster). This creates two second level clusters containing 11 components.

The numbers at a particular pass of the clustering process are defined in a different context than the numbers at the prior pass (because of the transformation made), and so numbers do not have a consistent meaning across passes. However, there is a partial ordering based upon bindings, defined among the clusters at the same level. For instance, Leading_Non_Blank_Position and String_End_Position are more tightly bound than Trailing_Nonblank_Position, String_End_Position, and Is_Empty_String.

The subtree to which a component belongs defines its clustering subgroup. For example, the Substring_Position and Character_Position cluster is grouped with the components Substitute_Substring and Substitute_Character, creating a dendrogram subtree. Finally, all the clusters coalesce into one clustering group, representing the entire system.

```
PACKAGE String_Utilities_Package          :> PACKAGE String_Utilities_Package

100                                            :> String_Equalities 2
                                                  Change_Character_Case_Lower
    0                                             Change_Character_Case_Lower
    Fill_String
    Clear_String                             :> String_Length 3
    Next_Blank_Position                         Is_Empty_String
    Is_Numeric_String                           Leading_Nonblank_Position
    Is_Alphabetic_String                        Trailing_Nonblank_Position
    Change_String_Case_Upper
    Change_Character_Case_Upper              :> String_End_Position 1
                                                  Leading_Nonblank_Position
   75
                                             :> Character_Position 2
    66                                            Change_Character_Case_Lower
    Trailing_Nonblank_Position                    Change_Character_Case_Lower
    String_Length
    Is_Empty_String                          :> Substring_Position 3
                                                  Character_Position
    50                                                Change_Character_Case_Lower
    Leading_Nonblank_Position                         Change_Character_Case_Lower
    String_End_Position                           String_Equalities
                                                      Change_Character_Case_Lower
   80                                                 Change_Character_Case_Lower
    Change_String_Case_Lower                      Character_Position
                                                      Change_Character_Case_Lower
    71                                                Change_Character_Case_Lower
    String_Equalities
    Change_Character_Case_Lower              :> Substitute_Character 1
                                                  Character_Position
    75                                                Change_Character_Case_Lower
    Substitute_Substring                              Change_Character_Case_Lower
    Substitute_Character
                                             :> Substitute_Substring 1
    66                                            Substring_Position
    Substring_Position                                Character_Position
    Character_Position                                    Change_Character_Case_Lower
                                                          Change_Character_Case_Lower
                                                      String_Equalities
                                                          Change_Character_Case_Lower
                                                          Change_Character_Case_Lower
                                                      Character_Position
                                                          Change_Character_Case_Lower
                                                          Change_Character_Case_Lower
```

Figure 2: Examples of Tools Output

The ctt outputs a tree showing the potential invocations of all *ABCs* within
a system. The call tree for the package String_Utilities_Package is
shown in figure 2. The *ABCs* that had no fan–in (were not invoked) are
not pictured. The mark ":>" indicates an *ABC* definition. The number
of calls made by the *ABC* is shown next to its definition, and underneath
each definition is the associated call tree. It can be seen that there are
several layers of invocation even for a relatively simple procedure such as
Substitute_Substring. Examination of that call tree shows that for one invocation of Substitute_Substring there are six unique potential invocations

of the leaf node **Change_Character_Case_Lower**. Since no main routine that
drives the program was identified, no counts of system usage were generated.
If a main routine is identified, then the output includes for each *ABC* the
number of times that it was invoked. The number of potential invocations
can be used as a rough measure of the value of the *ABC* to the system [BC88].

5 Design of the Tools

Both tools have been developed using an Ada grammar adapted for Lex
[Les75] and Yacc [Joh75] specifications. The generated compiler is used to
parse the input programs. The challenge was that implementing source code
metrics using Yacc specifications alone is not sufficient for complex structured
languages such as Ada. Intermediate language representations are rather
needed for an effective measurement process. The definitions of bindings
and the handling of procedure and function calls require information about
the use of globals and the association of program entities to correspondent
ABCs. Therefore, a pertinent symbol table for the parsed program needs to
be created.

The main idea behind the design of the tools is that the Ada source program
is transformed into an "intermediate" representation which is comprised of
an interconnected set of tables, called frames. Each lexical scope maintains
such a frame. Every subprogram, nested subprogram and package has its
own frame in the structure of this intermediate representation. Frames are
interconnected according to their scope position in the program. The resulting
structure is memory resident.

Each frame maintains information about the *ABC* it describes. Among other
pieces, it includes the following : the **name** of the elaborated *ABC*, the **type** of
the frame (i.e. subprogram, package, gen_package, function, etc.), a unique
numeric frame identifier **_num_id** that is used by the searching routines of
the tools. Navigation pointers that assist in traversing the structure are
provided such as **subord, superior, next**, etc. For example, **subord** is a
pointer providing access to *ABCs* nested in the current component. Every
frame maintains a list of the formal parameters (wherever applicable) along
with their types. Information about local types is kept in a list (pointed
to by **loc_types**) Types visible from the outside of the frame environment
are pointed by **exp_types**. The handling of local (**loc_vars**) and exported
(**exp_vars**) variables is done similarly. Variables are depicted by an object
name and their type descriptor.

A reasonably sized Ada program consists of a number of packages and subprograms compiled in a predefined order to produce object code. So far, just the description of simple *ABC* frames is given. The "partial" representations of packages and subprograms need to be connected in a way that establishes visibility via WITH and USE clauses. A top level structure that provides the capability to join the structure of the relevant compilation units is used at this point.

Ada's complex structure causes several problems in this phase of the tool design. Some of the more important ones are: separate compilation, renaming, generics and overloading.

The tools accept as input all compilation units described by the name of the files they reside in. Files are opened and closed in the order given in the command line. It is also assumed that files are given in the correct compilation order. The problem that still remains is that of subunits. A rather simple approach to overcome is to preprocess the source and expand the source code of the program with the subunit bodies.

Renaming can be applied to variables, exceptions, subprograms, task entries and packages. Renaming of variables is accommodated by maintaining pointers to the structure of the renamed object. Renaming of subprograms and task entries as well as packages can be handled pretty much the same way. For a renamed *ABC*, a new frame is set up in the system representation of type "renamed" and the field ren_frame points the renamed *ABC*. The cell is created within the scope the renaming was encountered.

Generics are kept in a separate structure where explicit references about the imported types and subprograms are maintained. Since bodies of generics are elaborated before instantiation, a record is maintained of which imported subprograms are invoked in the bodies of the generic. Imported *ABC* frames (i.e. imported functions and subprograms) are designed to be at the same lexical level as that of generic unit in the structure. The instantiation of a generic unit is basically a copy of the frame constructed in the generic form with the imported subprograms and types substituted accordingly. Upon a generic instantiation, bindings among the instantiated *ABC*s and the imported components can be easily computed. Bindings occurring among the instantiated *ABC*s and the rest of the system *ABC*s are calculated whenever needed thereafter.

Overloading is perhaps the most challenging problem to be dealt with in the design of an Ada based tool. Type information collected throughout parsing and stored in the "intermediate representation" of the Ada program is used to disambiguate the invocation of overloaded *ABC*s. A variation of the algorithm proposed in [Cor81] could be used to achieve resolution given the fact that the proposed representation resembles a decorated tree.

Once the intermediate representation is set up, the computation of the data bindings and call trees is performed. Finally, the data bindings and call trees are fed into programs for clustering and analysis. The current version of the tools makes some effort to disambiguate overloaded Ada Components and resolve generic instantiations, but it is rather limited.

6 Static Measures of Design Quality

Design assessment is used to obtain an indication of the product quality, allowing for corrective action to be taken if necessary. Goals of a quality modular design include inter–module independence and intra–module integrity [Mye78]. A well rated design should present a balance of these two major quality factors.

Several guidelines have been proposed on how assess design in a practical manner [JT79]. The Goal/Question/Metric paradigm ($G/Q/M$), as discussed in [BR88], provides such a framework for evaluation of products and processes viewed from different perspectives. The main idea is that in order to evaluate quality factors (goals) we need to refine them into a set of questions. Those questions deal with concepts and ideas on how to achieve these goals. In the next step down, the framework's questions are further decomposed to metrics. Metrics are designed around measurable entities which affect the design process and they may present the means for the automated measurement. Results of metrics can be examined to answer the questions asked and thus, to validate the quality factors at the first level. The validation of the $G/Q/M$ decision tree is carried out in a bottom–up way.

Questions that can be asked for the above mentioned quality factors include the following:

- What is the relative coupling among $ABCs$?

- How cohesive are the involved $ABCs$?

- Are there components with excessive external control flows?

- Are the interfaces defined at the appropriate level of abstraction?

Coupling measures the interaction between different software or design components. By minimizing the interaction among different entities, a greater degree of independence can be achieved. This independence helps to achieve the minimization of the effect of a change. We identify two types of coupling, data coupling and control coupling, dealing with inter–module data flows and control flows, respectively. More specifically, data coupling appears whenever there is a interaction of two or more components via a data element while control coupling (unlike the definition in [Mye78]) can be found if there is transfer of control between two elements. **dbt** has the capability to collect all data and some of the control couplings, and provides a view of the system focused on its coupling, while **ctt** computes all control couplings encountered into a system.

Cohesion measures the relative strength of a component, or how well related the internal objects are to one another. Using the **dbt** and **ctt** we can obtain measures of two types of cohesion, data cohesion and control cohesion. Data cohesion is defined as the degree to which the the internal objects utilize the same data elements (similar to the communication cohesion defined by Myers), while control cohesion measures the relative proximity of the internal objects invocation times (much like Myers' temporal cohesion). Control cohesion can be found in modules that execute predominantly in their locales. The **ctt** detects higher level *ABCs* (package level and above) with control coherence by identifying the location of the *ABCs'* subcomponents in the call tree. If they usually appear together in the tree, one can conclude that the *ABC* exhibits control cohesion. Examination of the system dendrogram can similarly provide indications of the degree of data cohesion in a higher level *ABC*. If the components of a particular *ABC* are clustered together at an early stage, we may conclude that the *ABC* in question is data cohesive. If however, these components are grouped in seperate clusters then the *ABC* does not exhibit data cohesion.

In the design of the components, it is desired that they have a clear, focused purpose. At the lower, or subprogram level, an estimate of the modules' integrity of purpose can be obtained by examination of its fan–out. Those with excessive fan–out values may have too broad a purpose, and perhaps should be further decomposed. **ctt** identifies *ABCs* with fan–out exceeding a threshold, facilitating further investigation. Evaluation of interfaces is essential is assessing design by deriving outliers that use a great number of interface items that lack abstraction and need to be redefined. **dbt** can detect such excessive interfaces (i.e. report *ABCs* that present more interface items that those of a threshold).

The **dbt** and **ctt** provide two complementary measures of coupling within a system, allowing for the analysis of both data coupling and control coupling. By providing the capability to analyze modules of varying granularity, we can determine the interaction of subprograms within a package and the interaction between packages. Taking this one step higher, by grouping packages and procedures into subsystems, one can analyze interaction within and across subsystems. This is how we see these tools being utilized for design assessment.

7 Interpretation of the Trees

Both dendrograms and call trees are used to get an assessment of the strength and the coupling of the various clusters in the system. Dendrograms for instance furnish abstracted information about the data flow of a system. On the other hand, call trees provide a picture of the potential control threads within the system. By analyzing both types of flow among the various $ABCs$ (at all levels), decisions about the design structure are obtained. The interpretation process for each of the trees is outlined below.

Dendrograms can be examined along the following lines:

- For any level n, each of the clusters at level $n - 1$ forms a subsystem usable for building n and higher level functions. If the binding within a cluster is strong, (i.e. the cluster number is small relative to the cluster number of the level n) then this cluster demonstrates close coupling among its components. This cluster would also be evaluated as having loose coupling to the other clusters at that level.

- If however, the binding within a cluster is weak, (i.e., the cluster number is close to the cluster number at level n) then the top level components of this cluster do not demonstrate tight coupling which, means that the cluster does not have high strength. Also its coupling to any other component at that level is weak. This would imply that even simple changes to the system might change the dendrogram structure with regard to the components in this cluster.

- In general, it could be said that for any level n of the dendrogram, the individual components at level n are auxiliary. They use clusters at $n - 1$ as "core" components to build on. They add functionality to the system at level n and may themselves be used as building blocks for level $n + 1$. If the number of siblings at every level of the dendrogram is small, e.g., at most 2, independent of the depth or cluster numbers, then a highly nested structure has been encountered.

Call trees can be interpreted in the following manner:

- If two components are invoked in close proximity throughout the call tree, and the invocation occurs frequently then there exists control coupling among these *ABC*s.

- Examination of the fan–out values of the various *ABC*s is used to detect possible needed abstractions. For example, if the fan-out of a particular *ABC* is much greater that of most other *ABC*s, then it may be the case that the level of abstraction of the design needs to be improved. The call tree can make such discrepancies apparent.

- Identifying *ABC*s that appear at widely varied levels throughout the call tree may indicate unsatisfactory distribution of calls throughout the system. This could be taken as a pointer to an unbalanced design.

When analyzed in isolation, the call tree and dendrogram each provide useful input for assessment of the structural quality of the system. However, taken together, one can readily identify discrepancies between the trees, thereby isolating potential problem areas that may warrant further examination.

8   Analysis Results

The software used in the analysis was supplied by the *RAPID Center Library* project and the Software Engineering Group at the University of Maryland. The *RAPID Center Library* consisted of 13 sets of Ada compilation units making up 15 systems. The University of Maryland test software contains 3 sets of Ada compilation units making up 4 systems. Their sizes range from a few hundred lines to approximately five thousand lines of source code. Reuse is a primary objective for the *RAPID Center*. Therefore, all of their systems were designed and implemented for reuse. All three techniques were used in the development of those systems. Programs provided by the Software Engineering Group were developed using predominantly Object–Oriented design.

Designing with one of the top–down methods produces systems with dendrograms and call trees resembling the functional decomposition that was followed. The components of a module predominately exhibit a high degree of data and control flow amongst themselves, implying that they are data and control cohesive. At a higher level, coupling is minimized, and is used to present the means for interconnection among groups of *ABC*s, providing a clear separation of component functionality. Although an exact match between the trees and the design decomposition was not found, it was possible to identify the general trend followed by the decomposition process. Examination of the leaf modes of the call tree and the other low level nodes shows they are clustered by **dbt** at an earlier phase than the components located near the root of the call tree. To summarize, for the TDD systems, if there is close resemblance between the decomposition and the two trees then the reviewer may have a greater confidence in the quality of the design.

Systems created with the bottom–up techniques tend to have fewer levels of depth and therefore furnish a flatter structure. In most cases, BUC systems start either with partial reuse of already existing systems or with exploratory development of low level functionalities. The remaining parts of the systems are built around these pieces. From the analyzed software, we have seen that such system are in all examined cases of utilitarian purpose. Examination of dendrograms showed that cohesive objects were supplied at the bottom level furnishing groups of these utility *ABC*s. Increased coupling was found among the higher level *ABC*s. Inconsistent structure of the call tree was observed due to variations of the fan–out values. One of the difficulties in designing a system bottom–up is the excessive growth due to unused code. It is worth mentioning that the tools can assist toward this direction. **dbt** clusters at zero level all *ABC*s not involved in data flow, while **ctt** enumerates all actually called components. These two results determine unused subprograms within a system. In two cases, more that half of the source code was found not to be called actually from any other component in the system. Given that typically the size of an Ada system is rather large, eliminating such code would significantly decrease compilation times.

Object–Oriented systems tend to be built as sets of packages located in layers. It is also expected that these layers are relatively flat, in the sense that they do not contain a great deal of language construct nesting (i.e. packages within other packages etc.). The findings for systems designed with this method are much different from those described above. Examination of the trees for such systems reveals low data and control cohesion (of package level *ABC*s). However, inspection of the packages in question showed that they are "conceptually cohesive", meaning that they consists of logically related entities.

The call tree indicates that a procedure call triggers a sequence of procedure calls throughout the system layers. Dendrograms and call trees of such systems group these sequences that carry out semantically related computations through the levels of abstraction. Figure 3 shows such a system with three layers and four objects. Each of them consists of a number of *ABC*s. The encapsulating bubbles indicate the clustered as they were generated by the **dbt**. These clusters go across the borders of the object in the system hierarchy. This indicates that the system was designed around conceptually coherent objects rather than minimization of coupling.

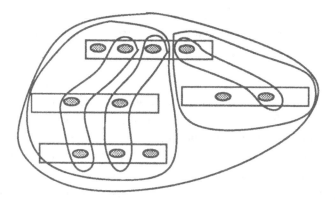

Figure 3: Clustring Across Object Boundaries

The call trees were typically well structured with consistently small fan–out values. Unlike TDD and BUC systems, where there was a clear tendency by **dbt** to cluster low level call tree components before high level *ABCs*, OOD systems show a greater mix in their groups. Both high and low level components were clustered early by **dbt**, implying a more even distribution of the computational effort across the system.

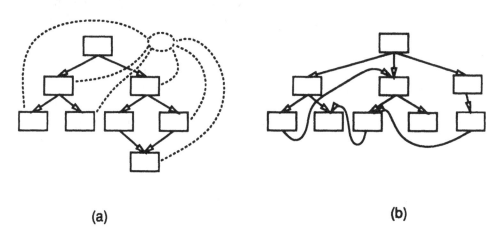

(a)   (b)

Figure 4: Irregular System Structures

On the other hand, a small number of systems gave trees not complying with the followed hierarchical methods (TDD and BUC). Possible explanations for these deviations include:

- Many parameterless calls: To utilize such techniques for carrying out a design may be valid but the **dbt** is unable to establish bindings (due to nonexistent data interfaces). Therefore, the clustering gives altered picture of the system. On the other hand, **ctt** gave a precise picture of such system since its very role is simply that. In such system use of bindings does not reveal the accurate decomposition and there is certain discrepancy between call tress and dendrograms.

- Use of large global data structures: This is a direct result of the large number of implicit data bindings derived from the interaction of the system *ABC*s with a particular data area. Figure 4(a) illustrates such a system. Solid lines indicate control flows among *ABC*s and dashed lines interaction with a global data store. The conformance between the dendrogram and the decomposition of the system was "altered" due to the large number of bindings established through the common data area. It is worth mentioning that the use of **ctt** alone will not detect such a discrepancy.

- Non–abstract interfaces: Their side effect is similar to that of the global data structures. An excessive number of interface items results in many bindings which alter the picture of the system under examination. Many simple bindings may force *ABC*s to cluster much earlier than would be expected. A possible means of alleviating this problem is to adapt to a weighting scheme for the differently typed interface parameters. For the time being, **dbt** has been modified so that it reports components that exceed a threshold number of interface items, but no weighting has been used.

- Poor design performed: As figure 4(b) depicts, there exist calls of components from deeper *ABC*s to shallower ones providing a mix in the procedure/function call ordering. The usefulness of the trees in the understanding of the systems – apart from the fact of verifying the bad design – is very limited.

9 Conclusions

An attempt to assist design assessment using automated tools for static analysis is reported in this study. Definitions of Data Bindings and Call Trees in Ada are given. The examination of **dbt** and **ctt** produced trees for the provided systems reveals insight on how the design techniques were applied in the development process.

An interpretation of the output trees for the various design methodologies is proposed and validated through the examination of several software systems. dbt dendrograms emphasize the data interaction of system components and

are complemented by **ctt** call trees, which allows for the inclusion of parameterless calls and identifies the flow of control. Therefore, it is our belief that
the tools work cooperatively.

Another important benefit of these tools is that they may be used throughout
the design process, so that design can be assessed at an early stage as well as
upon completion.

As future work, we plan to analyze more complex system and systems designed with hybrid methodologies. A weighting scheme for the data bindings
can be adapted to reflect in a more precise manner the established bindings.
Prototypes of the tools were developed as part of the *TAME* [BR88] and the
CARE [BC88] projects at the University of Maryland.

10   Acknowledgment

We are grateful for the guidance and support of Professor Victor R. Basili.

References

[BC88] V. R. Basili and G. Caldiera. Reusing Existing Software. Technical
report, Dept. of Computer Science, Un. of Maryland–CP, October
1988.

[Boo86] G. Booch. Object–Oriented Development. *IEEE Transactions on
Software Engineering*, 12(2), February 1986.

[BR88] V. R. Basili and H. D. Rombach. The TAME Project:Towards
Improvement–Oriented Software Environments. *IEEE Transactions
on Software Engineering*, 14(6), June 1988.

[BT75] V. R. Basili and A. Turner. Iterative enchancement: A practical
technique for software development. *IEEE Transactions on Software
Engineering*, 1(1):390–196, December 1975.

[Cam89] J. Cameron. *JSP & JSD: The Jackson Approach to Software Development.* IEEE Computer Society Press, 1989.

[Cor81] G. Cormack. An Algorithm for the selection of overloaded functions
in Ada. *SIGPLAN Notices*, 16(2):48–52, 1981.

[DB90] A. Delis and V. Basili. Data binding tool: a tool for measurement based ada source reusability and design assessment. Technical report, University of Maryland, Computer Science Dept. CS-TR-2470, May 1990.

[HB85] D. Hutchens and V. R. Basili. System Structure Analysis: Clustering with Data Bindings. *IEEE Transactions on Soft. Engineering*, 11(8), August 1985.

[HD84] C. Hammons and P. Dobbs. Coupling, Cohesion, and Package unity in Ada. *ACM Ada Letters*, IV(6):49–59, 1984.

[Joh75] S. Johnson. Yacc–yet another compiler compiler. Technical report, AT&T Bell Laboratories, 1975.

[JT79] R. W. Jensen and C. C. Tonies. *Software Engineering*. Prentice–Hall, Inc., 1979.

[KM90] T. Korson and J. McGregor. Understanding object–oriented: A unifying paradigm. *Communications of ACM*, 33(9), September 1990.

[Les75] M. Lesk. Lex–a lexical analyzer generator. Technical report, AT&T Bell Laboratories, 1975.

[LMW79] R. C. Linger, H. D. Mills, and B. I. Witt. *Structured Programming: Theory and Practice*. Addison–Wesley, 1979.

[Mye78] G. Myers. *Composite–Structured Design*. Van Nostrand Reinhold Company, 1978.

[Sho83] M. L. Shooman. *Software Engineering: Design, Reliability, and Management*. McGraw–Hill, 1983.

[YC79] E. Yourdon and L. Constantine. *Structured Design*. Prentice–Hall, first edition, 1979.

Part VI: Distribution

Using Ada to Implement the Transaction Mechanism of a Distributed Object-Oriented DBMS

P. SOUPOS, S. GOUTAS

Computer Engineering Dept.
and Computer Technology Institute
University of Patras,
26500 Patras, Greece

1 INTRODUCTION

In the recent years we have seen a substantial influx of ideas in the DBMS technology coming from object-oriented programming languages, logic programming and rule based systems. This stimulated a lot of research effort in the area and a number of object-oriented models and systems have been put forward [Kim89a, Su88, Banc87, Ait86]. In this frame we have developed a distributed object oriented DBMS which facilitates asynchronous communication among object types through a public communication area the blackboard [Tsic87], uses rules and relies on logic for retrieval.

More precisely imperative rules, ie. condition action pairs, are treated as object properties and are used to express explicit constraints [Brod78] and relationships between object types.

Relationships between objects are used to express interaction between objects. Taking advantage of this fact we have used Horn Clauses [Cloc81] as the formalism of the query language since Horn Clauses are based on this notion. By bringing the two together, namely our model and Horn Clauses, one has a very powerful formalism that treats rules in object type definitions, as logic predicates.

As already mentioned communication among object types is accommodated through the blackboard. This means that each object represented by its object class puts information on the blackboard or reads information from it. The context of this communication is data retrieval since we are dealing with a DBMS, or in other words the transaction mechanism is based on the asynchronous communication between the objects of the database. The design and implementation phase of the transaction mechanism of the DBMS were carried out using tools well accepted in application involving synchronization. More specifically we used Petri Nets for the specification and Ada for the implementation. This paper focusing on the use of Ada for such an implementation is yet another demonstration of its potential in applications where its tasking and structuring mechanisms of Ada simplify the implementation process. Indeed such is the case with the implementation of a distributed object oriented DBMS. Each Petri net produced during the design process was easily translated to Ada tasks.

This paper is organized as follows, in the next section we give a short description of the object oriented data model and the data manipulation mechanisms of the DBMS and we conclude with an overview of the Ada implementation of the data manipulation mechanisms.

2 THE DBMS

In the data model we distinguish between two object types. Collection objects which are types with an associated extension and type objects that are types without an associated extension. Object types are organized in an object lattice where there are two kinds of inheritance the ISA inheritance [Mylo80] and partial inheritance [Stro86]. Objects have two kind of properties, attributes and rules. Rules are imperative, ie. condition action pairs, and are used to express explicit constraints [Brod78] and to express relationships between object types. A thorough description of the data model can be found in [Gout90a, Gout90b].

Data manipulation is based on the fact that interaction between objects are expressed with relationships. In order to represent these relationships between objects we have used Horn Clauses [Cloc81] as the formalism of the query language since they are based on this notion. By bringing the two together, namely our model and Horn Clauses, one has a very powerful formalism that treats rules in object type definitions, as logic predicates. The advantage of such an approach is that since rules express constraints all interactions are certain to keep objects in a consistent state always. To put it differently this approach combines imperative and declarative rules. Imperative rules (condition action pairs), as it has already been stated in the preceding sections, allow for the declarative specification of the conditions under which a certain action is to be taken. Declarative rules (Horn Clauses) on the other hand, provide a logical declaration of what the user wants rather than a detailed specification of how the results are to be obtained.

The data manipulation language proposed does not turn the system into a typed logical system. It rather serves the manipulation of data organized according to a model that provides far more than typing, encapsulation. All objects are independent and transactions are carried out through message passing. The objects communicate asynchronously by exchanging messages through the blackboard. This process is transparent and is supervised by the administrator. The administrator is the tool responsible for evaluating queries and for that purpose it produces and receives the messages required for obtaining the answers. An overview of this process can be seen in figure 1.

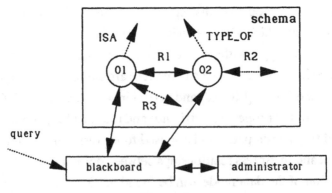

Figure 1.

To be more precise each query is analyzed so as to contain only base predicates. This is achieved using a variation of the connection graph [Hens84, Kowa75] called Modified Connection Graphs (MCG) [Soup90]. The connection graph has been used because it transforms recursion into iteration which in turn enables static determination of data and the modification was made in order to enhance its usage in the query language proposed.

3 THE TRANSACTION MECHANISM

The MCG is constructed by the administrator which in turn traverses it and in the process produces the appropriate messages to the objects in the database. An overview of this process is depicted in figure 2 using Petri Nets a powerful formalism to describe concurrent systems [Genr81], figure 2 is an elaboration on figure 1. The MSG fits well with the overall concept of independence and asynchronous communication between objects since it enables the separate evaluation of predicates at individual object types and the incorporation of the intermediate results into the evaluating process. The evaluation of logic queries using the MSG is discussed in detail in [Soup90].

The object types, the blackboard and the administrator, as can be seen in figure 2, contain one or more control processes which represent the activities carried out. They receive messages from the outside and can send messages to the outside. These control processes are implemented as Ada tasks. A type within an object type is an ordinary Ada type and a rule is implemented as a pair of a boolean function and a procedure.

Communication between the objects the blackboard and the administrator is performed using Ada rendezvous. A direct rendezvous between the objects and the administrator on the one side and the blackboard on the other, was not used, because as can be seen in the Petri net specification of the system sending a message to the blackboard is not blocking and the blackboard can receive one or more messages simultaneously. Instead a buffer was associated with the blackboard, so the calling task is released as soon as the message is put into the buffer.

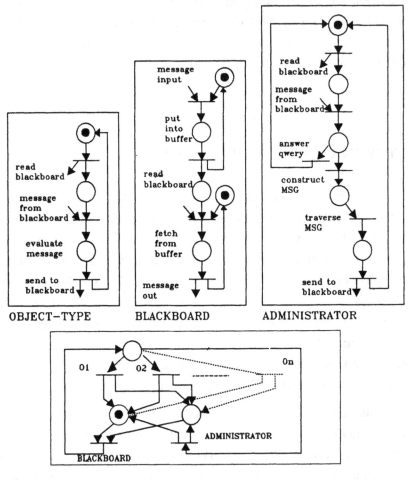

Figure 2.

The blackboard can receive many messages simultaneously. These messages are buffered separately. The sender is blocked while waiting for the message to be buffered and is then released when the message is buffered. It must be noted that the sending object type is not blocked with respect to the receiving object type which may be engaged in the evaluation of another message. This is much more convenient than the object types receiving and sending messages directly because then the sending object type would have to be blocked for longer. Each object type periodically checks whether there is a message on the blackboard addressed to it and if there is, it is received and evaluated using the instances of the particular object type. This answer is then placed on the blackboard.

The procedure that we followed in the implementation of the transaction mechanism comprises of the specification phase where the overall communication scheme is defined using Petri Nets and the translation phase where individual subsystems such as the blackboard and the administrator are translated into Ada packages. The object type subsystem is translated as a generic package since it is the class of all object types which have similar behaviour but involve different data types.

The translation phase is then followed by the gradual introduction of more information such as predicates and actions. Then follows the combination of the individual subsystems by establishing the proper connections between them. The proper connection involves the compatibility of types between connections of different object types with the blackboard and the administrator. Object types exchange "tokens" with the administrator. The "tokens" which are exchanged are predicates and the results of the evaluation of these predicates against the individual object instances.

The administrator sends predicates to the object types and the object types evaluate these predicates against their instances and then they send the results back to the administrator. Here we have an issue of compatibility of data types which can be settled automatically by a procedure which receives tokens of one type and translates them to tokens of another type.

The benefit of using Ada for the implementation which has been outlined above is that it simplifies the transition from the specification to the implementation which in turn can be carried out incrementally by introducing more information gradually. It is due to the rendezvous and the structuring capabilities of Ada that this methodology can be followed.

Acknowledgments

The authors would like to thank BYTE Computer Applications ltd. and especially Elias Spiropoulos for their support in the preparation of this paper.

REFERENCES

[Ait86]   H. Ait-Kasi and R. Nsr, "Logic and Inheritance", Proc. Symposium on Principles of Progr. Lang., St. Petersburg, Florida 1986, pp. 219-227.

[Banc87] F. Bancilhon, T. Biggs, S. Khoshafian and P. Valduriez, "FAD: A Powerful and Simple Database Language", Proc. of the 13th VLDB Conf. Brighton, UK 1987, pp. 97-107.

[Brod78] M. Brodie, "Specification and Verification of Data Base Semantic Integrity", Ph.D. Thesis, Dept. of Comp. Sci., Univ. of Toronto, 1978.

[Cloc81]   W.F. Clocksin and C.S. Mellish, "Programming in Prolog", Springer-Verlag, Berlin 1981. [Genr81] H.J. Genrich and K. Lautenbach, "System modelling with high-level Petri-Nets", Theoretical Computer Science, vol. 13, pp. 109-136, 1981.

[Gout90a]S. Goutas, P. Soupos and D. Christodoulakis, "Rules and Object-Oriented Database Systems", Proc. Future Databases '90 Workshop, Melbourne, Australia, Febr. 1990.

[Gout90b]S. Goutas, "The Incorporation of Imperative Rules in an Object-Oriented Data Model", PhD Thesis, Computer Engineering Dept., Univ. of Patras, Greece, 1990.

[Hens84] L. Hensen and S. Naqvi, "On Compiling Queries in Recursive First-Order Databases", Journal of the ACM, vol. 31, no. 1, Jan. 1984, pp. 47-85.

[Kim89]   "Object-Oriented Concepts, Databases and Applications", W. Kim and F. Lochovsky (Eds.), ACM Press, New York, 1989.

[Kowa75] R. Kowalski, "A Proof Procedure Using Connection Graphs", JACM, vol. 22, no. 4, October 1975, pp. 572-595.

[Mylo80] J. Mylopoulos, P. Bernstein and H.K.T. Wong, "A Language Facility for Designing Database-Intensive Applications", ACM Trans. on Database Syst., vol. 5, no. 2, June 1980, pp. 185-207.

[Soup90] P. Soupos, "Logic in Data Manipulation in an Object-Oriented DBMS", PhD Thesis, Computer Engineering Dept., University of Patras, Greece, 1990.

[Stro86] B. Stroustrup, "The C++ Programming Language", Addison-Welsey, Reading, Ma., 1986.

[Su88] S. Su, V. Krishnamurthy and H. Lam, "An Object-Oriented Semantic Association Model (OSAM*)", A.I. in Industrial Engineering and Manufacturing: Theoretical Issues and Applications, S. Kumara, A. L. Soyster and R. L. Kashayap (eds.), American Institute of Industrial Engineering, 1988.

[Tsic87] D. Tsichritzis, E. Fiume, S. Gibbs and O. Nierstrasz, "KNOs: KNowledge Acquisition, Dissemination and Manipulation Objects", ACM TOIS, vol. 5, no. 1, Jan. 1987, pp. 96-112.

Distributed Systems and Ada – Current Projects and Approaches Comparative Study's[1] Results –

U. BAUMGARTEN

University of Oldenburg
FB 10 (Informatics)
Postfach 2503
D – 2900 Oldenburg
GERMANY
Tel.: +49 441 798 4518
E-mail: baumgarten @ uniol.UUCP

1 INTRODUCTION

In the last decade the propagation and usage of *"Ada"* as well as the knowledge about theory and practice of *"Distributed Systems"* largely evolved. Accordingly the Ada community is clearly interested in programming distributed systems by means of Ada. The distributed execution of Ada programs is the main goal. Investigations about the subject of *Distributed Ada* have been made at Oldenburg University in the Department of Computer Science in 1990 in order to give a survey of this subject and to gain a deeper insight [SPE90].

The objectives of this paper are the

- motivation of the usage of Ada to program distributed systems,
- presentation of the main results of a survey of recent projects and approaches in the area of distributed Ada systems,
- presentation of a classification scheme to describe the approaches resp. systems,
- discussion of connections and relationships to the context of distributed applications and distributed operating systems in general, and the
- presentation of the objectives of the VERITOS distributed operating system project in progress at Oldenburg University and its results concerning the area of distributed Ada.

---

[1]This work has been supported by Competence Center Informatik (CCI), Meppen, Germany

The usage of the general purpose high level programming language Ada for programming distributed applications and distributed systems will be introduced and discussed.

Many projects, approaches, and systems exist in the area of *Distributed Ada²*. The study has been made in order to obtain an overview of current approaches by comparing them, by discussing the pros and cons, and by making evident some future trends. A summary of the study will be given in section 2. A simple model follows which introduces the processing of distributed programs by means of a set of transformations (cf. section 3).

A classification of these approaches is done in the frame of a general model which identifies several aspects of description (cf. section 4). These aspects, which are used as classification criteria, act as dimensions. Some of them are independent from each other, others are not. The list of aspects includes the underlying program model for distributed programs, the choice, definition, and establishment of distribution units, quality-oriented properties, applications, the target architectures, and the approaches' influence on the Ada language itself, its compilers, and its run-time systems. Some of these aspects may be found in [BIS89]. The model was chosen in a way such that all approaches can be classified in a satisfactory manner (cf. section 5). The approaches for *Distributed Ada* are classified along their main characteristics. Their contribution to the construction of distributed systems will be shown. The main results and the quintessence of the study will be presented in section 6 comparing the most interesting current approaches in the area of *Distributed Ada*. In section 7 a comparative description will be given. General conclusions and results from our own research and development in the area of distributed systems, the VERITOS project, will be outlined in the last section (cf. section 8).

2   STUDY'S SUMMARY

The public literature about the subject of *"Distributed Ada"* was the starting point for our study. The work originates from the *'Distributed Ada'* Conference in December 1989 [DAD89] held at Southampton. It comprises about 170 references in literature. The most valuable part with about 110 references was studied in detail. 13 most interesting approaches result, which are documented in depth [SPE90]. These 13 approaches fulfill three requirements, which we stated as necessary preconditions, namely that

1. they allow parallel processing,

---

²The meanings of the terms *project, approach,* and *system* are the following: projects follow approaches and approaches may result in systems or prototypes of systems. Often these three terms will be used synonymously.

2. their implementations are based upon multiprocessor configurations, and

3. the projects are in an advanced state which includes that projects are completed.

In addition ten approaches are regarded in less detail.

In this paper parallel processing is sometimes called abstract distribution.

The distributed execution of Ada programs is the main goal, which all approaches jointly pursue. Nevertheless, a few other aspects are taken into account, namely *(a)* fault tolerance, *(b)* software engineering, and *(c)* Ada 9X refinements and extensions.

Besides performance, *fault tolerance* is one of the most evident advantages of distributed systems over non-distributed systems. Many Ada applications belong to areas, where a high degree of fault tolerance is required. However, the question remains open, whether concepts and mechanisms, which enable the establishing of fault tolerance, should be integrated in the programming language in an explicit manner or should be hidden from application programmers. If concepts and mechanisms are hidden then they are transparent to the programmers. Possible mechanisms are hardware redundancy, software redundancy, or atomic actions for instance.

The necessity of Ada programming support environments must be emphasized for distributed programming. Therefore, *software engineering* methods and tools have to be provided.

The Ada language definition itself [ADA83] demarcates frames for the definition of distribution semantics. The semantics of Ada are not as clear as possible and necessary in many cases. They hamper simple straightforward solutions for distribution. The resulting necessity to modify or enhance Ada's concepts and constructs will be reflected in the Ada 9X requirements process [ADR90].

The results of the study can be found in section 8 for all three topics.

In general research and development in the area of *"Distributed Ada"* are of major interest in our study. Existing compilers and run-time systems, which are commercially available, are less important than research and development.

3 PROCESSING BY TRANSFORMATION

In order to reach distributed execution the preparation of source programs is performed by a set of transformations. The source program can be a single Ada program or a set of related Ada programs. Distributed execution means the execution in a distributed environment.

A distributable application program forms the starting point for the set of transformations. Fundamental parts of these distributable programs are Ada source programs. They will be processed by a sequence of transformations. The result is a program system, which can be executed on a given distributed hardware configuration in a distributed manner.

Figure 1 reflects these transformations. Basic terms are defined. All of these transformations are done by precompilers, compilers, linkers, and loaders. In addition further tools can be used to perform these transformations.

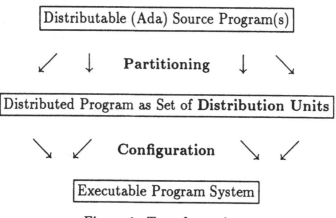

Figure 1: Transformations

First of all, the Ada source program, which defines an abstractly distributed system as a solution of a problem, has to be prepared for distributed execution. Distribution units must be defined. They are characterized by the fact, that each distribution unit has to be handled as a whole. The source program has to be separated. The resulting distribution units are separated from each other. Many Ada program units are eligible in order to be used as distribution units. But other concepts, which do not belong to the repertoire of Ada's concepts, may be introduced as well to define distribution units.

The transformation of separation is called **partitioning**. Its result is a distributed program as a set of distribution units. As far as possible partitioning should be independent of physical hardware configurations. In this sense partitioning does logical distribution.

A **configuration** is described as a mapping between a distributed program as a set of distribution units and a set of physical nodes on which the executable program system is running. The mapping can include replicas of distribution units. The appropriate transformations are called **configuring** transformations. They are used to construct these mappings and to process the representations of distribution units. Configuring transformations take into account the target hardware configuration. They map distribution units onto physical nodes of a distributed hardware configuration. This mapping can be performed in a static or dynamic manner. If it is dynamic then migration of distribution units may be possible. Distribution units may be replicated, for instance, for the purpose of fault tolerance.

4 DESCRIPTION SCHEME

In this section the aspects, which are used to define the classification criteria, will be sketched shortly. Descriptions of projects, approaches, and systems will be done in accordance with these aspects. The aspects are grouped into two major parts. Functionality predominates the first part which includes the aspects of the program model and the characteristics of units for building distributed programs.

The first part describes these aspects. The second part includes further aspects which extend functionality or enable it.

Functionality-related Aspects

First of all, the aspect concerning the underlying **model for distributed programs** will be discussed. A distributed program can be modeled following at least four categories.

1. It can be modeled as a single Ada program; distribution is transparent at the program level.
2. The distributed program can be seen as a collection of self-reliant Ada programs which are independent of each other.
3. In addition, these programs may be related to each other. Communication mechanisms of the underlying operating system or of the communication system are examples.
4. A separate model for distributed programs may be used defining functional properties and further properties, if appropriate.

The first and the third categories include most of the known approaches. Accordingly, transformations start with a single Ada program or a set of Ada programs.

A broad spectrum of Ada program **entities** exist which are **eligible** for building **distribution units**. These entities can be selected as possible **partitions**. The granularity of distribution units ranges from whole Ada programs to small units, which can be composite objects like record objects or array objects, simple objects like variables or constants, or parts of composite objects. Tasks can be viewed to be mid-sized distribution units. The upper range within the gamut of granularity – between tasks and whole programs – is covered by virtual nodes. On the one hand the size of a virtual node can extend to an entire programs. On the other hand the size can extend to single tasks or simple packages.

An early result of the study is evident. The larger the distribution units are the smaller the amount of work for their implementation can be. This general proposition holds with respect to the granularity of distribution units.

A great number of possible **definitions for distribution units** exist. Ada concepts – like tasks or library units – can be used to define distribution units implicitly. Otherwise they may be defined explicitly, for example by means of Ada language modifications, additional pragmas or separate languages.

Distribution units can be **established** resp. enforced in an implicit way or an explicit way in analogy to their definition. In case of implicit enforcement the mappings between distribution units and logical or physical nodes (computers, processors) may be transparent to a programmer of distributed Ada programs. They can be performed by compilers supported by language run-time systems, underlying operating systems, and communication systems. In case of explicit enforcement the configurations may be defined by means of Ada language extensions language or by means of a separate specification language. Other solutions are possible and known.

Further Aspects

Other properties are of great relevance as well. **Quality-oriented** properties may evolve from the area of dependability – with availability, fault tolerance and security as important topics – or from the area of real-time applications. The importance of these properties will grow in the near future. This study reports on investigations as to which extent current approaches support these quality-oriented properties (cf. the results in section 8).

Theoretically the kind of **applications**, for which a distributed Ada approach will be used, plays an important role. Applications influence the efforts spent for development and implementation of systems. Expressiveness and generality of approaches will be dependent of applications. In many cases specialized applications in the area of embedded systems lead to simple and effective but very restrictive solutions. Projects which provide solutions for general purpose applications have to solve many problems. Among these problems are the implementation of remote operations – like remote rendezvous or remote procedure calls. A problem is termination of tasks which are dependent of other tasks and which are executed on different nodes too. The absence of a clear semantic model of distribution is hampering.

Surprisingly we couldn't find characteristic applications which went beyond simple explanatory ones (cf. section 8) in the literature.

The **target architecture** for the distributed execution of Ada programs plays a predominant role with each approach. It strongly influences the design and implementation decisions. Every implementation relies heavily upon the underlying hardware architecture and software architecture. The hardware configuration may consist of loosely-coupled or of tightly-coupled multiprocessors or of processors (single processor systems or multiprocessor systems) in a local area network. The approaches support different storage models, like distributed memory, shared memory or global virtual memory. They use various communication models like message passing or remote operations. Host architectures, for example the development or the programming environment as known from software engineering, do not play an important role as compared to target architectures. They are neglected in this context.

Each project has its own **influence** on the **Ada language** itself, its **compilers**, and its **run-time systems**. The language remains unmodified. Its concepts and characteristics are not changed. But several limitations restrict the definition of distribution units. A remarkable advantage of this approach is that existing compilers can be used without any changes. The Ada language run-time system has to be modified or extended with many projects. This is necessary in contrast to the persistence of the compilers. New features have to be integrated into the run-time system especially from the area of communication in distributed systems.

The aspects mentioned above provide a useful model of dimensions, which will be used in order to describe and classify most approaches in the area of *"Distributed Ada"*. The descriptions will be completed by **state of the art** of the projects.

5 CLASSIFICATION OF APPROACHES

The approaches can be classified according to the dimensions mentioned in the section above. The result is shown in figure 2.

The systems belong to class 1 if partitioning and configuration is completely transparent to the application. The Ada source program reflects the solution of a problem just from the application programmer's point of view. The solution is abstractly distributed. Physical distribution is not visible at this level. Partitioning and configuration of programs are left to the compilers and to the run-time systems. Ada tasks are preferred as distribution units. The

Class 1	Ada systems with transparent partitioning and configuration	NYU Ada/Ed
		MUMS
		Encore
		Honeywell
		Source Translation
		TI-MPAR
Class 2	Ada systems with explicit partitioning in agreement with Ada language concepts (conform partitioning)	DIADEM
		ASPECT-YDA
		Michigan Ada
		SD-Ada
		Systeam
Class 3	Ada systems with concepts being not conform to the language and with explicit partitioning	DARK
		Alsys Transputer
		PULSE
		Chorus
		RTAda/OS
		FGAN Wachtberg

Figure 2: Classification of approaches (cf. next section for references)

Honeywell distributed Ada system plays a special role which will be explained later.

Partitioning is done in an explicit manner in those systems which belong to class 2. **Virtual nodes** [VOZ89] play the predominant role for distribution units in this class. They are oriented towards Ada library units. Application programs are specified as sets of cooperating virtual nodes.

Further concepts of partitioning and communication will be used in addition to the concepts of Ada for those projects which belongs to class 3. Partitioning is done explicitly by application programmers. Distribution units are entire Ada programs. These programs can cooperate by means of interface modules which, among other things, provide facilities for communication.

6 CHARACTERIZATION OF APPROACHES

In this section a short characterization will be given of the approaches mentioned above. A few key words are presented. This characterization extends and explains the classification of the approaches. Projects are listed according to the sequence in figure 2.

NYU Ada/Ed [DEW89]: Ada system for specialized IBM RP3 multiprocessor, memory architecture with shared and local memory, done at New York University, USA.

MUMS [ARD89]: multiprocessor implementation for sets of processor pairs (one processor for program execution and one for communication) interconnected by a communication system, shared virtual memory architecture, done at Lund University, Sweden.

Encore Multimax [RIC89]: tightly-coupled symmetric multiprocessor implementation, done by Encore, UK.

Honeywell Distributed Ada [JHA89] [EIH89]: explicit specification of partitions and configurations by means of an additional language called APPL (Ada Program Partitioning Language), distinction between application programming and distribution, flexibility with respect to the selection of distribution units, general with respect to target architectures, done by Honeywell, USA.

Source Translation [BIS87]: tools for transforming Ada programs at a source level, implementation for transputer configurations, done at Southampton University, UK.

TI-MPAR [LIN89]: multiprocessor implementation for TI-V1750A processors, done by Texas Instruments, USA.

DIADEM [MOR88]: one of the first projects in *"Distributed Ada"*, outrider favouring virtual nodes, providing many tools, followed by the DRAGON project, supported by European Community.

ASPECT-YDA [HUT89]: virtual nodes, integration of fault tolerance, done at York University, UK.

Michigan Distributed Ada [KRI89]: favouring virtual nodes, specification by means of pragmas, configuration and placing in an abstract manner, processing by means of a precompiler, done at Michigan University, USA.

SD-Ada Multiprocessor System [CHO89]: hardware configuration with tightly-coupled specialized processors, done by SD Scicon, Germany.

Systeam [JAN88]: compiler extension in sense of virtual nodes, by Systeam Corporation, Germany.

DARK Projekt [SCO90] [BAM89]: Distributed Ada Real-Time Kernel with its own process model intended for real-time applications, done at Carnegie Mellon University, USA.

Alsys Transputer Ada [DOB89]: Ada system for transputers supported by means of occam communication concepts, by Alsys, UK.

PULSE [KEE85]: Ada-oriented operating system with communication supported by buffer tasks, done at the University of York, UK.

Chorus [GUI89]: distributed operating system kernel usable for Ada with applications in the area of avionics, by Chorus Systèmes, France.

RTAda/OS [RAB89]: flexible Ada system including operating system for embedded systems, by Ready Systems, USA.

FGAN [GRU88]: tools to support distributed Ada programming, done at Wachtberg, Germany.

7 COMPARATIVE DESCRIPTION

The projects can be compared with respect to four aspects, which result from out study. These are the following. The first is the underlying target architecture. The second is the amount and kind of work, which is demanded from the application programmer. The decisions, which are in the responsibility of the programmer, are stated. The third are the potentialities of distribution units. The last is the degree of tailoring of target hardware architectures, software architectures, run-time systems, compilers, or the language Ada itself for distributed execution of Ada programs.

A distinction of systems can be made between loosely and tightly-coupled systems with regard to *target hardware configuration*. The distinction is summarized in figure 3. Specific characteristics cannot be derived for the classes. Systems which are based upon local area networks (LANs) and systems which are connected with high speed communication systems (like transputers) are examples for loosely-coupled systems. Most of the approaches support at least LAN configurations. Tightly-coupled systems include shared memory which is physically present. Otherwise shared memory may be emulated by means of the operating system. With MUMS, for example, the shared memory abstraction is provided by the operating system.

The *amount and kind of work* demanded from the application programmer varies in a broad spectrum from nothing at all to very much. This can be seen in figure 4.

On the one hand nothing must or can be specified by the application programmer. He isn't responsible for any decision with respect to distribution. Class 1 approaches show this absence of responsibility, because partitioning and configuration are transparent. On the other hand the programmer has to separate his solution into distribution units. This holds for all approaches of class 3. The relation to the classes 3 or 1 divides those systems which belong to class 2. A valuable degree of distribution will be reached within the projects DIA and AYD by means of elaborate specifications. In contrast, the projects MIC and SDA allow the specification of distributed programs by means of pragmas in a way which is very close to a pure Ada solution. All

Project	loosely-coupled		tightly-coupled				Cl.
	LAN	high speed	really existing homog.	really existing heterog.	emulated homog.	emulated heterog.	
NYU						⊗	1
MUM					⊗		1
ENC			⊗				1
HON	⊗						1
DIA	⊗						2
AYD	⊗						2
MIC	⊗	⊗					2
SDA				⊗			2
DAR	⊗						3
ALS		⊗					3
PUL	⊗						3
CHO	⊗						3
RTA	⊗	⊗	⊗	⊗			3

Abbreviations: NYA: NUY Ada/Ed, MUM: MUMS, ENC: Encore Multimax; HON: Honeywell Distributed Ada; DIA: DIADEM; AYD: ASPECT - YDA; MIC: Michigan Distributed Ada; SDA: SD-Ada Multiprocessor System; DAR: DARK Projekt; ALS: Alsys Transputer Ada; PUL: PULSE; CHO: Chorus; RTA: RTAda/OS.

Figure 3: Hardware configuration

projects in class 3 follow the multiple programs approach as can be seen in figure 4. All other projects favour the single program approach. Only a few extensions are applied.

The Honeywell distributed Ada approach plays a slightly different role. This approach is classified as a class 1 system with transparent partitioning and configuration. This is true from the application programmer's point of view. Nevertheless, both partitioning and configuration can explicitly be done by means of the APPL (Ada Program Partitioning Language). Default specifications are used if no APPL specification is given. Therefore, the programmer's responsibility can be very small. Otherwise very detailed specifications can be made. In this case a distribution programmer is responsible for many decisions, which are related to distribution.

In each class characteristic *distribution units* can be found. In class 1 these

Project	What is demanded? What is the programmer responsible for?					Cl.
	single program				multiple progs	
	Nothing	Something			All	
		Few	Some	Much		
NYU	⊗					1
MUM	⊗					1
ENC	⊗					1
HON		⊗	⊗	⊗		1
DIA				⊗		2
AYD				⊗		2
MIC		⊗				2
SDA		⊗				2
DAR					⊗	3
ALS					⊗	3
PUL					⊗	3
CHO					⊗	3
RTA					⊗	3

Abbreviations: NYA: NUY Ada/Ed; MUM: MUMS; ENC: Encore Multimax; HON: Honeywell Distributed Ada; DIA: DIADEM; AYD: ASPECT - YDA; MIC: Michigan Distributed Ada; SDA: SD-Ada Multiprocessor System; DAR: DARK Projekt; ALS: Alsys Transputer Ada; PUL: PULSE; CHO: Chorus; RTA: RTAda/OS.

Figure 4: Responsibility of application programmers

are primarily tasks. Honeywell's Ada is an exception too. It allows a broad range of units eligible for distribution. In class 2 virtual nodes are predominant. They are closely related to Ada library units and sets of library units. Several kinds of virtual nodes exist depending on the approach. The distribution units are complete Ada programs in those systems which belong to class 3.

The *tailoring* of approaches can be described as follows. As examples a few approaches are picked up from the study illustrating the way of tailoring. Ada systems and Ada applications may be tailored in order to use

- specialized hardware architectures for special purposes like embedded systems or other real-time applications (Distributed Ada Real-Time Kernel DARK, Alsys Transputer Ada),

- multiprocessor systems, which are not generally distributed systems, with different storage models and various task execution models (MUMS, Encore, NYU Ada/Ed), or
- existing conventional hardware and software systems (Chorus, Transputer).

An Ada application may tailored with respect to the model of partitioning. Pre-partitioning and post-partitioning define to alternatives. The virtual node approaches support pre-partitioning because systems have to be partitioned before the transformations be performed. Virtual nodes are defined like Ada library units. Several restrictions are applied to their structure and interference (Michican Ada, DIADEM, York Distributed Ada). Restrictions which are applied in the Honeywell system are based on considerations about the efficiency of implementations.

The Ada language itself [ADA83] can be tailored for distributed applications with explicitly defined and established distribution. Some requirements which concern distribution are collected in [TAY89]. They are integrated partially in the Ada 9X requirements document [ADA90]. [GAR90] offers a possible solution, which fulfills these requirements.

8 CONCLUSIONS

Some results of the study have been presented in the previous sections. A model for the description of the approaches has been developed (cf. section 4). The classification which is outlined in section 5 is very rigorous but expressive. Systems and approaches of class 3 can not be favoured by application programmers. They are interested in abstractly distributed solutions of problems. They do not want to know the details of hardware configurations. These programmers should use the approaches of the classes 1 and 2.

In our opinion the *best solution* for these programmers should be a class 1 solution, because partitioning and configuration is transparent. But the approaches in class 1 suffer from two general deficiencies. Firstly, most of them support only special hardware configurations (i.e. tightly-coupled multiprocessor systems). Secondly, in most cases tasks are the only eligible distribution units. Both deficiencies are obvious. The amount of work, which is to be done for implementation, is reduced. Vice versa class 1 systems are hard to implement without these restrictions. In this case different hardware configurations and many kinds of distribution units have to be implemented. In addition partitioning and configuration have to be done automatically by means of compiler and run-time system. This task seems to be very hard especially if no restrictions are applied. A difficult question arises. Can these tools produce optimal solutions for partitioning and configuration in an automatic way? In this situation pragmatic approaches involve programmers – i.e. distribution programmers – in the task of performing partitioning and configuration. This bridges the gap between approaches of class 1 and those of class 2. Virtual nodes are very close to library units, which have to be specified for a well-structured solution anyway. Therefore, the explicit specification of virtual nodes requires only small overhead. In this sense the additional expenditure can be kept small. A special opinion may even prefer this solution. This opinion says, that the application programmers (and not the transformation system) have the best knowledge for making the best decisions concerning distribution.

Concepts and mechanisms in the area of fault tolerance fall short of expectations in the evaluation. Only a few substantial results can be found though distributed systems stipulate the progress in this area. Most publications express only intentions or collect requirements. Shortcomings of Ada may be the reason. The implementation and usage of mechanisms of fault tolerance often belongs to the programmer's responsibility. Redundancy mechanisms are the only provisions for fault-tolerant executions. Details can be found in [KNI87] [KNI88] [ALV89] [HUT89].

The area of real-time applications accompanies distribution. But real-time requirements are directed mainly to Ada in general (for instance task scheduling, asynchronous communication and asynchronous transfer of control). Only a few hints for solutions can be found with respect to this topic.

But most of all we are astonished by the absence of typical and characteristic *distributed applications*. Only simple and illustrative examples are found in the literature.

Many projects outline requirements for software engineering support for programming distributed Ada systems. They declare their necessity. Many tools are provided, but most of them are closely related to the approaches they are belonging to. In this context design methods and higher levels of abstraction, for instance functional programming and object-oriented methods are requested. DRAGON [MAI89] and HOOD [GIO90] point out solutions in this direction. Further contributions, especially with respect to operating systems, can be expected from the PCEE project [BUR89] in a few years.

Class 1 solutions should be best suited with respect to future developments in distributed systems and distributed execution of Ada programs. They can be extended by class 2 facilities, where detailed knowledge of distribution is present at the application level. Nevertheless, future distributed systems will be language oriented, facing the programmer with abstractly distributed systems using concepts from the area of advanced programming languages. Most of the burden of partitioning and configuration must be taken away from the programmer. Compilers, run-time systems and distributed operating systems jointly have to solve all of these tasks. The languages have to support adequate concepts. We have made our own experience in this direction in the VERITOS project which is primarily influenced by the construction of distributed operating systems. Results of the VERITOS project [BAU90], whose objectives are defined in the area of general purpose distributed systems and distributed operating systems, can be taken into consideration. They are useful both in the area of distributed Ada and in the area of distributed systems in general. For example, the component concepts and component structures, as defined in the VERITOS project, support long-living reliable distributed applications. The definition of finely gradated static and dynamic components will be allowed.

The evaluation of the approaches yields hints for future usage of Ada in the area of distributed systems. These hints are guided by pragmatic aspects. The evaluation includes stimulations for further development of languages for distributed systems (e.g. Ada) though the study was not made in direct connection with the refinement of Ada.
Nevertheless, the integration of distribution in Ada 9X is of great importance. The final report on the Ada 9X requirements activities [ADR90] reflects this subject in two requirements. These are very general and allow many different solutions. Both the single program approach and the multiple programs approach are possible.

ACKNOWLEDGEMENTS

The work, which has been done to produce the results of the study, has been performed by U. Baumgarten, L. Bölke, C. Eckert, M. Lange, D. Marek, R. Radermacher, K. Röhrs and P.P. Spies supported by the Competence Center Informatik (CCI), Meppen, Germany.

REFERENCES

[ADA83]   Ada. The Programming Language ADA - Reference Manual. American National Standards Institute, Inc. ANSI/MIL-STD- 1815A-1983, LNCS, 155, Springer-Verlag, 1983, 1983.

[ADA90] unknown. Ada 9x requirements working draft version 3.3. Technical report, Software Engineering Institute, Carnegie Mellon University, Pittsburgh, Pennsylvania 15213, 1990.

[ADR90] *Ada 9X Project Report, Ada 9X Requirements*, Office of the Under Secretary of Defense for Acquisition, Washington, D. C. 20301, December 1990, Carnegie Mellon University, 1990

[ALV89] S. Arévalo and A. Alvarez. Fault Tolerant Distributed Ada. ACM Ada LETTERS, Vol. IX, No. 5, July 1989, pages 54–59, 1989.

[ARD89] A. Ardö and L. Lundberg. The MUMS Multiprocessor Ada Project. In Distributed Ada 1989, Proceedings of the Symposium, 1989.

[BAM89] R. Van Scoy, J. Bamberger, and R. Firth. An Overview of DARK. ACM Ada LETTERS, Vol. IX, No. 7, November 1989, pages 91–101, 1989.

[BAU90] U. Baumgarten. Veritos Distributed Operating System Project - An Overview -. In Proceedings of the Workshop on Computer Architectures to Support Security and Persistence of Information, Bremen, May 1990, 1990.

[BIS87] J.M. Bishop, S.R. Adams, and D.J. Pritchard. Distributing Concurrent Ada Programs by Source Translation. Software Practice & Experience, Volume 17, No.. 12, Dec. 1987, pages 859–884, 1987.

[BIS89] J.M. Bishop and M.J. Hasling. Distributed Ada - an Introduction. In Distributed Ada 1989, Proceedings of the Symposium, pages 3–16, 1989.

[BUR89] A. Burns and C.W. McKay. A Portable Common Execution Environment for Ada. In Proceedings of the Ada-Europe International Conference, Madrid 1989, 1989.

[CHO89] A. Cholerton. Ada for Closely Coupled Multiprocessor Targets. In Proceedings, TRI-Ada'89, David L. Lawrence Convention Center - Pittsburgh, PA, October 23 - 26, 1989.

[DAD89] Distributed Ada 1989, Proceedings of the Symposium, 1989.

[DEW89] R. Dewar, S. Flynn, E. Schonberg, and N. Shulman. Distributed Ada on Shared Memory Multiprocessors. In Distributed Ada 1989, Proceedings of the Symposium, pages 229–241, 1989.

[DOB89] B.J. Dobbing and I.C. Caldwell. A Pragmatic Approach to Distributing Ada for Transputers. In Distributed Ada 1989, Proceedings
of the Symposium, 1989.

[EIH89] G. Eisenhauer and R. Jha. Honeywell Distributed Ada - Implementation. In Distributed Ada 1989, Proceedings of the Symposium,
pages 163–181, 1989.

[GAR90] A.B. Gargaro, S.J. Goldsack, R.A. Volz, and A.J. Wellings. Towards Supporting Distributed Systems in Ada 9X. In Ada: Experiences and Prospects, Proceedings of the Ada-Europe International
Conference, Dublin, 12-14 June 1990, pages 301–323, 1990.

[GIO90] R. Di Giovanni. On the Translation of HOOD into Ada. In Ada:
Experiences and Prospects, Proceedings of the Ada-Europe International Conference, Dublin, 12-14 June 1990, 1990.

[GRU88] W.-J. Grünewald, J. Kutscher, and T. Schell. Ein Arbeitsplatz zur
Programmierung verteilter Systeme in Ada. In Ada-Symposium
1988/ Fa. Strässle, Mannheim, 1988.

[GUI89] M. Guillemont. Chorus: A Support for Distributed and Reconfigurable Ada Software. Technical report, Chorus Systemes, CS/TR-
89.40.2, Presented at the ESA Workshop on Communication Networks and Distributed Operating Systems within the Space Environment, 24-26 October 1989, 1989.

[HUT89] A.D. Hutcheon and A.J. Wellings. The York Distributed Ada Project. In Distributed Ada 1989, Proceedings of the Symposium,
1989.

[JAN88] H.-St. Jansohn. Ada for Distributed Systems. In Ada LETTERS,
A Special Edition from SIGAda, The ACM Special Interest Group
on Ada, Vol. VIII, No. 7, Fall 1988, International Workshop on
Real-Time Ada Issues, Moretonhampstead, Devon, UK, 1-3 June
1988, pages 101–103, 1988.

[JHA89] R. Jha and G. Eisenhauer. Honeywell Distributed Ada - Approach.
In Distributed Ada 1989, Proceedings of the Symposium, pages
141–161, 1989.

[KEE85] D. Keeffe, G.M. Tomlinson, I.C. Wand, and A.J. Wellings.
PULSE:An Ada-based Distributed Operating System, APIC Studies in Data Processing Series. Academic Press, London, UK, 1985.

[KNI87]   J.C. Knight and J.I.A. Urquhart. On the Implementation and Use of Ada on Fault-Tolerant Distributed Systems. IEEE Transactions on Software Engineering, Nr.SE-13(5), pages 553–563, 1987.

[KNI88]   J.C. Knight and M.E. Rouleau. A New Approach To Fault Tolerance In Distributed Ada Programs. In Ada LETTERS, A Special Edition from SIGAda, The ACM Special Interest Group on Ada, Vol. VIII, No. 7, Fall 1988, International Workshop on Real-Time Ada Issues, Moretonhampstead, Devon, UK, 1-3 June 1988, pages 123–126, 1988.

[KRI89]   R.A. Volz, P. Krishnan, and R. Theriault. Distributed Ada - A Case Study. In Distributed Ada 1989, Proceedings of the Symposium, pages 17–59, 1989.

[LIN89]   M. Linnig and D. Forinash. Ada Tasking and Parallel Processors. In Proceedings, TRI-Ada'89, David L. Lawrence Convention Center - Pittsburgh, PA, October 23 - 26, 1989.

[MAI89]   A.D. Maio. DRAGOON: An Ada-based Object Oriented Language for Concurrent, Realtime, Distributed Systems. In Proceedings of the Ada-Europe International Conference, Madrid 1989, 1989.

[MOR88]   C. Atkinson, T. Moreton, and A. Natali. Ada for Distributed Systems. Cambridge University Press, 1988.

[RAB89]   H.M. Rabbie and D.A. Nelson-Gal. An Operating System for Real-Time Ada. In Proceedings, TRI-Ada'89, David L. Lawrence Convention Center - Pittsburgh, PA, October 23 - 26, 1989.

[RIC89]   V.F. Rich. Parallel Ada for Symmetrical Multiprocessors. In Distributed Ada 1989, Proceedings of the Symposium, 1989.

[SCO90]   R. Van Scoy, J. Bamberger, and R. Firth. A Detailed View Of DARK. ACM, Ada LETTERS, Vol. X, No. 6, July/August 1990, pages 68–83, 1990.

[SPE90]   Baumgarten, U., Spies, P.P., *Ansätze zu verteiltem Ada und ihre Beiträge zur Konstruktion von Verteilten Systemen*, Interne Berichte, Fachbereich Informatik, Universität Oldenburg, Bericht SA/90/2, November 1990

[TAY89]   B. Taylor. Distributed Systems in Ada 9X. Ada User, Vol. 10, No. 3, pages 127–131, 1989.

[VOZ89]   R.A. Volz. Virtual Nodes and Units of Distribution for Distributed Ada. In Ada LETTERS, A Special Edition from SIGAda, The ACM Special Interest Group on Ada, Vol. X, No. 4, Spring 1990, Third International Workshop on Real-Time Ada Issues, Nemacolin Woodlands, Farmington, PA, 26-29 June 1989, pages 85–96, 1989.

Reconfigurable Ada Distributed Control System Software

D.C Levy, M.C. Randelhoff, J.L. Tokar[1]

University of Natal,
Durban,
South Africa

ABSTRACT

Distributed computer systems have proven cost effective and are finding increasing application in real-time systems [1,2]. In this project Ada is used to develop a flexible software environment for managing a set of tasks distributed across a network of PC's. The primary goal of this environment is to facilitate the implementation of real-time process control applications. This includes the ability to reconfigure the system without shutdown.

1 INTRODUCTION

An objective of this project is to take advantage of the tools available today to construct a flexible software environment to support process control applications distributed across a network of PC's. Netbios[2][3] is used to provide the necessary interprocessor communications. A number of Netbios emulators are available for local area networks including Ethernet and Arcnet[3]. Use of Netbios will allow flexibility, reusability and reconfigurability for systems across different networks.

---

[1] Dr Tokar is now with Pyrrhus Software, Pittsburgh, USA.

[2] Netbios is a trademark of IBM Corporation

[3] Arcnet is a trademark of Datapoint Corporation

Ada with its emphasis on modular software and reusability, is chosen to implement the communications package which will interface with Netbios. It is also used for the development of the application software which will call upon the communication package to establish and maintain the distributed system.

In this environment, construction of a small scale, low cost, distributed real-time process control applications will be facilitated. The functionality provided by Netbios together with the Ada communications package will permit the system to be reconfigured without shutdown.

2 SYSTEM DEFINITION
2.1 System Assumptions
Process control systems are often implemented on uniprocessors. For example, consider a soft drink bottling plant. The process consists of placing the empty bottles on the line, filling them, capping them, labelling them, and finally crating them. On a uniprocessor, the controlling software would be implemented in the form of multiple tasks.

Uniprocessor systems are being replaced by distributed systems, which have become widely used in industrial control applications for the following reasons [4]:

Faster response: Local processors may be dedicated to particular drives and are thus able to respond very quickly.

Reduction in wiring costs: Industrial sites extend over considerable distances and wiring often accounts for a substantial portion of the cost.

Simpler Development and Maintenance: Code development is easier as distributed software is inherently modular, and local intelligence allows a controller for example to be isolated for maintenance and/or testing.

Fault tolerance: Local intelligence allows degraded operation when central control has failed.

A fundamental question is: What is the granularity of the distribution unit [5]? Natural units of distribution in Ada are packages and tasks. The approach chosen in this project is distribution in terms of functionality.

A process control system may be viewed as a set of functions. Each processor (PC) will be responsible for a particular subset of functions. The collection of PCs will implement the entire system. The distribution of these functions is application dependent. The physical layout of the plant as well as the time dependencies influence how the distribution is done.

Thus because the configuration of the industrial process represented by the nodes is known, the data, the data paths and the required rates of transfer are to a large degree established during the design phase of a particular process control system. The communication system, however, must be capable of supporting whatever configuration is required [6].

2.2 A Layered Communications Interface

Netbios has been chosen as the communications protocol to provide the framework for the data transfer across the network. Netbios provides a high-level programming interface [7]. It operates at the session layer of the ISO model (figure 1). At the ISO application level, an Ada communications interface package has been written to provide the process control package with access to Netbios.

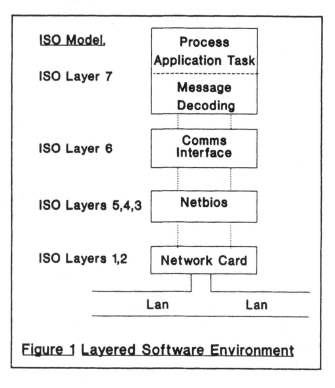

Figure 1 Layered Software Environment

The communications system maintains a table (invisible to the application) of the participating nodes in the system. The application is the process control task at each node. The communications interface will provide the process control task with a message of defined length and format. The process control task must decode the message into the application dependent process variables.

The communications environment must, under the above circumstances, provide facilities to transfer the information along the required data paths. Initially a set of network management primitives must allow an application to announce itself as a node on the network, or later deregister from the network.

Data transfer primitives allow an application to send or receive messages of a predefined format and length to previously identified nodes, with the knowledge that the data will retain its integrity in the transfer process.

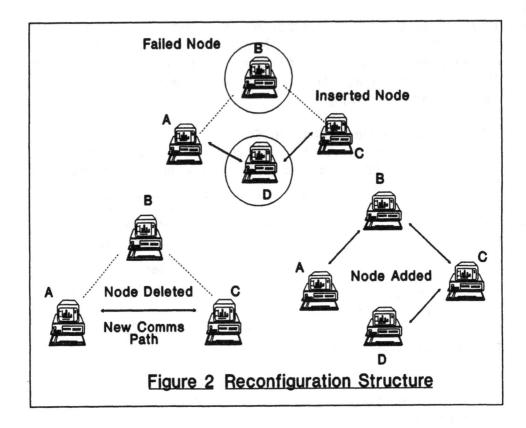

Figure 2 Reconfiguration Structure

Reconfiguration primitives must be provided to allow the system to reconfigure itself (figure 2). This implies the replacing of one processor in the system configuration with another. This could be necessitated by a hardware failure or simply to enable the processor to be serviced. Assuming that an industrial process will never perform exactly as designed, or that alterations might be required, it may often be highly desirable to add a step in the process and consequently alter the control system. It is usually costly to shut down a process and it would be desirable to include this next step while the process is on line. Primitives would have to be provided to allow for a node to be inserted or deleted and consequently to cause other communicating nodes to alter their data paths of their own accord with as little delay and disturbance as possible [8].

3 COMMUNICATIONS PACKAGE

3.1 Netbios Structures

The communications layer comprises three basic functions: peer to peer communication, network reliability testing, and network configuration control. Netbios[9] offers direct peer to peer communication in the form of session support. This requires that both partners have valid names entered into the

Netbios name table. To create a session, one partner listens for the other partner's call. If both the listen and call are successful a session is established. A local session number is associated with this session and is referred to in future communications.

Netbios also offers Datagram support, which provides short messages (up to 256 bytes) and does not have the management overhead associated with session support. It allows the use of the permanent node name as the adapter name and so alleviates the necessity of adding a name, listening and then calling to create a session. Datagram support, however, does not acknowledge successful transfer of information.

Applications issue Netbios commands by zeroing out a 64 byte area of memory to prevent residual data from producing erroneous results. This area of memory is used to construct a Netbios Control Block, which consists of a number of fields containing data relevant to the particular command issued. Once the Control Block is complete the ES:BX register is set to point to the first memory location of the block and an INT 5C interrupt request is generated. Discussion on the Netbios Control Block fields is contained within the appendices.

3.2 Peer to Peer Communication

This is established only for those processes which must exchange data during their normal operation. Two Netbios sessions are created per channel, for each direction of communication. Although the session is bidirectional, the overhead of an additional session for each channel is outweighed by the added complexity required of the controlling software to allow full duplex communication with one session; consequently, the communications package implements two directional sessions for each channel. The receiving end of the session is interrupt driven[10] to maximise the productive use of

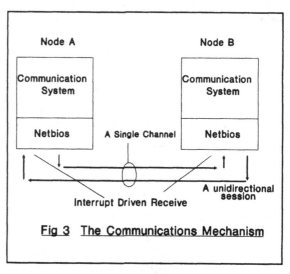

Fig 3 The Communications Mechanism

the processor and to eliminate the overhead and inefficiencies evident in polling (figure 3).

The package resets the network adapter upon initialisation, and then adds the network permanent node name to the Netbios name table. The initialisation routine calls a task that appends a datagram receive command to the Netbios command queue. This datagram facility is used to allow a remote node, that has no existing communications with the host node, to instruct the host node that there is an eligible partner. The communication package responds by listening for the remote node, and then calling it to create the bidirectional channel, using sessions. Netbios will allow a message to be sent to this datagram receive from any other adapter. When a message is successfully received the adapter interrupts the processor and in Ada an interrupt task entry has the highest priority; this will ensure that the communications routine has immediate access to the resources of the microprocessor.

3.3 Data Transfer
When the process tasks are updating critical information the possible interference through an adapter hardware interrupt (generally specifying a successfully received message) must be catered for. The communications interface provides semaphores which protect the system against this [11]. The package allows the application to set a guard while critical information is being updated, and remove it when the process has completed. The guard takes control of the network adapter's interrupt to the processor. The interrupt vector is altered so if the adapter interrupts while the host processor is updating, a new interrupt handler is invoked. This handler sets a flag indicating that an adapter interrupt has occurred. When the guard is released through a call by the application, the original interrupt handler is invoked to process the request.

When the application task instructs the communications facility to initiate a channel with a particular node, the package expects the new partner's permanent node name and alias to be passed as parameters. The package sends a datagram, containing the host's permanent node name, to the pended datagram receive at the remote node. The session is then established. The permanent node name, and the alias that it is known under, are added to a list local to the communications package.

3.4 Communications Failure
If communications with a particular node break down, the package will issue a failure code, specifying the cause of failure, to the calling application procedure. This failure code is based upon that which the underlying protocol, Netbios, returns to the communication package. It is the responsibility of the application program to decide what action to take.

4 APPLICATION TO COMMUNICATION INTERFACE (USER VIEW)
4.1 The Nodes Life Cycle
The communication layer provides primitives which permit the application to access remote nodes and control the network status of the application's host node.

The application is required to initialise itself as a member of the network. The communications system adds the node's network permanent node name to the Netbios name table. The application identifies with whom it wishes to communicate and then calls an initialise_channel routine to establish a bidirectional logical communication channel, passing as parameters the permanent node name of the remote node and an alias that it will use in future references. This is to facilitate programming the process control task. The communications system returns a failure code for any primitive called, indicating the status of the request. The application also has the facility to halt communications with a particular remote node. It

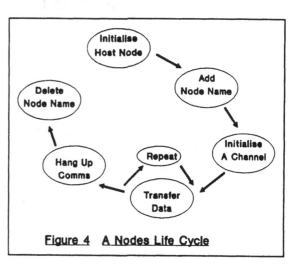

Figure 4   A Nodes Life Cycle

issues a hang_up_communications instruction, passing as parameters the node with which it wishes to terminate communication. When all communication channels are closed the application may then deregister from the network name list. This removes all trace of the node from the system as a whole (figure 4).

4.2 Data Transfer Operations
Data transfer primitives enable the applications running on a number of nodes to exchange information. The application may send or receive a message, of a predefined length, to or from a particular remote processor. The bidirectional communication channel comprises two independent directional channels, which deposit and retrieve data from information 'pools' at both ends (refer to figure 6). Thus the message transferred from Node A to Node B may have a different format and length from that of a message transferred from Node B to Node A. A multi-send routine is provided to send messages to a list of remote processors simultaneously. The receiving end of the bidirectional logical communication channel is interrupt driven. The network adapter issues a hardware interrupt

when it has data to transfer to the host processor. If the adapter interrupts the processor while the processor is updating or retrieving data from the information pool, the old Netbios interrupt vector is redirected and a flag is set until after the completion of the data transactions[11]. The process task issues an instruction to the communications package setting a guard which is released through a similar call when the updating is complete. The communication package restores the original interrupt vector and checks whether an adapter interrupt has occurred. If necessary the Netbios interrupt service routine will be invoked, and the flag will be cleared.

The communication channels are reliable; they will ensure that there is no unauthorised alteration of messages, no duplication or desequencing and no loss of messages [12]. Should this performance be impossible, the communications routine will return an error code expressing the reason for failure.

4.3 Control Operations

Control process primitives enable the application to alter its status in the network as a whole. These primitives are aimed at transforming the communications structure to suit the changed environment, not at directly altering the actual process executing at the remote nodes. The insert_node primitive allows an application to close the logical communication channel already existing between two nodes and reroute those communications through the new node that has just been inserted (refer to figure 5). The responsibility of supplying the two existing nodes, A and B, with their required data, to

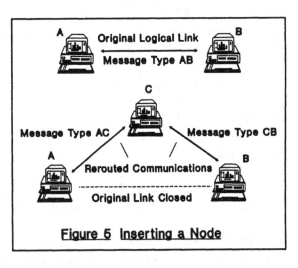

Figure 5 Inserting a Node

allow them to continue operating as before, rests with the new application program (C), otherwise the network will fail.

As discussed above, the original application running on node A, will have a maximum set of data that is relevant to any other partner's application, determined by the function that A performs. The existing partner (B) that A communicates with will only have access to this data, which A has made available for public use. The same logic applies to node B. The new inserted node (C) must be set up to handle the messages coming from and expected by nodes A and B. C must also be able to provide A and B with the data A and B provided to one another.

The remove_node primitive is provided to allow an application to remove itself from the structure (refer to figure 7). The partners (A and B) that C communicates with, are forced to redirect their communications. They begin communicating directly with one another since they may no longer communicate with node C (it has been removed). It is the responsibility of the application at node C to ensure that the Nodes A and B will be able to obtain the information that they require from one another to continue functioning. In the event that the particular function at node C is absolutely necessary for the integrity of the network as a whole, a node could be inserted to perform that function, as discussed above, and then node C removed (perhaps for maintenance).

Control information, such as instructing the partner nodes A and B to stop sending to C, will be sent through messages, as if it were conventional data, and decoded using the message decoding routines in the application package.

4.4 Failure Semantics
If a node fails this will be detected from failure codes returned to the application when communication is attempted. The application must provide the reconfiguration control, using the primitives provided, to communicate with the other nodes in the system.

The emphasis in the communications interface is on providing primitives for the reliable transfer of information. The application is responsible for the processing of the information and control of the industrial process.

5 THE APPLICATION PACKAGE
The application has two main sections. One section comprises the actual process tasks which implement the process functions and drive the process devices. The other comprises the interface to the communications system and the encoding and decoding of messages carrying process control data. The sections are interdependent, and cannot be separated because of the necessity of transferring data between the message decoding (and encoding) routines and tasks performing the control functions. The message decoding/encoding will be dealt with here, the specifics of the process control not being particularly relevant to this discussion, since the value of the communications software is in its applicability to more than one process control implementation.

The message decoding routines are expected to identify control protocols as opposed to straight data transfer messages. The control protocols must be defined by the particular implementation of the software environment, at the message decoding level, for a particular application.

5.1 Bidirectional Data Transfer

Each node is responsible for encoding its outgoing messages. Since all communication between two nodes will be carried on a common channel, all messages between those two nodes must be encoded into a single message format. Hence there may be a unique message format between each node pair. Assume that a particular node possesses two operating processes, involving two independent tasks, each with data that is relevant to functions dealt with on other nodes, and requiring data from other nodes. The data that is received by the message routine from a remote node must be made availabie to the operating tasks; if a remote request arrives for data it must be serviced with the most up to date information possible. Consequently, a vital facet of the package is the bidirectional transfer of the process data

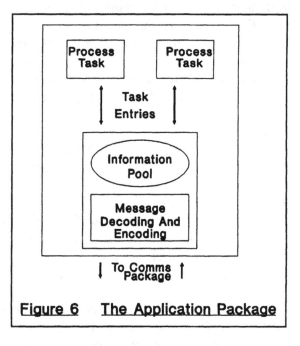

Figure 6   The Application Package

between the actual process task and the message handling routine. This data transfer occurs in the following way (figure 6).

The process task writes the process data into a pool of information which is accessible both to the process task and the message handling routine, through task entries. The entry passes two records; the one contains the data for the information pool while the other record is returned with data relevant to the process task.

Two distinct sets of data exist within the pool. The one set consists solely of locations defined to be 'deposit boxes' for the message routine to deposit updated information from a remote node. The other locations act as deposit boxes for the process tasks and are accessed by the message handling routine. This approach offers a clearly defined interface between the message handling routine and the process tasks.

5.2 Data Retrieval

A retrieve primitive is provided which allows the application to instruct the communications system to transfer the most recently received message from the decoding routines. The currency of the data is dependent upon the frequency with which the data both in the pool and the local process task is updated, and this is at the discretion of the application programmer. Before the transfer of data is made the process task must issue a guard request to the communications package to ensure that if a network adapter interrupt occurs, the transfer will be completed before new data is written into, or read from the pool. Upon completion of the data transfer the application issues a guard release directive to the communications package. The communications routine determines whether an adapter interrupt has occurred and if this is the case will return control to the original interrupt service routine.

A task within the message decoding system is set up to receive a message from a particular partner. The format of the partner's message is defined in this task. It is defined by the applications programmer and may be set at compile time if chosen to be constant. If the format may change, the programmer must include software to deal with this eventuality. The task dumps the data into the information pool. The process tasks retrieve the data when required through procedure calls to the pool.

5.3 Node Insertion

It must be emphasised that the status and requirements of the existing nodes, and the message format for data transfer where the new node will be included, are known and may thus be included at compile time. This allows the new node to be tailored to fit in the network as a whole and this is the programmer's responsibility. The insertion is accomplished by discontinuing the processing of the application at the remote nodes momentarily, to allow the construction of the new communications structure with the new node to be accomplished and to bring the new node on line.

5.4 Node Failure

As depicted in figure 7, if a node C fails and the application software deems that the process is capable of continuing without C, A and B must now begin to confer. To do so, A and B must have knowledge of one another's message structure, and this must be stored along with the information in the application which will define whether the process may continue or must be forced to fail gracefully.

The application is expected to take into account the possibility that an insertion of a new node or deletion of an old node may fail, and must be able to prevent the whole network from degrading in this event.

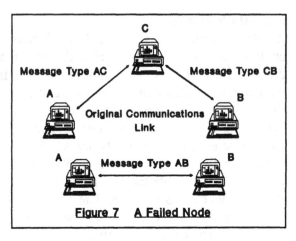

Figure 7   A Failed Node

The application layer of the software environment is the final decision making layer. It has the responsibility of deciding what to do with the network in the event of unexpected occurrences. The message decoding section, defined by the application, is the intelligent interface to the communications structure.

The users will be supplied with a set of packages comprised of a type definition package, an information pool package, and an example application package. The communications specification package will be supplied, but the body will be hidden.

Appendix C contains a simple example of an application.

6 CONCLUSION

The software is designed to provide a flexible environment for a distributed process control application. While the emphasis in the design has been placed on a flexible system that is reconfigurable and capable of handling dynamic changes in the constraints of the system, it has been seen that with an increase in flexibility there is a marked increase in the complexity of the software. There is thus an effective limitation placed upon the flexibility of the system by the necessity to minimise the complexity of the software. While flexibility is desired, it potentially allows uncontrolled changes to the detriment of system as a whole. This places a responsibility on the programmer of the individual unit, to ensure that he takes into account the integrity of the whole system. The solution has aimed at producing individually intelligent units, all of the same priority and status, other than that defined naturally by the industrial process functions they implement, to reduce the criticality of a failure in a single unit.

The system is currently being implemented. An Ada communications 'phone' program, over a local area network, has been implemented and used to test the underlying concepts on which the reconfigurable, flexible control system software described above, is based.

REFERENCES

1) Van Scoy R, Bamberger J, Firth R, "An Overview Of Dark", Ada Letters, Volume IX, Number 7, pp. 91-101, November/December 1989.

2) Alvarez A, Arevelo S, "Fault Tolerant Distributed Ada", Ada Letters, Volume IX, Number 5, pp. 54-59, July/August 1989.

3) Schwaderer W, "C Programmers Guide To Netbios", Howard Sams and Company, 1988.

4) Sloman M, Kramer J, "Distributed Systems and Computer Networks", Prentice-Hall(UK), 1987.

5) Volz R, "Virtual Nodes And Units of Distribution for Distributed Ada", Ada Letters, Volume X, Number 4, pp. 85-96, Spring 1990.

6) Buhr R, "System Design With Ada", Prentice Hall, 1984.

7) Jensen T, "Data Exchange Coordination on a Netbios Lan," Tech Specialist, Volume 1, Number 7, pp. 44-56, December 1990.

8) Van Scoy R, Bamberger J, "Returning Control To Where It Belongs", Software Engineering Institute, Carnegie Mellon University, 1989.

9) "IBM Technical Reference: PC Network", IBM Corporation, Personal Computer, 1984.

10) Allworth S, "Introduction To Real-Time Software Design", Springer-Verlag, New York, 1981.

11) Barnes J, "An Introduction To Real Time Programming", unpublished notes.

12) Raynal, M, "Networks & Distributed Computation Concepts Tools & Algorithms", North Oxford Academic, 1987.

APPENDIX A

The Communications primitives defined under the communications package are:
Note: The following primitives all return a failure code that specifies the status of the request.

Initialise. This primitive allows the application to announce itself to the network.
Initialise_channel(Remote_node_name, Alias). This primitive allows the application to open a bidirectional communication link with the remote node. It passes the remote nodes permanent node name and an alias that it will refer to in future communications.
Send_message(Remote_node_alias, Message). This primitive sends a message to the remote node denoted by the alias.
Multi_Send(Remote_node_alias_list, Message). This allows the message to be sent to a group of remote nodes, denoted by their aliases, simultaneously.
Receive(Message). This allows an application to specify the communications routine to return the latest message received to the requesting task.
Insert_Node(Remote_node_alias1, Remote_node_alias2). This inserts a new node between the two remote nodes specified and reroutes the connections through the inserted node.
Remove_Node. This removes the current node from the process structure and forces its partners to redirect their communications.
Hang_up_communications. The communication channels with the other nodes in the network are closed and the local network node name is removed from the Netbios name table.
Guard. The communications routine redirects the network adapters interrupt while data transfer is occurring between the message handling routine and the process tasks. The guard routine protects the integrity of the data.
Unguard. This routine resets the original adapter interrupt service routine. It removes the guard to allows the interrupt service routine to complete.

APPENDIX B

This Appendix contains the Ada Netbios package specifications for the Netbios Control Block and command options. The control block is the mechanism through which the communications package accesses Netbios.

PACKAGE NETBIOS IS

```
subtype byte is integer range 0..255;
subtype unsigned is integer range 0..65535;
type Mem_address is record
        Offset : Unsigned;
        Segment : Unsigned;
end record;  -- Mem Address
subtype String_16 is string(1..16);
subtype String_14 is string(1..14);
```

type Netbios_control_block is record
Command : Byte;
-- The Command field which tells Netbios which function is to execute. If the
-- high bit is set, the command is a "no-wait" command.
Retcode : Byte;
-- Returned by Netbios when the command completes, this field is zero if all
-- went well. Otherwise this field holds the error code.
Session_number : Byte;
-- When a call or listen command completes this field holds the number of the
-- established session. If you issue a send or receive command you must load
-- this field with the appropriate session number.
Name_number : Byte;
-- When an Add Name or Add Group Name command completes, this field
-- holds the number associated with that name; used with datagram commands.
Buffer : Mem_address;
-- For send commands, this field holds the offset and segment number of the
-- buffer holding the message to be transmitted. For receive commands, this field
-- points to the buffer where the incoming data is to be stored.
Length : Unsigned;
-- The number of bytes in the buffer pointed to by the buffer field.
Call_Name : String_16;
-- Used by the Call and Listen commands to hold the name of the remote station
-- that will become the session partner.
Name : String_16;
-- Holds the local name for the add name and delete name commands.

Receive_timeout : byte;
-- Indicates the time out in 1/2 second increments for receive commands.
Send_timeout : byte;
-- Indicates the time out in 1/2 second increments for send commands.
Post : Mem_address;
-- This filed points to a post routine which Netbios executes after completing
-- a no wait command; should be set to 0 if not used.
Adapter_number : Byte;
-- Network Adapter Number; indicates which network adapter card the command
-- should be issued to.
Command_Complete : Byte;
-- A value of 255 in this field indicates the command specified by the NCB has
-- not completed. Netbios sets this field to 0 when the command is finished.
Reserved : String_14;
-- Reserved by Netbios.
end record; -- Netbios_control_block.

--- Netbios Commands

Call	: constant byte: = 16#10#;
Listen	: constant byte: = 16#11#;
Hangup	: constant byte: = 16#12#;
Send	: constant byte: = 16#14#;
Receive	: constant byte: = 16#15#;
Receive_Any	: constant byte: = 16#16#;
Chain_Send	: constant byte: = 16#17#;
Send_Datagram	: constant byte: = 16#20#;
Receive_Datagram	: constant byte: = 16#21#;
Send_Broadcast	: constant byte: = 16#22#;
Receive_Broadcast	: constant byte: = 16#23#;
Add_Name	: constant byte: = 16#30#;
Delete_Name	: constant byte: = 16#31#;
Reset_Adaptor	: constant byte: = 16#32#;
Adaptor_Status	: constant byte: = 16#33#;
Session_Status	: constant byte: = 16#34#;
Cancel	: constant byte: = 16#35#;
Add_Group_Name	: constant byte: = 16#36#;
Unlink	: constant byte: = 16#70#;
Send_No_Ack	: constant byte: = 16#71#;
Chain_No_Ack	: constant byte: = 16#72#;

-- No Wait (Interrupt Driven) Option must be ORed with NCB command.
No_wait : constant_byte: = 16#80#;

-- Netbios Return Codes

Cmd_Completed	: constant byte: = 16#00#;
Invld_Buffer_Lgth	: constant byte: = 16#01#;
Invld_Cmd	: constant byte: = 16#03#;
Cmd_Timeout	: constant byte: = 16#05#;
Data_Overflow	: constant byte: = 16#06#;
Noack_Failed	: constant byte: = 16#07#;
Invld_Session_Nbr	: constant byte: = 16#08#;
No_Session_Space	: constant byte: = 16#09#;
Session_Closed	: constant byte: = 16#0A#;
Cmd_Cancelled	: constant byte: = 16#0B#;
Dupl_Local_Name	: constant byte: = 16#0D#;
Name_Table_Full	: constant byte: = 16#0E#;
Active_Name	: constant byte: = 16#0F#;
Sess_Table_Full	: constant byte: = 16#11#;
Bad_Open	: constant byte: = 16#12#;
Bad_Name_Nbr	: constant byte: = 16#13#;
No_Name	: constant byte: = 16#14#;
Bad_Name	: constant byte: = 16#15#;
Duplicate_Name	: constant byte: = 16#16#;
Name_Deleted	: constant byte: = 16#17#;
Session_End_Abl	: constant byte: = 16#18#;
Duplicate_Names	: constant byte: = 16#19#;
Bad_Protocol	: constant byte: = 16#1A#;
Busy	: constant byte: = 16#21#;
Max_Commands	: constant byte: = 16#22#;
Bad_Lan_Adapter	: constant byte: = 16#23#;
Complete_Cancel	: constant byte: = 16#24#;
Reserve_Addgn	: constant byte: = 16#25#;
Bad_Cancel	: constant byte: = 16#261;
Cmd_Pending	: constant byte: = 16#FF#;

END NETBIOS;

APPENDIX C

This Appendix contains some example code on how to set up a single task to communicate with one other node. It contains no shutdown code or reconfiguration code since only one node is considered.

```
--- *** Definitions of Data structures
package define_types is
message_length : constant := 65;
subtype message_type is string(1..message_length);
subtype node_name_type is string(1..16);
type array_of_node_name_type is array(1..10) of node_name_type;

--- *** Data structures used for task1 at node
   type type_info_task1_in is
   record
      var2 : string(1..16);
   end record;
   type type_info_task1_out is
   record
      var1 : integer;
   end record;

--- *** possible other data structures for other process tasks.

--- *** Data structures used for the message creation and decoding
--- routines
   type type_info_message_in is
   record
      task1 : type_info_task1_in;
   end record;
   type type_info_message_out is
   record
      task1 : type_info_task1_out;
   end record;
end define_types;

## -----------------------------------------------##

--- *** The Communications Specification file.

with define_types,text_io;
use define_types;
```

```
package comms is
  function initialise return integer;
  procedure initialise_channel(
        remote_processor_name : in node_name_type;
        failure_code : out integer);
  procedure send_message(
        remote_node_name : in node_name_type;
        message : in message_type;
        failure_code : out integer);
  procedure multi_send(
        remote_node_alias_list : array_of_node_name_type;
        message : in out message_type;
        failure_code : out integer);
  procedure receive(
        message : in out message_type;
        failure_code : out integer);
  procedure insert_node(
        remote_node_alias1 : in node_name_type;
        remote_node_alias2 : in node_name_type;
        failure_code       : out integer);
  function remove_node return integer;
  function hang_up_communications return integer;
  function guard return boolean;
  function unguard return boolean;
end comms;
```

--##

**** The Information Pool, Message Handling Specification File

```
with define_types; use define_types;
package info is
  task pool is
    entry task1(
        info_record_in : in type_info_task1_in;
        info_record_out : out type_info_task1_out);
    entry message(
        info_record_in : in type_info_message_in;
        info_record_out : out type_info_message_out);
    entry message_dump(
        info_record_in : in type_info_message_out);
    entry message_get(info_record_out : out type_info_message_in);
```

```
  end pool;
  task message is
     entry send(remote_node_alias : in node_name_type);
     entry receive;
  end message;
end info;
with define_types,tty,comms;
use define_types;
```

```
package body info is
--- *** This procedure transfers the data into the pool and will
--- *** provide to calling tasks data from the pool
task body pool is
        pool_record_in : define_types.type_info_message_in;
        pool_record_out : define_types.type_info_message_out;
begin
  loop
     select
        accept task1(
              info_record_in : in type_info_task1_in;
              info_record_out : out type_info_task1_out) do
        --- performs the transfer between a task and the pool ---
              pool_record_in.task1 := info_record_in;
              info_record_out := pool_record_out.task1;
        end task1;
     or
        accept message_dump(info_record_in : in type_info_message_out) do
        --- dumps data in the pool from a remote message ---
              pool_record_out := info_record_in;
        end message_dump;
     or
        accept message_get(info_record_out : out type_info_message_in) do
        --- provides the data for a remote message to be sent out ---
              info_record_out := pool_record_in;
        end message_get;
     end select;
  end loop;
end pool;
```

```
--- Procedure creates a message from pool data entered by the process tasks
function create_message return define_types.message_type is
        message : define_types.message_type;
        pool_record : type_info_message_in;
begin
  pool.message_get(info_record_out = > pool_record);
  tty.put_line(" Message Created");
  return message;
end;



--- **** This Procedure Decodes the information into a record
--- **** That is sent to the information pool
procedure decode(message : in define_types.message_type) is
        pool_record : define_types.type_info_message_out;
begin
  tty.put_line(" Decode");
  ---
  --- Decode message into variables that form components
  --- of those in pool_record input from messages according
  --- to the format defined by the application programmer for the task
  ---
  --- Now send the data to be dumped into the pool
  ---
  --- if not control function then
  ---     pool.message_dump(info_record_in = > pool_record);
  --- else
  ---     do possible control function operations
  ---     defined by the application programmer
  --- end if
end;

--- *** This task has entries to allow the application to send a message to
--- *** a remote node or cause a message that has been received to be
--- *** decoded
task body message is
  message_received : define_types.message_type;
  failure_code : integer;
begin
  loop
    select
      accept send(remote_node_alias : in define_types.node_name_type) do
```

```
        comms.send_message(
              remote_node_name = > remote_node_alias,
              message = > create_message,
              failure_code = > failure_code);
        end send;
    or
      accept receive do
        comms.receive(
              message = > message_received,
              failure_code = > failure_code);
        decode(message = > message_received);
      end receive;
    or
      terminate;
    end select;
  end loop;
end message;
end info;
```

--##

*** This package contains the process task and initialisation code

```
package a is
end a;

with comms,tty,info,define_types ;
--- A simple example setting up one task to communicate with one other node
--- Removal primitives are not included - nor is the process task function
package body a is
        failure : integer;
--- ***
--- *** Process function 1
--- ***
task task1 is
end task1;
task body task1 is
        information_out : define_types.type_info_task1_out;
        information_in : define_types.type_info_task1_in;
        variable1:integer;
```

```
            variable2 : string(1..16);
begin
  loop
     ---
     --- perform maintenance
     ---
     ---
     --- ** sends data to remote node name - first creates message in
     --- ** message routine
     info.message.send(remote_node_alias => "remote_node_name");
     info.message.receive;
--
-- ** Sets guard and transfer information to the information pool
     if comms.guard=true then
        information_out.var1 := variable1;
        info.pool.task1(
                info_record_in  => information_in ,
                info_record_out => information_out);
        variable2 := information_in.var2;
-- ** Will service any interrupt handling
        if comms.unguard=false then
           tty.put_line(" Fatal Error -- Use error handler");
        end if;
     end if;
--
-- ** End of Guarded Data Transfer.
--
     delay 0.0;  -- task switch
  end loop;
end task1;
--- ***
--- *** Possible other process functions.
--- ***
---
--- *** Initialisation code to set up the original communication paths
---
begin
declare
begin
  if comms.initialise=0 then
     comms.initialise_channel(
                remote_processor_name => "comms_package026",
```

```
            failure_code = > failure );
      if failure=1 then
        tty.put_line(" Channel Initialisation Failed ");
        tty.put_line(" The failure code is " & integer'image(integer(failure)));
      end if;
   end if;
end;
end a;
```

--##

********* This is the main procedure -- Tasks Do all the work ********

```
with a;
procedure app is
begin
      null;
end app;
```

Part VII: Faces of Reuse

ROSE-ADA :
a Method and a Tool to Help Reuse of Ada Codes[1]

N. BADARO and Th. MOINEAU

SEMA GROUP,
16 Rue Barbès, 92126 MONTROUGE (France)
E-mail : [nada,moineau]@metradt.metra.fr

Abstract :

We present in this paper a method and a tool to help retrieval and adaptation of Ada reusable components. Starting from a goal specification, expressed as a hierarchy of Ada package specifications, a base of reusable components is filtered in order to extract the components which correspond to the goal specification, modulo a renaming and the addition of some subprograms. The filtering method is based on a pattern matching on the profile of the subprograms. Once a component is selected, the renaming is built by the system with a little help from the user when there are some ambiguities. After that the adapted code is automatically built by encapsulating the code of the reused components into a set of packages, which behave exactly like the goal specification. The code of the reused components is absolutely not modified; this allows to keep the quality level of the reused code and to factorize the maintenance.

This tool, which was never intended to be a complete reuse environment, is integrated into the ESF-ROSE reuse system.

Key-words :

software reuse, software adaptation, software components retrieval, Ada, ESF-ROSE.

Introduction

Software reusability is a topic of first practical importance and of great practical difficulty. It has been recognized as such for a long time, since the first subroutine libraries. More recently, this problem has been addressed in term of reuse of some development steps [BR87, CHSW89], mainly design (as in [Wir88], [CCJ+91] among others), as well as in term of reuse of code. It seems obvious that these two approaches are complementary and that they correspond to different aims. In this paper, we discuss the second approach that we call *as-it-is reuse* : the aim is to identify possible reuses such that there is no need to modify the reused code. When it is possible, *as-it-is reuse* is especially interesting since the absence of

---

[1]This work was funded by the Eurêka Software Factory project.

code modifications results in important benefits : there is no need for retesting and redocumenting the reused components. But, the main benefit of *as-it-is* reuse arises during the maintenance phase [LG84, BR87]. One can explain that by the following facts :

- Reusable components are usually of greater quality level than those developed from scratch, because they have been developed more carefully and because they have been tested more extensively (at least because they have been used many times by different people).

- Reusable components maintenance can be performed only once by a central team. Bug corrections and enhancements can then be done and tested very carefully, avoiding waterfall errors. After that the enhanced component can be broadcasted and automatically reinstalled within the various applications that have reused this component.

As a consequence, we consider here only *black box* reuse : the reuser must only need to know the specification of the code he wants to reuse, and should not need to know anything about implementation details (see [PCW83]). Indeed, as exposed above, the maintenance is facilitated, because any modification of the reused code does not affect the other parts of the application, provided that the specification remains the same. Hence allowing the reuser to know about the implementation details of the reused component can lead him to profit from implementation tricks that can be no more valid for the next version of this component; this will then impede the use of the new versions of the reused component. Moreover *black box* reuse is the only possible approach when the source codes are not available (for instance when only the object codes are given).

Hence we need a specification language to describe reusable components; the kernel of such a specification language will be described in section 1.

But *as-it-is* reuse is difficult to achieve. Indeed, as cited in [Mey87], a needed component is "neither ever quite the same, nor ever quite another" as an existing reusable component. A common problem is the one of renaming : the reusable component actually corresponds to the needs at a semantical level, but not on a syntactical level (e.g. the function names do not correspond, or a function corresponds to a procedure). But we do not want to change the specifications of other components when we reuse an already existing component. Hence we need a method for adapting a reused component in such a way that the resulting code is actually an implementation of the goal specification, even when the specification of the reused component is not syntactically equivalent to the goal specification. Such a method will be described in the section 2.

In section 3, we will face the following problem : given a goal specification SP_G to be implemented and a reusable component $\mathcal{R}$ of specification SP_R, is $\mathcal{R}$

reusable for the implementation of SP_G ? We will give a precise definition of the relation "is implementable by reuse of" between a goal specification and a reusable component. Roughly speaking, SP_G is said to be possibly implementable by reuse of a component $\mathcal{R}$ of specification SP_R if SP_G is a subset of SP_R modulo a renaming and the addition of some types and subprograms. This definition will be proved to be fully compatible with the adaptation method of section 2.

Finding the good renaming between a goal specification and a reusable component is a tedious and error prone task. There is thus a need for a tool to help the programmer in this task. Implementing such a tool is usually considered as impossible because of the huge number of potential renamings between the specifications. We will see in section 4 that simple considerations allow to build such a tool. Moreover the good performances of the retrieval method allows us to run it as a filter on a not that small set of reusable components, so as to keep only those which correspond modulo a renaming to a given goal specification.

As usually stated in the reuse framework, genericity is a powerful mechanism for code reuse. We will see in section 5 how the above method and tool have been adapted to cope with generic packages.

Finally we will describe in section 6 a tool which supports our retrieval and adaptation methods and we will compare it with other tools devoted to software reuse.

1 Reusable Ada component specifications

As explained above, we need a specification language to express the needs and to describe the reusable components. But before to describe our specification language, we have to state what a reusable Ada component is. As usual in the Ada framework, a reusable component is a set of Ada packages. More precisely an Ada component mainly consists in three parts [2] :

- a **plug** which is the specification of the capabilities exported by the component,
- a **socket** which is the specification of the capabilities imported by the component, and
- a **code** which contains a set of Ada packages.

The code part of a component may contain hidden packages which are not exported in its plug, and it is not required to implement all the capabilities described in its plug : some of these capabilities may be imported by the socket.

Two Ada components C (client) and S (server) can be composed together provided that all the capabilities imported by the socket of C are exported by the plug of S

---

[2]Other information are definitely needed for reuse purpose such as informal description, example of use, etc. These information are not discussed in this paper (see for instance [FN87]).

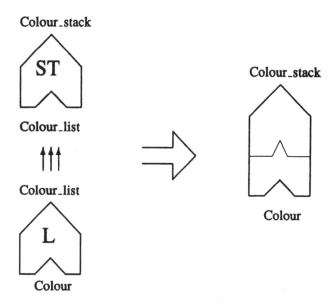

Figure 1: The plug-socket composition mechanism

(cf. figure 1). This composition results in a new Ada component whose plug is the one of C, whose socket is the one of S and whose code is built by merging the codes of C and S. This composition mechanism can be performed until all the sockets are filled, so as to get a complete hierarchy of Ada packages.

As an example, suppose we have a component ST for manipulation of stacks of colours

- whose plug exports stacks of colours,
- whose code contains a package implementing stacks by means of lists of colours, and
- whose socket imports lists of colours.

If we have another Ada component L exporting lists of colours, then we can plug L into ST so as to get a new component

- whose plug exports stacks of colours,
- whose code contains two packages implementing stacks and lists of colours, and
- whose socket imports colours.

The capabilities imported and exported by an Ada component are described using a rooted directed acyclic graph of Ada package specifications. The package specification part of the Ada language is used here, because it is obviously well adapted for Ada and because it should be well known by people developing Ada applications.

```
package COLOUR is
    -- <Types >
    type Colour is private ;
    -- <Generators >
    function blue return Colour ;
    function red return Colour ;
    function yellow return Colour ;
    -- <Basic Operations >
    function equal (a_colour1, a_colour2 : Colour) return Boolean ;
end COLOUR ;
```

```
with COLOUR;
package LIST is
    -- <Types >
    type List is private ;
    -- <Generators >
    function empty return List ; -- < raise no_more_room >
    procedure add (a_colour : in COLOUR.Colour; a_list : in out List) ;
                -- < raise no_more_room >
    -- <Basic Operations >
    function head (a_list : List) return COLOUR.Colour ; -- < raise empty_list >
    procedure remove_head (a_list : in out List) ; -- < raise empty_list >
    function is_empty (a_list : List) return Boolean ;
    -- <Extraneous Operations >
    function contains (a_list : List; a_colour : COLOUR.Colour) return Boolean ;
    function length (a_list : List) return Natural :
    -- <Exceptions >
    no_more_room : exception ;
    empty_list : exception ;
end LIST ;
```

Figure 2: Example of Ada specification : LIST

But the package specification part of Ada is not a specification language : it lacks some features that are definitely needed for describing components and it contains features which impede reuse. Hence we both extend and restrict the package specification part of Ada. But to be as compatible as possible with Ada syntax, the new information are added as comments.

Following [Ber86], we forbid usage of the use construct, because it decreases reusability; hence the hierarchy of the specification is expressed by means of the with construct. As explained by [Den87], we also forbid use of global data (i.e. the declaration of data within a package specification) and the types should be private types [3]. Moreover, a type should be defined in the same package as the subprograms

---

[3] We will see below that we have to forbid the use of limited private types.

acting on the data of this type. Hence a package should roughly correspond to an abstract data type definition or to an object class definition [GR83]. However thes rules are not a strict : one can define packages without any type definition (usually in the higher levels of the hierarchy) and one can have non private types (usually in the lower levels of the hierarchy).

We enrich the Ada language with the concept of generator as defined in [NS88]. Roughly speaking generators are the subprograms that generate the possible values of a data type, while non-generators can only yield values which are denotable by a composition of the generators. For instance possible generators for the List data type are a function returning the empty list and a procedure adding an element in the list; the procedure which removes the first element of a list is not a generator because the modified list can be obtained by successively adding elements to the empty list. As a consequence, any function or operator can be a generator, whereas a procedure can be a generator if one and only one of its parameter can be modified (i.e. of mode **out** or **in out**). To comply with our abstract data type orientation, a generator must be defined in the same package as its result type.

In Ada, the exceptions which can be raised by the subprograms of a package are declared in a global way at the end of the package specification. This is not precise enough for our purpose. Indeed the procedure which adds an element to a list can complain about lack of memory but is not likely to complain when the list is empty; on the other hand the function which gives the first element of a list is not likely to complain about lack of memory but should complain about an empty list. Hence we require to specify for each subprogram the exceptions it can raise. This allow to treat accurately the exceptions, so no blank exception propagates to the user.

A simple example of a component specification for list of colours is given in figure 2 (the distinction between basic and extraneous operations is explained below). Note that in the COLOUR package, one can also declare :

> **type** Colour **is** (blue , red , yellow) ;

Then the three constant functions blue, red and yellow are automatically added.

2   Implementation by reuse

Suppose that we have to implement the simple specification of list of colours given in figure 2 (for instance to fill the socket of the ST Ada component above), and suppose that we have an Ada component C_LIST whose plug is the specification COLOR_LIST of figure 3 (here nil, cons, car, cdr, nilp and member are the usual name in the Lisp community for empty, add, head, remove_head, is_empty and contains).

According to our experience of programmer, we know that we can reuse the component C_LIST to implement the specification LIST. But the specifications

```
package COLOR is
    -- <Types >
    type Color is private ;
    -- <Generators >
    function blue return Color ;
    function red return Color ;
    function yellow return Color ;
    -- <Operations >
    function equal (a_color1, a_color2 : Color) return Boolean ;
end COLOR ;
```

```
with COLOR;
package COLOR_LIST is
    -- <Types >
    type C_List is private ;
    -- <Generators >
    function nil return C_List ; -- < raise no_more_room >
    function cons (a_color : COLOR.Color; a_list : C_List) return C_List ;
                -- < raise no_more_room >
    -- <Basic Operations >
    function car (a_list : C_List) return COLOR.Color ; -- < raise empty_list >
    function cdr (a_list : C_List) return C_List ; -- < raise empty_list >
    function nilp (a_list : C_List) return Boolean ;
    -- <Extraneous Operations >
    function member (a_color : COLOR.Color; a_list : C_List) return Boolean ;
    -- <Exceptions >
    no_more_room : exception ;
    empty_list : exception ;
end LIST ;
```

Figure 3: Example of Ada reusable component specification : COLOR_LIST

COLOR_LIST and LIST are not equivalent : the names are not the same and some functions correspond to procedures. Hence we have to adapt the C_LIST component before to reuse it. As explained before we do not want to modify the code of C_LIST. Thus we encapsulate the reused code within packages which contain the relevant renamings [4], and we rewrite the package specifications of LIST and of COLOUR as follows (cf. figure 4) :

- The LIST package specification imports the COLOUR package (as requested by the goal specification) and imports the COLOR_LIST package (here comes the reuse of COLOR_LIST). It contains a subtype clause to rename C_List

---

[4]In this paper renaming means changing the names, but also permuting the order of the arguments and transforming functions into procedures or procedures into functions, as detailed below.

```
with COLOUR , — — as in the goal specification ;
     COLOR_LIST ; — — reuse of COLOR_LIST
package LIST is
     subtype List is COLOR_LIST.C_List ;
     function empty return List renames COLOR_LIST.nil ;
     procedure add (a_colour : in COLOUR.Colour; a_list : in out List) ;
     function head (a_list : List) return COLOUR.Colour renames COLOR_LIST.car ;
     procedure remove_head (a_list : in out List);
     function is_empty (a_list : List) return Boolean renames COLOR_LIST.nilp ;
     function contains (a_list : List; a_colour : COLOUR.Colour) return Boolean ;
     function length (a_list : List) return Natural ;
     no_more_room : exception renames COLOR_LIST.no_more_room ;
     empty_list : exception renames COLOR_LIST.empty_list ;
end LIST ;
```

```
package body LIST is
     procedure add (a_colour : in COLOUR.Colour; a_list : in out List) is
     begin
          a_list := COLOR_LIST.cons (a_colour, a_list);
     end ;
     procedure remove_head (a_list : in out List) is begin
          a_list := COLOR_LIST.cdr (a_list);
     end ;
     function contains (a_list : List; a_colour : COLOUR.Colour) return Boolean is
     begin
          return COLOR_LIST.member(a_color =>a_colour, a_list =>a_list);
     end ;
     function length (a_list : List) return Natural is
     begin
          null ; — — to be filled
     end ;
end LIST ;
```

Figure 4: Implementation of LIST by reuse of COLOR_LIST.

into List, and some renaming clauses to rename nil into empty, car into head, etc.

The LIST package body contains some code to implement the add procedure by means of the cons function, to implement the remove_head procedure by means of the cdr function and to implement the contains function by means of member [5]. This body also contains a skeleton to be filled out in order to provide an implementation for the length function.

- The package specification COLOUR imports the COLOR package. It contains the subtyping and the renaming clauses for Colour, blue, red, yellow and equal. Since all the subprograms of COLOUR are implemented by renaming, there is no need for a COLOUR package body.

In this example, we have considered permutation of the parameters between the goal specification and the existing component, for instance in the contains function, and we have created a stub to permute the order of the arguments. If only named association are used by the developers, this is no more necessary.

In the previous example, we can reuse COLOR_LIST for LIST even if the length function is not defined in COLOR_LIST. Indeed we do not need to know about the detailed implementation of the lists to implement length : we only have to remove the first element of the list and to increment a counter until the list is empty. The subprograms which can be implemented without any knowledge about the internal representation of the data types are called **extraneous** subprograms, the other ones are called **essential** subprograms. The generators are always essential. In the LIST specification for instance, empty, add, head, remove_head and is_empty are essential, while contains and length are extraneous. Implementing a goal specification by a reusable component is definitely not possible when an essential subprogram of the goal specification cannot be implemented by means of the subprograms exported by the reused component.

3 A definition of reusability

According to the above example, we see that a goal specification SP_G is implementable by reuse of a component $\mathcal{R}$ of specification SP_R if there exists a specification SP and a renaming ρ such that :

- SP imports SP_R (among others),
- each subprogram of SP can be implemented without knowing the actual implementation of the primitive types (i.e. those defined in the specifications imported by SP),
- after renaming by ρ, SP is equivalent to SP_G.

---

[5] We can also use the **inline pragma**, to avoid a function call and to have better performances.

Following the well-known maxim "one module ≡ one type", we forbid definition of new types in SP : if a type is needed in SP_G and is no exported by $\mathcal{R}$ then it has to be defined in a new specification imported by SP.

In the previous definition we used the concept of renaming that has to be precisely defined. A renaming is a relation which states by which type (resp. subprogram, exception) of SP_R a type (resp. subprogram, exception) of SP_G is implemented. More precisely a renaming ρ is a mapping which associates types with types, subprograms with subprograms and exceptions with exceptions and such that a subprogram is renamed into another subprogram if and only if we can implement the first one by means of the second one, as explained above. This implies that the two subprograms raise the exceptions modulo the renaming, i.e. the image by ρ of the set of exceptions raised by the first subprogram is exactly the set of exceptions raised by the second subprogram, and that we are in one of the following cases :

- A function `fun (a₁:t₁;...; aₘ:tₘ) return tₘ₊₁` can be implemented by means of another function `fun' (a'₁:t'₁;...; a'ₙ:t'ₙ) return t'ₙ₊₁` if they have the same number of arguments (i.e. $n = m$), and if the argument types in `fun` and `fun'` correspond modulo the renaming and a permutation (i.e. $\rho(t_{m+1}) = t'_{n+1}$ and there exists a permutation p such that $\forall i \in [1, m]$, $\rho(t_i) = t'_j$ with $j = p(i)$).

  The function `fun` can be implemented either by a renaming clause

      fun (a₁:t₁;...; aₘ:tₘ) return tₘ₊₁ renames fun' ;

  if there is no permutation of the arguments, or by the following code

  ```
  fun (a₁:t₁;...; aₘ:tₘ) return tₘ₊₁ is
  begin
      return fun' (a'ⱼ₁=>a₁,..., a'ⱼₘ=>aₘ);  --where jᵢ = p(i)
  end ;
  ```

  For instance, in the `LIST` and `C_LIST` example, `head` can be implemented by means of `car` and `contains` by means of `member`.

- A procedure `proc (a₁:m₁ t₁;...; aₘ:mₘ tₘ)` [6] can be implemented by reuse of a procedure `proc' (a'₁:m'₁ t'₁;...; a'ₙ:m'ₙ t'ₙ)` if they have the same number of arguments (i.e. $n = m$), and if the argument types and modes in `proc` and `proc'` correspond modulo the renaming and a permutation (i.e. there exists a permutation p such that $\forall i \in [1, m]$, $m_i = m'_j$ and $\rho(t_i) = t'_j$ with $j = p(i)$),

  The procedure `proc` can be implemented either by a renaming clause

      proc (a₁:m₁ t₁;...; aₘ:mₘ tₘ) renames proc' ;

  if there is no permutation of the arguments, or by the following code

---

[6] m_i denotes the mode of the i th parameter, i.e. **in**, **out** or **in out**.

```
proc (a₁:m₁ t₁;...;aₘ:mₘ tₘ) is
begin
    proc' (a'ⱼ₁=>a₁,...,a'ⱼₘ=>aₘ); --where jᵢ = p(i)
end ;
```

- A function $fun (a_1:t_1;...;a_m:t_m)$ $return$ t_{m+1} can be implemented by reuse of a procedure $proc' (a'_1:m'_1 \ t'_1;...;a'_n:m'_n \ t'_n)$ in the two following cases :

  - $proc'$ has one more argument than fun (i.e. $n = m + 1$), all the arguments of $proc$ are of mode **in** except one, $a'_{k'}$, which is of mode **out** and of the type returned by fun and the arguments types in fun and $proc'$ correspond modulo the renaming and a permutation (i.e. there exists a k' and a permutation p such that $m'_{k'} = $ **out**, $p(m + 1) = k'$, $\forall i \neq k'$, $m'_i = $ **in** and $\forall i \in [1, m + 1]$, $\rho(t_i) = t'_j$ with $j = p(i)$). The function fun is implemented by the following code

```
fun (a₁:t₁;...;aₘ:tₘ) return tₘ₊₁ is
x :  tₘ₊₁ ;
begin
    proc' (a'ⱼ₁=>a₁,...,a'ₖ'=>x,...,a'ⱼₘ=>aₘ);
            -- where jᵢ = p(i)
    return x ;
end ;
```

  - fun and $proc'$ have the same number of arguments (i.e. $n = m$), one of the arguments a_l of fun is of the type t_{m+1} returned by fun, all the arguments of $proc$ are of mode **in** except one, $a'_{k'}$, which is of mode **in out** and of the type returned by fun and the arguments types in fun and $proc'$ correspond modulo the renaming and a permutation (i.e. there exists a k', a l and a permutation p such that $t_l = t_{m+1}$, $p(m + 1) = k'$, $m'_{k'} = $ **in out**, $\forall i \neq k'$, $m'_i = $ **in** and $\forall i \in [1, n]$, $\rho(t_i) = t'_j$ with $j = p(i)$). The function fun is implemented by the following code

```
fun (a₁:t₁;...;aₘ:tₘ) return tₘ₊₁ is
x :  tₗ ;
begin
    x := aₗ;
    proc' (a'ⱼ₁=>a₁,...,a'ₖ'=>x,...,a'ⱼₘ=>aₘ);
            -- where jᵢ = p(i)
    return x ;  -- remember that tₘ₊₁ = tₗ
end ;
```

Note that we need to define here a new variable of type t_l and to assign it the value a_l. Because of this assignment, we have to forbid usage of limited private types.

- A procedure $\texttt{proc}(a_1{:}m_1\ t_1;\ldots;a_m{:}m_m\ t_m)$ can be implemented by means of a function $\texttt{fun}'\,(a_1'{:}t_1';\ldots;a_n'{:}t_n')$ `return` t_{n+1}' in two cases :

  - `proc` has one more argument than `fun` (i.e. $n + 1 = m$), all the arguments of `proc` are of mode **in** except one, a_k, which is in mode **out** and of the type returned by `fun`, and the arguments types in `proc` and `fun`' correspond modulo the renaming and a permutation (i.e. there exists a k and a permutation p such that $m_k = $ **out**, $p(k) = n + 1$, $\forall i \neq k,\ m_i = $ **in** and $\forall i \in [1, m],\ \rho(t_i) = t_j'$ with $j = p(i)$.

    The procedure `proc` is implemented by the following code

    ```
    proc (a₁:m₁ t₁;...;aₘ:mₘ tₘ) is
    begin
        aₖ := fun' (a'ⱼ₁=>a₁,..., a'ⱼₘ=>aₘ);  -- where jᵢ = p(i)
    end ;
    ```

    This case corresponds to the implementation of the procedure `add` by means of the function `cons` in the `LIST` and `C_LIST` example.

  - they have the same number of arguments (i.e. $n = m$), all the arguments of `proc` are of mode **in** except one, a_k, which is of mode **in out**, one of the arguments $a_{l'}'$ of `fun` is of the type t_{n+1}' returned by `fun` and the arguments types in `proc` and `fun`' correspond modulo the renaming and a permutation (i.e. there exists a permutation p, a k and a l' such that $t_{l'}' = t_{n+1}'$, $m_k = $ **in out** and $\forall i \neq k,\ m_i = $ **in**, $p(k) = l'$ and $\forall i \in [1, m],\ \rho(t_i) = t_j'$ with $j = p(i)$.

    The procedure `proc` is implemented by the following code

    ```
    proc (a₁:m₁ t₁;...;aₘ:mₘ tₘ) is
    begin
        aₖ := func' (a'ⱼ₁=>a₁,..., a'ⱼₘ=>aₘ);  -- where jᵢ = p(i)
    end ;
    ```

4 Searching for a component to reuse

Finding the good renaming between a goal specification and a reusable component is a tedious and error prone task. Hence we have decided to build a tool to assist Ada programmers in this task and to guarantee an errorless result (at least with respect to the static semantics of Ada).

The main problem with such a tool is the huge number of potential renamings. For instance there are 12 possible renamings between the COLOUR and the COLOR packages (including the permutations of the arguments of `equal`). Moreover the number of potential renamings usually increases as an exponential function of the number of subprograms of the specifications. The solution to this problem is to avoid constructing all the possible renamings : the time needed for that would be far too long, and the user wouldn't know what to do with such a long list of renamings. To reduce the computation duration, we only compute what we call fragments : a fragment is a part of renaming dealing only with one data type. We then let the user build incrementally the adequate renaming by choosing one fragment per data type. Of course we have to check that the selected fragments are compatible, and we only propose the user the fragments which are compatible with his previous choices.

To avoid dead-end choices (i.e. choosing a fragment which is correct for one package, but which is incompatible with all the fragments of another package), we have to propose only fragments that can actually lead to a correct renaming. For that purpose we begin by the so-called *check* phase which verifies that there exists at least one complete renaming between the goal specification and the reused components and which removes the fragments leading to dead-end choices. The good performances of this phase allow to run it as a filter so as to extract from a library all the components which correspond modulo a renaming to a given specification.

As explained above, some subprograms requested in the goal may be missing in in the reusable components, but can be implemented without knowing the actual implementation of the reused components (the extraneous subprograms of the section 2). Hence we ask the user to further split the non generator subprograms of his goal specification between essential and extraneous subprograms, and we search for the renamings that give a value to at least each essential subprogram.

To define more precisely our search method, we have to state how we associate subprograms with types and to define the so-called set of required types :

> *Given a goal specification* SP_G *and types* t *and* t' *defined respectively in the packages* P *and* P' *of* SP_G, *we say that* t **is more primitive than** t' *iff* P *is below* P' *w.r.t. the* **with** *hierarchy of* SP_G.

> *Given a goal specification* SP_G *and a subprogram* s, *we* **associate** s **with the types** *of its profile which are maximal w.r.t. the "is more primitive than" relationship.*

> *Given a goal specification* SP_G *and a set* S *of types of* SP_G, *we define the set* $\hat{S}$ *of the* **required types** *for* S *as the least set of types in* SP_G *verifying :*
> - *S is included in $\hat{S}$,*
> - *for each type t in $\hat{S}$ and for each essential subprogram s associated with t in SP_G, each type occurring in the profile of s also belongs to $\hat{S}$.*

For instance, the add function in LIST is associated with List and not with Colour because Colour is defined below List; the set of required types for

List is { List, Colour, Boolean }; this set does not contain Natural because length is not an essential function.

> *Given a goal specification* SP$_G$ *and a reusable component* R, *we say that a set of types* S *of* SP$_G$ *is perhaps implementable by reuse of* R *modulo a renaming* ρ [7] *if :*
> - *each type of the set* $\hat{S}$ *of required types for* S *has an image by* ρ,
> - *for each type t in* $\hat{S}$, *each essential subprogram s associated with t has an image by* ρ *and* $\rho(s)$ *is associated with* $\rho(t)$ *in* R,
> - *for each extraneous subprogram s of* SP$_G$, *if* $\rho(s)$ *is defined then the set of the types of the profile of s is perhaps implementable by reuse of* R *modulo* ρ.

In other words, we require to find modulo a renaming all the essential subprograms of the types in S and moreover to be able to implement by reuse all the types that occur in the profiles of these essential subprograms, and so on until an Ada predefined data type. Indeed the types in the profile of the essential subprograms of a type t are needed to implement the type t.

For instance, LIST can be implemented by reuse of COLOR_LIST, for all the required types (namely List, Colour and Boolean) can be found in COLOR_LIST. Since length is an extraneous subprogram, we can reuse COLOR_LIST to implement LIST, even if this function is missing in COLOR_LIST.

Clearly the above conditions are neither necessary nor sufficient : a reusable component can be found not *possibly reusable* for a goal specification SP even when reuse is possible and conversely a component can be found *possibly reusable* even if its semantics is completely different form those of SP (for instance a stack management package will usually be *possibly reusable* for implementing queue management). But due to the recursion in the above conditions, the number of junks is not too large. Moreover this method allows us to discover potential reuse we never though of before, as for instance implementing a tank temperature and pressure controller by reuse of an artificial heart controller [ESF90].

5 The case of generic components

It is necessary, when studying the reuse of Ada codes, to handle the case of generic units. Indeed, generic units are most frequently used as reusable software components [Boo87]. We will thus show how to implement a goal specification by reuse of a generic component. We have to consider two cases: the case of a non generic goal specification and the case of a generic goal specification.

The first case, which is the most common, will be illustrated by an example. Suppose that we want to implement the LIST specification of figure 2 and that

---

[7] or in short that R is perhaps reusable for (implementing) SP$_G$.

```
generic
    type Item is private ;
    with function eq (an_item1, an_item2 : Item) return Boolean ;
package GEN_LIST is
    -- <Types >
    type List is private ;
    -- <Generators >
    function nil return List ; -- < raise no_more_room >
    function cons (an_item : Item; a_list : List) return List ; -- < raise no_more_room >
    -- <Operations >
    function car (a_list : List) return Item ; -- < raise empty_list >
    function cdr (a_list : List) return List ; -- < raise empty_list >
    function nilp (a_list : List) return Boolean ;
    -- <Extraneous Operations >
    function member (an_item : Item; a_list : List) return Boolean ;
    -- <Exceptions >
    no_more_room : exception ;
    empty_list : exception ;
end GEN_LIST ;
```

Figure 5: Example of a generic component specification.

we have a reusable component corresponding to the generic package specification GEN_LIST of figure 5 (here the parameter function eq is used by the member function). We can clearly instantiate Item by COLOUR.Colour and eq by COLOUR.equal so as to implement LIST by GEN_LIST. After that we only have to implement (perhaps by reuse) the COLOUR specification.

A simple trick enables to extend our searching method to this case. First we consider the generic part of GEN_LIST as a package specification of kind parameter. Then we check that Item can be instantiated by COLOUR.Colour : we verify that all the types and generic subprograms of the parameter specification can be found modulo a renaming in COLOUR. Finally we check that all the types and essential subprograms of LIST can be found modulo a renaming in GEN_LIST.

Hence coping with genericity only requires to permute the arguments of the *check* procedure when the reusable package is a generic one.

The implementation of LIST by reuse of GEN_LIST will be achieved by renaming an instance of the generic package GEN_LIST. The instantiation process consists in associating the actual type COLOUR.Colour with the generic formal type GEN_LIST.Item and the actual subprogram COLOUR.equal with the generic formal subprogram GEN_LIST.eq. The association of the subprograms is possible because the formal parameter subprogram and the actual parameter subprogram have the same parameters and result type profile (both are functions and there is

```
generic
    type Elem is private ;
    with function equal (an_elem1, an_elem2 : Elem) return Boolean ;
package G_LIST is
    -- <Types >
    type List is private ;
    -- <Generators >
    function empty return List ; -- < raise no_more_room >
    procedure add (an_elem : in Elem; a_list : in out List) ; -- < raise no_more_room >
    -- <Basic Operations >
    function head (a_list : List) return Elem ; -- < raise empty_list >
    procedure remove_head (a_list : in out List) ; -- < raise empty_list >
    function is_empty (a_list : List) return Boolean ;
    -- <Extraneous Operations >
    function contains (a_list : List; an_elem : Elem) return Boolean ;
    function length (a_list : List) return Natural ;
    -- <Exceptions >
    no_more_room : exception ;
    empty_list : exception ;
end G_LIST ;
```

Figure 6: Example of a generic specification.

no permutation of arguments between them). If one of these two conditions comes not to be verified, it would have been necessary to define a new subprogram, in the goal specification, which would have been implemented by means of the actual subprogram, so that this new one would match the formal parameter subprogram.

The second case, the case of a generic goal specification, is very similar to the first one. All what has been said above concerning the search of a generic component and the implementation of the goal specification by reuse still holds. We just have to verify that a generic formal parameter type or subprogram in the goal corresponds to a generic formal parameter type or subprogram in the reused component, ensuring that any possible instantiation of the goal specification will correspond to a possible instantiation of the reused component. In other words, if the goal package is a generic package, we have to verify that all the types and subprograms of the parameter specification of the reused component can be found, modulo a renaming, in the generic parameter part of the goal package; then we have to check that all the types and essential operations of the goal can be found, modulo a renaming, in the reused component. Hence we can implement the specification G_LIST of figure 6 by reuse of the component GEN_LIST of figure 5, because we can associate Item and eq with Elem and equal and because all the essential subprograms in G_LIST can be implemented by subprograms in GEN_LIST.

```
with GEN_LIST ; -- reuse of GEN_LIST
package G_LIST is
    package NEW_GEN_LIST is new GEN_LIST (Item => Elem, eq => equal) ;
    subtype List is NEW_GEN_LIST.List ;
    function empty return List renames NEW_GEN_LIST.nil ;
    -- etc., as in figure 4
end G_LIST ;
```

Figure 7: Implementation of GEN_LIST by reuse of G_LIST.

The implementation by reuse will still be achieved by rename of an instance of the generic reused component (cf. figure 7). Indeed, since it is not possible to rename a generic unit, the generic component will be instantiated by the generic parameters of the goal package, resulting thus in a "generic instance" (NEW_GEN_LIST in figure 7), which is renamed, as in the non generic case, in order to implement the goal.

6 ROSE-ADA : the tool

This method for searching reusable component and implementing goal specification by reuse is supported by a tool called ROSE-ADA. This tool is implemented in Y3 (an object oriented environment on the top of Le_Lisp [Cal.86]) and use CENTAUR for parsing and building Ada code [BCD+87]. It has been tested on SUN workstation, but due to the portability of Le_Lisp is can be executed on many other platforms. Its user interface is based on X11 (version 4).

The current version of the tool supports almost all the Ada construct (except the multi-tasking aspect of Ada) and the predefined packages are correctly handled. Moreover it is possible to state in a goal specification that some packages are already implemented. This allows to cope with programming in the many and to use standard libraries (for instance a GKS library of graphical procedures).

The performances of the filter part of ROSE-ADA allows to use it on relatively big set of reusable components : the check phase for the LIST and COLOR_LIST example takes less than 0.05 seconds on a SUN3/60, and it take usually less than one second on components having around 50 packages. Hence filtering 200 components will usually take less than 2 minutes. Of course this tool is not meant to filter big reusable component libraries having millions of components; we consider that the user should use other tools before, like classification tools, in order to narrow the candidates before applying the ROSE-ADA filter.

Note that the ROSE-Ada filter can only check whether the goal specification and a given reusable component correspond at a static semantic level. Thus, the

Figure 8: User-interface of ROSE-ADA (part 1).

user may need to consult other information related to a reusable component in order to verify that it satisfies his needs (eg. informal description, target machine description, quality information).

Having chosen a reusable component $\mathcal{R}$, the user can reuse it to implement the goal specification. ROSE-Ada assists the user in building the corresponding renaming in an incremental way, as described in section 4. This is very useful since the number of possible renamings may be quite big (12 for the COLOUR type). A first window (cf. figure 8) enables the user to choose which type of $\mathcal{R}$ will implement a type of the goal specification. After that, he has to build the fragment corresponding to this goal type : he has to choose, for at least each essential subprogram of this type, the subprogram of $\mathcal{R}$ which will implement it, and the same for the exceptions raised by these essential subprograms. Whenever the user attempts to rename a type, a subprogram or an exception, he is supplied with all the possible choices which assure a compatibility between all the fragments. In case there is just one possible choice, it is automatically displayed, and the user has only to validate the choice. This is true, for instance, for the LIST type of figure 8. Once the renaming is built, the user may ask ROSE-Ada to implement the goal specification by reuse of $\mathcal{R}$ modulo this renaming. The corresponding package interfaces and package bodies are automatically deduced (cf. figure 9).

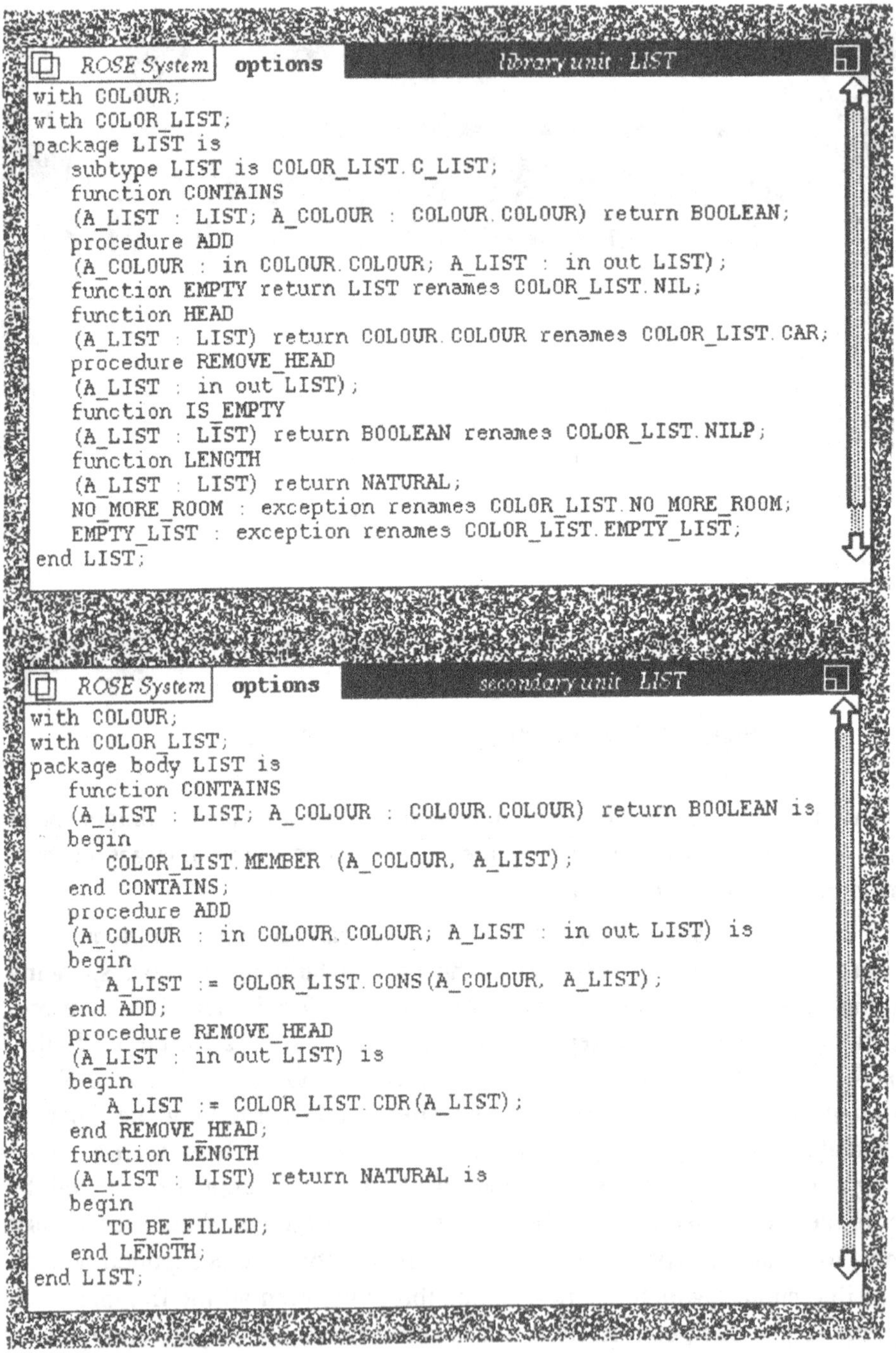
ROSE System
options
library unit LIST
with COLOUR;
with COLOR_LIST;
package LIST is
subtype LIST is COLOR_LIST.C_LIST;
function CONTAINS
(A_LIST : LIST; A_COLOUR : COLOUR.COLOUR) return BOOLEAN;
procedure ADD
(A_COLOUR : in COLOUR.COLOUR; A_LIST : in out LIST);
function EMPTY return LIST renames COLOR_LIST.NIL;
function HEAD
(A_LIST : LIST) return COLOUR.COLOUR renames COLOR_LIST.CAR;
procedure REMOVE_HEAD
(A_LIST : in out LIST);
function IS_EMPTY
(A_LIST : LIST) return BOOLEAN renames COLOR_LIST.NILP;
function LENGTH
(A_LIST : LIST) return NATURAL;
NO_MORE_ROOM : exception renames COLOR_LIST.NO_MORE_ROOM;
EMPTY_LIST : exception renames COLOR_LIST.EMPTY_LIST;
end LIST;
ROSE System
options
secondary unit LIST
with COLOUR;
with COLOR_LIST;
package body LIST is
function CONTAINS
(A_LIST : LIST; A_COLOUR : COLOUR.COLOUR) return BOOLEAN is
begin
COLOR_LIST.MEMBER (A_COLOUR, A_LIST);
end CONTAINS;
procedure ADD
(A_COLOUR : in COLOUR.COLOUR; A_LIST : in out LIST) is
begin
A_LIST := COLOR_LIST.CONS(A_COLOUR, A_LIST);
end ADD;
procedure REMOVE_HEAD
(A_LIST : in out LIST) is
begin
A_LIST := COLOR_LIST.CDR(A_LIST);
end REMOVE_HEAD;
function LENGTH
(A_LIST : LIST) return NATURAL is
begin
TO_BE_FILLED;
end LENGTH;
end LIST;

Figure 9: User-interface of ROSE-ADA (part 2).

The result may now be inserted in the development environment.

Conclusion

We have presented a method and a tool to help retrieval and adaptation of reusable Ada components. On the contrary of most of the others retrieval tools, which are based on classification schemes or on key-words, we do not impose the same names in the specification to be implemented and in the reusable component. For that aspect, our tool best compares with the PARIS system [KRKS87]. This system is, to some extend, more ambitious than our, because its retrieval method is based on the semantics of the reused components. But we consider that only very few developers currently use (and understand) formal specification. Hence we choose to base our retrieval method on a syntactical level and to use only Ada package specifications, which are well known by the developers.

As far as we know, our adaptation method does not relate to any other tool, except perhaps to application generators (but the reuse paradigm is not the component paradigm as in our work).

The ROSE-ADA tool is not meant to be a complete and stand-alone tool; it has to be coupled with classification or key-words based tools for the non functional aspects (performances, quality, ...). It can also be coupled with tools like PARIS if reuse is to be proved on a semantical level, for instance when very high reliability is requested. Hence ROSE-ADA is currently integrated within the ESF-ROSE reuse environment [MAR90], and is planned to be also integrated within the CONCERTO workbench.

We are currently adapting ROSE-ADA for HOOD specifications [Eur89] instead of Ada specifications, and we plan to study real-time aspects very soon.

Acknowledgement

A special thank to J.-C. Luchet for his help during the implementation of ROSE-ADA and to V. Dzuba for its comments on the first versions of this paper.

References

[BCD+87] P. Borras, D. Clement, Th. Despeyroux, J. Incerpi, G. Kahn, B. Lang, and V. Pascual. Centaur the system. Technical Report 777, INRIA, France, 1987.

[Ber86] E.V. Berard. Creating reusable Ada software. In *Proc. National Conference on Software Reusability and maintainability*, Tysons Corner, Virginia, 1986.

[Boo87] G. Booch. *Software Engineering with Ada*. Benjamin/Cummings Publishing Company, 1987.

[BR87]   T. Biggerstaff and Ch. Richter. Reusability framework, assessment and directions. In *Proc. 20th Annual Hawaii Int. Conf. on System Sciences*, 1987.

[Cal.86]   J. Chailloux and *al.* LE_LISP de l'INRIA, Version 15.2, Reference Manual. 1986.

[CCJ+91]   J. Cazin, P. Cros, R. Jacquart, M. Lemoine, and P. Michel. Construction and reuse of formal developments. In *Proc. TAPSoft'91*, 1991.

[CHSW89]   J. Cramer, H. Huenneken, W. Schäffer, and S. Wolf. A process oriented approach for software reuse. Technical report, Dortmund Universität, Germany, 1989.

[Den87]   R.J. St. Dennis. Reusable Ada software guideline. In *Proc. 20th Annual Hawaii Int. Conf. on System Sciences*, 1987.

[ESF90]   ESF-ROSE Consortium. Scenarii for HOOD reuse : analysis, method and examples. ESF-ROSE internal report, 1990.

[Eur89]   European Space Agency. HOOD Reference Manual. Issue 3.0, 1989.

[FN87]   W.E. Frakes and B.A. Nejmeh. An information system for software reuse. In *proc. 10th Minnowbrook Workshop for Software Reuse*, Blue Mountain Lake, NY, 1987.

[GR83]   A. Goldberg and D. Robson. *Smalltalk-80: The langage and its implementation*. Addison-Wesley, 1983.

[KRKS87]   S. Katz, C.A. Richter, and T. Khe-Sing. PARIS : A system for reusing partially interpreted schemas. In *Proc. 9th Int. Conf. on Software Engineering*, 1987.

[LG84]   R.G. Lanergan and C.A. Grasso. Software engineering with reusable design and code. *IEEE Transaction on Software Engineering*, SE-10(5), 1984.

[MAR90]   Th. Moineau, J. Abardir, and E. Rames. Toward a generic and extensible reuse environment. In P.A.V. Hall, editor, *Proc. SE'90*. Cambridge University Press, July 1990.

[Mey87]   B. Meyer. Reusability : The case for object-oriented design. *IEEE Software*, March 1987.

[NS88]   K. Nielsen and K. Shumate. *Designing Large Real-Time Systems with Ada*. McGraw-Hill, 1988.

[PCW83]   D.L. Parnas, P.C. Clements, and D.M. Weiss. Enhancing reusability with information hiding. In *ITT Workshop on Reusability in Programming*, 1983.

[Wir88]   M. Wirsing. Algebraic description of reusable software components. Technical Report MIP–8816, Passau University, Germany, Aug 1988.

Software Reuse: Customer vs. Contractor Point-Counterpoint

Trevor Syms
NATO CIS Ada Support and Control Capability
8 rue de Geneve
B-1120 Brussels, BELGIUM
011-322-728-8595

Christine L. Braun
Contel Technology Center
15000 Conference Center Drive
Chantilly, Virginia USA
703-818-4475
braun@ctc.contel.com

Abstract

Software reuse promises significant benefits to the software engineering profession, and is therefore an avowed goal of both organizations that contract for software ("customers") and those that develop it ("contractors"). Customer and contractor organizations are actively pursuing reuse programs, researching the technology and establishing libraries of reusable assets.

There are many technical challenges in achieving software reuse, but there are perhaps even more nontechnical challenges. Software reuse will require fundamental changes in business and contractual practices, organizational procedures, and the day-to-day activities of software engineers. Organizations naturally resist change; overcoming this resistance is a major consideration in moving toward an increased practice of reuse.

Many of the nontechnical issues related to reuse deal with the customer/contractor relationship. Reuse raises issues about financial incentives, software ownership, responsibility and liability, etc. that must be addressed in software development contracts. It also requires modifications to the software development process that must be recognized in program management procedures. A successful reuse program cannot be established without customer/contractor cooperation.

Unfortunately, such cooperation can be difficult to achieve. The customer and contractor necessarily have different perspectives and concerns in software contracting, and the contractual and program management processes are the formal mechanisms for managing these differences. There is a tendency for each "side" to view the other as an adversary, or an impediment in achieving its own goals. In particular, this conflict in viewpoints can appear when considering software reuse. Contractors believe the customer does not understand their concerns about reuse costs, risks, and liabilities; customers believe contractors do not support their goal of reducing software costs through reuse.

In fact, customers and contractors share the goal of reducing software cost and improving quality through reuse. Their differing perspectives, however, can obscure this basic agreement. To understand, and eventually to resolve, these differences, it is important that each side understand and appreciate the other's perspective. This paper seeks to further this understanding by examining some of these differences in perspective and suggesting common ground.

Common Goals, Different Perspectives

Software reuse is widely recognized as a key way to reduce software costs and improve software quality. Both customers and contractors are motivated by these benefits. Customers are clearly motivated to reduce costs -- to be able to obtain the best product available at the least possible expenditure of corporate or taxpayer money. As representatives of the end users, they are also vitally interested in quality.

It is less widely believed that contractors are motivated by cost reduction and quality. Cynical observers sometimes argue that contractors are opposed to cost-saving measures because they will make less money, and that there is not a financial incentive for the contractor to take an undue interest in quality. However, usual contracting systems create ample incentives for both cost reduction and quality. Contractors who can perform cost effectively can bid more competitively, thus increasing win percentage, and can achieve greater profit on development efforts. Contractors known to produce high-quality software have a distinct advantage in bidding on future programs. The incentives for reuse are there; the problem is to remove conflicting disincentives -- concerns about hidden costs, risk, and loss of competitive advantage.

A key understanding behind this problem is that customers and contractors have fundamentally different views of what "reuse" really means. The customer is primarily interested in getting more than one contractor to share software. The contractor, on the other hand, is primarily interested in reusing his own software for multiple customers. Both of these desires conflict with some of the standard practices in the customer/contractor relationship, and both threaten some of the accepted practices of the other side. The contractor is not eager to use other companies' software unless he can be guaranteed someone else (usually the customer) will absorb the risk of its failure. He is usually even less eager to allow other contractors to have his software, as this is perceived as giving up a competitive advantage. The customer, on the other hand, often questions the use of the contractor's existing software on his system. He gives up the opportunity to monitor its development, to have it built to his standards, to hold the exclusive right to its use, and perhaps to obtain the detailed documentation he wants. He may also fear having to compromise his system's functionality in order to conform to the existing software.

These are non-trivial issues -- important to the parties involved and sometimes difficult to resolve. However, they are clearly fundamental to achieving a significant practice of software reuse. They are not unsolvable problems, but they involve changes to accepted and institutionalized practice.

Reuse Opportunities

In considering the dimensions of software reuse, it is important to identify the *kinds of assets that can be reused.* The most obvious type of reuse is code reuse -- the use of the same code in more than one system. However, reuse of other kinds of assets is an important part of the overall practice of reuse, sometimes more important than code reuse. Other assets that can be reused include requirements and design. Each involves unique considerations.

Especially interesting to the subject of this paper is the *reuse of requirements.* In the traditional software life cycle observed in contract software development, requirements are prepared by the customer and put out for bid by contractors. The requirements specify the function and performance of the desired system. To a very great degree, the requirements determine the extent of reuse that is possible; the contractor can only reuse software that conforms to the specified requirements. Often, the requirements make it impossible to reuse existing software that performs the same basic function, because it differs in details such as appearance of the user interface. Even when the requirements specification comes from a customer agency for whom the contractor has built a previous similar system, "improvements" in the specification may preclude reuse. Sometimes, even two documents that describe identical behavior are written so differently that this is not apparent to the contractor.

Customers need to aware that there can be a negative correlation between the amount of detail in the requirements specification and the extent to which the contractor can practice reuse. Avoiding overspecification of behavior that is not really important to the end user can greatly increase reuse opportunities. One approach to this problem is to circulate a draft requirements specification to interested bidders, with a request for industry comments on areas in which minor requirements changes would permit reuse.

Reuse of design is possible in a wider of range of situations than code reuse. Often when requirements are similar but not identical, design can be reused. This is common practice within a single development organization, but is rare across organizations. Sharing design among multiple contractors faces many obstacles. Perhaps the most significant is a technical obstacle; it is very difficult to understand another person's design well enough to reuse it. However, there are also many contracting-related concerns. The same issues of ownership and liability apply. Because of the technical difficulty, the contractor who agrees to reuse a design incurs significant risk. The contractor who is asked to give his design to another company is not only threatened by potential loss of competitive advantage (as in code reuse), but faces a high probability that the other company will not be able to understand the design and will blame him for this failure.

Other reusable assets include documentation, test cases, and other by-products of the software development process. Typically these are reused along with design or code; it is important to recognize this need and allow for it in contracting.

Another dimension of reuse is *possible sources of reusable components.* These include:

- previously developed by the same contractor under contract to the same customer
- previously developed by the same contractor under contract to another customer

- previously developed by a different contractor under contract to the same customer

- previously developed by a different contractor under contract to a different customer

- developed by the contractor with internal funding, and hence contractor-owned

- Commercial-Off-the-Shelf (COTS) software products

Each raises interesting issues of ownership and responsibility, which will be discussed in later subsections.

Contractual Issues

In software contracting, many issues arise concerning ownership of and rights to the developed software. Ordinarily, both the customer and the contractor have some rights to the software, though the specific assignment of these rights should be delineated in the contract. In the usual case, a government customer pays for the full development effort, and obtains full rights to use the software for other government programs (for example, to give it to other contractors). Such software, because it is paid for by taxpayers, is often placed in the public domain, and is thus made available to anyone who will pay a nominal reproduction cost. In this typical scenario, the developer often (but not always, depending on the contract) also retains rights to the software. He may choose to offer it for sale -- in a sense competing with the government's "free" version, usually offering enhancements or customer support that may make it more attractive to a purchaser.

This model becomes more complicated in a reuse situation. If the contractor wishes to build and take advantage of a library of reusable assets, he faces some questions. If he wishes to stock his library with components built on a government contract, what guarantee does he have that those same components will not be made available to his competitors, either directly by the customer or through the public domain? If he wishes to perform the contract using software that he already owns, must he abandon his rights to it when delivering it to the customer? The typical contracting model described above will answer both these questions to the customer's disadvantage, providing a disincentive to reuse.

Similarly, the customer who wishes to practice reuse also has concerns. If he wishes to obtain software that can be reused on other programs, how does he ensure that the software will in fact be usable by another contractor? Will it be adequately documented and comprehensible? Who should bear the responsibility if the software does not meet expectations? How will he arrange for its maintenance? The typical contracting model does not adequately address these concerns. In fact, it might be considered to provide an incentive to the contractor to deliver software that *cannot* be easily reused.

However, the typical model is not the only possible one. Contract law (though it differs from country to country) is generally flexible enough to allow a contract that meets both parties' needs. However, both parties must be aware of the issues and explicitly address them. When issues are addressed up front, a satisfactory contract can usually be written. While each case will differ, some of the options that might be considered are:

- The contractor who wishes to restrict the government's right to distribute his software might negotiate a significantly reduced software development cost in return.

- The contractor who wishes to reuse to use software he already owns in a delivered system might restrict rights to only those components. (This is similar to a situation that arises frequently today, in which a delivered system includes a commercially-available software product such as an operating system or DBMS.)

- To address liability and maintenance issues, and to provide an incentive to the contractor to deliver software that can be reused by others, the customer might arrange a continuing support contract of some kind. One possibility is to pay the contractor a license fee for each "reuser" of the software, in return for support and maintenance.

- An award fee may be used to incentivize the contractor to produce software that meets measurable criteria for reusable software components.

Legal Issues

In addition to contract issues, a number of other legal considerations can impact the practice of software reuse. These considerations are significant not only in contract software development, but in the software products world at large. Software is protected legally as *intellectual property*; as such, a number of laws control its dissemination and use. While these laws differ from country to country, in general there are three basic types of protection afforded to software -- *trade secret* protection, *copyright* protection, and *patent* protection. A variety of rules and precedents determine whether a particular software entity can be protected in any one of these ways, and all have been the subject of court battles. In general, the most common form of protection for software is copyright protection.

Most commercial software products are protected by copyright. Developers of software under contract also often claim a software copyright, explicitly assigning a number of rights to the customer. Among the restricted rights usually held by the copyright owner are: the right to reproduce the software, the right to reuse the software, the right to maintain and adapt the software, the right to reverse engineer the software, the right to make backup copies of the software, and the right to authorize third parties to perform any of these restricted acts. This means that only the copyright holder and those to whom he specifically assigns such rights can perform any of these activities. (The particulars vary from country to country. For example, US law permits a software purchaser to make a single backup copy, which must be destroyed if he ceases to be the owner of the software.)

In writing contracts involving the reuse of software, it is important that both parties be aware of the legal implications of copyright law. Holding the copyright is often in the best interests of the contractor. It limits the rights of the customer, but often the assigned rights can be defined so that the customer can in fact accomplish all of his objectives, while at the same time allowing the contractor to retain some rights and thus providing more incentive for reuse. In this case, the customer must recognize his needs and negotiate for them.

When the contractor uses software he already owns in performing a development contract, he is particularly likely to protect that software by copyright. In this case, the customer can usually negotiate the rights necessary to use the software as required. If he wishes to obtain full ownership of the delivered product, and the right to distribute it freely, he might be asked to pay for these rights, since he has not paid for development of the reused software.

Ownership issues also arise when there is a desire to reuse software across customer organization boundaries. If a contractor develops a software component for one customer and then proposes to reuse it for another, he may find the assignment of ownership rights in his original contract prohibits him from doing so. This is even more likely to arise when both the contractor and customer organizations are different. It is important in negotiating rights to anticipate such potential needs in the future.

Responsibilities and Liabilities

The increased practice of reuse introduces a number of interesting new problems concerning responsibilities and liabilities. When a contractor is asked by the customer to reuse software developed by another company, he will (or should) have a number of questions. Who guarantees the software will work? If it doesn't work, will the customer arrange to have it fixed? If this unexpected problem impacts schedule or cost, will the customer absorb the difference? Or is the contractor expected to assume responsibility for the reused software?

Usually the customer asks the contractor to reuse software because he assumes it will reduce his cost and perhaps development time. However, unless he guarantees the software and accepts any consequences of its failure to perform as advertised, he must expect the contractor to include in his price and schedule some allowance for such failure. He can minimize this additional cost in several ways:

- He can provide advance copies of the source code and documentation -- with the bid package if not sooner -- to allow the contractor to develop a realistic assessment of the risk involved in reuse. The quality of this material will affect the contractor's estimate for its use.

- He can develop a work plan that allows the contractor time after contract award to evaluate the software and decide whether to use it or not, and if not allow the contractor to pursue an alternate (and separately priced) approach.

- He can arrange for maintenance by the original developer, perhaps guaranteeing some level of turn-around time for bug fixes, after which he might recognize the contractors claim for cost or schedule relief.

The customer can have similar concerns when a contractor proposes to reuse his existing software in the customer's development program. He will be buying software that he has not controlled and monitored during development. How does he know if it meets his quality standards? What assurance does he have that its documentation is acceptable? If he finds it doesn't meet his standards, what can he do about it? (A particularly interesting problem is proposed reuse of software in a secure system. Typically, the customer organization requires oversight of the complete development process as part of validating the software.)

Again, the contract can address these concerns. It can establish objective standards that must be met by all delivered software, and place the responsibility on the contractor to meet those standards. These requirements should be well thought out, so that the contractor does not spend time needlessly revising documentation (for example) at customer expense.

Another interesting issue is that of indemnity -- who is responsible if a malfunction of reused software causes financial loss or human injury? This is actually a gray area in software contracting in general; reuse only complicates the issue. It is not difficult to imagine a scenario in which one customer organization blames another for failure of software originally developed under that organization's contract. All development contracts should address indemnity, but many fail to specifically consider indemnity relating to reuse of the software. This should be made explicit in writing contracts that include software development.

Cost/Economic Issues

Most people in the reuse field believe that reusable software is most useful when it is explicitly crafted for reuse by applying particular design, coding, and documentation standards. This is often more than simply good quality software; extra generality and flexibility are usually built into the design. This is in effect an additional requirement placed on the software developer, and it usually adds to the cost of development. Who pays this added cost?

The ideal answer to this question is that he who profits from reuse (since it presumably leads to reduced costs) should pay. However, not all the "producer/consumer" pairings we identified earlier have that property. A contractor might be asked to make his software reusable with little recognition of the added cost required, so that he earns a lower profit. He may then be "rewarded" for this work by having his software given to a competitor to be reused, thus letting the competitor profit from his efforts. In an alternative worst case, the customer might pay an added cost for highly reusable software without realizing it, so that the contractor can reuse the software in his own future programs.

Some contractual arrangements that more closely fit the "he who profits, pays" goal are:

- The customer provides, with the solicitation, explicit design and coding standards for all software required to be reusable, so that the contractor can estimate the work accurately. He then pays the cost for this additional effort and profits from that benefit by writing the contract so that he has the right to reuse the software on future programs.

- The customer does not necessarily pay an extra cost to ensure software meets reusability criteria, but pays the contractor a "royalty" whenever his software is reused in another program.

- The customer provides reusability guidelines (as opposed to required standards) to the contractor, and pays an award fee or other incentive based on degree to which the guidelines are followed.

- The contractor invests the added cost of making the software more reusable than his contract requires so that he can gain competitive advantage and/or greater profit by using it on future contracts. He may be able to negotiate a contract that at least partially limits access to his software by other contractors, in return for his extra investment.

- The contractor develops software under contract that meets normal contractual criteria but does not have added reuse qualities, then enhances reusability at his own expense to provide him with leverage on future contracts.

Clearly these issues are closely related to the ownership issues discussed earlier. Typically, whoever owns rights to the software stands to profit from its reusability. Usually these rights are shared between customer and contractor in some way; cost should be shared accordingly.

Program Management Issues

As indicated previously, reuse must be addressed when establishing the contractual requirements for a software development effort. The anticipated development of software for reuse, or reuse of existing software, must be made explicit. Means of determining that these requirements are met must be established.

When a contractor is required to develop software that is reusable, there must some definition of "reusable". A common way to do this is to specify standards or guidelines that, when followed, produce reusable software. The customer might have a set of such standards/guidelines that are referenced in the contract. Conformance can be made a contractual requirement, or it can be rewarded by an award or incentive fee. Alternatively, the contractor might have an internal set of standards for producing reusable software. The customer can ask the contractor to set forth his own standards in a Software Development Plan or similar document. Once approved by the customer, they can be used similar to customer-provided guidelines. Ideally, these contractor-provided guidelines should be included in the proposal so that both parties know the particulars of the work being contracted. (Similarly, of course, the customer-provided guidelines should be provided with the solicitation.)

An alternative approach is to define "reusable software" as simply "software that is reused". Rather than relying on any standards or guidelines, the contractor is considered to have delivered reusable software when it is reused successfully. This is hard to enforce as a contractual requirement, as there is ample opportunity for the developer to blame the reuser. However, it may be a suitable basis for an award fee.

Once reusability criteria are established, they must be enforced. Thus, they must be enforceable -- that is, objective and measurable. The contractor should be asked to provide an approach to monitoring their use on a regular basis, perhaps combining a Quality Assurance function with automated tools that either require or check for conformance. The customer must also have a way to verify that the criteria are met. This should be a specific subject addressed at program reviews. In addition, the customer QA organization should perform some level of audit for conformance.

If reusability is extremely critical in a particular program, for example if a known upcoming program is dependent on reusing the software produced in this program, an actual test of reusability might be required. This might include an independent exercise wherein some portion of the software is adapted to the requirements of the upcoming program. The feasibility and ease of this adaptation can then be judged. Such a test, of course, should be an understood requirement from the beginning of the program, and the test details developed similarly to normal software test plan and procedure development.

Similarly, program management practices must address the reuse of existing software. As noted earlier, it is usually not realistic to demand that reused software conform to all program standards, particularly in such details as coding style. If the contractor proposes to reuse software, it is ordinarily his responsibility to demonstrate to the customer that the software, documentation, etc. are sufficient to meet his needs. If the customer asks the contractor to reuse the software, he normally should provide software and documentation of acceptable quality and not expect the contractor to improve them. It is particularly worth noting that customer flexibility regarding the use of a particular set of documentation standards can save significant cost. As long as documentation for reused components meets the customer's usability requirements, it is far more cost effective not to redo it to another standard. This will usually require a contractual modification, as the documentation standard is normally specified in the contract.

Another issue is the testing of reused software. Clearly, the software should participate in integration and system testing, but unit testing may not be required. This is a very situational judgement, however, based on the contractor's familiarity with and confidence in the reused software.

Commercial Software

It has already become fairly common for contractors to include commercial-off-the-shelf (COTS) software in systems they deliver to the government. Among the most common examples of this are commercial operating systems and data base management systems. Other commercial components are also becoming available, particularly since the advent of Ada.

In many ways, contracting for systems that include these commercial products is similar to contracting for systems that include reused software. There are many similar issues that must be addressed:

- What can/should the customer expect in rights to the software? Typically, it is not realistic to demand a source license nor rights to modify and redistribute the COTS software, unless some kind of secondary license fee is negotiated.

- What testing and documentation should be expected for the software? Typically, the customer does not expect additional unit testing, but requires testing as an integral part of the system. Usually existing user documentation is considered acceptable; because the customer ordinarily does not have the right nor the need to modify the software, design documentation is not necessary.

- What arrangements can be made for maintenance? Use of COTS software places the customer at risk if he cannot depend on the COTS product vendor to maintain the product. Some assurance of continued maintenance is essential before a customer can accept a COTS component as part of his system.

As previous sections have noted, all these concerns also apply to the reuse of existing software in a contractor's proposed solution. However, while the customer is usually ready to accept answers like those noted above in the case of COTS reuse, he is often more reluctant to do so when a contractor's existing software is proposed. If the customer can apply some of these same principles to contracting for reused software, the benefits of reuse can be significantly enhanced.

Present Initiatives

As the technical community increases its interest in software reuse, and as its benefits begin to be proven, these contractual issues are surfacing as real impediments to the adoption of reuse. Several organizations are beginning to consider these issues and to recommend solutions. Some of these activities are briefly described below. More information on these and other efforts can be found in the publications referenced in the bibliography to this paper.

NATO has begun an initiative focused on increasing the practice of reuse in NATO programs. As part of this effort, they are undertaking the development of a set of guidelines to be used in contracting for software. These guidelines will address the development of reusable components, the creation and operation of a reuse library organization, and interaction by a project with such a reuse organization.

The U.S. Software Technology for Adaptable, Reliable Systems (STARS) program is addressing the technical issues in software reuse, and is also planning for the establishment of a national reusable components library organization. A major focus of this organization will be to work with and modify contracting practices to facilitate the practice of reuse.

The U.S. Joint Integrated Avionics Working Group (JIAWG) includes a software task group that is addressing software reuse issues for a group of interrelated avionics programs (the A-12, Advanced Tactical Fighter, and Light Helicopter). This group has recently prepared a report recommending contract elements that specifically address reuse issues. These include: sample text for an award fee provision and for fee criteria, statement of work text to establish requirements for a reuse library and for the reuse of software, a set of "Special Provisions" appropriate to an effort involving reuse, an addendum to the "Instructions to Offerors" section that asks the offeror to identify restricted rights objects, and that asks for a draft Software

Development Plan describing the contractor's approach to reuse, a set of Evaluation Criteria that include software reuse, and additional contract text addressing software licensing agreements.

The National Securities Industries Association has formed a working group, at the request of government contracting organizations, to address contractual issues in reuse. A draft report has been prepared and a final should be available soon.

The U.S. government is developing proposed modifications to the Federal Acquisition Regulation (FAR) for Rights in Technical Data. A preliminary form of the proposed modifications has been prepared and published in the Federal Register, and several public hearings have recently been held.

A working group of the Association for Computing Machinery Special Interest Group on Ada (SIGAda) has been formed to address software reuse. A subgroup of this organization is considering contractual and legal issues. While no report has been published yet, this group provides an opportunity for interested members of the Ada community to participate in a public forum in this area. The group ordinarily meets at all U.S. SIGAda meetings.

The U.S. Army Information Systems Engineering Command has sponsored a reuse program -- Reusable Ada Parts for Information Systems Development (RAPID) -- that has established a reuse library organization. Among the activities of this program have been a study of the legal and contractual issues related to software reuse and a set of recommendations to the Army for dealing with these issues. RAPID has also produced a set of standards for coding and documentation of reusable software components.

Summary

As noted earlier, customers and contractors are not really that far apart. We share the same goals for software reuse -- reduced cost and improved quality through a significant shift in our approach to software engineering. We often seem at odds because we don't appreciate one another's concerns. In fact, compromises are possible and the mechanisms exist to effect them. However, significant awareness is necessary to use those mechanisms effectively to accomplish the desired result. This paper has attempted to increase that awareness.

One of the attractive things about the software reuse field is that incremental progress is possible. Even if we don't solve all of the problems addressed in this paper, we can all benefit from beginning to practice reuse on a more limited scale. Even reuse within the context of a single program, or by a single customer/contractor combination, has many benefits. The most important thing is simply to begin. As we learn from early practice we will see a clearer path to solutions to problems that now seem inapproachable.

Bibliography

Braun, C.L., J. Goodenough, and R.S. Eanes, *Ada Reusability Guidelines*, SofTech TN 3285-2-208/2, SofTech, Inc., April 1985.

Braun, C.L., "Development Methods Committee Report", *Ada Letters*, November/December 1989.

Department of Defense Software Master Plan (Preliminary Draft), Defense Acquisition Board, Science and Technology Committee, Software Working Group, 9 February 1990.

"Federal Acquisition Regulation (FAR); Rights in Technical Data", *Federal Register*, Vol. 55, No. 199, 15 October 1990.

Joint Integrated Avionics Working Group, "Contract Elements for Software Reuse", J89-S8, 15 March 1990.

Leavitt, R., *The Benefits of Software Reuse*, document number 90-0048-K, Prior Data Sciences Ltd., 6 September 1990.

Ruegsegger, T., *RAPID Center Policy Recommendation*, SofTech TN 3451-4-112/5.1, SofTech, Inc., September 1988.

Ruegsegger, T., *RAPID Center Standards for Reusable Software*, SofTech TN 3451-4-012/6.4, October 1990.

Sookman, B.B., "Intellectual Property Rights and Software Reuse: A Canadian and American Perspective", presented at SIGAda meeting, Ottawa, Canada, July 1989.

"Standardization in Specifying Requirements", Software Working Group Report, Electronics Industries Association meeting, February 1990.

Steadman, A.L., *A Study of the Air Force's Implementation of DOD Software Data Rights Policy for Reusable Software*, document number AFIT/GCM/LSL/88S-10, Air Force Institute of Technology, September 1988.

Syms, T., *Software Reuse Report, Ada Implementation Sub-Group*, NATO CIS Ada Support and Control Capability, 1989.

Reusable Input/Output Packages for Ada Avionic Applications

ALFRED ROSSKOPF

MBB GmbH
P.O. Box 801160, 8000 Munich 80
GERMANY
Tel. +89 6072 6939

Abstract

The availability of Ada packages that allow access to the facilities of MIL-STD-1553B bus interfaces is a recurring problem in – current and future – avionic applications. Basically, the problem arises for each system where communication between computers is based on MIL-STD-1553B and the implementation language is Ada. Since MIL-STD-1553B defines the lower-level communication protocol it favours the definition and development of reusable input/output interfaces. This paper presents Ada packages for target-independent input/output via MIL bus interfaces.

1 Introduction

Ada was defined for real-time embedded systems of which avionic applications are a part of. The use of Ada in this application domain has in the past led to the identification of a number of problems. Many of those were related to the performance of Ada systems and can meanwhile be considered resolved due to the availability of relatively mature Ada implementations.

However, for the use of Ada in avionic applications at least three problem areas remain where the facilities defined by the language or the support provided by off-the-shelf Ada systems is currently not – or only partly – sufficient to build applications using standardized, reusable building blocks. These areas are:

- suitable mathematics packages

- support for multi-processor target systems

- application-specific input/output packages

The lack of suitable support in the first two areas has forced users to develop their own non-standard solutions (see e.g. [TAS2-MP]). One can hope that Ada9X will alleviate some of these problems.

The availability of suitable input/output (I/O) packages is a key requirement in avionic applications. Ada provides only the predefined packages for Text I/O and File I/O which are not applicable to avionics applications. The package template for Low-Level I/O is also not very helpful for the definition of application-specific I/O packages.

Avionics software is known as being very I/O intensive and has to access many different types of I/O devices, including bus interfaces according to MIL-STD-1553B ("MIL bus"), discrete I/O, analog I/O and others. MIL bus interfaces, in particular, play a central role in the distributed architecture of modern avionic systems.

This paper presents the definition of a "Reusable MIL Bus Interface in Ada" (RUMBADA) that can serve as a basis for reusable input/output components in the avionics application domain.

The paper is organized as follows. At first, avionics systems are shortly characterized and some basic principles of communication via MIL bus are described. Then the major requirements for a standardized Ada MIL bus input/output interface are given and some of the related design issues are discussed. Following is an outline of the proposed approach, in terms of an abstract model of the user interface, extracts of the Ada package specifications and examples of their use. Finally, some references to related work are given.

2 The Application Domain

To aid the understanding of the input/output packages presented below it seems appropriate to briefly characterize the hardware environment and to describe some basic principles of communication via MIL bus.

2.1 Distributed Architecture of Avionic Systems

An avionic system can be seen as a distributed system, consisting of a collection of avionic computers. The individual computers roughly correspond to the functional subsystems of the avionic system, as for example flight control, navigation, displays and controls, etc.

The computers are typically linked together via several MIL-STD-1553B data buses. The topology of the connection network is determined by the functional and performance requirements of the overall avionic system. There are computers that are only connected to one data bus and others that have access to two (or more) buses. MIL-STD-1553B defines that for each bus there is one distinguished node, the "bus controller", that initiates all transfers on the bus.

A model of the distributed architecture of a typical avionic system is shown in figure 1. The bus controller of each bus is indicated through a thick line to the bus.

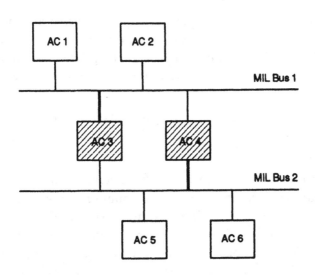

Figure 1: Distributed Architecture of a MIL Bus Based Avionic System (AC = Avionic Computer)

2.2 Hardware Architecture of Multi-Processor Avionic Computers

Typical avionic computers are based on a shared-memory multi-processor architecture, with the following characteristics :

- The computer contains one or more (standard) processors that are dedicated to the application software.

- There are one or more I/O processors that handle input/output from/to the MIL Bus interfaces. These interface processors operate in parallel with the application processors.

- Each of the application and I/O processors has private memory for program code and local data.

- For communication between processors, there are shared memories that can be accessed from several processors. In addition, the hardware provides the capability of inter-processor interrupts.

In figure 2, a typical example is given of a multi-processor avionic computer, containing three application processors and two MIL bus interface processors.

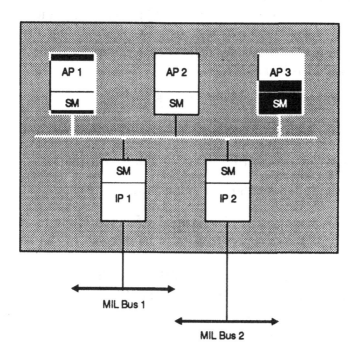

Legend : AP = Application Processor, IP = Bus Interface Processor,
          SM = Shared Memory

Figure 2: Example of a Multi-Processor Avionic Computer

2.3   Basic Principles of Communication via MIL Bus

The following is a short overview on the concepts and characteristics defined in MIL-STD-1553B for MIL Bus based systems. For further details the reader is referred to [MILBUS].

For each bus there is one master node (the "bus controller", BC) and up to 31 other nodes ("remote terminals", RT's). An RT can take over BC function, but there is only one active BC at a time.

The nodes connected to a bus send "messages" to each other, where each message transfer basically involves three components: a "command word" sent from the BC to an RT, a "status word" sent as a response from the RT to the BC and a sequence of up to 32 "data words". This command/response philosophy is central to MIL Bus communication: All message transfers are initiated by the BC and acknowledged by the RT's.

Each of the command, status and data words contains 16 bits of data. (For each such word an additional sync pattern (3 bit times long) and a parity bit (20 bits total) are transmitted over the bus.) The contents and interpretation of command and status words are defined by the standard, the contents of the data words is user-defined.

The command word consists of the following fields:

- RT Address (5 bits) : Identifies a specific RT

- Subaddress (5 bits) : An RT internal address/destination

- Word Count (5 bits) : Number of data words

- Transmit/Receive (1 bit) : "Transmit" refers to data to be transmitted by the RT, "Receive" refers to data to be received by the RT.

The status word contains (amongst other fields) the RT address of the sending RT to allow validation of the status word by the BC. For all message transfers that are not error-free the status word is suppressed. This allows the BC to time-out on this failure condition.

MIL-STD-1553B defines a low-level protocol for communication between bus nodes. The three basic types of message transfers are illustrated in figure 3:

- BC to RT Transfer :
  The BC sends a receive command word, followed by a sequence of up to 32 data words, the RT responds with a status word.

- RT to BC Transfer :
  The BC sends a transmit command word, the RT responds with a status word, followed by a sequence of up to 32 data words.

- RT to RT Transfer :
  The BC sends a receive command to one RT and a transmit command to a second RT. The latter RT sends a status word, followed by a sequence

of up to 32 data words, the first RT sends a status word. Both status words are evaluated by the BC to verify error-free message transmission.

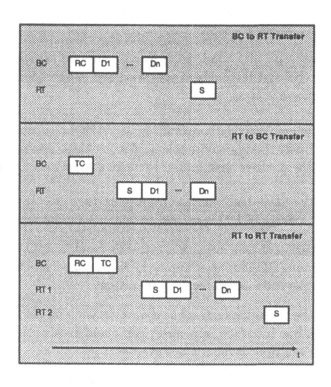

Legend: RC = Receive Command, TC = Transmit Command,
S = Status Word, Di = Data Word

Figure 3: Basic MIL Bus Message Transfers

3   The Requirements and Design Issues

Based on an analysis of the application domain, the following requirements have been identified for a reusable MIL Bus package to be used in Ada avionic applications.

- The interface provided by the package should be target-independent. The application program should be shielded from the details of specific bus interfaces. The I/O operations provided by the package should be uniform across different avionic computers. The basic hardware architecture assumptions shall be those defined in sections 2.1 and 2.2.

- The package should be compatible to MIL-STD-1553B and should allow to exploit all major features of the standard (including mode command transfers, dynamic bus control handover, handling of RT service requests etc., see [MILBUS]).

- The requirements of avionic applications must be satisfied, including support for BC and RT mode of operation and support for periodic and aperiodic message transfers.

There are a number of design issues resulting from the multi-processing architecture and the multi-tasking environment. Among these issues that need to be addressed in the package design (and implementation) are the following:

- Access to the same bus interface from more than one application processor and sharing of I/O resources by more than one task

- Synchronization of task execution with bus input/output (synchronous / asynchronous I/O) and overlapping I/O activity with both application processor operation and other I/O operations

- Notifying the multi-tasking application of asynchronous events identified by the bus interface (e.g. reset command received) and selective waiting for multiple asynchronous events

- The multi-tasking environment with preemptive scheduling of tasks must be taken into account. The I/O operations provided must be reentrant. The consistency of bus messages and of internal data structures must be guaranteed through appropriate protection of shared data and resources.

- Communication between application processors and interface processors must be minimized. Any unnecessary copying of data must be avoided.

As the I/O package is intended for Ada applications, a set of additional Ada related requirements and design issues can be identified, e.g.

- The user interface must be defined in the form of (one or more) Ada package specifications.

- The level of abstraction should be comparable to that of Ada's facilities for tasking or Ada's predefined I/O packages. Low-level internal details (e.g. buffer handling or synchronization) should be hidden from the user.

- The facilities provided should be compatible and well-integrated with Ada's concepts for task synchronization and communication and interrupt handling.

- The package interface shall allow the Ada application program to treat bus messages as Ada objects of appropriate types (e.g. integer, fixed point, array or record types).

- Error conditions shall be indicated to the user in the form of Ada exceptions defined in the I/O packages. An example of such an error situation is a mismatch between the expected length and the actual length of a received message.

- The package should exploit Ada's capabilities with respect to static type checking or the definition of abstract data types.

- The implementation must make use of appropriate facilities provided by the Ada runtime system for interrupt handling, task scheduling, time queue management and efficient mutual exclusion.

4   The Proposed Approach

4.1   An Abstract Model of the User Interface

The I/O packages presented below are based on an object-oriented view of MIL bus interfaces and its services. Various "I/O objects" are provided to the user. Each object is characterized by a number of associated properties and operations. The operations provided by an object are the only means available to the user to manipulate the object.

The major object types provided to the user of the I/O packages are bus interfaces, ports and channels, and transfers. In the following, for each of these object types a short overview is given in terms of its visible characteristics and its provided operations. Further details can be seen from the examples given later and the Ada package specifications included in the appendix.

Bus Interfaces

An (abstract) bus interface basically represents the physical MIL bus interface together with its software-implemented functionality. A bus interface has the following *visible characteristics* :

- It has some external name (a character string) that allows the user to distinguish it from other bus interfaces within the same computer.

- It has a current state that basically corresponds to the state of the physical I/O interface (e.g. ready, running, stopped).

- It has a number of additional attributes corresponding to features of the bus interface that can be influenced by the application software, e.g. parameters to control the error retry mechanism.

The names of the *basic operations* provided for bus interfaces are listed below.

- `create_bus_interface` / `delete_bus_interface`

- `start_bus_interface` / `stop_bus_interface`

Ports and Channels

Ports are used as the basic mechanism to identify source or destination in I/O transfer operations. A channel is defined as a pair of ports (a send port and a receive port) in two separate computers. The relationship between ports, channels and bus interfaces is illustrated in figure 4.

A port has the following *visible characteristics* :

- Each port belongs to a unique bus interface. It has a transfer direction and is either a send or a receive port.

- A port defines the addressing information required in MIL bus transfers: A port contained in the BC and connected to an RT defines the RT address and a subaddress within the RT, a port contained in an RT and connected to the BC or a second RT defines a subaddress within the (former) RT.

- For each port there exists an associated message buffer. It is automatically allocated by the system when the port object is created and can hold one message at a time. The message buffer temporarily holds a message before it is sent out on the bus by the bus interface processor or after it has been received from the bus.

- There are two types of ports ("unsynchronised" and "synchronised") that are selected by the user depending on the synchronisation behaviour of I/O transfer operations on that port.

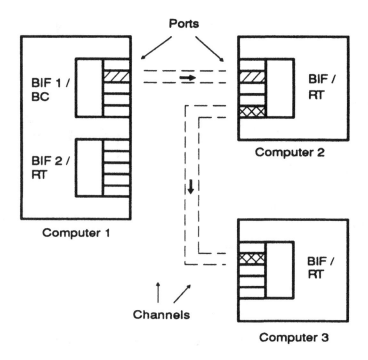

Figure 4: A Model of Bus Interfaces (BIF), Ports and Channels

- An unsynchronised port can be shared between tasks, i.e. it can be used by more than one task, a synchronised port is private to a task, i.e. it can only be used by one task at a time.

Figure 5 illustrates the simple model of the user interface that results from the definition of the above concepts.

The *basic operations* involving ports and channels are the following :

- `create_port / delete_port`
- `open_port / close_port`
- `create_rt_rt_channel / delete_rt_rt_channel`
- `open_rt_rt_channel / close_rt_rt_channel`

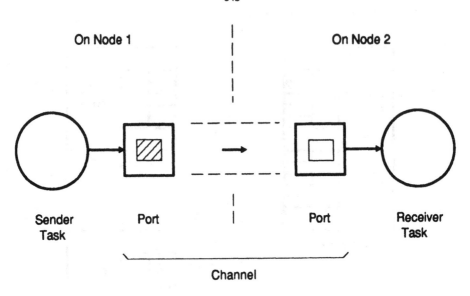

On Node 1

On Node 2

Sender
Task

Port

Port

Receiver
Task

Channel

Figure 5: User View of MIL Bus Input/Output

Transfers

A transfer is the exchange of a message between two bus nodes. The message is a user-defined sequence of data words to be transmitted over the bus. The *visible characteristics* of transfers can be summarized as follows:

- Each transfer is associated with a specific port or channel. Thereby source and/or destination of the transfer is uniquely defined.

- There are periodic and aperiodic transfers. Periodic transfers are defined by the user with all necessary parameters (e.g. the period) and then activated. They are then autonomously performed by the BC interface processor until they are deactivated by the user. Aperiodic transfers are implicitly defined by the user through send or receive transfer operations and initiated by the BC interface processor as a result of these operations.

- A bus message contains between 1 and 32 data words, each 16 bits wide. Bus messages can be treated by the application as Ada objects of appropriate types.

The *basic operations* relating to transfers are listed below by their names :

- **define_periodic_transfer / undefine_periodic_transfer**

- **read / write**

- **receive / conditional_receice / timed_receive**

- **send / timed_send**

- **initiate_aperiodic_transfer**

Some details of the concrete Ada user interface to the MIL bus services can be seen from the extracts of the package specifications in the appendix of this paper.

4.2 Example Uses

This section gives two simplified examples of the use of the I/O packages. They should be largely self-explanatory and are to give the reader an impression of the functionality and the level of abstraction provided by the packages.

The first example illustrates how an application on a BC node sends *periodic* messages to an application on an RT node.

```
procedure bc_application_1 is              -- on BC node
   ...
begin
   bc_bid  := bif_bc_create_bus_interface
      (bif_name           => "bif1" ) ;

   sender_pid  := bif_bc_create_port
      (bus_interface_id  => bc_bid ,
       rt_address        => c_rt_5 ,
       subaddress        => c_sa_msg1 ,
       send_or_receive   => send ) ;

   bif_bc_define_periodic_transfer
      (bc_port_id         => sender_pid ,
       period             => msec_20 ,
       msg_length         => c_len_amsg1 ) ;
   ...
                              -- activate periodic transfer
   bif_bc_open_port
      (port_id            => sender_pid ,
       sync_mode          => unsynchronised ) ;
```

```
   loop
        ...                        -- setup new message
                                   -- update message buffer
      bif_bc_write
         (port_id             => sender_pid ,
          message             => message1 ,
          result              => write_result ) ;
   end loop ;
end bc_application_1 ;
```

```
procedure rt_application_1 is           -- on RT node
   ...
begin
   rt_bid  := bif_rt_create_bus_interface
      (bif_name             =>  "bif1" ) ;

   receiver_pid  := bif_rt_create_port
      (bus_interface_id    =>  rt_bid ,
       subaddress          =>  c_sa_msg1 ,
       send_or_receive     =>  receive ) ;
   ...
   bif_rt_open_port
      (port_id              => receiver_pid ,
       sync_mode            => unsynchronised ) ;
   loop
                             -- take latest available message
      bif_rt_read
         (port_id            => receiver_pid ,
          message            => message1 ,
          result             => read_result ) ;
        ...                  -- process message
   end loop ;
end rt_application_1 ;
```

The second example demonstrates two application programs on separate computers that exchange *aperiodic* messages. An application task on an RT node waits for a message to be sent by the BC node. The RT application task is either resumed when a message has been received or after a specified time limit has expired.

```
procedure bc_application_2 is              -- on BC node
   ...
begin
   ...
   bif_bc_open_port
      (port_id          => sender_pid ,
       sync_mode        => synchronised ) ;
   loop
      ...                -- setup message
                         -- send aperiodic message
      bif_bc_send
         (port_id       => sender_pid ,
          message       => message2 ,
          result        => send_result ) ;
   end loop ;
end bc_application_2 ;
```

```
procedure rt_application_2 is              -- on RT node
   ...
begin
   ...
   bif_bc_open_port
      (port_id          => receiver_pid ,
       sync_mode        => synchronised ) ;
   loop
      bif_rt_timed_receive
         (port_id       => receiver_pid ,
          message       => message2 ,
          time_limit    => 0.1 ,
          result        => receive_result) ;

      if  receive_result = not_rec_time_out  then
         ...
      end if ;
   end loop ;
end rt_application_2 ;
```

5   Related Work

The availability of a suitable Ada interface to MIL bus services is a recurring problem in avionic applications. Therefore, the approach presented in this paper is not the first and sole attempt to define Ada packages for MIL bus input/output. The author is aware of at least three (European) projects where similar efforts have been made.

The Tornado Ada system (TAS-2) is a multi-processor Ada system targeted to an avionic computer of the Tornado aircraft. It implements a single-program approach for the shared-memory architecture of a multi-processor target (see [TAS2-MP]). Important components of TAS-2 are its Ada MIL bus packages that provide access to the bus interfaces of the target system (see [TAS2-IO]). It could be verified through successful flight tests that the TAS-2 runtime environment in general, and the I/O components in particular, are suitable for operational use – both with respect to functionality and efficiency.

The European Fighter Aircraft (EFA) programme has also been pursuing the goal of standardized Ada packages for MIL bus I/O. An Ada interface has been defined (see [EFA-IO]) that is currently being implemented by several suppliers of EFA avionic computers. A further variant of an Ada MIL bus interface has been defined in the European helicopter project PAH2/HAC-HAP. As for EFA, the implementation has not yet been finished and no practical experience from its use is available up to now.

The approach presented in this paper ("Reusable MIL Bus Interface in Ada", RUMBADA) was mostly influenced by the MIL bus interface implemented in TAS-2. The design of RUMBADA can be seen as an attempt to take over proven concepts, to avoid some of the weak points and to incorporate improvements resulting from practical experience. The goal was a complete and consistent interface that can serve as a sound basis for reusable software components.

At the moment, RUMBADA exists "only" as an interface definition. It is envisaged to verify the design of the interface in a prototype implementation and to use it in future Ada avionic applications.

6   Conclusion

The provision of an Ada interface to MIL bus input/output services has been identified as a key requirement and a recurring problem in the avionics application domain. The fact that the lower-level communication protocol in MIL bus based systems is standardized is favourable for the definition and development of target-independent, reusable input/output components.

Practical experience has shown that a high-level, target-independent Ada interface to MIL bus services can be implemented with the efficiency required in avionic systems. The approach presented in this paper is considered a suitable candidate for a standard interface and corresponding reusable software components for Ada avionic applications.

The benefits that can be expected from a reusable MIL bus interface in Ada include reduced application software complexity, reduced development costs and increased reliability and maintainability.

References

[MILBUS]   MIL-STD-1553 Designer's Guide,
            ILC Data Device Corporation, New York, 1987 (2nd Edition)

[TAS2-MP]   Ada for Closely Coupled Multiprocesor Targets,
            A. Cholerton, Proc. TRI-Ada 1989 (Pittsburgh)

[TAS2-IO]   Tornado Ada System for a Multiprocessor Avionic Computer,
            TAS-2 User and Design Documentation, MBB GmbH, 1989

[EFA-IO]   Target-Specific Ada Packages Requirements Specification,
            Eurofighter GmbH, 1990

Appendix: Outline of Ada Package Specifications

```
------------------------------------------------------------------------
--                         R U M B A D A
--                  ReUsable MILBus Interface in ADA
------------------------------------------------------------------------
-- MBB GmbH                                            September 1990
-- Military Aircraft Division
-- A. Rosskopf, Dept FE 363
------------------------------------------------------------------------
-- RUMBADA defines a target-independent, high-level interface to the
-- input/output facilities supported by MIL-STD-1553B (STANAG 3838)
-- bus interfaces. It consists of the following Ada packages:
--            bif_constants_and_types
--            bif_bc_services
--            bif_rt_services
------------------------------------------------------------------------


------------------------------------------------------------------------
package bif_constants_and_types is
------------------------------------------------------------------------

   -- The package bif_constants_and_types provides definitions that
   -- are used in both the BC mode and the RT mode packages.

                              -- external bus interface name
   type t_bif_name           is new string ;

   type t_bus_interface_id   is private ;

   type t_port_id            is private ;

   type t_channel_id         is private ;

   subtype t_rt_address      is natural range 0 .. 31 ;

   subtype t_subaddress      is natural range 1 .. 30 ;

   subtype t_msg_length      is natural range 1 .. 32 ;
```

```
                                -- port direction
   type t_send_or_receive    is
      (send, receive) ;
                                -- port synchronization mode
   type t_sync_mode          is
      (unsynchronised,        -- used for periodic transfers
                              -- (i.e. write or read)
       synchronised) ;        -- used for aperiodic transfers
                              -- (i.e. send or receive)

                                -- bus message related types
   type t_bus_data_word      is  range 0 .. (2**16) - 1 ;
   for  t_bus_data_word'size use 16 ;

   type t_msg_array  is array (t_msg_length range <>)
                                of t_bus_data_word ;

   type t_message  (msg_length  : t_msg_length := 32) is
      record
         msg_array  : t_msg_array (1..msg_length) ;
      end record ;
   ...
private
   ...
-----------------------------------------------------------------------
end bif_constants_and_types ;
-----------------------------------------------------------------------


-----------------------------------------------------------------------
package bif_bc_services is
-----------------------------------------------------------------------


   --   The package bif_bc_services  provides the following set of
   --   functions for use in BC mode:
   --
   --       bif_bc_create_bus_interface
   --       bif_bc_start_bus_interface
   --       bif_bc_stop_bus_interface
   --       bif_bc_delete_bus_interface
   --
   --       bif_bc_create_port
   --       bif_bc_open_port
```

```
--        bif_bc_close_port
--
--        bif_bc_create_rt_rt_channel
--        bif_bc_open_rt_rt_channel
--        bif_bc_close_rt_rt_channel
--
--        bif_bc_define_periodic_transfer
--        bif_bc_undefine_periodic_transfer
--        bif_bc_read
--        bif_bc_write
--
--        bif_bc_receive
--        bif_bc_send
--        bif_bc_initiate_aperiodic_transfer
--
--        bif_bc_send_mode_cmd
--        bif_bc_send_mode_cmd_and_data
--        bif_bc_send_mode_cmd_receive_data
```

--------------------------------- BC Services Exceptions ------

-- The following exceptions may be raised by bif_bc_services :

```
bif_exc_port_not_open        :   exception ;
bif_exc_length_mismatch      :   exception ;
    . . .
```

------------------------------- BC Bus Interface Operations ------

```
function  bif_bc_create_bus_interface
    (bif_name              : in     t_bif_name
      --  additional bus interface parameters
    )                            return t_bus_interface_id ;
```

-- Initialises the nominated (physical) bus interface for operation
-- as a bus controller and creates an (abstract) bus interface
-- object. The bus interface is placed in the ready state.
    . . .

------------------------------- Port And Channel Operations ------

```
function  bif_bc_create_port
```

```
(bus_interface_id     :  in      t_bus_interface_id ;
 rt_address           :  in      t_rt_address ;
 subaddress           :  in      t_subaddress ;
 send_or_receive      :  in      t_send_or_receive )
                         return  t_port_id ;
```

-- Creates a port within the specified bus interface and declares
-- it as either a send port or a receive port. The message buffer
-- that is associated with each port is automatically allocated
-- through this create operation. (The buffer is large enough to
-- hold one message with a maximum length of 32 data words.)
-- The parameters rt_address and subaddress identify the source or
-- destination of messages received from or sent via the port.

procedure bif_bc_open_port
```
    (port_id          :  in      t_port_id ;
     sync_mode        :  in      t_sync_mode ;
     initial_msg      :  in      t_message
                         := def_initial_message ) ;
```

-- Opens the given port for either synchronised or unsynchronised
-- mode. An application task must open a port before it can use it
-- in any transfer operation.
--
-- An "unsynchronised port" can only be used in unsynchronised,
-- periodic transfer operations (i.e. write and read).
-- A "synchronised port" can only be used in synchronised,
-- aperiodic transfer operations (i.e. send and receive).
--
-- An unsynchronised port can be "shared" between tasks, i.e. it
-- can be opened by more than one task. A synchronised port is
-- "private" to the task that has opened that port, i.e. it can
-- only be used by one task at a time. Opening a synchronised port
-- "allocates" the port to the calling task.
--
-- Opening an unsynchronised port within a BC bus interface (that
-- has not yet been opened by another task) "activates" any peri-
-- odic transfer that has previously been defined on that port.
-- ...

-------------------------------- *Periodic Transfer Operations* ------

procedure bif_bc_define_periodic_transfer
   (bc_port_id   : **in**   t_port_id ;
   period   : **in**   t_period ;
   msg_length   : **in**   t_msg_length) ;

-- *Defines a periodic transfer between a BC port and an RT port.*
-- *The transfer is activated with the first bc_open_port operation*
-- *called by an application task.*
  ...

---------------------- *Unsynchronised Read / Write Operations* ----

procedure bif_bc_read
   (port_id   : **in**   t_port_id ;
   message   : **in out** t_message ;
   result   :   **out** t_read_result) ;

-- *The latest available message is taken from the specified port's*
-- *message buffer.*
-- *The procedure provides a "non-blocking read" where the calling*
-- *task is never suspended. The same message may be read several*
-- *times ("non-consuming read").*
--
-- *Parameters :*
--   *port_id   receive port*
--   *message   msg_length : expected message length (in)*
--   *msg_array : contents of message buffer (out)*
--   ...
-- *Exceptions :*
--   *bif_exc_port_not_open*
--   *bif_exc_length_mismatch*
--   *raised if the length of the message received by the bus*
--   *interface and deposited in the buffer does not match the*
--   *expected message length (as provided in the message para-*
--   *meter of the read operation)*
--   ...

procedure bif_bc_write
   (port_id   : **in**   t_port_id ;
   message   : **in**   t_message ;
   result   :   **out** t_write_result) ;

-- *The given message is deposited in the specified port's message*
-- *buffer (from where it will eventually be sent out on the bus by*
-- *the bus interface).*
-- *The procedure provides a "non-blocking write" where the calling*
-- *task is never suspended. A message previously written into the*
-- *buffer and not yet sent out on the bus may be overwritten.*

------------------------------ *Aperiodic Transfer Operations* ------

--------------------- *Synchronised Receive / Send Operations* ------

procedure bif_bc_receive
    (port_id   : **in**   t_port_id ;
    message   : **in out** t_message ;
    result   :   **out** t_receive_result) ;

-- *The calling task waits for a message (from a remote node) via*
-- *the given port.*
-- *This procedure provides a "synchronised receive" where the*
-- *calling task waits for the completion of the corresponding bus*
-- *transaction. A message deposited in the buffer can only be read*
-- *once by an application task ("consuming receive").*
-- ...

procedure bif_bc_send
    (port_id   : **in**   t_port_id ;
    message   : **in**   t_message ;
    result   :   **out** t_send_result) ;

-- *The given message is sent (to a remote node) via the given*
-- *port. This procedure provides a "synchronised send" where the*
-- *calling task waits for the completion of the corresponding bus*
-- *transaction.*
-- ...

----

end bif_bc_services ;

```
-------------------------------------------------------------------------
package bif_rt_services is
-------------------------------------------------------------------------


    --    The package bif_rt_services  provides the following set of
    --    functions for use in RT mode:
    --
    --        bif_rt_create_bus_interface
    --        bif_rt_start_bus_interface
    --        bif_rt_stop_bus_interface
    --        bif_rt_delete_bus_interface
    --
    --        bif_rt_create_port
    --        bif_rt_open_port
    --        bif_rt_close_port
    --
    --        bif_rt_read
    --        bif_rt_write
    --
    --        bif_rt_receive
    --        bif_rt_conditional_receive
    --        bif_rt_timed_receive
    --        bif_rt_send
    --        bif_rt_timed_send
    --
    --        bif_rt_indicate_service_request
    --        bif_rt_send_service_request
    --
    --        bif_rt_indicate_fault_cond
    --        bif_rt_indicate_bus_control_acc


-------------------------------------------------------------------------
end bif_rt_services ;
-------------------------------------------------------------------------
```

Part VIII: Project Reports

Constructing a Pilot Library of Components for Avionic Systems[1]

JOSÉ L. FERNÁNDEZ
ISDEFE, Madrid

JUAN A. DE LA PUENTE
Universidad Politécnica de Madrid

Abstract

The BCA[2] research project, whose aim is to investigate the viability of Ada for the development of reusable software for avionics systems, is being carried out by a consortium of Spanish companies. A pilot component library has been built with this purpose. In addition to the usual abstract data structures and mathematical functions, navigation and executive components have been built. Some design decisions are discussed in the paper. Documentation and testing issues are also briefly dealt with.

1 INTRODUCTION

At the end of 1,989 the *Subdirección General de Tecnología e Investigación* provided funding for an eighteen month research project to investigate the viability of Ada in the development of reusable software components for their use in future projects by the Spanish aerospace industry.

The project participants were ISDEFE as the prime contractor, and CASA and the Technical University of Madrid (UPM) as subcontractors.

The project was started without any previous experience in component reusability design and without access to the complete source code of any of the similar reusable software components projects which had been carried out before. This paper illustrates those aspects of the project that may be helpful to develop similar projects.

The aspects considered in this paper are those closely related to the characteristics of the development of reusable software components. Those aspects can be grouped into the following sections: Component Selection, Overall Library Structure, Overview of Design Decisions, Reusability Documentation and Testing activities.

---

[1]This research was funded by contract No. 508/24/90 from the *Subdirección General de Tecnología e Investigación, Ministerio de Defensa de España.*

[2]Biblioteca de Componentes Ada

2 COMPONENT SELECTION

The purpose of this activity was to identify those reusable components that could be of use for the development of Real Time Systems, emphasizing those applied to Avionic systems.

Some of the components that are implemented were selected based in the work done in similar projects. The projects considered were the CAMP project, the GRACE and BOOCH COMPONENTS libraries and mathematical libraries [PFTV88][FKR86]. The CAMP project [And88] developed software components for their application in real time embedded missile systems. The GRACE [MB87] and the BOOCH COMPONENTS [Boo87] libraries dealt both with Abstract Data Types.

The experience acquired from those projects served to identify a group of basic components that are widely used. The development of those basic components served the purpose of familiarizing the design team with the design and implementation of reusable components.

The more specific components (those related to the avionics system) were selected taking into consideration the *Core Software Concept*:

> This study involved reviewing selected data on existing aircraft software and analyzing the data to extract algorithms having a great deal of commonality which could be used across a wide spectrum of aircraft [HKB81].

The design team perceived the navigation functions as the most widely used and consequently identified the subfunctions that could be designed as reusable software components.

The analysis of the Operational Flight Program of an aircraft trainer by the design team provided the requirements for the navigation components that were selected to be developed. In some cases a component has more than one implementation depending on the availability of data inputs from the Inertial Navigation System, the Air Data Computer or other systems, to perform the calculations.

The last group of components selected were those related to reusable avionics executive software [Bou81]. This concept can be adapted to the conditions imposed by the Ada programming language and it can be applied to other hard real time systems. The analysis of executive functions led to the design of two kinds of reusable executive subsystems, one based on the cyclic executive model and the other one based on Ada tasks.

3 OVERALL LIBRARY STRUCTURE

The components library was divided into the five groups of components described below with some of the components that form them.

3.1 Basic Components

These are well known data structures such as Stacks, Lists, Queues and Rings which can have different forms: bounded, unbounded, protected, guarded, priority etc. as defined in the taxonomies of GRACE [MB87] and BOOCH COMPONENTS [Boo87]. Other basic components are sychronization mechanisms, such as semaphores and monitors, which are used in protected, guarded and multiple forms of abstract data types, and finite state and combinational machines.

3.2 Matrices, Vectors and Quaternions

These components include general vector matrix algebra and quaternion operations.

Constrained arrays were used to improve the time and space efficiency of these components after considering the loss of reusability.

The use of quaternions is indicated in certain applications where the main computational effort is spent updating the vehicle attitude itself.

3.3 Trigonometry and General Purpose Mathematical Components

These components were selected because they were used as subcomponents by the navigation parts.

3.4 Navigation Components

The components that were selected perform the functions described in the Trainer Aircraft's Operational Flight Program (OFP). Each of these functions was broken down into its most fundamental elements. The Navigation Component Library is made by the association of some of the lowest level algorithms by components.

The Navigation Components developed are: *Transformation Aircraft Platform, Aircraft Body Velocity, Turn Rate, Wind Velocity, Attitude Angles, Ground Velocity, Convergence, Lambert Coordinates, Track Angle, Next Desired Track* and *Steering Parameters Calculation*. Some of these components have various implementations depending of the validity of the input data.

Other components also included in this library are the Kalman Filter and the implementation of dimensional units as components (*Unit Operations, Product Unit, Quotient Unit* and *Unit Conversion*).

3.5 Reusable Executive Components

Executive components provide a toolkit to build an executive subsystem on top of which application tasks can run. Two kinds of executives have been devised: A *safety-critical executive* and a *mission critical executive*. Both executives are designed in such a way that hard real-time deadlines can be guaranteed for periodic tasks. The executives also support aperiodic tasks, mode changes and error recovery.

The first executive is intended to be used in safety-critical applications. Since compliance with *safe Ada* [HW88] was required, tasks and some other Ada features could not be used. The executive design is based on the *cyclic executive* model [BJ87] instead. The main component is a generic *cyclic scheduler* which can be instantiated to fit the characteristics of different applications. Other components provide executive data structures and templates for building application processes and interrupt handlers from Ada procedures.

The *mission critical* executive does not have the same restrictions, and is thus based on Ada tasks. The theoretical foundation is based on *rate monotonic scheduling* [SG90]. Although most of the theory can be applied with the Ada mechanisms, some components were designed to provide extensions to the basic Ada features and mechanisms for mode change and error recovery.

4   OVERVIEW OF DESIGN DECISIONS

This section describes the use of the Ada language in the design of the components, and specifically in the design of the navigation components.

The navigation components include some features supported by the Ada programming language such as generics, strong typing, dimensional units [Gro88], and exceptions [BGE88].

Figure 1 shows a simple component that calculates the aircraft's body velocity based on the available air data.

The instantiation parameters include the type of the physical magnitudes that are used, the maximum and minimum input values and the functions that are imported by the component (the function "*" is overloaded so that the component can use dimensional magnitudes). It will be discussed later on how the component is instantiated using an engineering units package created from objects that implement dimensional magnitudes.

If the input parameters are not in the range defined by their minimum and maximum values, an exception is raised. This parameter check could be avoided if it is done somewhere else in the application.

The way to interface exceptions and reusable components is to have the generic unit depend on a specification package of exceptions declarations. This technique is consistent with "top down" methodologies.

For the instantiation of the components the library provides an *Engineering Units* package created from the components BASIC_TYPES, UNIT_OPERATIONS, PRODUCT_UNIT, QUOTIENT_UNIT and UNIT (Figure 2).

The component BASIC_TYPES is used only to increase the portability of the package.

```
with NAVIGATION_EXCEPTIONS;
generic
  type T_VELOCITY is digits <>;
  type T_ANGLE    is digits <>;
  type T_DIMENSIONLESS is digits <>;
  TAS_MIN : in T_VELOCITY;
  TAS_MAX : in T_VELOCITY;
  AOA_MIN : in T_ANGLE;
  AOA_MAX : in T_ANGLE;
  with function SIN (X: T_ANGLE) return T_DIMENSIONLESS is <>;
  with function COS (X: T_ANGLE) return T_DIMENSIONLESS is <>;
  with function "*" (LEFT  : T_VELOCITY;
                     RIGHT : T_DIMENSIONLESS)
                     return  T_VELOCITY is <>;
procedure AIRCRAFT_BODY_VELOCITY_A
          (TAS : in     T_VELOCITY;
           AOA : in     T_ANGLE;
           U   : in out T_VELOCITY;
           V   : in out T_VELOCITY;
           W   : in out T_VELOCITY);
```

Figure 1: (a) AIRCRAFT_BODY_VELOCITY Component Specification.

```
procedure AIRCRAFT_BODY_VELOCITY_A (...) is
begin
  if (TAS not in TAS_MIN..TAS_MAX) or
     (AOA not in AOA_MIN..AOA_MAX) then
       raise NAVIGATION_EXCEPTIONS.PARAMETER.ERROR;
  end if;
  U := TAS * COS (AOA);
  V := 0.0;
  W := TAS * SIN (AOA);
exception
  when NAVIGATION_EXCEPTIONS.PARAMETER_ERROR =>
    raise NAVIGATION_EXCEPTIONS.PARAMETER_ERROR;
  when others => raise;
end AIRCRAFT_BODY_VELOCITY_A;
```

Figure 1: (b) AIRCRAFT_BODY_VELOCITY Component Body.

```
with SYSTEM;
package BASIC_TYPES is
  type T_REAL    is digits SYSTEM.MAX_DIGITS;
  type T_INTEGER is range SYSTEM.MIN_INT..SYSTEM.MAX_INT;
end BASIC_TYPES;
```

Figure 2: (a) BASIC_TYPES Component.

```
with BASIC_TYPES; use BASIC_TYPES;
package UNIT_OPERATIONS is
  type T_DIMENSION is new T_REAL;
  UNITS_ERROR : exception;
  ...
  -- The exception UNITS_ERROR will be raised when the
  -- required operation results in a non homogeneous dimension
  function "*" (LEFT  : T_DIMENSION;
                RIGHT : T_DIMENSION) return T_DIMENSION;
  function "*" (LEFT  : T_REAL;
                RIGHT : T_DIMENSION) return T_DIMENSION;
  function "*" (LEFT  : T_DIMENSION;
                RIGHT : T_REAL)      return T_DIMENSION;
  function "*" (LEFT  : T_DIMENSION;
                RIGHT : INTEGER)     return T_DIMENSION;
  ...
  -- The exception UNITS_ERROR will be raised when the
  -- required operation results in a non homogeneous dimension
  function "/" (LEFT  : T_DIMENSION;
                RIGHT : T_DIMENSION) return T_DIMENSION;
  ...
end UNIT_OPERATIONS;
```

Figure 2: (b) UNIT_OPERATIONS Component Specification.

The package UNIT_OPERATIONS and the generic package UNIT [Gro88] allow the creation of objects that implement dimensional magnitudes. Ada features are used to detect and reject incorrect utilization of the units package at compilation or at run time, ie. multiplying two magnitudes of the same dimension to obtain a magnitude of the same dimension.

```
with UNIT_OPERATIONS;
generic
package UNIT is
   type T_DIMENSION is new UNIT_OPERATIONS.T_DIMENSION;
end UNIT;
```

Figure 2: (c) UNIT Generic Package.

```
with UNIT;
with PRODUCT_UNIT;
with QUOTIENT_UNIT;
package ENGINEERING_UNITS is
  package FEET is new UNIT;
   ...
  package SECONDS is new UNIT;
   ...
  package FEET_PER_SECOND is new QUOTIENT_UNIT
            (NUMERATOR_DIMENSION   => FEET.T_DIMENSION;
             DENOMINATOR_DIMENSION => SECONDS.T_DIMENSION);
   ...
end ENGINEERING_UNITS;
```

Figure 2: (d) ENGINEERING_UNITS Package.

Using these components and others that allow to create derived magnitudes such as PRODUCT_UNIT and QUOTIENT_UNIT it is possible to create an ENGINEERING_UNITS package that can be used in the instantiation of the Navigation Components.

5   REUSABILITY DOCUMENTATION

The documentation for reusable software components includes some items not found in normal circumstances in the development of software. Besides the development documentation, there has to be a specific document (Component

User's Manual [BG85]) in which it is described what the component does and how it can be used. The Components User's Manual describes the following :

- **Functional Summary.** Concise description of the basic function performed by the component.

- **Documentation References.**

- **Performance Characteristics.** The total number of assignments multiplications, additions and other basic operations performed by the component.

- **Known Limitations.** The kind of inputs that the component can handle and dependence on any particular characteristic of the hardware.

- **User Modifications and Customization.** Provisions for modifications and/or customization by the user.

- **Partial Reuse Potential.** Capability of the component to be reused partially.

- **Special Design Considerations.** Design decisions considered to be of interest to the user.

- **Error Handling.** Component response to incorrect inputs.

- **Examples of Use.**

- **Interface Descriptions.** Enumerates the interfaces of the component and describes how each one is going to be used.

6 TESTING ACTIVITIES

Testing is of great importance in the development of a reusable software component. The validation of the individual components was realized performing a group of tests with both black box and white box approaches.

Black box testing includes equivalence partitioning, boundary values analysis and error guessing.

White box testing is achieved through structured testing techniques calculating the cyclomatic complexity metric and using the baseline method to identify a set of control paths and test data to satisfy the testing criteria.

The validation of the more complex components (especially executive components) includes additional tests, checking for timing requirements and developing test scenarios.

7 CONCLUSIONS

The viability of the Ada programming language to be used for the development of reusable software components has been corroborated, building simple components which implement well-know algorithms with input and output data validation is straightforward. Exceptions and dimensional units can be helpful for this. Nevertheless, component selection and complex component building are much more difficult issues which need further research. This is especially true in real-time systems, where the functionality of each component has to be matched with schedulability requirements in order to guarantee hard real-time constraints.

Productivity metrics are not provided because they would not give a meaningful evaluation of the project due to the additional efforts that are inherent to a pilot project; similar conditions would not prevail in full scale development activities.

The project has also provided us with valuable experience for the development of future projects.

Acknowledgements

We would like to thank the members of the Design Team for their dedication and support:

Jose Acuña	(ISDEFE)
Alejandro Alonso	(U.P.M.)
Juan L. Freniche	(CASA)
Enrique Martín	(CASA)
Carmen Muñoz	(ISDEFE)
Juan L. Redondo	(U.P.M)
Nicolás Suárez	(ISDEFE)
Juan Zamorano	(U.P.M.)

We appreciate and would like to thank the support of the contracting agency's representative Mr. Manuel Golmayo (Centro de Investigación y Desarrollo de la Armada).

References

[And88] Chris Anderson. The CAMP approach to software reuse. *Defense Computing*, September 1988.

[BG85] C.L. Braun and J.B. Goodenough. *Ada reusability guidelines*. Softech, 1985.

[BGE88]   M.F. Bott, G.J. Gautier, and A. Elliot. Guidelines for the use of ada in reusable software components. In *Ada-Europe reuse seminar*, 1988.

[BJ87]   T.P. Baker and K. Jeffay. Corset and Lace: adapting Ada runtime support to real-time systems. In *IEEE Real-Time Systems Symposium*, 1987.

[Boo87]   Grady Booch. *Software components with Ada*. Benjamin Cummings, 1987.

[Bou81]   R. Bousley. Reusable avionics executive software. In *IEEE National Aerospace and Electronics Conference*, 1981.

[FKR86]   B. Ford, J. Kok, and N.W. Rogers. *Scientific Ada*. Cambridge University Press, 1986.

[Gro88]   J.A. Grossberg. Object-oriented dimensional units. *Dr. Dobb's Journal*, September 1988.

[HKB81]   E.F. Hitt, M. Kluse, and R. Broderson. Integrated control core software concept. In *4th AIAA/IEEE Digital Avionics Systems Conference*, 1981.

[HW88]   R. Holzapfel and G. Winterstein. Ada in safety critical applications. In S. Heilbrunner, editor, *Ada in Industry*. Cambridge University Press, 1988.

[MB87]   J. Margono and Edgar Berard. A modified booch's taxonomy for ada generic data-structure components and their implementation. In S. Tafvelin, editor, *Ada components: Libraries and tools*. Cambridge University Press, 1987.

[PFTV88] W.H. Press, B.P. Flannery, S.A. Teukolsky, and W.T. Vetterling. *Numerical Recipes in C: the Art of Scientific Computing*. Cambridge University Press, 1988.

[SG90]   Lui Sha and John B. Goodenough. Real-time scheduling theory and Ada. *IEEE Computer*, 23(4), 1990.

Formally specifying the logic of an automatic guidance controller [1]

DAVID GUASPARI

ORA Corporation, 301A Dates Drive, Ithaca NY, USA 14850-1313

The Transportation Systems Research Vehicle (TSRV) is a specially equipped Boeing 737 operated by NASA's Langley Research Center as part of the Advanced Transport Operating Systems program. It is used as a laboratory to study the development, implementation, and certification of digital flight control systems.

The logic of the interface through which the pilot communicates with the flight control software of the TSRV is quite complex, and is difficult to describe clearly by *ad hoc* means. This paper describes work-in-progress, the development of a *formal* specification of an Ada implementation using the Larch/Ada specification language, the language of the Penelope verification system [GMP 90].

1 A SESSION WITH THE FLIGHT CONTROLLER

The pilot communicates with the flight control system through the Control Mode Panel, which contains four knobs, four windows, and eleven switches. The knobs and switches are used to request various kinds and degrees of automatic flight control—for example, to maintain a given airspeed or altitude, to follow a preset flight plan, or to land automatically. These requests may be honored, ignored, or "put on hold" awaiting appropriate external conditions; and the the resulting state of the flight control must be displayed via the windows and various colored lights.

Figure 1 shows the physical layout of part of the Control Mode Panel:

- Two of the four windows, each with its associated knob and switch.

[1]This work was supported by the STARS program of the Defense Advanced Research Projects Agency under Contract No. BOA#3695.STARS-043 and by the National Aeronautics and Space Administration under Contract No. NAS1-18972. The views and conclusions contained in this paper are those of the author and should not be interpreted as necessarily representing the official policies, either expressed or implied, of DARPA, NASA, or the U.S. Government.

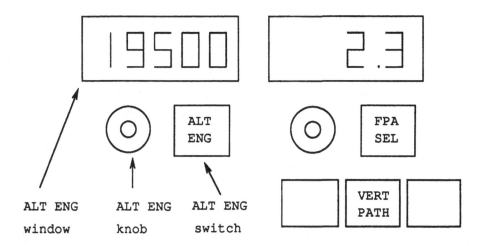

Figure 1: Part of the Control Mode Panel

The ALT ENG window displays altitude in feet and the FPA SEL window displays the flight path angle in degrees. Associated with each window is a knob (which can be used to change the value displayed in the window) and a switch (which can be used to request engagement or disengagement of the corresponding mode of flight control).

- Three of the seven switches governing flight control modes not directly associated with any of the windows.

  VERT PATH, for example, governs the vertical-path mode, instructing the flight control to follow a stored flight plan from one waypoint to another.

Here is a brief narrative of one possible "session" with the Control Mode Panel. Initially, the panel's windows read actual (sensed) values. Suppose that the pilot wishes to climb from 19,500 to 25,000 feet and to hold that altitude. The knob of the ALT ENG window can be used to dial 25,000 into the window, at which point the window should stop displaying the actual altitude and, instead, freeze on the *preselected* value of 25,000. To indicate that the window is displaying a preselected (rather than a current) value, a blue lamp should light in one quadrant of the translucent ALT ENG switch.

Preselecting an altitude should not by itself engage the *altitude* mode of the flight control system (which can automatically fly to and maintain a preselected altitude). Instead, the pilot must explicitly request the altitude mode by pushing the ALT ENG switch. When the difference between the actual altitude and the preselected altitude is large—more than 1,200 feet—the ALT ENG switch should not immediately engage the altitude mode, because it is the pilot's responsibility to choose the *flight path angle* (the angle of ascent or descent) at which the plane should approach the preselected altitude. In our scenario, therefore, the request made by pushing the ALT ENG switch should be "put on hold." The altitude mode is then said to be *armed* but not *engaged* (a situation indicated by turning off the blue lamp and turning on an amber lamp behind the ALT ENG switch).

When the altitude mode is thus put on hold, the flight path angle mode should engage automatically (indicated by lighting a green lamp in one quadrant of the FPA SEL switch). If the pilot dials an angle into the FPA SEL window when the flight path angle mode is engaged and the altitude mode armed, the flight control system will be instructed to climb at that angle until the plane is "close enough" to the preselected altitude—at which point the flight path angle mode should disengage (the green lamp in the FPA SEL switch goes off, the FPA SEL window returns to showing the plane's actual flight path angle) and the altitude mode of the flight control system should become engaged (ALT ENG switch light becomes green), instructing the flight control system to fly to and maintain the preselected altitude of 25,000 feet. An armed or engaged altitude mode may be cancelled at any time by pushing the ALT ENG switch.

This rather intricate scenario is only one out of a large number of possibilities. A little thought raises a number of questions, and not all of the answers are easy to find. For example:

- If the altitude mode is armed and the pilot cancels it by pushing the ALT ENG switch, should the flight path angle mode also disengage or should the plane continue its automatically controlled ascent or descent?

- If the preselected altitude is higher than the actual altitude, but the pilot selects a negative flight path angle, will this instruction to descend be obeyed?

- If the altitude mode is armed, and the flight path angle mode engaged, can the pilot cancel the flight path angle mode and fly the plane to the desired altitude manually?

The imaginative reader can supply others.

2 FORMAL SPECIFICATIONS

2.1 The role of a formal specification

This interface is difficult to describe clearly and succinctly using conventional styles of documentation, as can be seen by considering some examples taken from one English-language description of the Control Mode Panel. This description presents, roughly, a pilot's-eye-view, and well illustrates some of the common problems with informal specifications:

Ambiguity: Both the physical act of pushing a switch and the logical act of engaging the corresponding flight control mode are referred to as "selection." It is not always clear which is meant.

Incompleteness: The airspeed mode maintains a preselected airspeed and the time-path mode attempts to maintain a predefined schedule from waypoint to waypoint. The informal documentation notes that these two functions are incompatible, but does not indicate how conflicts between them are resolved. For example, what happens if the pilot attempts to invoke the airspeed mode when time-path is engaged: is the command ignored, or does airspeed engage and time-path disengage?

Inconsistency: It is said in one place that the flight path angle mode cannot be "directly deselected"—i.e., when the flight path angle mode is engaged it cannot be cancelled by pushing the FPA SEL switch. Elsewhere, the document lists the effects of directly deselecting the flight path angle mode.

It is obviously desirable to have systematic techniques for developing and analyzing complex specifications, and a clear notation for communicating them to others. A *formal* specification notation is one with a mathematically defined syntax and semantics. Formal specifications are conceptually useful because they provide an unambiguous medium for communication among users, designers, and implementors. In addition, they make it possible to apply semantically-based tools to the analysis of design and implementation. For example, there are mathematical techniques for checking various completeness and consistency properties of formal specifications, and for demonstrating the consistency between a formal specification and its implementation. These possibilities can be exploited with any desired level of rigor—from informal walk-throughs, to the pencil and paper analyses of ordinary mathematics, to machine-checkable results supported by theorem provers, proof checkers, etc.

2.2 The Larch/Ada specification language

Larch/Ada is the formal specification language for Ada that is accepted by the Penelope verification system [GMP 90],[Gu 89]. It is a *two-tiered* formalism,

[Wi 87]: Each specification consists of a *mathematical tier*, which is essentially a collection of definitions, and an *interface tier*, which describes the behavior of the code in terms of those definitions.

Consider, for example, an "infinite precision" integer package

```
package arbitrary_integer
    type super_int is private;
    --| BASED ON Int;  -- the *mathematical* integers
    function ''+''(x,y: super_int) return super_int;
    --| WHERE
    --|    RETURN x+y;  -- the *mathematical* sum
    --|    RAISE too_big <=> (|x+y| > 10**(2**16));
     ..
```

Type super_integer might be implemented as an unconstrained array of digits. The BASED ON annotation says that each value of super_int is to be regarded as a value in *Int*, the set of mathematical integers. (The definition of *Int* and its operations belongs automatically to every mathematical tier.)

The RETURN annotation says that when execution terminates normally, the value returned by x+y is that of the mathematical sum x+y. The RAISE annotation says that the exception too_big is raised if and only if the mathematical sum is greater (in absolute value) than $10^{2^{16}}$. Thus, the type super_int and the executable operation "+" are *described* in the vocabulary of idealized arithmetic, but are not required to *implement* any of that vocabulary. For example, most values from *Int* do *not* correspond to values of super_int, and "+" can raise an exception even though (mathematical) + cannot. A two-tiered specification can be thought of as a simple, idealized, abstraction together with a description of how the executable operations deviate from that abstraction.

The interface component of a Larch/Ada specification is written in a notation tailored to the specifics of Ada, and the mathematical tier in the Larch Shared Language [GGH 90].

3 DEVELOPING THE SPECIFICATION

The avionics software of the TSRV (and, in particular, of the Control Mode Panel) was originally developed by the Computer Services Corporation. In 1986, NASA conducted an internal research project to recode the software of the Control Mode Panel using systematic "AI" techniques [HM 88]. Our project has been to devise an Ada design (an appropriate collection of packages) and then to specify the packages formally.

The first draft of the specification was based on the English-language description of the Control Mode Panel already mentioned. As formal specification methods are highly intolerant of ambiguity, this raised a large number of precise questions. Answers generously supplied by R.M. Hueschen were factored into a second draft, which was then compared to the C code produced by NASA's 1986 recoding project (new questions arising at each stage). In its current state the specification is "wrong," in the sense of not fully expressing the intentions of the system's designers, but has the virtue of being wrong *clearly*. The discipline of formal specification has meant that all our problems resulted in efficiently communicable questions, and not in states of mere confusion.

3.1 The mathematical tier

The first step was to make an unambiguous model of the vocabulary used in the English-language description of the Mode Control Panel. We first defined the following sets of values (others are omitted for lack of space):

- Sets of values representing states:

  The states of the Control Mode Panel are represented by values in AGCS_state; the states of the aircraft's sensors are represented by values in Sensor_state; etc. This will be formally expressed by the "based on" relation described in section 2.2. Not all the values in AGCS_state will correspond to states that can actually be reached by a properly functioning system.

- A set of values representing actions:

  $$\text{Action} = \{\text{alt\_eng\_switch}, \ldots, \text{alt\_eng\_knob(i)}, \ldots, \text{alt\_capture}, \ldots\}$$

  For example, alt_eng_switch represents the action of pushing the ALT ENG switch. The action alt_capture is not an action of the pilot, but represents the system's detection that a desired altitude has been attained.

- A set of values representing modes of automatic flight control:

  $$\text{Mode} = \{\text{alt\_eng}, \text{fpa\_sel}, \text{vert\_path}, \ldots\}$$

We define, in addition, various operations on these values, such as

- An operation *transition*, describing the results of various actions on values of AGCS_state.

  The bulk of the mathematical tier is devoted to defining this operation.

- A predicate *good*, formulating various properties that should be possessed by all reachable values of AGCS_state.

- Various observer operations reporting on properties of Sensor_state values, Display_state values, etc.

These definitions are provided in modular pieces, of which we give two examples.

The structure of AGCS_state values A *trait* is the Larch Shared Language construct for presenting axiomatic definitions in a structured way. (The examples in this paper show none of the interesting features of the Larch Shared Language.)

AgcsStructure : **trait**
    AGCS_state **tuple of**
        on: Bool, modes: Set_of_modes, engaged: Engagement_status,
        setting: Value_settings, window: Window_array
   includes Modes, Actions, Windows, Engagements, Externals
   introduces
        transition: AGCS_state, Action, Sensor_state, Flight_plan $\rightarrow$
             AGCS_state
        good: AGCS_state $\rightarrow$ Bool

The "tuple" construct says that an AGCS_state can be characterized by five components, containing the following information: whether the flight control system is on; which modes of automatic flight control have been selected; which of the selected modes are engaged; what settings have been preselected in the windows; whether windows are showing current or preselected values.

The "includes" clause adds the definitions and declarations provided by other traits named Modes, Actions, etc., which are not shown here. An "introduces" clause is used to declare mathematical operations (inputs to the left of the arrow and outputs to the right). The declaration of *transition* indicates that changes to AGCS_state values are determined not only by the current state and the instigating action, but also by the state of the sensors and of the currently active flight plan. A trait may also supply axioms about any operations introduced by itself or those traits it includes. We decided to omit from AgcsStructure any axioms about the complex operations transition and good, leaving their definitions to be filled in by other traits.

Changes of window status The next example provides part of the definition of the transition operation. If a window is dislaying a current, sensed, value it is said to be *current*; if it displays a value that has been preselected it is said to be *chosen*. The way in which windows change their status is completely uniform, regarded as a function of the changes in the set of selected modes:

- Any action selecting the w-mode makes the w-window chosen.

- Any action deselecting the w-mode makes the w-window current.

- Use of the w_knob makes the w-window chosen.

- Any other action leaves the status of the w-window unchanged.

where the placeholder w may be replaced throughout by one the names ALT ENG, FPA SEL, etc.

The behavior of the windows is highly *non*-uniform if we try to describe it as a function of actions; the informal specification, expressed from this point of view, is rather confusing. Larch notation allows us to define, in effect, a "generic" trait capturing the description given above:

StatusShell : **trait**
  includes AgcsStructure
  introduces
    _.component : Window_array → Window_status
    md: → Mode
    knob : Value → Action
  asserts for all [agcs:AGCS_state, act:Action, sens:Sensor_state,
                 plan: Flight_plan]
  abbreviation agcs' == transition(agcs,act,sens,plan)
    agcs'.window.component =
      if md ∈ agcs'.modes - acgs.modes **then** chosen
      elsif md ∈ agcs.mode − agcs'.modes **then** current
      elsif act = knob(i) **then** chosen
      else agcs.window.component

In these axioms, _.component represents the window, md its corresponding mode, and knob its corresponding knob. The behavior of all the windows is thus described by appropriately instantiating StatusShell four times.

Note: the "abbreviation" construct is a syntactical extension of the Larch Shared Language that we have found quite useful.

3.2 An Ada design

We choose to organize the Ada code into five packages, called panel_logic, display_manager, sensor_data, flight_plan, and flight_control. The package panel_logic, which calls on all the others, encapsulates the "state-changing" logic of the Control Mode Panel. This is the package we specify. The other packages encapsulate interactions with devices, as suggested by their names.

The state of panel_logic will be based on AGCS_state. That is, the local variables of this package are regarded as an implementation of the state of an abstract state machine whose states are values in AGCS_state. Similarly, the state of package display_manager is based on Display_state, etc. The set of Action values is *not* mapped to an Ada data type. Instead, each such value corresponds to a procedure exported by package panel_logic, which effects the appropriate response to the action.

This design makes panel_logic compatible with various designs for the overall system: For example, the main program could be structured as a loop that polls the switches and knobs and, upon detecting an action, calls the corresponding subprogram. Alternately, some of the responses to actions could be interrupt-driven, with the corresponding subprogram invoked by the interrupt handler. (The cost of the subprogram calls can be avoided by compiling them in-line.)

3.3 The interface tier

Two extracts from the specification of panel_logic should give a reasonable idea of the Larch/Ada style.

```
--| WITH TRAIT AgcsLogic, AgcsProperties, LogicalDisplay
--| WITH sensor_data, flight_plan, display_manager,
--|      flight_control
with sensor_data_types; use sensor_data_types;
package panel_logic
   --| BASED ON AGCS_state
   --| INVARIANT  panel_logic.on -> good(panel_logic)
```

```
--| INITIALLY not panel_logic.on
            ...
end panel_logic;
```

All lines containing Larch/Ada specification constructs are prefaced by the symbol --|. The two dashes mean that Ada compilers treat them as comments, while the following bar indicates to our Larch/Ada tools that what follows is part of a specification.

The "with trait" clause names all the traits needed to supply all the definitions used in the specification. In addition to the Ada context clause "with sensor_data_types ..." we include a Larch/Ada context clause "--| WITH sensor_data ..." The Ada context clause names units needed to compile the (Ada) specification of panel_logic, while the Larch/Ada context clause names any additional units referred to by the Larch/Ada specification. This separation allows us to avoid introducing unnecessary compilation dependences solely for the sake of writing Larch/Ada specifications.

As mentioned above, the "based on" construct treats the package as a state machine whose local state can, abstractly, be thought of as having a value in AGCS_state. The "invariant" clause says that all reachable states of the package must satisfy the predicate *good*; and the "initially" clause says that immediately after the package is elaborated the system is not on.

The procedure att_cws_switch_effect effects the correct response to the action of pushing the att_cws switch. (Note: In Larch/Ada specifications the name of a package denotes the current value of the package state.)

```
procedure att_cws_switch_effect;
--| WHERE
--|   GLOBALS IN  panel_logic
--|   GLOBALS OUT display_manager, flight_control, panel_logic

--|   IN panel_logic.on

--|   OUT panel_logic = transition(IN panel_logic,
--|                                att_cws_switch,*,*)
--|   OUT FORALL ss: Sensor_state::
--|     look(display_manager,ss) = display(panel_logic,ss)
--|   OUT FORALL md:mode ::
--|     fc_engaged(md,flight_control) = engaged(md,panel_logic)
--| END WHERE;
```

The "globals" clause says that this procedure reads the state of `panel_logic` and may modify the states of packages `display_manager`, `flight_control`, and `panel_logic`. The "in" clause says that the procedure may only be invoked when the system is on.

The first of the "out" clauses specifies the value of the (abstract) state of package `panel_logic` upon termination of a call to `att_cws_switch_effect`. In this equation the term "IN `panel_logic`" refers to the state of `panel_logic` at the time of the call, and the two *'s are a shorthand indicating that the other parameters to the transition operation are irrelevant.

The second of the "out" clauses is explained as follows: The operation *look* is defined in the mathematical tier of the specification of `display_manager`. It defines the actual look of the display that results from a given state of packages `display_manager` and `sensor_state`. The operation *display* is provided by the mathematical tier of the specification of `panel_logic`, and it defines what the display *should* look like given the states of `panel_logic` and `sensor_state`. The "out" clause says that the action of this procedure brings the whole system of packages into a state in which the actual look of the display is what it should be. The third "out" clause performs a similar service for the actions of the `flight_control` package.

4 CONCLUSION

The complex logic of the Control Model Panel can be intelligibly described, with reasonable effort, in the Larch/Ada specification language. As might be expected, the construction of the specification brought to light many ambiguities, inconsistencies, and oversights in the limited documentation we possessed, flaws that could easily persist even in carefully written informal descriptions. Expertise in both formal specification and avionics was necessary to construct the Larch/Ada specification, but these two forms of expertise did not reside in a single person. Two important tests of this specification have not been performed: its comprehensibility by a person (e.g., a programmer) expert in *neither* formal specifications nor avionics, and its usefulness and adaptability throughout the life of an implementation derived from it.

For a comparison of various specification methods applied to this problem, and an account of its use as a classroom exercise, see [Ar 91].

References

[Ar 91]   Mark A. Ardis. *A comparison of specification methods.* Technical Report, Software Engineering Institute, Carnegie-Mellon University, 1991.

[GGH 90] S.J. Garland, J.V. Guttag, and J.J. Horning. Debugging Larch Shared Language specifications. *IEEE Transactions on Software Engineering*, 16(9):1044–1057, September 1990.

[Gu 89]   David Guaspari. Penelope, an Ada verification system. In *Proceedings of Tri-Ada '89*, pages 216–224, Pittsburgh, PA, October 1989.

[GMP 90] David Guaspari, Carla Marceau, and Wolfgang Polak. Formal verification of Ada programs. *IEEE Transactions on Software Engineering*, 16(9):1058–1075, September 1990.

[HM 88]   R.M. Hueschen and J.W. McManus. *Flight software requirements for the AI-developed control mode panel logic on Advanced Transport Operating Systems Transportation Systems Research Vehicle.* Technical Report, NASA, 1988.

[Wi 87]   Jeannette M. Wing. Writing Larch interface language specifications. *ACM Transactions on Programming Languages and Systems*, 9(1):1–24, January 1987.

Ada as High Level Language for Real Time Systems exploiting RDBMS Techniques

C. COLOMBINI, A. DELLA TORRE, R. PALOTTI

Carlo Gavazzi Space S.p.A - Milan - Italy

1 INTRODUCTION

The more evident trend in the aerospace programmes over the past years is constituted by the growing complexity of the future on-board systems, like Columbus and Hermes. This evolution has consequently deeply influenced the functional, performance and architectural requirements of the Spacecraft integration, test and validation systems, conventionally called Electrical Ground Support Equipments (EGSE).

The present trend in the EGSE design is characterized by the following major requirements:
- test system performances enhancement;
- improvement of the human-computer interface design, in order to simplify the test engineer tasks and eventually reduce the spacecraft integration and test time;
- increased amount of real time test data to be handled on line;
- use of the most recent equipments, tools and technologies available on the market, in order to reduce the development costs by introducing off-the-shelf building blocks in the design;
- enforce the protability of the design over several Spacecraft Programmes, in order to recover the initial design investments.

Current generation EGSE's are typically based on a distributed architecture, with dedicated intelligent front-end equipments (Special Checkout Equipments - SCOE's) in charge of the data preprocessing from the various Spacecraft Subsystems.
The core of the Spacecraft test and integration system is constituted by a Master Test Processor (MTP), in charge of centralized test control, monitoring, data archive and retrieval tasks, according to the European Space Agency Spacecraft Overall Checkout Equipment (OCOE) reference architecture. MTP is interfaced to the various SCOE's via the EGSE Local Area Network (LAN).
The test engineers control the test session evolution via Test Conductor Consolles (TCC), interfaced onto the EGSE LAN.

The Spacecraft test and validation activities require that all the data relevant to each test session must be stored into a test Data Base, to be kept under configuration control.

The above mentioned increased performance requirements, together with the more recent trends in distributed systems architectures and Database technologies, have led to identify in the MTP design a dedicated equipment for the test data handling, the Data Server (DS) equipment, while the "conventional" MTP test data processing operations are performed by another dedicated equipment, the Checkout Manager (CM) equipment.

2 THE DATA SERVER

The Data Server equipment is required to manage the real-time archiving and the consequent organization of a large amount of test data, in order to make them available to be processed and analyzed in pseudo real-time by the Spacecraft test engineers.
The test data retrieval operation must be available both to Data Server local operators and to remote users, connected onto the EGSE LAN.
The Data Server required functionalities can be

classified into the following main categories:
- Test Execution functions
- Test Evaluation/Support functions

Among the <u>Test Execution functions,</u> it can be identified the archiving of test results onto the mass memory devices and the management of the interfaces with the local operator and with the CM.

The test results data to be archived belong to different categories:
- Telemetry and Telecommand data (TM/TC), which are respectively the application, experimental and housekeeping data transmitted from the Spacecraft to ground and the commands transmitted from the ground control centre to the Spacecraft.
- SCOE-links data, i.e. the data exchanged during the test session between the MTP and the Special Checkout Equipments (SCOE's) associated to the various Spacecraft Subsystems under test.
- Logbook files, where all the test engineers actions and all the error/event messages are time tagged and recorded.
- Test Sequence generated files, i.e. the data files generated during the run of the Test Procedures (Test Sequences) specifically designed by the test engineers for the Spacecraft integration, validation and test purposes.

Among the <u>Test Evaluation/Support functions</u> it is possible to identify:
- Consultation by local or remote users of the archived test results (event, parameter, file fetch and complex items queries).
- Replay of the archived TM/TC files to CM, in order to perform the related data processing as during the real time test operations.
- Conversion of Telemetry raw data into Engineering Units, according to the sensors conversion tables stored into the Spacecraft Database
- Recovery of test data not yet eventually archived (due for example to a DS failure) during a test session.

The main features of the DS design, elaborated on the base of the above mentioned functional requirements, are listed in the following:
- the DS equipment S/W runs on a Microvax 3400 DEC computer system, under VMS Operating System;
- the selected programming language is Ada;
- Test Data are stored into a Relational Database.
  The DS equipment provides on the EGSE LAN the capabilities of a SQL Server, allowing a centralized real time archiving and a distributed on line retrieval of Spacecraft tests data (by local or remote users connected via the EGSE LAN); the design exploits the wide range of tools provided by the ORACLE RDBMS (SQL*PLUS, SQL*NET, SQL*MENU, SQL*FORMS, SQL*REPORT_WRITER, PRO*ADA precompiler).
  A high rate of input data (more than 15 kbytes/sec) is processed in real time, inserted into the Test Data Base and eventually archived.
- Bulk data transfer from test data major source (CM) and DS is achieved via a Shared Disc Subsystem, to which both equipments are interfaced.
- an Optical Disk Subsystem is used in order to eventually store (and to maintain over the Spacecraft overall lifecycle) this big amount of data.

As said above, the Data Server S/W is implemented in Ada and SQL languages; two major subsystems can be identified:
- the data archiving subsystem, which is and Ada/SQL application, constituted of 11 ADA tasks.
- the data retrieval subsystem, which is constituted of 3 main command files, resulting from Ada/SQL*PLUS/SQL*FORMS applications.

The overall dimensions of the DS application is of the order of 15.000 Ada source lines.

Besides the above described functional requirements, the DS equipment must fulfil general requirements, coming from the specific application area, like:

- improved Human-Computer Interface (HCI),
- design portability over different spacecraft programmes
- adoption of modern S/W design and development methodologies,
- maintainability over a long time period, of the order of tenth of years,
- capability of coping with technology evolution during the equipment life cycle,
- Reliability and Safety.

The main goal of optimizing the cost/performance ratio during the project development phase is achieved by:
- designing the S/W system according to sound S/W engineering principles
- enhancing the portability, maintainability and reusability of the produced S/W
- making a large use, whenever compatible with the equipment requirements, of off-the-shelf products and tools available on the market.

Moreover, the HCI improvements achieved with respect to the past generation Spacecraft EGSE's enforces the cost reduction in the overall Spacecraft Assembling, Integration and Test activities over the entire project lifecycle, since the integration and test time can be significantly decreased.

The reason of the key choices of the Ada environment for the Data Server S/W design/development and of a RDBMS for the test data handling is derived direcly from the above defined primary project objectives.

3 THE ADA CHOICE

The choice of the Ada environment for the design and development of DS S/W perfectly meets the main project requirements, providing several major advantages, like:
- Maintainability, Porting, Reusability.
  The maintainability, the porting and the code reusability are key features necessary to reduce costs in the overall S/W life-cycle.
  This is true especially for the DS, which has to be reused in different EGSE configurations and in the frame of several Spacecraft testing programmes, typically requiring adaptations during their life cycle in order to cope with different testing specifications and EGSE architectures.
  Moreover, the areas of application of this equipment are potentially very large, not only limited to Spacecraft testing, and also the hardware platforms on which the S/W has to run may be very different.

The adoption of the Ada environment ensures a high level of maintainability; this means that typically the design can be easily modified, without increasing the complexity of the S/W, with consequent lower efforts and resulting costs.

All that is majorly true if the design and development phase is performed following sound S/W engineering priciples, like design modularity, clear interfaces between modules and code readibility.
The phylosophy that is at the base of the Ada language perfectly copes with these aspects, providing syntax rules to implement important features like abstraction and information hiding, besides readibility.
The same features improve the design portability, allowing to port an application through different programmes, with the minimum reconfigurations required by programmes specific requirements.

From the programming techniques point of view, the

portability can be increased if the above described features are fully implemented (in fact the machine dependent code, if any, can be isolated in well identified modules).

At programming language level, the standardization of the language can significantly influence the porting of code among different environments.

At this purpose, one of the main benefits coming from the adoption of the Ada language is the standardization.

All the Ada compilers must be in fact validated each year by the ACVC (Ada Compiler Validation Capability); that avoids the raising and growth of dialects and permits a high level of standardization between different compilers. Moreover, also a standardization of the development environment is in progress.

All these characteristics promote the porting of S/W among different target systems.

Also the reusability of the code over different programmes takes advantage from the same Ada features as discussed above.

- Maturity.
  Ada has now to be considered as a "mature" language; currently, it is supported on the most diffused and popular H/W platforms and S/W environments, from different H/W and S/W manufacturers.

- Productivity.
  Another advantage in using Ada is the achievable high productivity with respect to the conventional languages and environments.

- Ease of Integration.
  Due to the adopted methodology and to the specific characteristics of the Ada environment, the time required for final integration of complex modules (and related risks) are reduced to minimum, having been obliged to face and solve all the potential integration and interface problems in an early design stage.

- Suitability for Prototyping.
  Another important feature of Ada is its suitability
  for prototype development, which is very useful for
  the selection of the system architecture and the
  validation of performance requirements, at an early
  stage of the system design.

- Suitability to exploitation of S/W Design
  Methodologies.
  Another advantage of Ada is provided by its
  suitability to be employed in conjunction with modern
  S/W Design Methodologies, like Hierarchical Object
  Oriented Design (HOOD), which, for large projects,
  allows a significant save of development time by
  mixing the power of the object oriented design
  methodology with a hierarchical conception of the
  objects and of their relations.

All the above Ada key features, are fully in line with
the DS general and application specific project
requirements and this justifies the choice of Ada as
programming environment.

4 THE CHOICE OF RDBMS

The choice of exploiting an off-the-shelf Relational
Database Management System (ORACLE) for the DS archive
and retrieval functions meets the project functional
and performance requirements, by limiting at the same
time the data retrieval applications development costs.

This choice comes from the following major reasons:

- System Architecture: the Data Server must perform a
  centralized massive archiving of a wide range of data
  types and allow both local and remote data retrieval
  operations by users distributed over the EGSE LAN;
  the availability of an off-the-shelf product
  providing a wide set of tools already suited for
  handling the data archiving and retrieval, also via

LAN, is obviously welcome for the Data Server application.

- Human-Computer Interface: the RDBMS makes available the Data Server user with SQL, which is a very powerful and expressive language to manipulate and interrogate the Data Base; it provides also a large set of tools oriented to make easier the access to the Data Base by non-expert users; the high-quality of man-machine interface meets also the DS major requirement of reducing the Spacecraft test and integration time, with important benefits on the overall Spacecraft programme costs.

- Reduction of the development costs: by using off-the-shelf RDBMS tools, it is very easy and cost effective to build applications related to the Data Base.
The improvement with respect to past generation EGSE's, where every data retrieval and post processing operation had to be implemented via complex programs designed ad hoc, is dramatic.

- Performances improvement: it is ensured by the good performances of the RDBMS; moreover, it is possible to use precompilers, which allow to embed SQL statements directly into high-level Ada code.

- Power and flexibility: it is ensured by the RDBMS tools powerful features, complemented by the flexibility made available by SQL.

- Program to data independence, also in this case ensured by the RDBMS.

5 CONCLUSIONS
Our experience about the DS application comprises at the present two generations of equipments, with the same general functional requirements, but with some peculiar differences mainly related to different test data formats, input/output data flow and performance requirements.

Both projects exploit Ada and SQL languages, and make and extensive use of ORACLE RDBMS facilities and tools. From our experience, Ada has fulfilled all the DS project related requirements.

The potential advantages associated to the language choice (i.e. ease of maintenance, portability, reusability, productivity, ease of integration, suitability to modern S/W technologies and prototyping activities, maturity) have been effectively proven in the course of the two mentioned projects.

Especially about reusability and portability, Ada has shown its great flexibility, because in the two projects it was possible to reuse both large and complete packages, with few modifications, and functions libraries from packages not completely reusable.

The exploitation of Ada as PDL has permitted the availability of a DS prototype during an early programme design phase, without major additional efforts with respect to the ones related to the performance of architectural design phase.

The prototype has allowed the early verification of the most critical elements of the design.

The efforts related to the design of the data storage and retrieval functions have been minimized by the exploitation of the ORACLE RDBMS and related tools, including the ones supporting the design of the operator interface and the provision of RDBMS services to remote users, connected to DS via the EGSE LAN.

The interfacing of the Ada application programs to RDBMS has been greatly simplified by the capability of embedding SQL statements in the Ada source code, thanks to the availability of a precompiler.

Due to the exploitation of an etherogeneous environment with products from different suppliers, the verification of the overall environment compatibility was confirmed to be a key factor to be assessed during an early program phase; change in revision of one S/W component needs to be verified for compatibility before introducing it into the design.

Experience Developing Two Ada Applications For Embedded Real-Time Systems Using Different Software Processes.

Brian Gilbert

AWA Defence Industries

Mike Taylor

RADE Systems

Greg Bek

Rational

1 INTRODUCTION

This paper provides a description of the development of two embedded real-time systems. Descriptions of applications are provided, followed by a discussion of our experiences with using Ada for this type of application, with particular emphasis on Ada tasking.

We also compare the two different software development processes used on the project. The comparison of the two development methods will show that the choice of development process can affect developer productivity and project schedules.

The lessons learnt show that a growing awareness of developers, management and customer in understanding the nature of software development in Ada is key to achieving project success.

2 APPLICATION DESCRIPTION

Our project was to develop two separate applications to be executed in embedded computers. The applications were built as turnkey systems, and were delivered to the customer in EPROM as part of a larger system.

A variety of external equipment connected to the system required a number of different interfacing methods. Some equipment was connected through direct control circuits; other equipment was connected by serial communications links. The applications implemented a layered protocol on the serial links to provided a reliable method for passing both application and control messages.

The communications requirements of the systems meant that our applications had to process interrupts occurring with a frequency of over several kilohertz during peak load periods.

The common target processor used was a Motorola MC68020 with a MC68881 Floating Point co-processor. The cross compiler used for target-code generation was the Rational Motorola Cross-Development Facility.

3 ADA TASKING

The most important feature of Ada for use in real-time applications is tasking. A thorough understanding of the Ada Tasking model and the problems that can be encountered is necessary to be successful when using Ada for embedded real-time applications.

Our customer was aware of the criticisms frequently made of tasking, and expressed concern about our designs with respect to performance and reliability.

The specific areas of concern are discussed in the following sections.

3.1 Rendezvous Performance

Each application consisted of a significant number of Ada tasks. Application A had over thirty tasks and application B had over forty. Our customer was concerned that the interactions between this number of tasks would require a significant amount of runtime performance to operate.

We found that rendezvous performance was more than adequate to support the number of tasks we used. The number of tasks in an application had no effect on rendezvous performance.

3.2 Task Scheduling

One of the most important points to consider when developing a real-time system using Ada is the scheduling characteristics of the runtime kernel. The runtime kernel used by the Rational Cross-Development Facility implements a preemptive scheduler. This kernel makes a scheduling decision every time a delay expiration occurs. This preemptive scheduling ensured consistent runtime behaviour of our applications.

The use of preemptive scheduling allowed us to guarantee that any high-priority cyclic tasks would be made eligible for execution when the tasks cyclic delay expired. Our delay expiration was accurate to within 1 millisecond of the delay requested, which was sufficient to meet the timing requirements of the system.

Our experience shows that applications containing large numbers of tasks can be developed even without the use of specialised scheduling algorithms such as Rate Monotonic Scheduling as described by Sha and Goodenough. [Sha 1990]

3.3 Interrupt processing
Ada provides an elegant method for interrupt processing which is consistent with the underlying tasking model. Because of the semantics of the Ada rendezvous however, an Ada implementation must perform a significant amount of processing before the code within an interrupt entry can begin execution.

Both applications had to process a large number of interrupts, and it was important to have efficient interrupt processing.

The target hardware implementation limited the amount of interrupts that could be processed using standard Ada to 2000 per second. The limiting factor was the speed of the CPU memory. To ensure no data was lost it was necessary to implement a faster handling method for the high frequency interrupt sources.

The Rational Cross-Development Facility provides two alternate methods of handling interrupts. The method we chose to use for fast processing was procedural interrupts, which allow an Ada procedure to be bound to a hardware interrupt vector. When the interrupt occurs, the run time system generates a call to the appropriate procedure. When the procedure completes, the run time system returns control to the task that was executing prior to the interrupt. These procedures execute using the CPU interrupt stack, so no context save/restore cycle is necessary.

Although this method was non standard, it allowed the interrupt processing to be written in Ada. At one point it was suggested that the interrupt procedures be coded in assembler, however, when the compiler generated code for the Ada routines was examined it was concluded that the small gain in speed was offset by the difficulty in developing and maintaining any assembler routines.

3.4 Unsafe Tasking Practices
The development team were trained not to use tasking practices that were known to have a potential to cause problems. Specifically they were taught not to make any assumptions about the order of evaluation within select statements, and not to use task priorities as a mechanism to ensure task execution.

No need was found for using the potentially dangerous attributes of 'Callable, 'Count and 'Terminated.

3.5 Memory Usage Of Tasks

Our customer was concerned that the number of tasks would consume significant amounts of memory in what were memory constrained targets.

Each task requires an amount of of memory for storing a Task Control Block (TCB) that the runtime uses for task management. Each TCB contains space for saving the processor state when the task is not executing. Each task also requires an amount of memory for use as a program stack, the size of this stack is usually controlled by using the 'Storage_Size representation clause.

Early versions of the applications exceeded the amount of available memory. However, using target memory analysis tools we were able to examine each tasks specific memory usage and reduce the required amount of storage accordingly.

4 USE OF TWO DIFFERENT DEVELOPMENT PROCESSES

The two applications discussed in this paper were developed sequentially, using different development processes.

The use of the different development processes provides an opportunity to compare and contrast both the reasons for taking the different approaches and the lessons learnt as a result of using the different processes.

4.1 Application A

The contract specified that a standard DOD-STD-2167 approach should be followed. Little or no tailoring of the development process and the deliverable documentation was specified in the contract or allowed during the development of application A.

It was decided early in the project to use OOD as the basic design methodology. This decision was made due to negative experience on previous projects using Functional Decomposition methodologies. Prior to commencing development members of the team received some training in OOD.

The use of ODD was hampered for Application A as the original requirements supplied by the customer had been analysed using Functional Decomposition, which hindered the mapping from top level specifications to lower level design documentation.

After installation of the Rational Development Environment, the team received a series of training courses in how to use the environment. This training resulted in a increase in Ada literacy as well as the acquisition of knowledge about use of Rational Environment. The team utilised the development environment quickly; at the end of the first month they had moved their design to the environment and were producing updated SRS's and Design Documents using the Rational's Design Facility for DOD-STD-2167.

4.2 Results Of The Waterfall Approach

The development of application A could be described as very typical of the waterfall approach. The amount of effort required at integration was considerable. This amount of integration effort made planning and resource allocation difficult for the manager of application B who was expecting to have resources shifted across from application A after completion of integration.

As development for the first release of application A progressed it became clear to the customer that the workload and time associated with using a waterfall approach and strict compliance with the standard would impact upon delivery schedules. This helped motivate both parties to investigate an alternate development process for application B.

At the time of writing application A is preparing for Factory Acceptance Testing of the last release of the software. After this release is made the software will be transitioned to maintenance by the customer.

Statistics for the code produced for application A are listed in the following tables:

Total Lines	Comment Lines	Blank Lines	Semicolons
49566	15530	6471	15395

Man Months	Single Lines Of Code/MM	Non-Comment Non Blank/MM	Terminal Semicolons/MM
60	718	460	256

4.3 Application B

The development of application B was started when application A was at the integration and testing phase. Because of the difficulties encountered during the development of application A and the lessons learnt, it was appropriate to reexamine the use of DOD-STD-2167 development process and the DOD-STD-2167 deliverable documentation requirements.

DOD-STD-2167 imposes the waterfall life cycle as the software process model and development is split into phases which are document- and review-based. The customer, who was initially comfortable with these concepts, realised that documents and associated reviews were cumbersome, inflexible and did not measure real progress.

A major problem with the waterfall model is that it delays integration until late in the process. A large amount of risk was associated with performing integration, making schedules unpredictable and resource allocation difficult.

These factors were instrumental in rewriting the Software Management Plan for the development of application B. The new plan differed in two ways. Firstly, the contents of the deliverable documents were changed so that the information contained was more object oriented. In particular, a decision was made to use object oriented requirements analysis and document it in the SRS. Secondly, the software process was altered from the waterfall model to an incremental build approach.

4.4 Defining a new Software Process

The software process defined in the management plan was based on TRW's Ada Process Model. The software would be demonstrated to the customer during development as a series of incremental "builds". A document pack consisting of partially complete SDDD, test descriptions and test procedures would be delivered to the customer prior to a build review. Builds would progress from the "bottom up"; low level services and processor/throughput load tests would be demonstrated first, followed by more and more functionality in later builds.

Traditional Analysis and Top Level Design phase activities focused on architectural analysis, design and demonstration. Detailed Design, Coding and Testing phase activities were replaced by the builds, which allowed gradual integration of the functionality onto the target hardware.

The traditional phases and the new activities are outlined in the following table:

Traditional Phase	Application A Activity	Application B Activity
Analysis	Analysis	Design Top Level Architecture
Top Level Design	Top Level Design	Implement top level, 2 recursions
Detailed Design	Detailed Design	Implement build 1. Formal CDR
Code	Code	Implement build 2. Formal CDR
Test	Test	Implement build 3. Formal CDR

This incremental approach gave the customer much greater confidence that the project would succeed. At each review, the software was demonstrated in its current form and the customer was able to provide immediate feedback on each occasion.

4.5 Implementation

Having gained approval of the new software management plan, development of application B started in earnest.

The system architecture was determined during the requirements analysis phase. The OORA was based on Ed Colbert's methodology [Colbert 1989]. Objects and their interfaces were analysed, and the static and dynamic interactions between them defined for the various system modes and states.

A new SRS was produced to capture this analysis. Using a liberal interpretation of the DID paragraphs, SRS Functions represented objects, and each Subfunction represented an exported service. Object interaction diagrams were inserted in an appendix with a full description of system behaviour. This appendix became the focal point of discussions of the system architecture as it clearly showed system dynamic and static behaviour.

The customer was very pleased with the outcome of the SRS, which built confidence in the new approach. The transition to Top-Level Design was simple because the concepts developed in the SRS mapped directly to the TLCSC's in the STLDD. A function-oriented requirements model cannot map easily to an object-oriented design, as the Top-Level Design document has to introduce new components (objects) and relationships to the reader. Since it was not necessary to document a new set of software components, the STLDD document could be directed to more important issues such Ada tasking and introduction of the next abstract layer of "solution space" objects of the software.

The main activity in the Top-Level design phase was implementing the OORA model in Ada on the host machine. Embedded debugging statements were used to update status displays on the terminal as the model was tested through system modes and states to prove that the architecture worked.

4.6 Results of the iterative approach

At the time of writing application B was just about to complete the review process for Build 3, the final build before delivery.

Each build review has become easier as both development team and customer have gained familiarity with the new process. The increased visibility of development progress has helped the customer to monitor progress more easily, and has enabled both parties to communicate more effectively.

Productivity figures for the development using the iterative process indicate an almost 40% increase over the waterfall approach.

Statistics for the code produced for application B are listed in the following tables:

Total Lines	Comment Lines	Blank Lines	Semicolons
37995	8760	8057	12200

Man Months	Single Lines Of Code/MM	Non-Comment Non-Blank/MM	Terminal Semicolons/MM
30	997	705	406

5 DEVELOPMENT ENVIRONMENT SUPPORT

The development environment used was the Rational Environment. Target computers were connected to the development Ethernet, thus permitting fast downloading and a degree of remote control through the use of intelligent Ethernet cards within the target computer.

5.1 Rational Subsystems

We found the most important feature of the Rational Environment for our development effort was Rational Subsystems. Rational Subsystems allowed us to partition and manage our designs at a much higher level than that of managing individual Ada units.

Rational Subsystems provide facilities for managing multiple development paths for a single partition of an Ada application. These paths can be used for host development, target development or integration. Subsystems also provide the focus for configuration management within the Rational Environment.

Each developer managed two paths of their allocated development subsystem: a host path for fast unit testing and a target path for target testing.

When multiple developers were allocated to a subsystem, an integration path was maintained where all developer code was synchronised for final target integration testing.

After initial delivery of software, we found that we had to maintain three different development paths for the software. All these paths contained common code for the majority of Ada units, but each path had its own specific code differences that needed to be managed. The three paths were: Normal Development, for continued software development; Metrics, for specially instrumented code; Calibration, for code modified to interact with experimental external equipment.

Rational Subsystems provided the facilities to manage these multiple software variants and their integration. This would be have been extremely difficult using a conventional configuration management product.

5.2 DOD-STD-2167 Support

Rational's Design Facility for DOD-STD-2167 was used to produce the delivered Software Requirements Specifications, Software Top Level Design Documents and Software Detailed Design Documents. This automated support helped to remove a significant workload from the development team.

The flexibility of the Design Facility allowed the team to: customise the format of the documents so that they conformed to company standards for layout; and to include more information in the documents that was requested by the customer.

5.3 Target Support

The Rational Environment provided us with a range of software interfaces that aided the integration of our software into the targets. A programmatic interface is provided to the Rational object-module format. This interface was used to convert object modules to a form suitable for downloading to the intelligent Ethernet cards.

The object-module interface was also used to produce tools that generated reports on static memory usage for the software, and to produce a dynamic analysis tool that reported on the dynamic memory usage of the software. This tool reported on heap usage and task stack dynamics. The values obtained where then cross referenced back to the source code and link map, with the tool recommending ways to reduce the amount of target resources required.

6 CONCLUSION

From our experience on this project it is clear that Ada is a very suitable language for the development of Embedded Real-Time Systems. The language allows the designer to reason about a design at various levels of abstraction ranging from Top Level Design down to specific hardware interfaces.

Ada Tasking need not be a problem, so long as the designer recognises the potential for misuse of tasking that can occur with careless design changes and priority assignments. Developers should be made aware of the limitations of Ada tasking and should be trained in the correct use of Tasks.

Object Oriented techniques were used successfully for the Design and Documentation of both Projects through to delivery, by engineers with varying levels of Software Engineering experience. OOD was found to fit extremely well with the real-time hardware underlying the software development.

When using Development Standards such as DOD-STD-2167 it is important that both the Project Management and the Customer understand the requirements and implications of the standard. When tailoring of the standard is permissible, careful consideration of the tailoring should be made prior to contract signing.

The use of a well defined iterative process, publicised in advance to both developers and customer, is the most important single criteria in building software systems correct to specification and with a high degree of confidence of delivery dates. Morale within the organisation and with the customer was maintained at a high level throughout application B as a result.

The use of an integrated development environment can have a significant impact upon project performance. The Rational Environment provided us with a powerful integrated set of tools and allowed us to customise and develop specific tools for our special requirements.

7 ACKNOWLEDGMENTS
The authors would like to thank John Makepeace of AWA for his support during the development of the project software and during the preparation of this paper.

8 REFERENCES
[Sha 1990]. Sha, L. and Goodenough, J., "Real-Time Scheduling Theory and Ada" IEEE Computer, April 1990

[Colbert 1989] Colbert, E., "The Object Oriented Development Method: A Practical Approach to Object-Oriented Development.", TRI-Ada Proceedings, Pittsburgh, October 1989

TESTING AND INTEGRATING A LARGE EMBEDDED REAL-TIME SYSTEM

J.-M. Lippens, J. Arnol

1. INTRODUCTION

How can 60 modules, written in ADA, and developed with OOD, be tested ?
How can these modules be integrated, when most target hardware is late ?

Subsequent to the ADA Europe 90 presentation (an Ada OOD'ed application On Board a Submarine), this paper intends to use the experience acquired to answer these two questions. After a quick presentation of the system and a review of the development phase, we shall mainly discuss phases relating to module testing and module and system integration.

2. GENERAL POINTS

2 . 1   THE COMPUTER SYSTEM

The computer system is an Action and Information Organization (AIO) system which is part of the combat system to be installed in a newly designed French ship.
The responsibility for the AIO system is assumed by a department of the DCAN (*Direction des Constructions et Armes Navales*) in Toulon (FRENCH NAVY). The task of software design and development has been granted to SYSECA.

The AIO system shall perform the following operational functions :

- acquire information from the sensor suite
- correlate the information with that from other sources
- develop and display resulting tactical
- evaluate the corresponding threat and situation
- suggest actions to the Commanding Officer.

Such on-board systems generally use specific hardware in order to withstand the required environment constraints and conditions. The hardware architecture in this case, therefore, consists of over a dozen signal and display processing units, based on 68K family processors, interconnected by two high-speed communications buses.
The software design and development is planned for 2.5 years, requiring an estimated 100,000 man-hours.

2.2 DEVELOPMENT METHODOLOGY

Development is based on SYSECA's development method called MEDOC, which calls for a traditional V cycle, in order to control complexity. It is made of a downward designed phase, followed by an upward integration and validation phase. Regarding the development of this system, the following cycle has been identified :

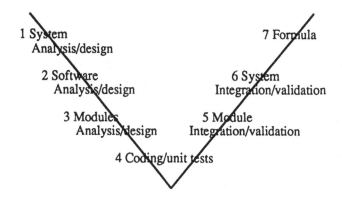

Please note that the software integration/validation phase has not been maintained. The project includes producing the system and its associated software (no work is sub-contracted). This phase would have required complex simulation means, out of proportion with expected benefits.

Remember that with a traditional system design, a dozen CSCI* had been identified, each being run on a processor.
This CSCI design, based on an OOD approach, with the STROOD method, has produced some sixty modules, ten of which can be reused.
Remember also that a module corresponds to an object and is implemented as an ADA package.
Module design, which has also been developed using OOD, identifies components. A component is a package (call sub package), a procedure, a function, or an ADA task.

3. TESTS

3.1 MODULE UNIT TESTS

They are "white box" tests ; they deal with each module component, and help validate the algorithm and comprehensively test all its branches.

The system requested must be extremely reliable ; for this reason, the constraint of testing most branches has been imposed ; such a testing is only possible at that moment in the system life cycle.

These tests are carried out on test beds, without any specific tools, using :
- a TEST entry point declared in the module package specification, so that the component to be tested can be called with the adequate parameters.

- a test procedure per component

- a symbolic debugger authorizing access to the component local variables ; the tests are then archived, using macro files so non regression (non regression test : test done after any modification, to check that the code has not been damaged) tests may be carried out.

Through experience, we noticed some difficulty for the developers to adjust the level of these tests, some of them performing useless while others did not do adequate coverage.

Therefore, we have defined two reasons for interrupting the unitary tests, that is:
not to test : - trivial branches
- the compiler

3 . 2   INTEGRATION/VALIDATION MODULE

INTEGRATION

When all components, (or a consistent sub-set of components) in a module have all been unit tested, it is possible to integrate them to make up the module (or the consistent sub-set of a module).

This inter-component integration is validated by component integration tests carried out by calling module package methods, from a test procedure, which may also manage the listing of results.

Surrounding modules are scantily simulated (listing of call parameters, and positioning of return parameters, for example.)
These tests are especially interesting when several tasks must be synchronized, since this synchronization has not been studied during unit testing.

Please note that component unit testing at the higher module level, completes all or part of integration tests of lower level components, when calls between components are implemented.

More specifically, when a module design has led to several ADA packages, (called sub-packages later on), module component integration tests are then carried out in two steps :

- integration tests for each sub-package

- integration test for the module package.

MODULE VALIDATION

This validation entails verifying whether the module complies with its specification, in an environment simulation.

This validation is carried out into two steps :

- a mono-machine integration on a single target machine, emitting the validation of interfaces with other software modules, with the executive and the libraries.

- on the same principle as for the integration tests, the validation is executed on a host machine in the form of :
    - specifications of the inputs applied to the module (call for the methods)
    - expected results or module outputs

There are two types of validation tests :
- functional : the outputs are checked functionally
- quantitative : the suitability of the module to its environment restraint is checked

3 . 3   INTEGRATION/VALIDATION SYSTEM

The main features of this phase are that it is very long, and that only a part of the target hardware is available at the beginning of integration.

We have therefore considered two phases located, in time, before and after hardware availability date.

Before the availability date, only partial integration shall be mentioned, since the available hardware did not make it possible to set up the system as a whole. After the availability date, the integration is global.

PARTIAL INTEGRATION

It is broken down in several steps, corresponding to different integration levels.
Each level of integration is defined according to :

- software development

- hardware availability

- system functional lay out

It is therefore possible, while following a nominal information path, to isolate, within the system, functionally consistent sub-sets, which each have a minimum interface with the others.

At each step, checkpoints are defined. Checkpoints are an image and its associated dialogues, which help with integration follow-up.

For each CSCI an integration plan of the software is elaborated, which defines and orders tests around:
- mono-machine tests described previously
- bi-machine tests allowing to check the correctness of the exchanges between two CSCI
- tests allowing to check the outcome of each step

The advantage of this situation is for the client to quickly be able to visualize the advancement of the work.

GLOBAL INTEGRATION

In this phase, the system surrounding the target hardware is set up, and its compliance with specifications is verified.

In order to do this, after a first phase where software is adapted to the final hardware, the modules in the system are assembled.

The assembly is carried out, as previously done, by following the functional layout, and adding the different functions one after the other.

Each function has been validated earlier during partial integration ; the main efforts are now therefore targeted towards communication between functions.

Validation is completed by carrying out the system validation catalog.

3 . 4 EFFECTS OF THE ADA OOD'ED APPLICATION ON VALIDATION INTEGRATION

Two important points should be noticed concerning the module and system integration validation phases :
- the implementation of STROOD, including the writing of a framework in Ada at the end of the conception phase (phases 2 or 3) leads to achieve the writing of the framework in order to anticipate the integration validation phase.
This leads to a clear distinction between the integration tests and the validation tests.

- It is impossible to execute a module validation in the system environment, depending on the operator interfaces, as it used to be done for classic conception modules (through the functions), because the functional requests involve, for an OOD, the implementation of several modules; and this does not permit to validate them separately as it should be done.

4. THE PRODUCTION PLATFORM

4.1 ORGANIZATION

Organized in a network around some fifteen work sttations (2 Gbytes of disk memory), it shows the development steps, that is to say a tree-like structure in which the system, the softwares and the modules can be found.

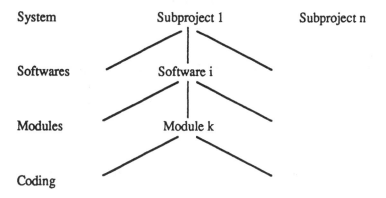

SYSTEM
It is divided into subprojects, each subproject covering a functional unit (from the system functional division) and organizational unit (from the realization team organization (project manager, group manager, designer)).

SOFTWARES
This level gathers, for each identified subproject, the softwares issued from the system analysis design.

MODULES
The modules issued from each software conception appear at this level.

CODING
At this level for each module, there are libraries containing operational sources, tests sources as well as the host and target softwares.

4 . 2   CONFIGURATION MANAGEMENT

The entities to be managed in configuration during the execution are the modules and the softwares.

The configuration management defines itself by the different steps forward, each step corresponding to the phases of the life cycle.

The action of getting from one level to another is called the catalog and consists of , for the modules, recopying the operational Ada sources from a library to another, and for the softwares of emitting a form indexing the implied modules.

Three advance levels per module are retained :

- Realization integration level (phases 4 and 5)
At this level, the module is under the responsability of the designer.
This phase ends when the validation tests and the mono-machine integration are successfully carried out. The module is then catalogued to the evaluation level.

- Evaluation level (phase 6)
This level is characteristic of an evaluating module during the system integration validation phase. It is under responsability of the realization group manager. It is catalogued to the following level when the system validation catalog relating to the functional unit to which the module belongs is successfully carried out.

- Delivery level
This level receives the modules ready for shipping. It is under the responsability of the product manager.

There are two advance levels to be remembered.

- Evaluation level
It contains a software made of evaluation level catalogued modules.

- Delivery level
It contains a software made of delivery level modules.

The production platform organization, that takes this management into account, can be simplified with a diagram as follows :

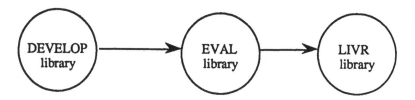

5. CONCLUSION

Through the experience, we can draw the following lessons :

- By the perpendicularity induced between abstraction levels and life-cycle, the OOD, and STROOD particularly, entail a particular care, as far as the separation between validation tests and integration tests are concerned.

- The use of Ada enables, thanks to the strictness of the language, to lighten the unitary tests so as to concentrate the efforts on the integration validation tests.

- The implementation of the configuration management, tools being unavailable, is easily done only on the sources (without managing the documentation in configuration), but needs a lot of memory.

Moreover, it seems that the configuration management during the development is more complex to process than the configuration management in the maintenance phase because of the flexibility required.

Bibliography :

- Ada-Europe Conference Dublin 90
  "an Ada OOD'ed application on board a submarine"